# Applying Techniques to Common Encounters in School Counseling

## A Case-Based Approach

Edited by

**Rebekah Byrd**

*East Tennessee State University*

and

**Bradley T. Erford**

*Loyola University Maryland*

Boston   Columbus   Indianapolis   New York   San Francisco   Upper Saddle River
Amsterdam   Cape Town   Dubai   London   Madrid   Milan   Munich   Paris   Montreal   Toronto
Delhi   Mexico City   São Paulo   Sydney   Hong Kong   Seoul   Singapore   Taipei   Tokyo

**Vice President and Editorial Director:** Jeffery W. Johnston
**Senior Acquisitions Editor:** Meredith Fossel
**Editorial Assistant:** Krista Slavicek
**Vice President and Director of Marketing:** Margaret Waples
**Senior Marketing Manager:** Christopher Barry
**Senior Managing Editor:** Pamela D. Bennett
**Production Manager:** Maggie Brobeck
**Manager, Central Design:** Jayne Conte
**Cover Designer:** Karen Salzbach
**Cover Photo:** lkunl/Fotolia
**Full-Service Project Management and Composition:** Kailash Jadli, Aptara®, Inc.
**Printer/Binder:** Courier Westford
**Cover Printer:** Courier Westford
**Text Font:** Palatino LT Std

Credits and acknowledgments for material borrowed from other sources and reproduced, with permission, in this text appear on the appropriate page within the text.

Every effort has been made to provide accurate and current Internet information in this text. However, the Internet and information posted on it are constantly changing, so it is inevitable that some of the Internet addresses listed in this text will change.

**Library of Congress Cataloging-in-Publication Data: Cataloging-in-Publication data not available at time of publication**

2 3 4 5 6 7 8 9 10 V092 16 15

ISBN 10:     0-13-284238-6
ISBN 13: 978-0-13-284238-9

*I would like to dedicate this text to my grandparents and my parents—the people in my life who introduced me to the concepts of warmth, genuineness, and unconditional positive regard. Norma Jane & Odell Baker and Carolyn & Gary Byrd, I love you. —RB*

*This effort is dedicated to The One: the Giver of energy, passion, and understanding; who makes life worth living and endeavors worth pursuing and accomplishing; the Teacher of love and forgiveness. —BTE*

# ABOUT THE EDITORS

*Rebekah Byrd*, PhD, LPC, NCC, RPT, is an assistant professor of counseling and the school counseling program coordinator in the Department of Counseling and Human Services at East Tennessee State University (ETSU). She serves on many national and state-wide committees for associations including Association for Assessment and Research in Counseling (AARC), Counselors for Social Justice (CSJ), Chi Sigma Iota (CSI), Safe Schools Task Force, and the Tennessee Counseling Association (TCA). In the past, she has also served as the Human Rights and Social Justice Chair for the Virginia School Counselor Association (VSCA), and as President of the Old Dominion University chapter of Chi Sigma Iota International. She is the recipient of a research grant from the Association for Counselor Education and Supervision and a research grant from the Association for Specialists in Group Work. Dr. Byrd was recently selected to receive the Distinguished Alumni Award from Old Dominion University. Other awards include the O'Hana Award from Counselors for Social Justice and the Young Emerging Leader Award from Association for Multicultural Counseling and Development. She was also selected to be a Chi Sigma Iota International Leadership Fellow. She has written many refereed journal articles and multiple text chapters, and her research specialization falls primarily in issues pertaining to children and adolescents, school counseling, and LGBTQ concerns. Other major research interests include play therapy, human rights and social justice, group work, self-injury in adolescents, women's wellness, and Adlerian theory. Dr. Byrd has been a faculty member at ETSU since 2010 and is a Licensed Professional Counselor, a Nationally Certified Counselor, and a Registered Play Therapist. Prior to arriving at ETSU, Dr. Byrd was the director and developer of a character education program in a middle school and a school counselor in both middle and elementary school settings. She maintains a client caseload specializing in children and adolescents and play therapy. Dr. Byrd holds a PhD in counselor education and an M.S.Ed. in counseling with a concentration in school counseling from Old Dominion University in Norfolk, Virginia. She holds a B.A. in psychology from the University of North Carolina at Asheville. She teaches courses in counseling children and adolescents, school counseling, psycho-educational groups, legal and ethical issues in counseling, social and cultural foundations, women's wellness, play therapy, practicum, and internship. Dr. Byrd lives in Asheville, North Carolina, with her partner Alex, and their three dogs (Neptune, Gemini, and Joe) and two cats (Adhara and Faun).

*Bradley T. Erford*, PhD, LCPC, LPC, NCC, LP, LSP, is a professor in the school counseling program of the Educational Specialties Department in the School of Education at Loyola University Maryland. He is President of the American Counseling Association (2012–2013) and the recipient of the American Counseling Association (ACA) Research Award, ACA Hitchcock Distinguished Professional Service Award, ACA Professional Development Award, and ACA Carl D. Perkins Government Relations Award. He has also been inducted as an ACA Fellow. In addition, he has received the Association for Assessment in Counseling and Education/Measurement and Evaluation in Counseling and Development (AACE/MECD) Research Award, the AACE Exemplary Practices Award, the AACE President's Special Merit Award, the Association for Counselor

Education and Supervision's Robert O. Stripling Award for Excellence in Standards, Maryland Association for Counseling and Development (MACD) Maryland Counselor of the Year, the MACD Counselor Advocacy Award, the MACD Professional Development Award, the MACD Professional Service Award, the MACD Outstanding Programming Award, and the MACD Counselor Visibility Award. He has coauthored and edited/coedited a number of texts, including *The ACA Encyclopedia of Counseling* (ACA, 2009); *Transforming the School Counseling Profession* (Pearson, 2002, 2006, 2010); *Professional School Counseling: A Handbook of Theories, Programs and Practices* (Pro-Ed, 2004, 2009); *Orientation to the Counseling Profession: Advocacy, Ethics, and Essential Professional Foundations* (Pearson, 2010, 2014); *Developing Multicultural Competence: A Systems Approach* (Pearson, 2010, 2014); *35 Techniques Every Counselor Should Know* (Pearson, 2010); *Group Work in the Schools* (Pearson, 2010); *Group Work: Processes and Applications* (Pearson, 2010); *Crisis Intervention and Prevention* (Pearson, 2010, 2014); *Group Activities: Firing Up for Performance* (Pearson, 2007); *Assessment for Counselors* (Houghton Mifflin/Lahaska Press, 2007, 2013); *Research and Evaluation in Counseling* (Houghton Mifflin/Lahaska Press, 2008); *Educational Applications of the WISC-IV* (Western Psychological Services, 2006); and *The Counselor's Guide to Clinical, Personality, and Behavioral Assessment* (Houghton Mifflin/Lahaska Press, 2005). His research specialization falls primarily in development and technical analysis of psycho-educational tests and has resulted in the publication of more than 60 refereed journal articles, 100 text chapters, and a dozen published tests. He is a Past ACA Governing Council Representative; Past President of the AACE; Past Chair and Parliamentarian of the ACA—Southern Region; Past President of the MACD; Past Chair of the ACA's Task Force on High Stakes Testing, Standards for Test Users Task Force, Interprofessional Committee, and Public Awareness and Support Committee; Chair of the Convention Committee and Past Chair of the Screening Assessment Instruments Committee for the AACE; Past President of Maryland Association for Counselor Education and Supervision; Past President of Maryland Association for Measurement and Evaluation; and Past President of the Maryland Association for Mental Health Counselors. He is also an editorial board member of the *Journal of Counseling & Development*, and an ad hoc reviewer for *Counselor Education and Supervision*, *Measurement and Evaluation in Counseling and Development*, and *Psychological Reports*. Dr. Erford has been a faculty member at Loyola since 1993 and is a Licensed Clinical Professional Counselor, Licensed Professional Counselor, Nationally Certified Counselor, Licensed Psychologist, and Licensed School Psychologist. Prior to arriving at Loyola, Dr. Erford was a school psychologist/counselor in the Chesterfield County (VA) Public Schools. He maintains a private practice specializing in assessment and treatment of children and adolescents. He holds a PhD in counselor education from The University of Virginia, an M.A. in school psychology from Bucknell University, and a BS in biology from Grove City College (PA). He teaches courses in testing and measurement, psycho-educational assessment, life-span development, research and evaluation in counseling, school counseling, counseling techniques, and stress management (not that he needs it).

# ABOUT THE CONTRIBUTING AUTHORS

**Kie Anderson** received an MA in school counseling from Marymount University. She is a school counselor in Fairfax County Public Schools, VA.

**Laura Bell** is a graduate student at Marymount University and an intern in Prince William County Schools, VA.

**Elisabeth Bennett** chairs the Department of Counselor Education at Gonzaga University in Spokane, WA. In addition to educating and training school counselors, she consults with local school districts and provides training to school personnel.

**Melissa Beverly** is a high school counselor in Arizona. She was the 2011–2012 Arizona School Counselor Association president and is an adjunct faculty member for the School Counseling Program at the Northern Arizona University North Valley Campus, Phoenix, AZ.

**Jeffrey Brown** is a licensed professional school counselor with the District of Columbia Public School System. Prior to his tenure with the district, he served as a consultant to the Charles County Maryland School System for at risk-youth at the elementary level.

**Mary Brown** is a retired certified school counselor and administrator. She is presently a professor at Gonzaga University in Spokane, WA. She has been celebrated as the counselor educator of the year by the Washington School Counseling Association and has recently been a major contributor to the state's professional certification requirement for school counselors.

**Rhonda M. Bryant,** PhD, LPC, is a professional school counselor and counselor educator at Albany State University in Albany, GA.

**Catherine Y. Chang,** PhD, NCC, LPC, is an associate professor and program co-ordinator for the Counselor Education and Practice Doctoral Program at Georgia State University.

**Rebecca Christiansen,** LPC, NCC, is a certified professional school counselor for the self-contained behavioral classroom at Aberdeen Central High School, Aberdeen, South Dakota. Christiansen implements a combination of reality therapy, solution-focused therapy, and Boys Town behavior management to increase the level of student success in academic and social settings.

**Caron N. Coles** is a professional school counselor in Newport News Public Schools, VA.

**Kimere K. Corthell,** MA, APC, is a doctoral student in the Counselor Education and Practice Program at Georgia State University. She has clinical experience working in an alternative school setting and directing a community-based Adolescent Drug and Alcohol Transitional Program funded by the Department of Juvenile Justice.

**Hugh C. Crethar,** PhD, is an associate professor and the co-ordinator of the Counseling Program at Oklahoma State University.

**Laurie Curran** is a school counselor for Spokane Public Schools in Spokane, WA. She provides school counseling services to elementary school children and serves on the Master of Arts in School Counseling Professional Education Advisory Board at Gonzaga University.

**Alissa Darnell,** LAPC, is doctoral student in counselor education at Ohio University. Her areas of interest include theory development, multicultural issues in counseling, and counselor wellness.

**Charlotte Daughhetee** is a professor of counseling at the University of Montevallo in Montevallo, Alabama. She has a BS in Early Childhood Education from Indiana University, an M.Ed. in Counseling, and a PhD in Counselor Education from the University of South Carolina. She is an LPC and an LMFT in the state of Alabama. Her clinical experience includes working with children and adults in K12, college, agency and private practice settings.

**Tammy Davis,** PhD, is a professor in the Department of Counseling at Marymount University in Arlington, VA.

**Joyce A. DeVoss** is a full professor in the Department of Educational Psychology at Northern Arizona University, co-ordinator of the MEd School Counseling Program in Tucson, Arizona, and cochair of the Arizona School Counseling Association (AzSCA) Research Committee. She co-authored the book, *School Counselors as Educational Leaders* (2006) and has published numerous articles and book chapters.

**Kelly Duncan** is an associate professor in the Division of Counseling and Psychology in Education at the University of South Dakota. Her research and presentation interests include comprehensive school counseling models, career and lifespan development, accountability measures, and supervision of school counselors.

**Denise B. Ebersole,** MEd, NCC, NCSC, is a professional school counselor at Hershey High School in Hershey, PA, and a PhD student in counselor education and supervision at Regent University. She earned her MEd in school counseling and certificate in supervision of guidance services from Millersville University of PA. She integrates a solution-focused counseling approach into her comprehensive developmental school counseling program.

**Miriam Eisenmenger** graduated from New Jersey City University in May 2012, receiving an MA in counseling with school counseling certification. Miriam received her BA in psychology from Concordia University in Chicago, Illinois, in 2007. Her current research topics include issues in immigration counseling, college and career planning for students with learning disabilities, trauma counseling, and sand-tray therapy.

**Nadine E. Garner,** EdD, LPC, is an associate professor of psychology and the Graduate Program co-ordinator for school counseling at Millersville University, PA. She is co-author of the ASCA-published book, *A School with Solutions: Implementing a Solution-focused/Adlerian-based Comprehensive School Counseling Program.* Dr. Garner consults with schools that seek to implement a solution-focused approach in their comprehensive developmental counseling curriculum and presents workshops on solution-focused counseling both in the United States and abroad.

**Jasmine Graham,** MEd, NCC, LCPC, is a freelance writer and speaker. Graham serves as the department chair for a counseling department of a large magnet school in Maryland. She is a member and past president of the Alpha Iota chapter of the Chi Sigma Iota Honor Society, a member of the American Counseling Association, a member of the Association for Multicultural Counseling and Development (AMCD), a member of Counselors for Social Justice (CSJ), and a member of the ACA School Counseling Task Force.

**Tim Grothaus** is an associate professor and School Counseling Program co-ordinator at Old Dominion University, Norfolk, VA.

**Natalie Grubbs,** MEd, is a full-time school counselor at Whitefield Academy and a full-time doctoral student in the Counselor Education and Practice Doctoral Program at Georgia State University.

**Nadine Hartig** is an assistant professor in counselor education at Radford University. She has counseling experience in a variety of settings, including K-12 schools, universities, and community mental health centers.

**Tara Hill,** PhD, is a licensed clinical counselor and supervisor and works as an assistant professor at Old Dominion University, Norfolk, VA.

**James Jackson** is an assistant professor at the University of Montevallo in Montevallo, AL. He is a licensed professional counselor and national certified counselor and has experience as a preK–12 teacher, community counselor, and school counselor. He holds a PhD in counselor education and supervision from the University of Alabama.

**Stefanie Johnson,** MEd, is a professional school counselor in the Chatham County School System. She completed an MEd in the Department of Counselor Education at North Carolina State University.

**Sandy Kay** is a Certified Rehabilitation Counselor (CRC), a Certified Substance Abuse Counselor (CSAC), and Licensed School Counselor (PreK-12) currently serving as a school counselor in Montgomery County Public Schools, VA. She has over 20 years of experience providing counseling services to children, adolescents, and families.

**Megan Kidron** has worked for more than three years as a school counselor, school therapist, and school social worker. She is currently living in San Diego, CA, where she is taking classes and pursuing the Licensed Professional Clinical Counselor.

**Tracy Knighton,** PhD, is a professional school counselor in southwestern Georgia. She is very active in her community performing outreach and service in urban and rural settings.

**Dana Heller Levitt,** PhD, is an associate professor of counselor education at Montclair State University. She received her master's and doctoral degrees from the University of Virginia. Dr. Levitt's research focuses on ethics and counselor development, eating disorders, and body image.

**Katie Liebers** is a professional school counselor in the Bristol Tennessee City School System. She received her MA in school counseling from East Tennessee State University.

**Tracy MacDonald** is a professional school counselor at Chesapeake Middle School in Anne Arundel County Public Schools, MD.

**Heather McCarthy** is a professional school counselor at the middle school level in Fairfax County Public Schools, VA.

**Catalina Morillas,** MEd, is a certified school counselor at an alternative school. She has clinical experience working with minority student populations focusing on social justice issues within school and community settings. Advocacy on behalf of Latino and LGBTQIQ students has been a focus in her career. She has also worked on bullying intervention projects and international mental health projects.

**Latisha Walker Nelson,** MEd, is a graduate of the University of North Carolina at Chapel Hill's School Counseling Program. She has counseled children in grades K-12 for 12 years in rural, urban, and suburban areas throughout the Mid-Atlantic region of the United States.

**Audrey Neuschafer,** NCC, LPC, is a counselor and consultant with Southwest Plains Regional Service Center in Sublette, Kansas. She works as a part-time, K-12 school counselor for three rural districts in southwest Kansas and facilitates student assemblies in the areas of student leadership, bullying prevention, and character education in Western Kansas. She also provides professional development on topics of social and emotional student health to teachers and counselors in her region.

**Lindsey M. Nichols** is a former school counselor and currently assistant professor of Counselor Education at the University of Montana.

**Tom O'Connor** is a school counselor in Spokane Public Schools in Spokane, Washington. He has devoted 30 years to public education, the last ten of which have been as an elementary school counselor.

**Delila Owens**, PhD, LPC, is a professional school counselor and counselor educator at Indiana Wesleyan University in Marion, IN.

**Lindy K. Parker**, EdS, LPC, NCC, is a doctoral student in the Counselor Education and Practice Program at Georgia State University. She has clinical experience working in an alternative school setting, and in an adolescent inpatient and outpatient psychiatric and substance abuse hospital.

**Molly B. Quick**, MEd, is a language arts teacher in a Seattle-area private high school and is currently pursuing her PhD in education at Seattle Pacific University.

**Brandy K. Richeson,** PhD, is a professional school counselor for Newport News Public Schools, VA and completed her PhD in counselor education at Old Dominion University, Norfolk, VA.

**Morgan Kiper Riechel,** MA, has seven years of experience as a full-time professional school counselor. She is currently pursuing her doctorate in counselor education at the College of William and Mary, VA, where she continues to work with children and adolescents in schools.

**Helen Runyan** is the director of a Character Education Program in middle and high school settings and a doctoral student at Old Dominion University, Norfolk, VA.

**Adria Shipp,** PhD, is a school counselor with experience at the elementary, middle, and high school levels. She is currently working as an elementary school counselor at Sylvan Elementary School in Alamance County, NC.

**Christopher A. Sink**, PhD, LMHC, NCC, is a professor of Counselor Education at Seattle Pacific University, School of Education. Prior to serving in a professorial role, Chris was a secondary school and community college counselor. He also has many years of editorial experience in counseling-related journals and has extensively published and presented on, among other areas, issues related to comprehensive school counseling programs, research methods in counseling, and the intersections between student spirituality and positive psychology.

**Stacy Solsaa** is a K-12 counselor in a small rural community with approximately 300 students. Stacy also works in the agency setting part-time and has been involved with the counseling association and school counseling association in her state.

**Fran Steigerwald** is currently the associate dean of the College of Education and Human Development at Radford University in Radford, Virginia. Previously, she was associate professor in their Department of Counselor Education. She has been a college and community mental health and substance abuse counselor and has worked with children and families in private practice.

**Tori Stone** is a professional school counselor in Prince William County, VA.

**Jill M. Thompson,** PhD, is an associate professor of counselor education at the University of the District of Columbia, in Washington, DC. She serves as program co-ordinator for the school counseling master's program. Her teaching and research interests are in school counselors' accountability and development, attachment issues across a lifespan, and constructivism as an approach to counselor supervision/skill development. She has 15 years of experience as a public school counselor and teacher, and is a licensed professional counselor, licensed marriage and family therapist and an approved clinical supervisor.

**Shannon Trice-Black,** PhD, LPC, is an assistant professor in counselor education at the College of William and Mary, VA. She has over ten years' experience as a professional school counselor and a licensed professional counselor.

**Tricia Uppercue** is a professional school counselor at Aberdeen High School in Harford County, Maryland. She is also a licensed clinical professional counselor and nationally certified counselor.

**Amy Upton** is the school counseling department chair at Great Neck Middle School in Virginia Beach, VA.

**Brielle E. Valle** is an admissions counselor at Philadelphia University. She has a BS in Speech Communication: Public Relations from Millersville University, PA.

**Laurie A. Vargas,** MS, is a full-time counselor with San Francisco Unified School District.

**Ann Vernon,** PhD, NCC, LMHC, is professor emeritus and former coordinator of counseling at the University of Northern Iowa, and a counselor in private practice where she works extensively with children, adolescents, and their parents.

**Maegan Vick** is a graduate of the Counseling Program at the University of Montevallo, AL, and a school counselor at Helena Elementary School in Shelby County Public Schools, AL. Prior to becoming a school counselor, Maegan was a special education teacher in both inclusion and self-contained classrooms in Shelby County Public School in Alabama.

**Kami Wagner** is a professional school counselor and department chair at Mt. Hebron High School in Howard County Public School System in Maryland.

**Lacey L. Wallace,** MEd, is a professional school counselor at Manor View Elementary School in Anne Arundel County Public Schools, MD. She has worked with the military population for several years on Fort George M. Meade, MD. Lacey obtained her degree in school counseling at Loyola University Maryland.

**Christine Ward** is an assistant professor of counseling at Old Dominion University, Norfolk, VA.

**Jeffrey M. Warren,** PhD, is an assistant professor of professional school counseling in the Department of School Administration & Counseling at the University of North Carolina at Pembroke. He is a national certified school counselor.

**Jenna N. Warren,** MS, is a professional school counselor in the Wake County Public School System in North Carolina.

**Bianca Bekker Willman** is a professional school counselor at Lee Elementary School in Cypress-Fairbanks ISD, Houston, TX.

# PREFACE

Thank you for choosing *Applying Techniques to Common Encounters in School Counseling: A Case-Based Approach*! The idea for this text came from years of working with school counselors in training, professional school counselors in the field, and counselor educators, all of whom expressed the desire to have a text that ties theory to practice in the school setting. Specifically, graduate counseling students often report a need to understand theories taught in the classroom and how to apply those theories in the school setting. Most graduate training programs teach theory and practice from a general counseling perspective and rarely reference its application for counseling in the schools.

In practicum and internship classes especially, students have expressed a desire to understand theory as it relates to work in the school with individual students, groups, classroom guidance, and work with teachers, administrators, and school staff—which are all important components of a comprehensive school counseling program. Further, these practicum and internship experiences are often not of sufficient length or depth for students to acquire a strong foundation in a particular theoretical framework. This results in counselors in training and new school counselors having great difficulty linking theory and practice. Whether during graduate training or in full-time employment, professional school counselors face myriad challenges, which can lead to their having feelings of uncertainty about what goals to address or how to theoretically frame the specific issue at hand. In the development of training and practice, as a student and as a professional school counselor, counselors are searching for tangible, grounded real life examples of how to transfer and apply theory into practice for commonly encountered counseling situations.

The purpose of this text is to introduce students in training and new professional school counselors to various situations each is likely to come across during training and the first 5 years of practice. It is our hope that exposure to these experiences and attention to the diverse theoretical approaches that can be applied to resolve these student situations will enhance your training and better prepare you to deal with a variety of situations. In other words, our aim is that the use of these case scenarios and a flexible case conceptualization model early in your career as a professional school counselor will accelerate your growth and development, and assist in building self-confidence for the trials and triumphs that await you. Your career will have many challenges and countless rewards. While on your journey to becoming a seasoned, knowledgeable, and experienced school counselor, we hope this text is beneficial in your developmental process of learning and applying the school counseling trade.

## ACKNOWLEDGMENTS

All of the contributing authors are to be commended for lending their expertise in the various topical areas and for being dedicated and courageous school counselors and educators. As always, Meredith Fossel of Pearson has been wonderfully responsive and supportive. We also would like to thank the following reviewers who offered useful suggestions for this edition: Mary L. Anderson, Western Michigan University; Tim Grothaus, Old Dominion University; Toni R. Tellerud, Northern Illinois University; and Debra J. Woodard, University of Missouri–Kansas City.

# CONTENTS

# Chapter *1*

# Case Studies in School Counseling

REBEKAH BYRD AND BRADLEY T. ERFORD

W elcome to the school counseling profession! By this point in your journey toward becoming a professional school counselor, you probably feel not only a mixture of emotions, including excitement and anticipation, but also some trepidation. You may be lacking self-confidence, asking, "Can I really do this?" It is not unusual for us to hear school counselors in training say something like this: "I think I understand the theories, and I seem to be able to put them into practice in role play, but how am I supposed to know what to do when I encounter new situations?" The purpose of this text is to answer this common question.

The truth is that the journey toward becoming a professional school counselor will continue for many years to come. The journey starts with foundational course work that is often general and theoretical, but quickly becomes more real world oriented and pragmatic when a graduate counseling student gets to the practicum experience. This is often a student's first experience with clients with real life problems. The culminating experience in most school counseling training programs is the internship, in which the student actually gets to live the life of the professional school counselor. Unfortunately, most interns have had limited exposure to the types of real life problems that school students and their families present with. In both the practicum and the internship, school counselors in training rely heavily on supervisors for guidance about the best ways to address student issues. In seminars, school counselors in training quickly learn that supervisors vary in experience, expertise, and favored approaches. As a result, some student issues seem easier to resolve than others, whereas other issues linger and may even seem impossible to resolve. Quality of experiences and supervision makes a huge difference in whether the student will be able to "hit the ground running" as a professional school counselor.

If all goes as planned, the school counselor in training will graduate and begin year one of a lengthy and fulfilling career. However, the rookie school counselor quickly encounters challenging new situations and circumstances that often require additional supervision and training. Sometimes these challenging new situations can become overwhelming and frustrating, and it is not unusual for the rookie school counselor to question whether the training received was adequate for the job. The truth of the matter is that no school counseling training can prepare a student for *all* of the new and dynamic

1

circumstances encountered; indeed, one who experienced *most* of the situations encountered during the training program would count himself or herself very fortunate! School counseling is a fluid and dynamic occupation because every student, guardian, teacher, or administrator who seeks the school counselor's advice presents with a slightly different case and slightly different details. It is the responsibility of the rookie school counselor to assimilate all these details to address the issue at hand effectively.

By about the fifth year of experience as a full-time professional school counselor, one finally reaches the point of diminishing returns; the counselor encounters fewer and fewer truly "new" cases that have never been previously encountered and needs less and less consultation with and supervision from colleagues. Interestingly, at about the five-year mark most professional school counselors will decide whether they have reached their life calling and remain a school counselor for another 20 plus years. On the other hand, many professional school counselors (and teachers) leave the profession around their fifth year for a host of reasons, including poor training, burnout, unfulfilling work (expectations), poor compensation, or a mismatched person–environment fit. For the majority who do stay beyond the fifth year and through retirement, societal, systemic, and individual changes continue to permeate schools and school students. Therefore, they must continue to adapt to changing circumstances throughout the remainder of their careers. In other words, becoming a professional school counselor, from training through retirement, is developmental. All school counselors accumulate experiences that are generally similar to those of their colleagues, yet do so at somewhat different rates.

With this developmental trajectory as context, the purpose of this text is to expose students in training and new professional school counselors to numerous situations each is likely to encounter during training and the first five years of practice. It is our hope that this exposure, as well as attention to the diverse theoretical approaches that can be applied to resolve these student situations, will better prepare students in training to deal with each dilemma using a fluid, dynamic, and flexible approach to school counseling. In other words, we hope that using these cases and a flexible case conceptualization model early in your career as a professional school counselor will speed up your development, better prepare you, and give you confidence for meeting the trials ahead.

## APPLYING THEORY TO PRACTICE: IT'S NOT A CLICHÉ!

Applying theory to practice can seem like a daunting task. School counselors in training thirst for real life stories of how to help students, families, and teachers using a viable and effective theoretical orientation. Specifically, graduate counseling students want to know what it is like to live the life of the professional school counselor. They often report disconnects between the theories taught in the classroom and the application of those theories in the school setting. Oftentimes their practicum and internship experiences are not enough to gain a sense of theoretical grounding, making it difficult to bridge the gap between theory and practice. Once working full-time in the field, school counselors are confronted with new cases daily and sometimes feel at a loss about how to proceed, how to theoretically frame the problems and issues they are encountering, and what action steps to take. In the early stages of training and practice, counselors are searching for concrete, grounded, real life examples of how to transfer and apply theory into practice for commonly encountered situations.

Practicum and internship experiences are intended to serve as opportunities to integrate and apply classroom-derived knowledge and skills to field-based experiences. However, school counseling students frequently find themselves struggling to navigate a particular school system and meet with students the required number of hours. They are challenged to find the time and to obtain the supervision needed in order to draw a conclusion about what is happening in a student's life and then apply it in the midst of a pressured situation. Additionally, graduate school counselor supervisors find themselves struggling to meet the demands of their school as well as to discuss every "teachable moment" with their intern. Often professional school counselors are so busy striving to meet the needs of their extremely large caseloads, school responsibilities, and requirements as a supervisor to their practicum/internship student that there is limited time left for adequate supervision.

Supervision is also an extremely critical aspect of the professional school counselor's career, training, development, and success. As a field, we understand that supervision is imperative for ethical decision making, growth, and the prevention of burnout (Remley & Herlihy, 2010). Supervision could take place in the school if other school counselors are available to discuss ethical and legal aspects of cases and to consult with the new school counselor. Supervision is also available outside of the school with licensed professional counselors trained specifically to supervise. Additionally, staying in touch with one's supervisor from graduate school provides a means for supervision and consultation in the field.

Continued professional development throughout one's career is also an important aspect of professional identity and ethical practice. As students change, so does relevant and up-to-date research on working with children, adolescents, and special populations. Therefore, professional school counselors must stay abreast of current research and trends in the field (American School Counselor Association [ASCA], 2012) not only for assessing changes in the field but also for maintaining their ethical practice, conceptualization skills, and intervention techniques. Continued professional development is sometimes offered at the school; however, at times it may not be specifically geared to the professional school counselor's role and responsibilities. Local and state counseling organizations, local colleges and universities, national counseling associations, and online resources also provide continuing education for counselors. Such training is essential for continued development, competence, and enhancing one's professional identity (Remley & Herlihy, 2010).

This text seeks to bridge an existing gap between theory and school counseling practice by offering a collection of applications-based, school counselor experiences. These case scenarios show how actual school counselors in their own voices explain and handle similar real life situations. This text represents the combined wisdom of about 60 current and former school counselors across the nation who have confronted real life student problems; thought deeply about how to conceptualize the concerns using one or more theoretical models or frameworks; and implemented appropriate strategies, techniques, and interventions to address the presenting concerns in an efficient, culturally sensitive, ethical, and professional manner. It teaches school counseling students how to deal effectively with common, real life problems *before* they encounter them in practice.

It is important to be mindful that many school counselors do not have the time or resources to spend on each issue covered in this text. Also, in many of the scenarios, stakeholders such as teachers, parents, and others acted cooperatively. Although this does happen in real life, there are also situations in which this type of open assistance does not occur or is sabotaged in some way. Regardless, these case studies are true and certainly invite us to think critically about similar situations in which we may be involved. Our hope is that readers of this text will gain vicarious experience with the pragmatic, effective solutions applied to help vulnerable students, families, and educators.

## STRUCTURE OF THIS TEXT

The bridge between theory and practice begins in Chapter 2 with an overview of the primary theories of counseling used by school counselors today. These theories were grouped by paradigm: psychodynamic, humanistic/existential, behavioral/cognitive-behavioral, family systems, and emergent theories. This paradigmatic presentation then serves as the organizational structure for how school counselors draw a conclusion about each case. Most important, there are many ways to address student concerns, and the approaches chosen by the authors of each case scenario are not the only ways to resolve an issue. Indeed, often school counselors will need to approach a student concern from several different angles and use a number of strategies to resolve it. Thus, Chapter 2 strives to provide "choices" for how school counselors can frame, approach, and resolve myriad student concerns.

Next, Chapters 3–45 present cases thematically clustered into sections:

- *Section II: Social Justice and Diversity Issues in School Counseling* Chapter 3: Social Justice; Chapter 4: Advocacy (and the Use of Small Group Counseling for Students with AD/HD); Chapter 5: Multicultural Counseling in the Schools; Chapter 6: Immigration; Chapter 7: Racism; Chapter 8: Existential-Spirituality in School Counseling; Chapter 9: English Language Learners; Chapter 10: Lesbian, Gay, Bisexual, Transgender, and Questioning (LGBTQ) Issues in School Counseling
- *Section III: Academic Considerations in School Counseling* Chapter 11: Motivating the Unmotivated Student; Chapter 12: Working with Gifted Children; Chapter 13: College Access; Chapter 14: Counselors in Alternative Schools: The Last Line of Defense; Chapter 15: Transitions and Student Attendance
- *Section IV: Relational Aggression, Bullying, and Violence in School Counseling* Chapter 16: Bullying (Relational Aggression); Chapter 17: Bullying (Physical Aggression; Chapter 18: Helping Students Who Are Lesbian, Gay, Bisexual, Transgender, and Questioning (LGBTQ); Chapter 19: Dating and Relational Violence
- *Section V: Individual Issues/Coping in School Counseling* Chapter 20: Chronic Illness; Chapter 21: Helping Students with Grief and Loss Experiences; Chapter 22: Addressing Disruptive Behavior in the Classroom Using an Ecological Approach; Chapter 23: Social Isolation; Chapter 24: Working with Students Displaying Defi-

ant Behavior; Chapter 25: Helping Students with Anxiety; Chapter 26: Helping Students with Depression; Chapter 27: Self-Injury
- *Section VI: Parental/Family Issues in School Counseling* Chapter 28: Working with Families; Chapter 29: Children of Deployed Parents; Chapter 30: Children of Divorce; Chapter 31: Helping Children of Incarcerated Parents; Chapter 32: Children of Parents who Abuse Substances; Chapter 33: Physical Abuse; Chapter 34: Helping Students Living in Poverty; Chapter 35: Working with Samantha, a Homeless Child
- *Section VII: Risky Behavior and Crisis Intervention in School Counseling* Chapter 36: Substance Use; Chapter 37: Adolescents, Sex, and STDs; Chapter 38: Helping Students with Eating Disorders; Chapter 39: De-escalating Extreme Behaviors/Emotions; Chapter 40: Gang Involvement; Chapter 41: Suicide Prevention; Chapter 42: Helping Students Who Experience Disasters and Post Traumatic Stress Disorder (PTSD)
- *Section VIII: Legal and Ethical Considerations in School Counseling* Chapter 43: Responsible Technology Use (Social Networking); Chapter 44: FERPA Issues in School Counseling; Chapter 45: Confidentiality with Minors

## CASE SCENARIOS

School counselors in training will encounter each case's presenting problem or concern during their training and certainly during their first few years in the field. This text helps to raise the self-efficacy levels of counselors as the underlying dynamics of the situation are explained from one or more theoretical perspectives. Specifically, each case scenario follows this outline:

- *Case Background:* The school counselor describes a brief case scenario and background.
- *Initial Process Questions:* Initial process questions help the reader react to and process the specific case before proceeding further. They also can point to related issues to address.
- *Addressing the Issues:* This section explains the theoretical frameworks/models and any techniques specific to the theoretical orientation the authors applied to the situation. A table that addresses multiple theoretical techniques by grade level broadens understanding of the issue as it presents interventions for children at the elementary, middle, and high school levels.
- *In Session:* A brief transcript of essential portions of the actual intervention gives an idea of what a counselor actually said and did in session.
- *Outcome:* This is a summary of how the intervention turned out.
- *Final Process Questions:* Final process questions facilitate deeper exploration and understanding of the issues.
- *Resources*

## Conclusion

The purpose of this text is to expose you to numerous situations you are likely to encounter during training and the first five years of practice. It is our hope that this exposure as well as attention to the diverse theoretical approaches that can be applied to resolve these student situations will better prepare you to deal with each dilemma using a fluid, dynamic, and flexible approach to school counseling. As you delve into your training, we hope that using these cases and a flexible case conceptualization model early in your career as a professional school counselor will speed up your development, better prepare you, and give you confidence for meeting the trials ahead. You have chosen an admirable, honorable, and respectable career path full of challenges and rewards. While embarking on your journey to becoming a professional school counselor, we hope this text aids you in addressing some of these challenges so that you can hit the ground running!

*Chapter 2*

# Theories of Counseling

DANA HELLER LEVITT, ALISSA DARNELL, BRADLEY T. ERFORD, AND ANN VERNON

## THE SIGNIFICANCE OF THEORY

Theories ground us as professional school counselors by providing a means to understand what we are doing, how we are serving students, and how to explain counseling to students. Students entering counseling are generally not interested in hearing a detailed description of their school counselor's philosophical beliefs about the nature of the counseling relationship and human change. Rather, they are seeking guidance in the change process and are interested in how the professional school counselor can help them. Regardless, theories represent students' realities and what we know to be important and effective elements of the counseling relationship (Hansen, 2006a). Professional school counselors therefore must have a firm sense of the counseling process as well as their own philosophies about what works in counseling and how individuals change and grow.

An understanding of one's beliefs about counseling can help in explaining the process to students, so that they understand the nature of counseling and what can be expected (Gladding, 2012). This road map for counseling can help the school counselor generate new ideas with the student to determine the best course of action to reach goals.

Theories provide a framework for conceptualizing student problems and determining a course of action in counseling (Halbur & Halbur, 2006). For example, a professional school counselor who operates from a cognitive-behavioral standpoint would identify a student's struggle with bulimia as faulty logic and plan a course of treatment to reshape thoughts and behaviors. On the other hand, a professional school counselor who is psychodynamically oriented would view the issue through the lens of the student's past and therefore spend counseling time uncovering early triggers and sustaining factors for the disorder.

## THEORETICAL PARADIGMS

Through self-awareness, professional school counselors strengthen their approaches and learn new ways to work with students. Theoretical orientation usually remains relatively constant through most school counselors' development given its connection to personal philosophy. Changes that occur tend to be within general categories of theories, referred to as paradigms, which are a means of grouping theories based on common characteristics. Multiple theories exist within each paradigm. Tables 2-1

| TABLE 2-1   Theoretical Paradigms: Theories and Theorists | | |
|---|---|---|
| **Paradigm** | **Major Theories** | **Prominent Theorists** |
| Psychodynamic | Psychoanalysis | Sigmund Freud |
| | Adlerian | Alfred Adler |
| | Ego Psychology | Carl Jung |
| Humanistic/Existential | Person-Centered | Carl Rogers |
| | Existential | Viktor Frankl, Irvin Yalom, Rollo May |
| | Gestalt | Fritz Perls |
| Behavioral/Cognitive-Behavioral | Behavioral | John Watson, B. F. Skinner, Albert Bandura |
| | Cognitive | Aaron Beck |
| | Cognitive-Behavioral Therapy | Donald Meichenbaum |
| | Rational Emotive Behavior Therapy | Albert Ellis |
| | Reality Therapy | William Glasser |
| | Solution-Focused Brief Counseling | Steven de Shazer |
| Systems | Family Systems | Murray Bowen, Virginia Satir |
| Emergent | Narrative | Michael White, David Epston |
| | Constructivist | George Kelly |
| | Feminist | |
| | Interpersonal Psychotherapy (IPT) | |

and 2-2 provide a summary of the five most prominent paradigms: psychodynamic, humanistic/existential, behavioral/cognitive-behavioral, systems, and emergent.

Theories can be described as having specific and common factors. Specific factors are the unique characteristics of a given theory—those elements that distinguish one theory from another and are often the basis of association with a theory. For example, the empty chair technique is a specific factor for Gestalt, a humanistic/existential theory. Disputing irrational beliefs is unique to Albert Ellis's rational emotive behavior therapy (REBT) and the behavioral/cognitive-behavioral paradigm. Common factors are characteristics that appear in all theoretical perspectives. For example, a therapeutic alliance and a healing setting that promotes student trust through professional counselor competence are common factors. A coherent rationale and set of procedures are also common to all theories. These are important principles for graduate counseling students to keep in mind as they review the major paradigms and begin to formulate their own approach to counseling.

The following discussion of theories and paradigms is broad in nature. We encourage you to read further about theories in the references provided throughout this chapter and to research specific theories of interest in greater depth.

**TABLE 2-2   Theoretical Paradigms: Principles, Techniques, and Multicultural Considerations**

| Paradigm | Principles | Techniques | Considerations |
|---|---|---|---|
| Psychodynamic | Predetermined<br>Relationship of events and current functioning<br>Bring unconscious into conscious | Free association<br>Interpretation<br>Dream analysis<br>Analysis of transference | Ego and past cultural identity development<br>Id, ego, superego development<br>Limited views of women |
| Humanistic/Existential | Innate goodness of people<br>Self-actualization<br>Freedom and responsibility<br>Finding meaning<br>Anxiety | Counseling relationship<br>Empty chair, "I" statements<br>Genuineness, unconditional positive regard, empathy<br>Role play, role reversal | Attention to individual's unique perspective<br>Lack of structure<br>Limited attention to external factors<br>Common values of love, death, and anxiety |
| Behavioral/Cognitive behavioral | Changing behavior, negative thought patterns, beliefs<br>ABCDEs of REBT<br>Disputing irrational beliefs | Specify automatic thoughts<br>Token economy, homework<br>Cognitive restructuring<br>Thought stopping | Understanding beliefs as identity<br>Structure<br>Caution when challenging belief systems |
| Systems | Family provides framework for understanding individual<br>Differentiation of self | Genograms, questions<br>Coaching, "I" position<br>De-triangulation | Identity patterns<br>Caution when attempting to change multigenerational patterns<br>Resistance to external input on family |
| Emergent (Narrative) | Retell story to create favorable outcomes<br>Person is not the problem | Deconstruct problems<br>Externalize problems<br>Miracle question<br>Sparkling moments | Many cultures emphasize storytelling<br>High-level processing required |
| (Constructivism) | Personal reality<br>Personal construct | Card sort, repertory<br>Identify constructs | Insight required<br>Challenges test beliefs and principles |

*(continued)*

| TABLE 2-2 (continued) | | | |
|---|---|---|---|
| **Paradigm** | **Principles** | **Techniques** | **Considerations** |
| (Feminist) | Application of feminist principles: equality, empowerment<br>Mutuality<br>Androgyny | Gender role analysis<br>Empowerment<br>Egalitarian relationship<br>Sociocultural exploration of gender | Addresses shared experiences of oppression<br>Political action may be against belief<br>Limited application with men |
| (Interpersonal Psychotherapy) | Improve interpersonal functioning, social network<br>Attachment, social, and communication theories<br>Present focus | Therapeutic alliance<br>Communication analysis<br>Interpersonal incidents<br>Content and process affect<br>Role playing | Flexible and adaptable to unique individuals |

## PSYCHODYNAMIC PARADIGM

At the time of his work, Sigmund Freud's thinking and conceptualizing of the problems experienced by people, primarily women, was considered revolutionary. Today, many theories are based upon Freud's work, either added to what he developed or created as an alternate explanation to a theory heavily focused on the past and the subconscious mind. For this reason, the psychodynamic paradigm serves as an introduction to and foundation of the other paradigms of counseling theories.

Theories that fall under the psychodynamic paradigm are based largely on insight, unconscious motivation, and personality reconstruction. The psychodynamic paradigm holds that most issues students face are the result of unresolved issues from their early development. The focus in counseling from a psychodynamic framework is on the relationship of past events to current functioning. For example, the professional school counselor may question how childhood messages of expected success are affecting current student performance in school and the subsequent feelings experienced. The psychodynamic approach is very analytic in nature, and it may require a good deal of time to uncover past issues and make headway into current and future functioning.

### Psychoanalysis

Freud's psychoanalytic theory is probably the most widely recognized theory in the psychodynamic paradigm. Many people may have the image of a wise therapist sitting behind a couch on which a client lies and contemplates the meaning of past events. Many popular media depictions do little to ameliorate this stereotype and may perpetuate the public's beliefs about the nature of counseling in general. Although this image may have been the form of psychoanalysis in early renditions of the theory, much has changed since Freud's groundbreaking approach to counseling to challenge the means by which professional school counselors with a psychoanalytic orientation help their students.

Freud believed that personality is completely formed in childhood and that challenges later in life are the result of unresolved conflicts. Consistent with the idea that theories emerge from our personal philosophies and experiences, Freud's background demonstrates his emphasis on childhood and the family. The eldest of eight siblings of an authoritarian father, Freud was particularly close to his mother. His upbringing and religious affiliation (a Jew in Vienna, Austria, in the mid- to late 1800s) limited his career aspirations to medicine or law. One might then see his own life experiences as the basis of Freud's intense self-analysis and his subsequent theories of personality dynamics.

In psychoanalysis, the personality is perceived as being composed of three parts: the id, or pleasure principle; ego, or reality principle; and superego, or morality principle (conscience). Conflict among these structures creates anxiety in the individual. The ego often manages the subsequent anxiety by employing defense mechanisms, which can be either adaptive or damaging. These mechanisms help the individual to cope with the anxiety and not feel overwhelmed.

The goal of psychoanalytic counseling is to bring unconscious drives into consciousness and thereby develop insight into intrapsychic conflicts. Techniques such as free association, interpretation, dream analysis, and analysis of resistance and transference may be employed to assist in the development of insight. As might be expected (and often a criticism of this approach), this process can be quite lengthy and time consuming.

The psychoanalytic counselor is like a blank screen. Listening, analyzing, and attending to transference and countertransference issues are essential to successful counseling in the psychoanalytic approach. The therapeutic relationship takes the form of professional school counselor as expert, teaching students about the intrapsychic processes occurring.

Concepts such as defense mechanisms and transference seem to be relevant for individuals from various backgrounds. The culturally sensitive school counselor may encourage individuals from ethnic, racial, or sexual minority groups to develop an overall ego identity as well as a cultural identity. It is also important for psychoanalytic counselors to address their own potential biases and recognize how countertransference could unintentionally play a part in the counseling process. A limitation for multicultural counseling in psychoanalysis is in the area of gender issues. Women are seen as inferior to men because they do not resolve the Electra complex as completely as it is thought that men resolve the Oedipus complex. This concept and other similar concepts, such as penis envy, have been largely discredited and discontinued. For independent study on psychoanalysis, these foundational resources will be helpful:

Freud, A. (1936). *The ego and the mechanisms of defense* (J. Strachey, Trans.). New York, NY: International Universities Press.

Freud, S. (1900/1955). *The interpretations of dreams* (J. Strachey, Trans.). London, UK: Hogarth.

Freud, S. (1923/1933). *New introductory lectures on psychoanalysis* (W. J. H. Sprott, Trans.). New York, NY: Norton.

Freud, S. (1923/1947). *The ego and the id* (J. Strachey, Trans.). London, UK: Hogarth.

## Adlerian Counseling

Alfred Adler, a student of Freud's, developed his theory as a result of disagreeing with many of the principles his mentor proposed. Adler commended Freud's work on dream interpretation, yet the generalizations Freud drew from dreams and his emphasis on sexual trauma and development did not resonate with Adler. Herein lies another example of the need to formulate a specifically personally relevant theory of counseling. Adler left Freud's tutelage to develop his holistic approach of focusing on the client as a whole person, an indivisible being capable of growth and seeking social interest and connections with others. Similar to Freud, Adler emphasized the role of childhood in personality development and problem (and solution) formation.

Adler's work has been widely used, yet not widely researched or developed. It is best known for its emphasis on and analysis of birth order and sibling relationships. Tom Sweeney (1998), Terry Kottman, Don Dinkmeyer, James Bitter, and Richard Watts are a few modern Adlerian scholars. Traces of Adler's work are evident in the wellness movement in the counseling profession. Commonly used Adlerian-based techniques include the use of "I" messages, "acting as if," and "spitting in the client's soup."

The Adlerian concept of social interest supports the theory's cultural sensitivity. Individuals are encouraged to move beyond themselves to learn about and understand different cultural groups and how they may contribute to the greater society. Cultures that emphasize the family find that many Adlerian concepts align with their value systems. However, limitations exist when emphasis is placed on changing the autonomous self and on exploration of early childhood experiences. Some students may find it inappropriate to reveal family information, or may not want to delve into the past as they may not see the connection to current pressing concerns. For more information regarding Adlerian counseling, the following resources will be useful:

Adler, A. (1927). *Understanding human nature.* Greenwich, CT: Fawcett.

Adler, A. (1964). *Social interest. A challenge to mankind.* New York, NY: Capricorn.

Adler, A. (1969). *The practice and theory of individual psychology.* Patterson, NJ: Little-field, Adams.

Dreikurs, R. (1953). *Fundamentals of Adlerian psychology.* Chicago, IL: Alfred Adler Institute.

Sweeney, T. J. (1998). *Adlerian counseling: A practitioner's approach* (4th ed.). Philadelphia, PA: Accelerated Development.

## Other Psychodynamic Theories

Jungian theory, also referred to as ego psychology, and object relations theory are other approaches that fit within this paradigm. Although many principles of these theories are used today, more modern adaptations of psychoanalysis and Adlerian counseling are seen more readily in practice. To study a foundational work by Carl Jung, refer to the following resource:

Jung, C. G. (1961). *Memories, dreams, reflections.* New York, NY: Vintage.

Table 2-3 provides a listing of strategies and techniques aligned with the psycho-dynamic paradigm.

**TABLE 2-3    Psychodynamic Strategies and Interventions**

- Analysis of transference and countertransference
- Analysis of private logic
- Parent or teacher consultations
- Encouragement
- Analysis of Adlerian goals of misbehavior (attention, power, inadequacy) and building social interest through group activities
- Teaching "I" statements and other skills
- Encouraging insight into unconscious aspects of problem through creative processes
- Adlerian play therapy to discover the child's lifestyle and private logic
- Teaching parents techniques for encouraging the child
- Family constellation and family atmosphere
- Lifestyle analysis
- Striving for significance and belonging
- Natural and logical consequences
- Early recollections to understand the child's behavior patterns
- Adlerian family counseling for family to learn to operate cooperatively
- Variation of activities between play and talking can be used such as during sand play or drawing
- The use of metaphor and the exploration of developmental themes highlighted in movies, TV, and books
- Focus on helping the student become more self-aware through the use of pictures, stories, and metaphors
- Helping the student to accept responsibility for the life choices that come with becoming an adult and to avoid regression toward childhood, where decisions were made on his or her behalf
- Assisting with adult identity formation in a culturally sensitive fashion
- Exploration of recurrent themes in the child's fantasies and play
- Using play therapy techniques to understand the student's current emotional state
- "Acting as if"
- Free association
- Determining events of childhood that may have a larger impact later in life
- Empty chair
- Role play
- Sand tray play and puppets to help younger children project angry feelings outside of themselves

*(continued)*

**TABLE 2-3**  *(continued)*

- Trying a projection game such as "Parallels with Animals" in which the counselor asks the child what different animals look, act, and sound like when they are angry (Vernon, 2004)
- Artwork
- Incomplete sentences
- Psycho-educational lessons/handouts on self-understanding
- Recognizing feelings and basic motivation
- Mutual storytelling
- Drawing a tree and making a branch for each person the student feels he or she can trust
- Analysis of avoidance (e.g., refusing to come to school)
- Talking about the fears and worries that may be embedded in the unconscious
- Relationship of events and current functioning
- Dream analysis
- Analysis of ego development (fragile ego, under-/overdeveloped superego)
- Analysis of anxiety and defense mechanisms (especially avoidance)
- Use of sand tray and symbolic play to better understand conscious and unconscious struggles
- Patterns of similar behavior of family members
- Interpreting the reason for behavior based on dialogue, drawings, or dreams
- Exploration of relationships between current behavior and past or current life events
- Attachment assessment and introduction of stable adult figure
- Exploration of relationships with teachers perceived as "safe" or "unsafe"
- Exploration of unconscious themes through use of a timeline to chart significant life events
- Verbally explore the student's past and how this affects current behavior
- Use of various art mediums such as drawing and sculpture to allow students to explore and work through early childhood stressors
- Listing some positive things about self to draw on strengths, encourage and build self-esteem
- Analysis of relationship with father and mother throughout childhood
- Assistance in achieving industry versus inferiority, identity versus role confusion
- Expressive techniques in uncovering unconscious struggles
- Uncovering and processing attachment issues, childhood conflicts, and motivation for behavior
- Exploration of conflicts regarding maintaining power/status quo in classroom
- Processing childhood interests and experiences, and how one views family and self roles
- Exploration of the use of emotion (e.g., anger) to mask hurt
- Analysis of immature/neurotic defenses (projection, regression, acting out, splitting, devaluation, displacement, rationalization, intellectualization)

# HUMANISTIC/EXISTENTIAL PARADIGM

In contrast to the subconscious focus of the psychodynamic paradigm, the humanistic/ existential paradigm is relationship-oriented. Rather than concentrating on an individual's unresolved conflicts in the past, the emphasis of this paradigm is on current and future functioning. Humanism and existentialism are similar in the belief that human nature is fundamentally good, and people have the freedom and responsibility to grow and develop.

Humanists believe that goodness and worth are qualities that people possess. In the journey toward self-actualization, people are considered purposeful, active, and capable of determining their own behavior (Jones & Nugent, 2008). Similarly, existentialists emphasize the importance of anxiety, freedom, values, and responsibility and finding meaning in one's actions (Gladding, 2012). Another parallel between humanists and existentialists is that both stress the importance of the student–counselor relationship. The professional counselor must enter the student's subjective world in order to focus on student perceptions of the presenting issue.

## Person-Centered Counseling

Person-centered counseling, developed by Carl Rogers (1951, 1957), is a major theoretical approach in the humanistic framework. Over time, this method has also been identified as nondirective, client-centered, and Rogerian. According to Rogers, the primary motivating force of humans is self-actualization, the tendency to move in the direction of growth, adjustment, socialization, independence, and self-realization (McWhirter & Ishikawa, 2005).

Because people have the basic need for a high self-regard, they attempt to organize their internal and external experiences into an integrated self. During this process of self-actualizing, unhealthy psychological or social influences may hinder an individual from realizing his or her potential as an integrated, productive self. In other words, conflicts develop when individuals' basic needs and their needs to obtain approval from others are inconsistent.

Rogers (1957) identified three essential characteristics a professional counselor must employ for a therapeutic relationship to be established: genuineness (or congruence), unconditional positive regard, and empathy. Genuineness is displaying honesty, sincerity, and directness while avoiding any personal or professional façade. Unconditional positive regard is the professional counselor's ability to accept every aspect of the student's personality while remaining nonjudgmental and nonevaluative toward the student's feelings, thoughts, and behaviors. Empathy is the ability to understand the student's world in the way the student understands it. Creating a nonthreatening, anxiety-free relationship will allow students to resolve conflicts and reach self-understanding.

Person-centered counseling has had a significant impact on the area of human relations with diverse cultural groups. Many countries have adopted person-centered concepts in counseling as well as in cross-cultural communication and education. Multicultural limitations include lack of structure, difficulty translating core conditions to practice, and focus on internal evaluation, rather than external evaluation (Corey, 2009). The following resources provide more information about person-centered counseling:

Rogers, C. (1942). *Counseling and psychotherapy.* Boston, MA: Houghton Mifflin.

Rogers, C. (1951). *Student-centered therapy.* Boston, MA: Houghton Mifflin.

Rogers, C. (1961). *On becoming a person.* Boston, MA: Houghton Mifflin.

Rogers, C. (1980). *A way of being.* Boston, MA: Houghton Mifflin.

## Existential Theory

Existentialism stems from the work of Søren Kierkegaard, a 19th-century philosopher who focused on the pursuit of becoming an individual. There are many contributors to existentialism as a therapeutic approach including Ludwig Binswanger, Fyodor Dostoyevsky, Friedrich Nietzsche, and Abraham Maslow. In more recent years, notable figures in existential psychotherapy include Rollo May, Viktor Frankl, and Irvin Yalom.

The essence of existentialism is the belief that humans have the capacity for self-awareness and the freedom and responsibility to make choices that would bring about meaning in their lives. However, along with this freedom comes the reality of living with the consequences of those choices, which could lead to existential anxiety. May (1977) asserted that normal anxiety can be healthy and motivational.

Frankl (1963) maintained that, despite negative conditions, individuals can preserve their own independent thinking, spiritual freedom, and opportunities for choice. In contrast, an individual who sees life as meaningless and without value would be thought to be in what Frankl termed an *existential vacuum.* A well-functioning person is an individual who authentically experiences reality and expresses needs in a way that is not determined by others.

Other than concentrating on the student–counselor relationship, there is no systematic way that existential counselors help others. Still, Yalom (2002) was able to emphasize three significant qualities within the existential counseling process: (1) helping students attend to the here and now, (2) being open and authentic with their students, and (3) cautiously using self-disclosure.

Specific goals in existential counseling include the following: encouraging students to be sensitive to their own existence, identifying characteristics unique to each student, assisting students in enhancing interactions with others, helping students pursue meaning in life, and promoting present and future decision making that will impact one's direction in life. Few specific techniques are offered in an existential approach. All interventions are undertaken with the intention of assisting students to find meaning in their own actions.

The existential focus on love, suffering, anxiety, and death—the universal elements of human life—makes this theory quite applicable cross-culturally. In contrast, a limitation of multicultural existential counseling involves the emphasis on self-determination and the lack of focus on the environment and the social context. Some students may feel powerless in the face of external realities such as discrimination, racism, and oppression. Refer to the following resources for more information on existential counseling:

Frankl, V. (1963). *Man's search for meaning.* Boston, MA: Beacon.

May, R. (1953). *Man's search for himself.* New York, NY: Dell.

May, R. (Ed.). (1961). *Existential psychology.* New York, NY: Random House.

Yalom, I. D. (1980). *Existential psychotherapy.* New York, NY: Basic Books.

# Gestalt Therapy

Gestalt therapy began in response to the reductionist emphasis in schools of counseling such as psychoanalysis and behaviorism, which attempted to break an individual's personality or behaviors into understandable parts. In contrast, Gestalt therapy promoted the idea of wholeness. Frederick (Fritz) Perls and his wife, Laura Perls, were the major theorists associated with this school of thought.

Similar to the view of person-centered counselors, Gestaltists believe that people have the tendency to move toward wholeness or self-actualization. They emphasize the present, as indicated by Perls's (1970) statement: "To me, nothing exists except the now. Now = experience = awareness = reality. The past is no more and the future is not yet. Only the *now* exists" (p. 14).

In contrast to psychoanalysis, which focuses on predetermined and unconscious forces, the Gestalt view of human nature is antideterministic, meaning that people can become responsible, grow, and change from past events. Sometimes people experience difficulties in life that are a result of earlier thoughts, feelings, or experiences—a phenomenon referred to as unfinished business. The role of the Gestalt counselor is (1) to provide an atmosphere that allows students to identify and pursue growth, and (2) to help redirect energy into more positive and adaptive ways of functioning.

Gestalt counselors also directly confront students with their inconsistencies. They focus on the polarities within people and push students to correct misconceptions, to genuinely express emotions, and to take responsibility for change. Gestalt techniques may include exercises and experiments such as empty chair, role playing, role reversal, dream analysis, exaggerated body movements, and the use of "I" statements (Erford, Eaves, Bryant, & Young, 2010). Other characteristics of Gestalt counseling that help students develop and become mature in the "now" include awareness of nonverbal and verbal expressions and shedding neurotic tendencies. Perls (1970) identified five layers of neurosis that were thought to impede a student's ability to be in touch with himself or herself. Only when individuals reach the final, or explosive, layer can they be truly authentic and in touch with themselves and others.

Gestalt counseling can be viewed as a culturally sensitive theory because the experiments employed by professional school counselors may encourage students to integrate the polarities that exist between the cultures to which they belong. Further, Gestalt techniques can also be tailored to fit a student's distinct perception and interpretation of his or her own cultural framework. However, the individualistic focus of Gestalt counseling may engender conflict for people from cultures that emphasize group values. The following resources will be useful in the further study of Gestalt therapy:

Perls, F. (1969). *Gestalt therapy verbatim.* Moab, UT: Real People Press.

Perls, F. (1972). *In and out of the garbage pail.* New York, NY: Bantam.

Polster, E., & Polster, M. (1973). *Gestalt therapy integrated: Contours of theory and practice.* New York, NY: Brunner/Mazel.

Zinker, J. (1978). *Creative process in Gestalt therapy.* New York, NY: Random House.

Table 2-4 provides strategies and techniques aligned with the humanistic/existential paradigm.

**TABLE 2-4**   **Humanistic/Existential Strategies and Interventions**

- Therapeutic conditions (genuineness, unconditional positive regard, empathy)
- Modeling active listening, congruence, unconditional positive regard, and empathy with family
- Use of role play and reverse role play to assist student in finding meaning of current behavior while encouraging responsibility
- "I" statements
- Focus on the present, immediacy
- Active listening and reflection of feelings
- Building relationship
- Providing opportunity for empathy and safe exploration of thoughts, feelings, and behaviors
- Encouraging self-awareness and choice, leading to acceptance of self and others
- Gently confronting inconsistencies
- Teaching family members to (1) focus on the here and now, (2) take responsibility for their own thoughts, actions, feelings, and sensations, and (3) accept personal responsibility for change
- Teaching family members to substitute the use of *won't* for *can't* and to substitute the use of *what* and *how* for *why*
- Teaching parents to use self-esteem–building activities with child
- Encouragement of self-exploration and self-discovery through a warm, supportive, and affirming therapeutic relationship
- Through the relationship, the student learns to accept himself or herself and begin the journey toward self-actualization
- Providing support around goal setting
- Counseling seen as a way of *being with*, rather than *doing to* the student
- Culturally sensitive play therapy techniques, giving children the opportunity to *play out* rather than *talk out* feelings
- Appreciation for student uniqueness
- Focus on choice, taking responsibility for actions, and the present and future
- Redirecting energy or actions
- Focus on the person the student desires to be through art therapy techniques (mask activity)
- Avoiding use of desks in order to be more personal than authoritative
- Respecting the student regardless of acting-out behaviors
- Creating a job or role for the student to feel a sense of meaning
- Creating a memory box to feel a sense of accomplishment and connection when he or she adds to the box
- Examination of anxiety and behavioral issues related to safety, belonging, and personal and global responsibility and freedom (to classmates, classroom, school, community)
- Mentoring relationship
- Minimal encouragers and few questions

- Acceptance and trust
- Puppets and expressive art therapies for social issues and familial issues
- Reflective play therapy to process anxiety and substance abuse
- Cautious self-disclosure
- Music and art as adjunctive techniques
- Helping parents and staff understand the student's perspective
- Role playing potential scenarios relevant to responsible and irresponsible behavior
- Identifying emotions and appropriate expression
- Examination of anxiety and behavioral issues and a sense of belonging to classmates, classroom, school, and community
- Informal "lunch bunches" with student and potential friends to foster relationships among peers and a sense of accomplishment and connection
- Redirection of energy or actions
- Encouraging student to write a letter to his or her ideal self
- Use of humor to lighten the mood
- Exploration of significant changes in life, both good and bad
- Helping to find meaning by having student work with even younger students
- Development of self-awareness
- Demonstrating respect for the student's unique self
- Consultations with familial environments/guardians
- Framing student understanding of self in the context of community
- Helping student to find a place through a major life transition
- Developing activities that correct behavior but with respect and regard for the student as an individual
- Exploration of parent feelings toward students and any incongruence
- Helping to provide a sense of belonging by creating a special role for the student (i.e., mentor younger students, special job to complete daily)
- Helping the client to work through the feelings of "stuckness" that can accompany transitions
- Exploration of life scripts
- Allowing student to analyze ads for messages
- Consideration of students' roles in society and the meaning of their choices
- Exploration of conflict regarding future plans
- Providing decision-making models for present and future use
- Exploration of scenarios using the empty chair technique
- Exploration of the meaning of place in the world at this time
- Identification and resolution of incongruences

# BEHAVIORAL/COGNITIVE-BEHAVIORAL PARADIGM

Students seek action to change a current dilemma. The behavioral/cognitive-behavioral paradigm is the most action-oriented of the theoretical groupings. Students are guided to pursue specific tangible changes in behavior and thought. From a practical standpoint, many beginning professional school counselors are drawn to this paradigm because of its many tools and techniques. Additionally, professional school counselors and students alike can more readily observe progress in counseling from this perspective.

## Behavioral Counseling

John B. Watson was one of the first advocates for behaviorism as he was able to establish that human emotions were receptive to conditioning. Over time, behaviorism has incorporated various ideas, practices, and theorists. Other theorists associated with this approach include Burrhus Frederic (B. F.) Skinner, Joseph Wolpe, Hans Eysenck, Albert Bandura, and John Krumboltz.

Behavioral theory focuses on how to reinforce, extinguish, or modify a wide range of behaviors. Specifically, it emphasizes the association between feelings and environmental stimuli, and the learning or unlearning of behaviors accordingly. Professional school counselors are mainly concerned with the science of observing behavior with the resulting consequence of whether to reward positive or extinguish negative behavior. This is accomplished by eliminating the cause or condition that triggered the behavior. A specific behavioral technique is the token economy, whereby students gain or lose tokens depending on whether they have reached a mutually agreed-upon target behavior. Other behavioral techniques include use of the Premack principle (i.e., do what you don't want to do before you do what you do want to do), behavioral contract, time-out, response cost, and overcorrection (Erford et al., 2010). Techniques based upon social learning theory include modeling, behavior rehearsal, and role play.

Another behavioral approach involves the stimulus-response model, which applies classical conditioning, or learning through the association of two stimuli. The most well-known example of this model is Ivan Pavlov's laboratory experiments with dogs. He found that when he paired two stimuli, food and the sound of a bell, the dogs would eventually associate the sound of the bell with food and begin salivating in response to the bell before the food was served. Similarly, certain human emotions such as phobias develop because of paired associations. Once these associations are learned, they can be unlearned and replaced through procedures referred to as counterconditioning or systematic desensitization.

The nature of the student–counselor relationship in behavioral counseling differs dramatically from that in the humanistic/existential approaches. Behavioral counselors function as active teachers, reinforcers, and facilitators who help students learn, unlearn, or relearn specific ways of behaving. It is also common for professional school counselors to enter into the student's environment to instruct people who are a part of helping the student's change process. Beyond the usage of reinforcers, behavioral counselors may use other techniques including systematic desensitization, assertiveness training, implosion and flooding, contingency contracts, and aversive techniques. The ideal outcome of most behavior modification programs is to have the student's new behavior continue after the program has terminated (response maintenance) and to have the desired behaviors generalized to environments outside of the counseling setting (Cottone, 1992).

Behavioral counseling has advantages for individuals who are from cultures that do not focus on the experience of catharsis. For example, its emphasis is on specific behaviors that the student wants to change and the development of problem-solving skills applicable to the issue being addressed. Behavioral counseling takes into account an individual's environmental conditions—such as sociocultural, political, and social influences—that could be contributing to psychological problems. Yet when professional school counselors fail to recognize conditions beyond the individual, such as a cultural emphasis on family, the success of the counseling is limited. Other resources on behavioral counseling include the following:

Bandura, A. (1969). *Principles of behavior modification.* New York, NY: Holt, Rinehart & Winston.

Skinner, B. F. (1953). *Science and human behavior.* New York, NY: Macmillan.

Watson, J. B. (1925). *Behaviorism.* New York, NY: Norton.

## Cognitive and Cognitive-Behavioral Therapies

In the 1970s, many mental health professionals recognized that behavioral approaches were too limited and saw value in combining them with cognitive approaches. Aaron Beck developed cognitive therapy, which focuses on recognizing and changing negative thoughts and maladaptive beliefs into more realistic and constructive thoughts and beliefs. The essence of cognitive therapy is the cognitive content or automatic thoughts associated with an individual's reaction to an event. Beck asserted that psychological problems were derived from common processes such as making incorrect inferences on the basis of incorrect information, being unable to distinguish between reality and fantasy, and faulty thinking. In short, he maintained that how people think basically determines how they feel and behave.

Donald Meichenbaum (1995) is one of the founding theorists of the cognitive-behavioral therapy (CBT) approach. Similar to Beck, Meichenbaum thought that helping people change the way they talk to themselves into more constructive cognitions was central to the counseling process. The maladaptive self-statements that affect individuals' behaviors are termed *cognitive distortions.* The nine ways of mentally assessing a situation are all-or-nothing thinking, catastrophizing, labeling and mislabeling, magnification and minimization, mind reading, negative predictions, overgeneralization, personalization, and selective abstraction (Gladding, 2012).

The CBT counselor collaborates with the student by sharing the responsibility of selecting goals and bringing about change. Specific techniques, such as specifying automatic thoughts, assigning homework, thought stopping, and cognitive restructuring, are useful in identifying and challenging distorted thoughts. Homework and practicing skills and self-talk learned in session help to challenge cognitive distortions. The dozens of creative CBT techniques are usually active, time-limited, and structured. Consulting the following resources will be helpful for further study of cognitive and cognitive-behavioral counseling:

Beck, A. T. (1976). *Cognitive therapy and emotional disorders.* New York, NY: New American Library.

Beck, A. T. (1987). *Love is never enough.* New York, NY: Harper & Row.

Meichenbaum, D. (1977). *Cognitive behavior modification: An integrative approach.* New York, NY: Plenum.

## Rational Emotive Behavior Therapy

Rational emotive behavior therapy (REBT) is similar to counseling theories that stress behaviors and cognitions by placing emphasis on thinking, judging, deciding, analyzing, and doing. Albert Ellis (1996), the founder of REBT, assumed that people contribute to their psychological problems by how they interpret life circumstances and events. The basis of his assumption is the idea of a cause-and-effect relationship between behaviors, cognitions, and emotions. This theory maintains that people have the potential for both rational and irrational thinking.

In other words, although people have a tendency to move toward growth, self-preservation, happiness, and self-actualization, they also have a propensity for self-destruction, intolerance, and self-blame. Ellis (1996) stressed that people generally feel the way they think. Minimizing irrational beliefs and replacing them with practical and effective beliefs is central to REBT.

The REBT counselor encourages students to identify irrational ideas that contribute to their disturbed behavior, challenges students to validate their beliefs, uses logical analysis to dispute the irrational beliefs, and teaches students how to replace their ideas with more rational beliefs. One way to accomplish these goals is to use the ABCDEs of REBT. The letter *A* (Activating Event) represents the activating experience, the letter *B* (Belief) represents what the person believes about the experience, and the letter *C* (Consequence) refers to the subsequent emotional reaction or behavioral response to *B*. The letter *D* (Disputing) represents disputing irrational beliefs, and the letter *E* (Evaluation) points to the development of a new response. Other specific techniques that REBT uses include humor, changing one's language, rational-emotive imagery, role playing, and other behavioral techniques.

The cognitive-behavioral counseling approaches have advantages from a cultural perspective. For example, in the process of identifying and understanding students' values and beliefs, professional school counselors are able to understand fully students' conflicting feelings. Also, the emphasis on cognition, behavior, and relationship issues, and the structure provided, can benefit people from various populations. However, these approaches are limited when the professional school counselor does not fully understand the student's cultural background. It is important for professional school counselors to proceed with sensitivity and caution when challenging beliefs, values, and ideas. For more information on REBT, refer to the following resources:

Ellis, A. (1973). *Humanistic psychotherapy: The rational-emotive approach.* New York, NY: Julian Press.

Ellis, A. (1994). *Reason and emotion in psychotherapy revised.* Secaucus, NJ: Birch Lane.

Ellis, A. (1996). *Better, deeper, and more enduring brief therapy: The rational emotive behavior therapy approach.* New York, NY: Brunner/Mazel.

## Reality Therapy

William Glasser developed choice theory, which is based on the assumption that all behavior is purposeful and is a choice. Glasser contended that most people do not have a clear understanding of why they behave as they do; they choose behaviors they think will help them cope with frustrations caused by dissatisfactory relationships, which constitute many of the problems people have.

Also central to choice theory is that humans make choices based on the physiological need of survival and four psychological needs: love and belonging, power, freedom, and fun. Survival relates to how to maintain good health and a satisfying life. Love and belonging signify the importance of involvement with people and the need to love and be loved. Power refers to the need to be in charge of one's life and to have a sense of accomplishment. Freedom is the need to make choices, whereas fun is the need to laugh, experience humor, and enjoy life. Individuals attempt to control their world in order to satisfy these five basic needs, which differ in degree. Importantly, choice theory provides the theoretical underpinnings of Glasser's approach, and reality therapy is the counseling application of choice theory.

Reality therapy stresses the present, thereby helping people solve current problems. Instead of emphasizing feelings, its focus is on thinking and acting in order to initiate change (Glasser, 1999). Reality therapy, whether employed in an individual or a group setting, is active, didactic, and directive. It teaches students to look at whether their actions are getting them what they want, examine their needs and perceptions, and make a plan for change.

One of the basic premises of reality therapy is that connection and interpersonal relationships are very important, which leads to wide applicability of reality therapy to groups. With this in mind, a primary role of a school counselor is to establish a good relationship with the student by engaging in not only warm and caring interactions but also direct and confrontational interactions, as appropriate.

According to Glasser (1999), professional school counselors need to demonstrate openness to their own growth and a willingness to explore their own values with the student. They must be responsible individuals who can fulfill their own needs in order to help others do the same. Therefore, they must be mentally and emotionally mature, supportive, involved, accepting, and respectful of all students so they can serve as role models of responsible behavior. Professional school counselors help students to find effective ways to meet their needs and to develop specific action plans so that students can make the necessary changes to attain their goals.

Wubbolding (1991) identified four techniques commonly employed in reality therapy: humor, paradox, skillful questioning, and self-help procedures. According to Wubbolding, humor helps students to develop an awareness of a situation and should be used only after considering the timing, focus, and degree of trust. Paradox, whereby students are asked to perform the problematic behavior under certain circumstances while restraining the behavior's expression under all other circumstances, can be effective for some students, but should be used cautiously in school settings. Skillful questioning involves using open-ended questions to help students explore issues. It is also important to focus on positive behaviors that students would like to target.

Advantages of reality therapy are that it stresses accountability and includes a structure that helps individuals develop action plans for change. In addition, choice theory is a straightforward, flexible, and relatively brief approach to counseling. Students learn to accept responsibility for their behavior, realize that they can control themselves but not others, and develop their problem-solving abilities. Limitations of this approach include the de-emphasis on feelings and lack of exploration of the past, and counselors are cautioned against being too simplistic or acting as moral experts.

## Solution-Focused Brief Counseling

Brief counseling approaches have become increasingly popular since the 1980s due to managed care and other accountability initiatives. Currently the most prominent orientation is solution-focused brief counseling (SFBC). Although SFBC could easily be placed under the emergent paradigm, given its action-oriented brief strategies, we have included it under the behavioral/cognitive-behavioral paradigm.

SFBC is a social constructivist model by which students derive personal meaning from the events of their lives as they explain them with personal narratives. SFBC counselors value a therapeutic alliance that stresses empathy, collaboration, curiosity, and respectful understanding, but not expertness. de Shazer (1988; 1991) and O'Hanlon and Weiner-Davis (1989) are often credited as being the scholarly and theoretical forces behind SFBC. This model de-emphasizes the traditional therapeutic focus on a student's problems and instead stresses what works for the student (i.e., successes and solutions) and the times in the student's life during which the problems are not occurring. Berg and Miller (1992, p. 17) proposed three basic rules by which SFB counselors operate: (1) "If it ain't broke, don't fix it"; (2) "once you know what works, do more of it"; and (3) "if it doesn't work, don't do it again." It is easy to see the basic appeal of this commonsense approach to counseling.

Walter and Peller (1992) proposed five assumptions that expand upon these three basic rules: (1) Concentrating on successes leads to constructive change; (2) students realize that for every problem that exists, exceptions can be found during which the problem does not exist, effectively giving them the solutions to their problems; (3) small positive changes lead to bigger positive changes; (4) all students can solve their own problems by exposing, detailing, and replicating successes during exceptions; and (5) goals need to be stated in positive, measurable, and active terms. Sklare (2005) successfully applied SFBC to children and adolescents using these rules and assumptions to focus on changing student actions, rather than insights. Sklare concluded that insights do not lead to solutions; successful actions lead to solutions.

Five techniques are commonly associated with SFBC (Erford et al., 2010): scaling, exceptions, problem-free and preferred future dialogue, miracle question, and flagging the minefield. Scaling, a very quick and helpful assessment technique with wide applicability, can be used when counseling individuals of nearly any age and from any theoretical perspective. Basically, scaling presents students with a 10-point (or 100-point) continuum and asks students to rate where they currently are with regard to, for example, sadness (1) or happiness (10); calm (1) or irate (10); hate (1) or love (10); totally unmotivated (1) or motivated (10). Scaling is helpful not only in gauging a student's current status on a wide range of issues but also when it is reused periodically to gauge student progress.

In addition, exceptions (Erford et al., 2010) are essential to the SFBC approach because they provide the solutions to the student's "problems." Counselors probe the student's background for times when the problem wasn't a problem, thereby determining exceptions and providing the student with alternative solutions to act upon. Problem-free and preferred future dialogue is the technique that allows the counselor to turn the counseling intervention from a problem-focused environment to a solution-focused environment. SFB counselors hold the core belief that when students focus on problems they become discouraged and disempowered, and any insight they might gain into the origin and sustenance of the problem is not therapeutically valuable. A complementary belief is that finding exceptions/solutions to problematic circumstances encourages and empowers students, leading to actions and successes. The miracle question helps to reconstruct the way a student perceives a problematic circumstance into a vision for success, which motivates the student to pursue the actions that will lead to successes.

The final technique is a treatment adherence technique called flagging the minefield (Erford et al., 2010). Treatment adherence is critical in any field in which individuals seek and receive help. Many, even most, receive the help they seek but then do not follow the treatment regimen, for whatever reason, which basically guarantees the treatment will not be effective. For example, a patient may go to a doctor to address a medical condition, but then not follow the doctor's advice. Flagging the minefield, a technique ordinarily implemented during termination of treatment, facilitates students' thinking about situations during which the positive outcomes and strategies learned during counseling may not work, and thinking ahead of time about what should be done in those circumstances to persevere and succeed. Treatment adherence is a critical issue in counseling; what good is all that hard work and effort to alter problematic thoughts, feelings, and behaviors if the student will return to problematic functioning shortly after termination of treatment?

SFBC is a culturally respectful approach to working with students of diverse backgrounds because it discourages diagnoses, focuses on the student's personal frame of reference, and encourages the student to integrate and increase actions that have already been shown to be a successful fit for that personal frame of reference. The SFBC approach empowers students' personal values, beliefs, and behaviors, and does not try to dispute or alter these. It proposes that the student is the leading expert on what works for the student, and the counselor's role is to help the student recognize what the student knows to already work. The professional school counselor then encourages the student to alter his or her actions and "cheerleads" for the student's successes. SFBC approaches are particularly appreciated by students who prefer action-oriented, directive interventions and concrete goals (e.g., men, Arab Americans, Asian American, and Latinos).

Table 2-5 provides strategies and techniques aligned with the behavioral/CBT paradigm.

**TABLE 2-5   Behavioral/CBT Strategies and Interventions**

- Positive reinforcement
- Token economy
- Premack principle
- Behavior charts
- Behavior contracts
- Disputing irrational beliefs
- Cognitive restructuring
- Specifying automatic thoughts
- Analyzing negative self-talk and practicing positive self-talk

*(continued)*

**TABLE 2-5** *(continued)*

- Visual imagery
- Modeling
- Behavioral rehearsal
- Role playing
- Time-out
- "Picture in your mind"; what it would look like if . . .
- Exceptions
- Miracle question
- Overcorrection
- Response cost
- Flagging the minefield
- Behavioral play therapy
- Parent/guardian or teacher consultations
- Brainstorming
- Bibliotherapy/biblioguidance
- Recognizing and disputing negative thoughts and beliefs, and replacing with rational self-talk
- Thought stopping
- Behavioral homework
- Developing action plans for change
- Identifying positive behaviors and exceptions to the problem and striving to do more of the positive behaviors
- Scaling
- Teaching family about basic needs (survival, autonomy, control, belonging)
- Responsibility
- Teaching parents about the common irrational beliefs of children and parents
- ABCDE model
- Analysis of the client's shoulds, oughts, musts, catastrophizing, and awfulizing
- With children younger than 8 years old, focusing on concrete skills such as problem solving and behavior rehearsal
- With older children, the therapeutic alliance is essential to help the child "buy in" to the therapeutic process and establish goals for behavioral change
- Solution-focused brief counseling
- Development of coping strategies
- Consideration of contextual/environmental factors
- Guided imagery/relaxation

- Behavior intervention plans
- Scaling questions to address degree of catastrophizing
- Positive reframing to challenge negative predictions
- Assessment of triggers through drawing, role play, puppets, or sentence completion
- Postulating different points of view
- Practice of healthier self-talk
- "Picture on paper"
- Examination of a recent situation in which the student may have made a bad choice and asking the student what a better choice may have been
- Setting up a reward system for completed class work and homework
- Development of coping strategies
- Psycho-educational groups (e.g., friendship building, conflict resolution, emotional regulation)
- Positive feedback focusing on resources
- Reframing weaknesses into strengths
- Journaling or drawing about feelings and thoughts
- Understanding of one's perceptions of the issue and how those perceptions lead to feelings and actions
- Addressing negative predictions
- Boffey map
- Functional behavior assessment
- Instruction of parents to assist in helping the student change the behavior
- Assigning a job to foster a sense of belonging and responsibility
- Teaching students the stages of change with emphasis on timing and choice to modify behavior
- Building on perceived strengths and using culturally relevant examples
- Helping students understand that people think (and therefore feel) differently
- Teaching about choice theory and helping the student make a list of some of the good and poor choices made that have contributed to the current situation.
- Monitoring the student to determine compliance with writing homework assignments down and coming to school prepared
- Adopting a strengths-based approach that emphasizes successes not failures
- Making situationally intelligent decisions based on the context and salient cultural factors
- Consideration of the consequences of behavior to manage and direct thinking and actions to meet personal goals
- Collaboration to set up clear and tangible goals
- Exploration of realities of impact of behaviors/circumstances on future life plans (e.g., relationships, family planning)
- Facilitating an increasing awareness of reality testing to discover how the world works

## SYSTEMS PARADIGM

In contrast to the counseling approaches discussed thus far, the systems approach focuses on the interactive perspective, or the communication patterns within the student's family system. In other words, the family provides the framework for understanding how the student behaves in interpersonal relationships. As a pioneer in family therapy, Murray Bowen developed one of the most comprehensive views of human behavior of any approach to family therapy. The essence of Bowen's model is differentiation of self, which is the ability to maintain one's individuality in the face of group influences, namely, the pressures of a person's family (Nichols & Schwartz, 2005).

Bowen asserted that students have less emotional autonomy than they imagine, and that students are more dependent and reactive than we realize. Bowenian theory explains how the family, as a multigenerational structure of relationships, shapes the interaction of individuality and togetherness using these six concepts: differentiation of self, triangles, emotional cutoff, nuclear family emotional process, multigenerational transmission process, and societal emotional process (Bowen, 1966, 1976).

Normal family development is thought to occur when anxiety is low, family members are well differentiated, and partners are emotionally sound within their families of origin. This becomes difficult as most people leave home during the adolescence-to-adulthood transformation. The result often is that adult individuals react with adolescent sensitivity in their relationships with their parents and with others who interact in a way that is reminiscent of their parents (Nichols & Schwartz, 2005). Bowen stated that individuals are likely to repeat problematic behaviors in their own families that have been passed down from past generations unless they explore and resolve these patterns (Kerr & Bowen, 1988).

To help family members identify intergenerational patterns, and to help members differentiate from one another, a professional school counselor must remain calm and objective as well as be differentiated from his or her own family. A Bowenian counselor may work with all members of a family, although it is not necessary due to the belief that changing just one person may have a direct impact on the entire family system. Specific techniques that may be used include genograms, asking questions, "going home again," de-triangulation, person-to-person relationships, differentiation of self, coaching, and the "I" position (Gladding, 2012; Nichols & Schwartz, 2005).

The genogram can be an appropriate tool for professional school counselors to identify cultural aspects that influence family members' behavior. Also, evidence suggests that differentiation can be applied to individuals from different backgrounds. In contrast, some concepts may be limited in their application to people from diverse backgrounds. For more information regarding family systems counseling, refer to the following resources:

> Bowen, M. (1972). On the differentiation of self. In J. Framo (Ed.), *Family interaction: A dialogue between family researchers and family therapists* (pp. 111–173). New York, NY: Springer.

> Bowen, M. (1976). Theory in the practice of psychotherapy. In P. J. Guerin Jr. (Ed.), *Family therapy: Theory and practice* (pp. 42–90). New York, NY: Gardner Press.

> Bowen, M. (1978). *Family therapy in clinical practice.* New York, NY: Aronson.

Table 2-6 provides strategies and techniques aligned with the family systems paradigm.

**TABLE 2-6    Family Systems Strategies and Interventions**

- Caregiver or teacher training for dealing with relevant behavioral, academic, and social issues, and family dynamics
- Play therapy
- Parent/guardian or teacher consultations
- Teacher training on helping children cope with relevant issues
- Reaching out to caregivers to engage them in school
- Exploration of the family system through development of a genogram to identify behaviors and patterns passed down
- Coaching
- "I" position
- Teaching family members to recognize harmful communication patterns
- Assistance in building each family member's self-esteem
- Teaching family members differentiation by modeling "I" statements
- Focus on familial relationships and times when the family successfully overcame difficulties
- Emphasis on strengths, community, and resources
- Education of parents on signs, process, and interventions related to issues (e.g., bullying, divorce)
- Focus on interpersonal relationships
- Family as framework for understanding individual
- Use of parent skills training for promoting family connectedness and involvement
- Analysis of family rules and expectations
- Evaluation of family communication style
- Exploration of family conflict management techniques
- If family members are unavailable, asking students what they would be doing or saying if family members were there
- Highlighting strengths in the existing system
- Use of metaphors and narrative to indirectly guide students to healthier ways of behaving and coping
- Miracle question
- Sparkling moments
- Exploring interpersonal incidents
- Role playing
- Exceptions
- Flagging the minefield
- Providing resources in the community to support the family
- Teaching individuality despite family pressure

*(continued)*

**TABLE 2-6** *(continued)*

- Collaboration with parents about expectations
- Counseling for siblings and/or parents
- Parent education about school support systems available
- Education and collaboration with school personnel to assist student
- Assessment of family needs
- Teaching caregiver skills to support developmental needs, consistency, and availability, and exploring alternative solutions
- Autobiography/timeline of family events through sand, art, or play
- Family sculpting
- Analysis of family dynamics
- Referral to local agency for family intervention
- Identifying triggers
- Coaching
- Assessing basic needs of family
- Building a pattern of communication conducive to emotional expression
- Identification of key school and community persons who can assist the family in getting an evaluation for student
- Consultation with faith-based and community leaders for assistance
- Community member participation in career day
- Getting students involved in job shadowing programs
- Teacher training on exposing all students to the college option
- Education of families on the change in family dynamics common in transitional situations
- Linking with community resources to support family stability and locate extracurricular activities
- Discussion of triangulation and working toward de-triangulation
- Helping the client to differentiate between self and family and to develop mature peer relationships
- When working with parents, trying to reframe misbehavior using a developmental and emotional context
- Using family dynamics as framework for understanding the situation
- Communication analysis
- Trying to learn what values are important to the student's family
- Assisting student in discussing feelings with parents
- Consultation with parole officers, community counselors, and other community service agents working with the student
- Determining student's perceived and actual role in the family, school, and community
- Facilitation of healthy peer relationships and connections with mentors
- Revisiting discipline policies that continue to affect student academic progress

- Although the student must follow the school protocol, exploring ways that school staff, students, and parents can reinforce success
- Encouragement of adolescent to explore "going home again" and work on differentiation from emotional reactivity in family of origin
- Supporting the client through identity development
- Helping the family to understand changing parent–child relationships and the need for independence that defines adolescence
- Connecting the family to resources to support the student in pursuing postsecondary options
- Working with parents to identify possible community resources to assist in understanding student behavior
- Identifying cultural beliefs and values that will help contextualize student behavior

## EMERGENT THEORIES PARADIGM

The theories included in the preceding paradigms have the distinct quality of being supported and implemented over time. Theories take time to develop and become empirically validated for use in the counseling profession. This fifth paradigm of counseling theory includes the theories that are newer, or emerging, in the profession. Many can fall into this paradigm, including postmodernism (Hansen, 2006a), decisional counseling (Ivey & Ivey, 2007), motivational interviewing, narrative or constructivist approaches, and feminist counseling.

Some emergent theories were developed for specific purposes. For example, the motivational interviewing approach was designed to work with persons struggling with chemical dependency. Many emergent theories have been criticized for lacking empirical evidence that the approach works. Some (e.g., feminist) have even been viewed as lacking specific techniques and being more of a philosophy. Hansen (2006b) has posited that it is one's philosophical perspective that indeed makes a professional school counselor effective. Because theories take time to develop, professional school counselors want to avoid the "conference syndrome" approach of applying any new theory they hear or read about to professional development opportunities.

Instead, we propose a more systematic approach to learning about newer theories as they are emerging by first seeing what fits with one's personal style of counseling and then applying principles as opportunities arise and the theories become more solidified. So as not to overwhelm the reader, this chapter addresses only four emergent theories in counseling: narrative, constructivist, feminist, and interpersonal psychotherapy.

### Narrative Theory

Students have a story to tell. Students create a story about their lives and present situations, one that needs to be retold. The professional school counselor can encourage students to see and create success by helping them retell their stories and helping to alter the stories to more accurately fit student goals and desires. Such is the nature of narrative counseling: helping students to retell the stories of their lives to create outcomes that better reflect what they would like to be (Monk, Winslade, Crocket, & Epston, 1997).

One way of conceptualizing narrative counseling is to consider a book with many chapters. We can read a book and think we know how it will end in the final chapter. As a metaphor for our lives, we may be comfortable with the opening chapter and a few in between, but we may be dissatisfied with the contents of the book as a whole. Rather than looking to change the problems, a narrative approach suggests rewriting the chapters themselves to create a better perspective on the problems that lie therein. In essence, narrative counseling holds that we are the authors of our own lives (White & Epston, 1990).

Michael White and David Epston are the primary individuals associated with narrative counseling. The concepts of the theory are originally derived from family counseling. White and Epston drew from family therapy expert Gregory Bateson, who suggested that the means for change is to compare one set of events in time with another (White & Epston, 1990). In counseling practice, the goal of narrative counseling is to develop alternative stories for one's life.

The narrative counselor asks many investigative questions to understand what underlies the story and the student's self-perception. The narrative counselor helps to deconstruct problems, thus externalizing and separating them from the person and avoiding blame and self-recrimination (Monk et al., 1997). The professional school counselor seeks exceptions to the story, times when the outcome of one's actions is inconsistent with what one says or does in the story. These exceptions are referred to as sparkling moments, the positive shifts that begin to occur when one can exert control over the problem and begin to create a new story (White & Epston, 1990).

The student and professional school counselor work together "against" the problem to identify more favorable stories (Monk et al., 1997). From a cultural standpoint, narrative therapy is consistent with the storytelling nature of some ethnic populations. For example, the Chinese culture is built upon a series of stories handed down from generation to generation that appear in the form of mythical beliefs. For individuals who come from cultures in which storytelling is a part of their practice, narrative therapy can feel familiar and productive. The shift toward identifying one's role in changing stories can be challenging, and the narrative counselor must exercise patience and caution to deconstruct problems and not beliefs.

Because narrative theory tends to provide an overarching and organizing vision of the problem as separate from the person, it can be quite empowering and eye-opening. Narrative therapy requires a certain level of insight from the student to be able to tell and then retell the story. For more information on narrative theory, refer to the following resources:

White, M., & Epston, D. (1989). *Literate means to therapeutic ends*. Adelaide, Australia: Dulwich Centre Publications.

White, M., & Epston, D. (1990). *Narrative means to therapeutic ends*. New York, NY: Norton.

Winslade, J., & Monk, G. (2007). *Narrative counseling in schools*: *Powerful and brief* (2nd ed.). Thousand Oaks, CA: Corwin Press.

## Constructivist Theory

Is one person's perception of a problem another person's reality? How do we derive meaning from our lives, and how do we then make sense of this reality? Constructivist theory, based upon the personal constructs of George Kelly (1963), suggests that people create their own meaning and realities based upon personal experiences. Constructivism holds that it is the job of the counselor to respect and work with a person's particular reality, not to contradict or deny it (Hansen, 2006a). Personal constructs, as defined by Kelly, are self-beliefs that guide us in determining courses of action, the people with whom we associate, and the decisions we make about our own lives. The process of identifying and integrating these personal constructs is at the heart of constructivist counseling.

The constructivist counselor is inquisitive, often pairing constructivism with narrative techniques such as storytelling and searching for alternative explanations to problems. The goal of constructivism is to actively create and interpret personal reality through examination of personal constructs. The professional school counselor and student work collaboratively to identify personal constructs and their origins. Often students do not emerge with specific strategies to handle situations, but instead focus on personal learning and examination of how they are living authentic lives based upon these identified constructs.

One specific technique that stands out from this theory is the use of a card sort, a means of organizing beliefs into categories to help illustrate the organization of one's system of understanding and operating (Kelly, 1963). The constructivist counselor might help the student to develop a repertory test or grid to illustrate and organize belief systems. For example, the professional counselor might assist a student in determining his or her major beliefs about family, achievement, success, and failure. The counselor and student may identify the basic belief systems to explore further how these systems are operating in the student's interactions and decisions regarding the future. In so doing, the student develops insight and explores the personal meaning placed on constructs and the actions being taken to find meaning in life.

Similar to narrative theory, constructivism requires significant insight and a higher level of processing than do many traditional approaches. Constructivist theory may have limitations in its cross-cultural application in that some cultures expect adherence to their principles. Students engaged in constructivist counseling are questioning and at times even challenging fundamental belief systems. Conversely, proponents of constructivist counseling hold that the exploration of beliefs can be the ultimate goal of the theory and therefore can work effectively with most cultures. Resources for further reading about constructivist counseling are as follows:

Kelly, G. A. (1955). *The psychology of personal constructs: A theory of personality.* New York, NY: Norton.

Neimeyer, G. (1992). *Constructivist assessment: A casebook.* Newbury Park, CA: Sage.

## Feminist Counseling

A feminist approach to counseling has been greatly criticized as challenging fundamental cultural beliefs. Feminist counselors operate from the basic philosophy of feminism and support, respect, and highly value the role of culture in one's life.

The feminist philosophy espouses equality and rights of women. The feminist movement began as far back as the 1800s and abolition, wherein women were fighting for their voices to be heard (Wood, 2005). This movement continued through voting rights, suffrage, and what is more commonly perceived as the start of feminism, the women's rights movements of the 1960s. The principles of feminism held that women should be perceived as equals with men, have equal rights for employment and opportunities, be given certain inalienable rights to make their own choices, and essentially be treated with fundamental human respect.

Because of this history, many often perceive feminist counseling as benefiting (or being provided by, for that matter) only women. Much of the literature regarding feminist counseling suggests a woman-centered focus. Chester and Bretherton (2001) identified six themes in feminist counseling: woman-centered, egalitarian, feminism as belief, feminism as action, critique of patriarchy, and a positive vision of the future. Gilbert and Scher (1999) further assert elements of feminist counseling to include empowerment, androgyny, and mutuality within the counseling relationship. The latter citation emphasizes the importance of equality in counseling and in one's life, and therefore carries a more universal position that can benefit both women and men. Gender sensitivity in counseling may be a more accurate (and perhaps more palatable) position in applying feminist principles to counseling (Bartholomew, 2003).

Just how feminist counseling appears to the observer is more questionable. The very fact that this approach is an application of feminist principles makes it difficult to identify key feminist counseling theorists. We may look to the work of Carol Gilligan, a preeminent theorist on women's development, Judith Jordan and her colleagues at the Stone Center, and others who have all had an important role in the creation and proliferation of feminist approaches to counseling. The feminist counselor values the female as well as the male perspective, placing value on the role of both genders in our lives (Bartholomew, 2003).

This perspective uses gender role analysis as one of its primary techniques. Gender role analysis is a means of examining with students the messages they have received about what it means to be male or female, where these messages are derived, and how these messages have been employed and are affecting one's functioning (Bartholomew, 2003). Gender role analysis may address another important principle of feminist counseling: androgyny.

Based on the pioneering work of Sandra Bem (1981), androgyny challenges traditional gender roles for men and women. Androgyny suggests that we should value individual characteristics for what they are, regardless of a predefined category. Professional school counselors addressing androgyny see that stereotypically masculine and feminine roles are valuable within each individual. A woman who is more aggressive in the workplace and athletic with her peers may also be very sensitive and caring with her partner. Feminist counselors employ gender role analysis to examine these roles and to help the individual put them in a historical and societal context (Hoffman, 2001). The student is helped to see that all of these attributes create uniqueness. It is often society's views that perpetuate beliefs that a particular person is somehow aberrant or unacceptable (Chester & Bretherton, 2001). Feminist counseling addresses the societal perceptions and the means by which the individual can take action to implement change. This sociocultural perspective and action, as well as a degree of assertiveness, is the goal of feminist counseling.

The sociocultural history and viewpoint of feminism contribute to the multicultural sensitivity of this approach in counseling. Feminism has a rich history of working toward equality. Pioneers such as bell hooks and Alice Walker in the 1970s addressed the concern that feminism addressed only the concerns of White upper-class women (Wood, 2005). Current feminist movements emphasize and work toward the equal rights of all, attending to issues of gender, race, ethnicity, and other cultural variables.

Challenges with feminist theory may be its push for political action. Critics argue that suggesting that individuals must see personal issues as political and engage in social change imposes the counselor's values, which may be inconsistent with one's cultural beliefs. We instead argue that feminist counselors simply suggest the societal context of issues and explore what, if any, role the student would like to have in shaping an understanding of his or her issues from a broader perspective. Additional resources regarding feminist counseling include the following:

Bem, S. L. (1993). *The lenses of gender.* New Haven, CT: Yale University Press.

Brown, L. S. (1994). *Subversive dialogues: Theory in feminist therapy.* New York, NY: Basic Books.

Enns, C. Z. (1997). *Feminist theories and feminist psychotherapies: Origins, themes, and variations.* New York, NY: Haworth.

## Interpersonal Psychotherapy

Interpersonal psychotherapy (IPT), originally developed for adults with depression, is time-limited and specifically focuses on interpersonal relationships. The goals of IPT include helping students improve their relationships or their expectations of them, and helping students improve their social support systems in order to alleviate their presenting distress. For IPT, the view of human nature is based on the assertion that psychological symptoms are connected to interpersonal distress (Stuart & Robertson, 2003). Accordingly, this approach is derived from three theories: (1) attachment theory, (2) communication theory, and (3) social theory.

Attachment theory is based on the premise that individuals have the intrinsic drive to form interpersonal relationships, a result of the need for reassurance and the desire to be loved. Attachment theory describes the way individuals form, maintain, and end relationships, and hypothesizes that distress occurs as a result of disruptions in an individual's attachment with others. Problem areas specifically addressed by IPT include interpersonal disputes, role transitions, and grief and loss.

Although attachment theory is useful in understanding the broader, or macro, social context, communication theory works on a micro level, describing the specific ways in which individuals communicate their attachment needs to significant others. In other words, maladaptive attachment styles lead to specific ineffective communications with the result being that the individual's attachment needs are not met.

Social theory contributes to IPT by emphasizing interpersonal factors and how those factors contribute to depression or anxiety. One's social support system may be disturbed as a result of an individual's maladaptive response to a particular life event. One's level of social support directly influences how one handles interpersonal stress. Furthermore, social theory hypothesizes that poor social support is a fundamental factor in the development of psychological distress (Stuart & Robertson, 2003).

There are three main goals of counseling with IPT: (1) relief of the student's disturbing psychological symptoms; (2) examination of conflict, loss, and transition in the student's relationships; and (3) establishment of the student's needs in order to aid in more effective use of his or her social support system. In contrast to CBT in which the focus is on the student's internal cognitions, IPT emphasizes interpersonal communication. IPT may focus on cognitions in certain instances, yet they are not its primary targets. Likewise, CBT and other theories of counseling may touch on interpersonal issues, yet interpersonal issues are not their focus.

In contrast to analytically oriented theories, which tend to concentrate on early life experiences in relation to current psychological distress, IPT's present, here-and-now focus helps the student improve current communication and social support systems. In light of its time-limited approach and particular focus, IPT aims to resolve psychological distress and improve interpersonal communication, rather than to change underlying cognitions. The IPT counselor uses the student–counselor relationship to develop insight into the student's interpersonal functioning and to assess the student's attachment style.

Common techniques of IPT include establishing a therapeutic alliance, communication analysis, describing interpersonal incidents, using content to process affect, and role playing. Because of IPT's solid theoretical foundation, solid structure, flexibility, and adaptability, it can be useful for students from diverse backgrounds. IPT takes into account the components of several theoretical paradigms and creates a unique approach to address the individual needs of the student. For further reading on IPT, the following resources will be useful:

Bowlby, J. (1969). *Attachment.* New York, NY: Basic Books.

Kiesler, D. J. (1996). *Contemporary interpersonal theory and research: Personality, psychopathology, and psychotherapy.* New York, NY: Wiley.

Sullivan, H. S. (1953). *The interpersonal theory of psychiatry.* New York, NY: Norton.

Weissman, M. M., Markowitz, J. C., & Kleman, G. L. (2000). *Comprehensive guide to interpersonal psychotherapy.* New York, NY: Basic Books.

Table 2-7 provides strategies and techniques aligned with the emergent theories paradigm.

**TABLE 2-7    Emergent Strategies and Interventions**

- Miracle question
- Sparkling moments
- Empowerment
- Communication analysis
- Interpersonal incidents
- Role play
- Reading stories (bibliotherapy)
- Creating drawings
- Storytelling
- Providing student with age-appropriate information about various aspects of issues
- Deconstructing the problem-laden story, identifying unique outcomes, and helping students coauthor a new story that is strength based
- Externalizing the problem and working against the problem
- Celebrating success
- Addressing attachment issues
- Here-and-now focus

- Working on communication skills and accessing social support
- The process of change results from dialogue between counselor and family members
- Empowering each family member to re-author a more successful story
- Focus on communication skills, building friendships, and development of personal goals
- If the student and family desire it, attending to development of identity and fluency in both the mainstream and native cultures
- Examination of interpersonal relationships
- Social support system analysis and improvement
- Motivational interviewing
- Narrative therapy to deconstruct and externalize problems
- Examination of personal constructs
- Identifying and improving personal support systems
- Fill-in-the-blank exercises
- Sentence stems
- Word sort activities
- Coat of arms
- Listening to student's story without blame
- Exploration of gender roles
- Empowering student in healthy ways to decrease feelings of helplessness
- Using content of current situations to process affect
- Parent–student collaboration building and negotiating
- Caregiver/teacher training for dealing with relevant behavioral, academic, and social issues
- Exploration of family, school, and community dynamics
- Writing a short story about how the student successfully accomplished a goal
- Bibliotherapy about other students' experiences that are similar
- Exploration of alternative explanations to problems
- Questioning and challenge of the status quo
- Focus on resiliency factors
- Mentoring
- Encouraging student to self-advocate and be competent and confident
- Scaling to determine needs and levels of anxiety

(continued)

---

**TABLE 2-7**    *(continued)*

---

- Using expressive therapies (art, music, play) to tell life stories
- Stress reduction and mindfulness
- Psycho-educational and support groups to construct new realities
- Assisting the student in developing positive social networks
- Assisting the student in creating a story about the situation and identifying a more favorable outcome
- Breaking problems down into pieces
- Assessing ability to code switch in the school environment, if applicable
- Exploration of beliefs and attitudes toward working with diverse students. What are these beliefs, assumptions, and how do they affect interactions?
- Helping school staff ponder multicultural considerations and biases regardless of racial self-identification
- Analyzing your expectations of teachers and what historical life events have shaped your expectations or concerns about school staff
- Reading stories about different careers and issues
- Creating drawings to understand career interests
- Focus on positive relationships with peers and adults
- Providing students with age-appropriate information about various issues
- Improving interpersonal relationships by rehearsing behaviors to achieve desired goals
- Identifying someone in the student's life who would be the least surprised to see the student planning for the future
- Shape application of discipline policy
- Identifying cultural strengths the student and family bring to the school
- Identifying cultural strengths and capital within the family and community and harnessing these strengths to gain support and encouragement for parenting student
- Sharing stories about people the student might be aware of, their learning process, and how they pursued their careers

---

## APPLYING THEORY TO PRACTICE

These discussions of the various counseling paradigms offer a sampling of the many theories that exist. It can be very challenging to digest the information provided, and even more challenging to determine what theory fits a particular professional school counselor. After reviewing the paradigms and considering culture, professional school counselors must begin to apply theory to their counseling practice. A beginning counselor needs to determine what the critical components are of his or her approach.

A means of organizing thoughts about theory selection is to consider whether the underpinnings of a theory are aligned with one's basic beliefs about counseling. The elements of each theory will highlight the specific and common factors, personal philosophy, and multicultural considerations, as discussed in this chapter. But to be philosophically aligned with a paradigm or theory, professional school counselors should consider each of the following features: view of human nature, goals of counseling, role of the professional counselor, the techniques or approaches used, and flexibility.

## View of Human Nature

The first important aspect of applying theory to practice is one's view of human nature. How do people change? What motivates people to behave, think, and feel the ways that they do? What does the school counselor believe will best help someone grow and develop? These are important questions to ask oneself when considering one's own view of human nature. The manner in which one believes persons change will be directly related to the counseling theories to which one subscribes. For example, if one believes that personality is more or less fully constructed in childhood and change can occur only through regression back to those times, one may be more suited to one of the psychodynamic theories. Conversely, if one believes people are self-determined and control their own destinies, a humanistic/existential approach may be a better match.

Regardless of varying beliefs about how people change, practitioners across settings can agree that change happens only when one is ready to engage in the process. The pioneering work of Prochaska and DiClemente (1982) proposed stages of the change process to explain the manner in which individuals move through changes in thought, behavior, or emotion. Their work originally studied smoking cessation in an adult population and has since been adapted to many issues and populations. Table 2-8 outlines Prochaska and DiClemente's five stages of change and how they might appear in counseling practice.

## Goals of Counseling

The second important aspect of applying theory to practice is the perceived goals of counseling. Students may enter counseling wanting immediate answers to difficult problems. As a profession, school counselors are not prone to give direct advice or be problem solvers. Instead, they supply individuals with the tools to manage their own problems and to apply them in future situations. An overarching goal of all counseling is to help individuals more effectively manage the problems of everyday living.

At first glance, the identification of an overarching goal of counseling may seem to answer all of our questions about this subtopic. However, further examination demonstrates that theories hold different beliefs about what counseling should accomplish. Person-centered counselors believe counseling should result in greater self-awareness, behaviorists want to see physical evidence of change in actions, and REBT-oriented counselors assert that changes in thinking and behavior are the ultimate goals of the counseling experience. A school counselor's personal beliefs about what individuals should gain from their time in counseling will again dictate his or her determination of approach.

A word of caution: Many new professional school counselors jump to the conclusion that it is their role to determine specific goals for their students. However, specific goals, such as to stop smoking, build a healthy romantic relationship, stay out of detention, or get into college, must be established by the individual seeking counseling. Goal setting is a collaborative venture between professional school counselors and students. The emphasis on elements of the goals and the manner in which counseling can assist in reaching them is determined by counselor orientation.

| TABLE 2-8    Stages of Change | | |
|---|---|---|
| **Stage** | **Description** | **Application in Practice** |
| Precontemplation | No intent to change<br>Unaware that problem exists | Identify the problem as others have presented it to the individual; create ownership |
| Contemplation | Awareness of problem, but not yet committed to act to change | Weigh pros and cons of the problem and solutions |
| Preparation | Intent and commitment to take action | Address fears, impact of possible change in life |
| Action | Modify behavior, experiences, or environment to overcome problem | Discuss experience of the change and subsequent feelings<br>Consider means to sustain change |
| Maintenance | Prevent relapse and sustain gains achieved through change | Monitor and discuss new approach to the problem |

Adapted from Prochaska, J. O., & DiClemente, C. C. (1982). Transtheoretical therapy: Toward a more integrative model of change. *Psychotherapy: Theory, Research and Practice, 20*, 161–173.

## Role of the Professional School Counselor

The third aspect of applying theory to practice is the role of the professional school counselor. Relative activity or passivity as a professional school counselor will help apply theory to practice. As has been addressed in this chapter, theories differ in their perceptions of the roles professional school counselors play in the therapeutic process. Whether one is collaborative, expert, equal, or indifferent, the role of the professional counselor differs across theories. As has been discussed, many theorists were most successful by being true to their own preferences for interactions with one another. Although the professional counselor's role must be consistent with the other elements of a theory, it can in great part be determined by one's personality and style of interaction. In fact, some professional school counselors teeter on the edge of offering advice, whereas others may utter only a few words throughout their time with students.

## Techniques and Approaches

The fourth aspect of applying theory to practice is the techniques or approaches used. Professional school counselors entering the profession may be drawn to approaches that outline specific techniques to be used with students. For this reason, we have seen many professional school counselors begin with a cognitive-behavioral orientation and gradually shift to approaches that offer more flexibility in the process. This phenomenon may be due in part to the level of ambiguity school counselors are willing to endure as they enter new situations. So much of what is done as professional school counselors does not follow a "how-to" manual. There is no set of guidelines suggesting, for example, that if a student states his disdain for his mother, the counselor should offer him the opportunity to role-play a preferred interaction with her. Professional school counselors must instead rely on what seems to be consistent with their beliefs about counseling as outlined in the other elements of theory selection.

Certain theories are more heavily laden with techniques, whereas others are more amorphous in providing general guidelines about approaches. The new school counselor will need to review the theories to determine what stands out as most meaningful and effective. As he or she enters into the professional school counselor role, the school counselor must notice what is consistent about the approach chosen and its techniques. Does the counselor work more effectively when he or she can rely on a general approach and employ techniques as needed? Bear in mind that flexibility is a critical quality of effective counseling. What works well in one counseling interaction may not in another. An excellent guide to understanding and applying techniques to counseling practice is Erford et al.'s (2010) *35 Techniques Every Counselor Should Know* (Pearson Merrill).

## Flexibility

Beginning to apply theory to practice requires contemplation of the aforementioned elements, and the final important aspect is flexibility. No two counseling interactions are alike. What works well with one individual may fall flat with another. As will be discussed shortly, few professional school counselors operate from a truly purist perspective; instead they combine principles that fit best with their goals, beliefs, and desired roles in counseling. Selecting a theory relies on a careful examination of one's own personal style.

## THEORETICAL INTEGRATION

With so many sound theories from which to choose, it is challenging to select just one. Many professional school counselors, as previously stated, rely on more than one theoretical perspective. Theoretical integration is the synthesis of the best aspects of several theories with the belief that such a viewpoint will produce richer and more meaningful outcomes (Bradley, Parr, & Gould, 1999). Professional school counselors operating from an integrative perspective combine the best of what works for them with intentionality. While employing diverse perspectives and techniques, the integrative counselor holds fast to one underlying, foundational theoretical orientation. For example, one might at one's core believe and operate from the existential standpoint of finding meaning in life and searching for ultimate existence. Yet working with adolescents with alcohol or other drug abuse issues might require employing person-centered techniques to build rapport and behavioral techniques to demonstrate necessary behavioral changes. At the core, however, remains the fundamental belief system of existentialism, which guides the use of supplemental approaches.

## Integrative Versus Eclectic Counseling

It is critical to be intentional in differentiating integrative and eclectic modes of counseling. Eclecticism, in contrast to theoretical integration, is more haphazard in nature. The eclectic counselor is a technical expert, relying on knowledge of approaches and applying what seems to fit at a given time. Eclectic counselors select approaches based on student presenting issues and symptoms. There is a lack of a unified or guiding theory for the professional school counselor employing this approach. In many ways, eclecticism feels safe for beginning school counselors who feel that they are "flying by the seat of their pants" every time they face a new student and presenting issue.

Although such an approach is tempting, the professional school counselor must always consider more fully what he or she believes about counseling and use that as a guide.

## Why an Integrative Approach?

With the myriad research studies that demonstrate best practices in counseling, there is ironically a lack of consensus on a single most effective theory. Professional school counselors rely instead on the "it depends" mentality of counseling. Not to be confused with eclecticism, theoretical integration offers the professional school counselor flexibility in working with various issues and presenting concerns. There exists a level of multicultural responsibility to meet students where they are when they enter counseling. Also, one must be sure that what one does matches what students need. Professional school counselors can remain authentic in so doing, as the application of elements of theories will differ based upon one's underlying belief system.

One must also acknowledge the limitations of a purist approach. As discussed earlier, professional school counselors work in settings with specific requirements for their students. In a school setting, which often offers limited time for individual counseling, existentially oriented counselors can help youth explore what is most meaningful in their lives by challenging them to face issues and work in the present-focused framework of reality therapy or Gestalt theory.

Being an integrative counselor will require one to be a knowledgeable counselor. Knowledge of the many theories, or at minimum the paradigms, is required to determine consistency in applying varying techniques to support one's foundation. Additionally, exploring one's own beliefs about counseling, as in the previous section, builds a better foundation on which to add supporting approaches. Counseling is a profession valued for flexibility and the ability to see multiple dimensions of a problem. Professional school counselors must put this into practice by employing what works best to meet a student's needs.

In the case scenarios that follow, the reader will see the integrative approach in action, as most problems students experience can be resolved in multiple ways. The more adept the professional school counselor is at applying multiple theoretical approaches to the resolution of a problem, the more likely the counselor and the student will accomplish their collaborative goals. Also, the more complex the student's problem, the more likely that a multidimensional (trans-theoretical) approach will be required to achieve a successful outcome.

## Conclusion

Developing a personal counseling theory is an involved and lengthy process. The five paradigms discussed here provide a starting point to learn more about prominent counseling theories as you enter into practice. Before foreclosing on a specific theory, we strongly encourage beginning counselors to reflect upon their beliefs about themselves, human nature, and counseling. Aside from the ethical and professional responsibilities for using theory in practice, understanding how counseling works will better prepare you to help students. A unique perspective on your student's issues that is embedded in your beliefs about how people change and develop will enable you to select appropriate interventions to assist students to reach their goals. An intentional counselor is a successful counselor, employing a unique integration of personal characteristics, counseling theories, and evidence-based practices.

## Chapter 3

# Social Justice

Rhonda M. Bryant, Tracy Knighton, and Delila Owens

## CASE BACKGROUND

An emerging counseling paradigm describes social justice counseling as the fifth force in counseling, which is "complementary to the psychodynamic, cognitive-behavioral, existential-humanistic, and multicultural forces" that have shaped the profession since its inception (Ratts, 2009, p. 160). Social justice counselors use a multifaceted approach to simultaneously promote human development and the common good through addressing challenges related to both individual and distributive justice. Social justice counseling promotes empowerment of the individual as well as active confrontation of injustice and inequality in society as they impact clientele. In doing so, social justice counselors direct attention to the promotion of four critical principles that guide their work: equity, access, participation, and harmony. This work is done with a focus on the cultural, contextual, and individual needs of those served (Counselors for Social Justice, 2011). With these principles in mind, in this case scenario we employed social justice counseling principles to address the concerns of a student, his family, and a gap in services in the community.

We work and live in a school district located in the southeastern United States. The district has documented an increase in student behavioral issues that have resulted in increased disciplinary actions such as in-school suspension, out-of-school suspension, placement in alternative educational settings, or entrance into the criminal justice system. Although the district neighbors rural communities, it has an "urban flavor," which presents both strengths and challenges. For example, the district has access to Title I funding that supports instruction and staff development opportunities. However, the recession has limited community-based mental health prevention/intervention services for K through 12 students. Few community resources exist to assess or counsel students who exhibit behavior possibly related to undiagnosed or unmet mental health needs. Typically, only students who have significant mental health symptomatology (e.g., disordered/paranoid thinking, suicidal ideation) receive crisis management services.

In our role as professional school counselors, we collaborate with other professionals within and outside of the school to reduce systemic barriers that affect students experiencing school difficulties or failure. In this case scenario we attempted to address the four principles of social justice counseling—equity, access, participation, and harmony—in our interventions

43

with our student, Timothy, his parents, and the larger school and geographical community. The American Counseling Association's Advocacy Competencies (Lewis, Arnold, House, & Toporek, 2003) and the Association for Multicultural Counseling and Development's (AMCD) Multicultural Competencies (Arredondo et al., 1996) guided our efforts to broaden the focus beyond the student's particular circumstances and consider how school policies and community resources affect students with unmet mental health needs.

We first met Timothy after he transferred to the high school from a neighboring rural county. Timothy, an African American male, lives with his mother, father, and his aging grandmother. The family moved because of his father's new job opportunity and almost immediately found their niche by getting involved with the local church and its community service activities. Tracy, the school counselor, used the peer-mentoring program to match Timothy with a ninth-grade buddy to ease transition from middle school. She also worked with a school counseling intern in Rhonda's (a counselor educator) master's level fieldwork class to develop a transition plan for Timothy.

As the semester progressed, Timothy's teachers began to notice that he was becoming very active and, at times, very irritable. His initially quiet demeanor shifted from frustration to anger, and teachers would refer him for discipline and even to the school's safety resource officer. Timothy's grades were in the C to B- range, but his unpredictable outbursts and difficulty staying on task prevented him from participating more fully with his peers. Tracy became even more alarmed when Timothy reported that he did not sleep very often but had lots of energy. Concerned about Timothy's academic and personal/social success in school, Tracy consulted with the administration about a possible referral to the Student Support Team (SST).

Because Tracy and Timothy had developed a solid rapport, she explained the possibility of an SST referral to him and his parents. Timothy expressed a desire to follow school rules but reported feeling frustrated that he "just keeps getting in trouble." His parents noted that Timothy sleeps very little at home, and they are concerned about his inability to focus on one project at a time. They welcomed any insight the school might be able to offer. The administration informed Tracy that it would prefer to assess Timothy later in the school year to see whether the discipline referrals would curtail the problematic behavior. One day, Timothy was having what he described as a "tough" day and asked his teacher whether he could go to see Tracy for a "breather." The teacher informed him that he could not miss any more class time. When he asked again, he sent him to the office for a disciplinary referral for "disrespect." At this point, Timothy stormed out of the classroom and slammed the door so hard that the glass broke. The principal notified Timothy's family that Timothy had destroyed school property and faced possible referral to the alternative school or the Youth Detention Center based on district policy. His parents maintained that had the teacher consented to the time-out intervention previously suggested by Tracy, Timothy would have missed 10 minutes of class rather than getting suspended and facing alternative school. The counselors recognized Timothy's effort to self-regulate given his request to see the counselor.

## INITIAL PROCESS QUESTIONS

We were concerned that Timothy's behavior indicates an unmet mental health need. Lack of sleep (coupled with excessive energy), irritability, and angry mood troubled us enough that we wanted to meet with him and his family. Limited adolescent mental health resources in the community and lack of insurance might mean that Timothy would continue to have difficulty in school. Such difficulties could easily lead to legal trouble for him and his parents, whom the law would hold responsible for his actions. Indeed, we are aware that youth of color nationwide are less likely to obtain mental health wellness prevention and intervention than their peers. Further, youth of color tend to receive mental health services only after involvement with foster care or the criminal justice system (U.S. Department of Health and Human Services, Substance Abuse and Mental Health Services Administration [SAMHSA], 2001). Initial process questions include consideration of the micro, meso, and macro systems in our school and communities.

## Micro Level

- How can we use empowerment strategies in our direct counseling with Timothy and his family?

Continued discipline referrals have undermined Timothy's self-confidence and his self-esteem. Federal data indicate that mental health service providers underserve minorities, especially African Americans and Latinos (SAMHSA, 2001). SAMSHA also reports that over 70% of all children and adolescents who need mental health treatment do not receive these services. African American and Latino children have the lowest rates of service even when researchers controlled for insurance status (Ringel & Sturm, 2001). Untreated conditions persist and can "lead to school failure, poor employment opportunities, and poverty in adulthood" (Palpant, Steimnitz, Bornemann, & Hawkins, 2006). Unfortunately, our state's mental health program does not discuss mental health services for children and adolescents. We see this as a social justice issue.

- How can we address cultural considerations that may influence Timothy and his family's help-seeking behaviors?

The ACA Multicultural Competencies (Arredondo et al., 1996) indicate that culturally competent counselors (1) maintain awareness of how their personal beliefs and knowledge affect their counseling and (2) consider how clients' cultural worldviews shape attitudes and participation in counseling. The Competencies also stress the development of culturally appropriate counseling strategies and interventions that reflect clients' beliefs, accurate cultural knowledge, and, where possible, indigenous ways of helping. If Timothy does have an unmet mental health need, what is our role in helping him and his family obtain appropriate interventions?

- How might school and teacher attitudes contribute to Timothy's ongoing difficulties?

A partnership between the American School Counselor Association (ASCA) and the American Psychiatric Foundation (APF) indicates the benefits of training  school staff in distinguishing "typical" adolescent behavior from "troubled" behavior, symptomatic of unmet mental health needs. How could our staff benefit from such training?

- How can we use our comprehensive developmental school counseling program to assist Timothy in managing his behavior?

### Meso Level

- How can we collaborate with our school and community colleagues to ensure that Timothy and other students in need receive necessary services? Given that the community does not have mental health services for adolescents and many parents do not have insurance, what is our responsibility in helping these students succeed in school despite lack of resources?
- What district discipline policies contribute to the suspension or expulsion of students with unmet or undiagnosed mental health needs? Again, what training assists educators in distinguishing typical adolescent behavior from troubled behavior?

### Macro Level

- How can we negotiate mental health evaluation and intervention services on behalf of students in our state?

As professional school counselors, we recognize that, at the macro level, students with unmet mental health needs are more likely to drop out, face school discipline and sanctions, and become incarcerated. This not only affects district educational outcomes but also compromises the quality of life for these individuals and the well-being of our state's economy and productivity. The ACA Advocacy Competencies advise, "when counselors identify systemic factors that act as barriers to their students' or clients' development" . . . they can exert "systems-change leadership . . . in collaboration with other stakeholders . . . to develop a vision to guide change" (Lewis et al., 2003).

Although we hold counseling credentials, we understand that as school counselors we do not diagnose or provide ongoing treatment services. How can we use our professional expertise to add to the discourse on meeting children's mental health needs in our state?

## ADDRESSING THE ISSUES

Timothy expresses a desire to perform well in school by following classroom rules and behavior norms, but finds himself easily distracted, unfocused, and easily frustrated to the point of anger. His teachers, having "had it with him," acknowledge that he can be cooperative at times, but his unpredictability leads them to sanction him (and, they concede, at times more harshly than other students) to send him the message that he must follow the rules. This results in continued suspensions and grades of zero. Falling further behind in his work and grades, Timothy is discouraged because he feels that there is no way to catch up. His teachers shyly admit that they feel relieved when he is out of class. Timothy's parents are very involved with his schooling but are at a loss to explain or control his behavior; they believe that the school staff members think that they are not effective parents. They have not considered counseling as an option but have looked to pastoral input for guidance. Because of the behaviors that Timothy continues to present, despite consistent discipline at home and school, we felt it wise to make sure that he does not have unmet mental health needs. The community lacks viable referral alternatives for Timothy and his family to pursue, and now that he has damaged school property he could face criminal charges and his parents might face liability for the damage to the classroom door. Timothy's parents noted that they have dealt with Timothy's troubled behavior since fourth grade.

The usual approach to working with a student with concerns such as Timothy's involves meeting at the school with all the stakeholders. Because we wanted to demonstrate to Timothy and his parents that we fully valued their input, we decided to first meet with them to discuss their ideas about how to assist Timothy. The parents knew Rhonda from the community and agreed to have her consult with them and Tracy. We decided to ask Timothy to lead the meeting with his parents. He expressed surprise and said that he wasn't sure what we wanted him to do. Rhonda explained to him that we valued his opinion, and we weren't sure that anyone had asked him about his ideas or thoughts.

Timothy told us that there are times when his thinking is so clear that he can think for "days." During these times, he doesn't need much sleep and feels so energized that he knows he can do anything he wants. Other times, Timothy feels so sad and tired that he just wants to sleep. He told his parents that he didn't use drugs but had tried marijuana a few times in seventh grade. Timothy stated that he wants to stop getting in trouble and finish ninth grade. Timothy's father told us that his brother, Timothy's uncle, had had similar behaviors in school and "never got straightened out." When asked how the family tried to help Timothy's uncle, he told us that the uncle had a "nervous breakdown" and never fully recovered. Timothy's parents are concerned their son is dealing with the same condition as his uncle's.

With this information, next we arranged a meeting with Timothy, his parents, an administrator, and the lead teacher for Timothy's grade level. We did not ask all of his teachers to attend because we did not want the family to feel overwhelmed. We encouraged Timothy to lead this meeting as well, and he agreed, albeit reluctantly. Tracy and the intern worked with Timothy to identify his goals for the meeting. Timothy explained to the meeting attendees that he wants to do well but doesn't know how. His parents explained that they want to assist him and at this point would make an appointment to have him evaluated by a professional counselor outside of school if they had the funds. They expressed fear that if Timothy continues this behavior, he will repeat the ninth grade.

The principal indicated that safety for all students is the school's paramount concern but conceded that the discipline has not shifted Timothy's behavior toward desired outcomes. Teachers are very busy and refer him to the office because other steps, such as behavioral interventions and token economies, are too time consuming. The community advocate indicated that a local church offers pro bono counseling services by pastoral counselors trained at the master's level. If the family and school were willing, a referral for services could be made and collaborative efforts could be undertaken to help Timothy achieve his goals. The principal suggested that the counselor and Timothy develop "time-out" in the classroom, and the lead teacher noted that she would work with the ninth-grade team to redirect Timothy in a nonthreatening way. Rhonda, as a counselor educator, offered to conduct an in-service training with teachers at the local and district levels on how to distinguish a discipline problem from a possible unmet mental health need. Table 3-1 lists additional counseling approaches commensurate with a social justice and multicultural perspective.

**TABLE 3-1** Additional Approaches Commensurate with Social Justice Counseling

| Paradigm | Elementary School | Middle School | High School |
|---|---|---|---|
| Psychodynamic | *Student*: Exploring relationship with teachers perceived as "safe" or "unsafe"<br>*School staff and parents*: Exploring defense mechanisms related to dealing with parents and power differential | *Student*: Exploring defense mechanisms with a safe and trusted adult<br>*School staff*: Exploring defense mechanisms and conflicts regarding maintaining power/status quo in classroom; examining how these defense mechanisms shape application of discipline policy<br>*Parents*: Exploring defense mechanisms as they relate to student behavior and their role as "effective" parents | *Student*: Exploring defense mechanisms and resolving associated fears or beliefs<br>*School staff*: Exploring defense mechanisms and conflicts regarding maintaining power/status quo in classroom; examining how these defense mechanisms shape application of discipline policy<br>*Parents*: Exploring and resolving defense mechanisms used when interacting with school staff regarding student behavior |
| Humanistic/Existential | *Student*: Teaching basic empathy, particularly in the older elementary student<br>*School staff*: Using opportunities to model appropriate social behavior and how to get needs met<br>*Parents*: Using empathy and unconditional positive regard to support parents when they feel embarrassed or unsure about student behavior and how to correct it | *Student*: Framing student understanding of self in the context of community; helping student to find a place as he makes a major life transition<br>*School staff*: Developing activities that correct behavior but with respect and regard for the student as an individual<br>*Parents*: Exploring parent feelings toward students and any incongruence | *Student*: Exploring the meaning of place in the world at this time; framing self-understanding in terms of place in the world now that student is preparing to leave childhood<br>*School staff and parents*: Focus on unconditional positive regard for student even when behavior is unacceptable; identifying and resolving incongruence |
| Behavioral/CBT | Developing a token economy system to reward and reinforce desired behavior | Developing a token economy system to reward and reinforce desired behavior; adopting a strengths-based approach that emphasizes successes, not failures | Developing a token economy system to reward and reinforce desired behavior; using journaling to reduce stress and teach coping skills |
| Systems | Identifying key school and community persons who can assist family in getting an evaluation for student; consulting with faith-based and community leaders for assistance | Revisiting discipline policies that continue to affect student academic progress; while student must follow school protocol, exploring ways that school staff, student, and parents can use to reinforce success | Working with parents to identify possible community resources to assist in understanding student behavior; identifying cultural beliefs and values that will help contextualize student behavior; exploring possible ways to partner with community resources to have students assessed |

| Paradigm | Elementary School | Middle School | High School |
|---|---|---|---|
| Emergent/ Multicultural | *Student*: Assessing ability to code switch in the school environment, if applicable<br><br>*School staff*: Exploring beliefs and attitudes toward working with an African American male. What are these beliefs, assumptions, and how do they affect interactions? These considerations are necessary for all staff, regardless of racial self-identification<br><br>*Parents*: What are your expectations of teachers, and what historical life events have shaped your expectations or concerns about school staff? | *Student*: Exploring how racial and gender identity shape peer and adult interactions<br><br>*School staff*: Exploring how student physical maturation and build trigger stereotypical expectations of young African American males<br><br>*Parents*: Exploring how expectations about adolescence shape handling of student emotional and spiritual development | *Student*: Exploring how racial and gender identity shape peer and adult interactions and expectations of self in social situations<br><br>*School staff*: Exploring how student physical maturation and build trigger stereotypical expectations of young African American males and how this may shape application of discipline policy; identifying cultural strengths that student and family bring to the school<br><br>*Parents*: Identifying cultural strengths and capital within the family and community; harnessing these strengths to gain support and encouragement for parenting student |

## IN SESSION

We decided to conduct the next meeting in the afternoon to accommodate Timothy's parents' schedules. His parents, a community organizer, an educational activist affiliated with the church, the lead teacher of Timothy's grade, and an assistant administrator attended the meeting. About a week before the meeting, we asked each attendee to identify two meeting outcomes he or she hoped to achieve. Further, we asked the attendees not to share these goals with anyone but, rather, to bring them to the meeting. Timothy asked to role-play opening the meeting in the week leading to the appointment. We assured him that we would be there the entire time and that the meeting was his opportunity to share his experiences. Following is a brief synopsis of the session.

| | |
|---|---|
| TIMOTHY (T): | I'm a little nervous doing this meeting. All the meetings end up with me being in trouble or fussed at. |
| TRACY: (COUNSELOR, C) | Timothy, what happens here affects you the most, so we want you to be in the driver's seat. (*Timothy looks at the counselors for direction and hesitates*) |
| RHONDA (R): | Tim, maybe you can begin with sharing your goals for the meeting's outcome. |
| T: | (*Smiles nervously*) Well, I want to learn how to get along better with everybody—even my teachers. I want to learn how to not get so mad or down that I can't talk right. |
| C: | Talk right? |

| | |
|---|---|
| T: | You know. Tell what I'm so mad about instead of just blowing up. Or finding things to feel good about. |
| C: | (*Nods her head*) Gotcha. |
| T: | And, I want a fresh start with my teachers—most of them are done with me. |
| FATHER (F): | Son, after this meeting, your mother and I want you to have an action plan for catching up on your schoolwork. (*Mother nods in agreement*) |
| LEAD TEACHER (L): | Tim, I came to this meeting hoping that we could develop a plan to assist you in working with your teachers more effectively. |
| T: | Yes, ma'am. |
| R: | Timothy, I can tell that your parents have really stressed the importance of being respectful. And you're showing that to Mrs. Thomas [lead teacher]. This is a time when we really need to know your thoughts beyond "yes, ma'am." It's OK. (*Smiles*) |
| T: | (*Looks at his parents, who nod their heads in encouragement*) Well, I know that sometimes I don't act right, but Ms. Jones tells me before class that every day is new and let's begin again. I like her class. My other teachers don't like me. |
| L: | Tim, some of your teachers are frustrated because they believe you can do the work and succeed, but they can't reach you. I do see that Ms. Jones's class is one you have attended regularly and your grades are a bit higher in that class. |
| T: | If I get frustrated, she tells me to just put my paper down and wait for her to come to my desk. She says that even if she comes over at the end of class, she will do it. No zeros. She has written me up, but we talked about it after and she told me that her classroom is a no disrespect zone. That even goes for the teacher! |
| F: | Teachers routinely give students zeros if there is a problem in the class? |
| PRINCIPAL (P): | This is left up to the teachers but it is a practice in the school, yes. |
| T: | I'll never catch up! Sometimes I feel really good but at other times I don't feel like trying or even coming to school. |
| C: | So here are two important areas, then. First, Timothy is doing better in a class with a teacher who is building a relationship with him but still has high expectations. Second, Timothy wants to perform better in school but really, up to this point, has been struggling with the best way to do this. Timothy, what do you think? |

| T: | Yeah! That's it. Talking to you [speaking to Tracy] helps me handle things even when I get upset or feel really down. |
| R: | So talking with the school counselor helps you plan how to deal with a tough situation. |
| T: | Yes, ma'am. |
| MOTHER (M): | Tim, we have the counselor at church who works with the youth ministry. Do you talk with her? |
| T: | Sometimes after youth meeting. I like talking with her. She's all right. |
| C: | Because you like talking with her, perhaps this is something you and your parents could explore further. |
| F: | My wife and I have discussed this before but didn't know how Timothy would respond. We can make an appointment and see how it goes. |
| L: | I can speak with Ms. Jones to share her teaching and community-building strategies with Timothy's other teachers so that they can learn about how to work with him more effectively. |
| T: | I really want to do well. |

## Outcome

Timothy and his parents went to an intake appointment with the pastoral counselor at the local church, who then asked his parents to make an appointment with the local pediatrician at the health department. An initial diagnosis of bipolar disorder was made, and the pastoral counselor began to collaborate with the school social worker to arrange state insurance services for Timothy. One unexpected benefit of the meeting was that Timothy's uncle was also seen at the local pastoral counseling center. He subsequently received a referral to the Veterans Administration Center, as he is a veteran of the U.S. Army.

Timothy and his family had a hard time understanding and accepting the diagnosis at first. Tracy met with Timothy and his family to discuss how the school could provide accommodations through Section 504. She also understood the concerns that Timothy's parents had about his being "labeled" with a diagnosis. The school counselor placed Timothy in small group sessions at school on managing anxiety and self-care. Although they initially refused to consider medication management, Timothy's parents agreed to try a regimen at his doctor's recommendation. Outside counseling, school counselor intervention, and the willingness of school staff to use different approaches to redirect and shape Timothy's behavior led to a more successful school year. Timothy successfully completed the ninth grade and looked forward to the next academic year.

Our collaboration with the community advocate and the church resulted in the implementation of culturally meaningful and relevant services for Timothy and his family. Collaboration with Timothy, his parents, and the school staff helped satisfy the need for order, discipline, and high expectations for all students in the school environment. Timothy learned valuable self-advocacy skills, which we hope he will continue to hone.

Encouraged by Timothy's success, we recognized that other students in our region and the state face similar tough situations. Mindful of our social justice orientation, we pondered how to add to the discourse on students' unmet mental health needs and their impact on educational and developmental outcomes. Therefore, we collaborated with our state professional counseling association to share strategies that included working with community advocates, organizers, and pro bono organizations that assist children, adolescents, and their families in accessing mental health services. We also

decided to highlight this issue during our work with state committees charged with retooling and improving our state's school counseling services. School counselors "promote equity for all students through community resources" (ASCA Ethical Standards, D.2.c, American School Counselor Association, 2010). The lack of community resources for adolescents' mental health treatment did not negate our ethical responsibility. We chose to meet the spirit of this ethical standard by advocating for these paramount services and social justice both within and beyond the school walls.

## Final Process Questions

- How did this incident with one student shape how our school approaches similar situations in the future?
- How did our approach shift the paradigm from focusing solely on Timothy to taking an approach that considers all persons who shape Timothy's school and community experiences?
- How can we modify our policies, informal behaviors, and attitudes so that other students with similar concerns get their needs met?
- How can professional school counselors use collaboration and consultation to promote equity, access, fairness, and harmony in minority adolescents' mental health care?

## Resources

Counselors for Social Justice. (2011). *What is social justice in counseling?* Retrieved from http://counselorsforsocialjustice.com/

Owens, D., Henfield, M., Bryant, R. M., & Simmons, R. W. (2011). Urban African American males' perceptions of school counseling services. *Urban Education, 46*, 165–177.

Ratts, M. J. (2009). Social justice counseling: Toward the development of a fifth force among counseling paradigms. *Journal of Humanistic Counseling, Education, and Development, 48*, 160–172.

Wrenn, G. C. (1962). The culturally encapsulated counselor. *Harvard Educational Review, 32*, 444–449.

*Chapter 4*

# Advocacy (and the Use of Small Group Counseling for Students with AD/HD)

Melissa Beverly and Joyce A. DeVoss

## CASE BACKGROUND

"To be effective in their professional mission, school counselors not only can but must play an active part in addressing societal issues" (DeVoss & Andrews, 2006, p. 132). Advocacy is one of the key components of the *ASCA National Model* (American School Counselor Association, 2012), a leadership practice that professional school counselors must embody to fully serve students. The ASCA model aligns well with the American Counseling Association Advocacy Competencies (Lewis, Arnold, House, & Toporek, 2003), and their four key components are infused with themes of leadership, advocacy, teaming, collaboration, and systemic change. Professional school counselors who implement the ASCA model are well versed in addressing the ACA Advocacy Competencies at all three levels: client–student, school–community, and the public arena. Advocating for students means that school counselors assist students by removing barriers that prevent success. Advocacy can involve an entire student body or a smaller group in need of special attention.

Recently, at our suburban public high school with approximately 2,000 students, the counseling department set goals to improve our comprehensive school counseling program services by offering more targeted small group interventions. To accomplish these goals, we chose to partner with licensed mental health professionals, our school psychologist, and a social worker. We shared frequent concerns from our students and based our initial list for potential group members on our own perspectives and anecdotal information. Then we agreed to review disaggregated student data to see whether the data supported our perceptions of student needs.

## INITIAL PROCESS QUESTIONS

- According to our data, who are the struggling students in need of advocacy?
- What are some of the barriers to academic success for these students?
- What theoretical and evidence-based interventions are available to help these students?
- What are some of the multicultural implications of working students with AD/HD?

"When working to change the *status quo*, data can reveal areas of need or disparity" (Ratts, DeKruyf, & Chen-Hayes, 2007). One surprising finding in the disaggregated data we reviewed was a large number of students either in special education or on a 504 plan with a diagnosis of attention-deficit/hyperactivity disorder (AD/HD). Many students on a 504 plan were behind in credits. We believed that this culturally diverse group of students warranted our advocacy efforts. In considering interventions for these students, we were aware of the implications of their diverse ethnic backgrounds as well as their unique learning styles that are affected by AD/HD. After consultation with the school psychologist, we decided that a small group intervention could be a starting point to support these students' academic success. We obtained support from administrators to present to our teachers the data, the proposed small group, the parent component, and possible teacher interventions.

## ADDRESSING THE ISSUES

At a faculty and staff meeting, we gave the rationale for the AD/HD small group, shared data supporting the need for the group, and shared data demonstrating the effectiveness of previously offered small groups for academically struggling students. We offered a small group as one of several evidence-based interventions for our students with AD/HD and their parents and encouraged staff to think about evidenced-based interventions they could provide for students. We also encouraged teachers to collaborate with us by referring students to participate in the AD/HD group. The majority of teachers were supportive. The following activities are examples of school counselor advocacy at the client–student and school–community levels (Lewis et al., 2003).

We outlined eight topics covered in the group, including making connections with other group members, time management, self-monitoring, organization, routine, study skills, motivation, and closure/review. In designing the format for our eight-session AD/HD support group, we used concepts from family systems theory, solution-focused counseling, behavioral counseling, and Adlerian psychology. We advertised the group by e-mailing a flyer to all students and parents. Interested students and parents submitted signed consent forms. We met with parents three times: at the initial meeting, at the fourth week, and at the eighth week.

### Session 1: Making Connections

Our objectives for the first group session were to facilitate a sense of connection and to foster goal orientation among the students. We explained confidentiality and created group norms. We did introductions using a Thumball™ and a game to help everyone remember each other's names. Students completed the Conners 3—Self-Report—Short version (Conners, 2008) as a pretest with the expectation that, using the same posttest measure, we would find a decrease in AD/HD symptoms. This instrument contains subscales measuring inattention, hyperactivity/impulsivity, learning problems, aggression, and family relations. The Conners 3 rating scales are some of the most commonly used assessments for AD/HD. We discussed members' goals for the group and had students create a plan to remember dates and time of follow-up meetings. We included the family system by arranging to host three parent meetings over the semester.

## Session 2: Time Management

We began by introducing new members and reviewing group norms. We played a game in which students had to predict how long it would take to list five animal names that began with a letter they drew out of a cup. All but one student predicted it would take less time than it actually did, and we discussed the implications of this activity for time management. We also covered four time-management personalities included in the book, *The Seven Habits of Highly Effective Teens* by Stephen Covey (1998): the procrastinator, the prioritizer, the yes man, and the slacker. Students completed a worksheet reflecting on times they had displayed behaviors of each of the personalities. They each made a commitment to use a time-management technique selected from a list to help in achieving their goals. Students also agreed to document on a worksheet how they spent their time on a given day before the next group meeting.

## Session 3: Self-Monitoring

We reviewed the time-management techniques group members had chosen the previous week and how each one had worked. We played two self-monitoring games. Students observed one of the facilitators over 3 minutes and documented every 20 seconds whether the facilitator was on or off task. Students then created a to-do list for the rest of the week and charted whether they were on task during this activity in 20-second intervals over 3 minutes. We debriefed and brainstormed strategies to assist with self-monitoring. For homework, students agreed to chart how they were feeling at 10:00 a.m. every day until the next group meeting. Students set their alarms on their cell phones for 10 a.m.

## Session 4: Organization

We reviewed the self-monitoring homework activity followed with an icebreaker in which a note card with the name of a famous person was placed on the back of each student. Students then worked with a partner to ask yes or no questions until each figured out which famous person he or she was. In a second activity, students wrote on a note card a problem they were facing. Each card was passed around the group and each group member wrote a solution to the problem. Students were encouraged to share their favorite solution. Both activities were designed to facilitate the use of organizational as well as solution-focused skills. We decided to continue with the topic of organization in session 5 and asked students to bring in their backpacks and binders to organize them and share organizational tips.

## Session 5: Organization

Students brought in their backpacks and binders. We discussed what organizational methods students could use, and students worked on backpack and binder organization.

## Session 6: Routine

Students reflected on their usual routine and wrote down an hour-by-hour list of their activities in a typical day in their lives. We discussed changes students needed to make to improve the effectiveness of their routine and brainstormed solutions to challenges of keeping a routine.

## Session 7: Study Skills

Students completed a Learning Style Inventory by Human eSources (2011) through the Family Connection website (http://www.navariance.com/), which identified how they learn best. They were given suggestions on strategies to improve their study habits. We planned to discuss the results at our next student group meeting.

## Session 8: Motivation/Group Closure

Students reviewed their Learning Style Inventory results and discussed their motivation levels and what motivates them to complete tasks. We asked what students found interesting about the inventory results and what strategies they could implement. Then we reviewed the benefits the students felt they had gotten from the group and offered the option of continuing the group. They shared that they wanted to keep meeting. We agreed to resume meeting following the winter break as long as the students were benefiting. Students completed the Conners 3—Self-Report—Short version (Conners, 2008) as a posttest. Table 4-1 provides ideas for additional approaches for advocating for and working with students with AD/HD.

## IN SESSION

| | |
|---|---|
| COUNSELOR (C): | Hi! It's great to see everyone today. How are you doing? |
| MARTIN: | Fine. |
| SHIRONDA: | I did well on my math test today! |
| LUPITA: | Stressed out. I have a paper to write. |
| TOM: | I have a test coming up. |
| C: | I have an activity I think will help. I want to check in with everyone about the homework from last week. How were you feeling when your alarm went off at 10:00 a.m. each day? |
| MARTIN: | I was happy. |
| TOM: | I was happy on the weekends and felt bored in school. |
| C: | When you noticed you were feeling bored in school, how did you respond? |
| TOM: | I worked harder to pay attention. |
| C: | It is really important to be aware of how you are feeling because our feelings can impact our actions. If we are aware of our feelings, we can think before acting on our feelings. Let's go back to some of the struggles you have had this week. Pick one problem that you would like the group to help with. Write this problem on a note card. We are going to pass around the note cards to each group member and write a possible solution on each card. |
| C: | Did everyone have a chance to write on each note card? |
| MARTIN: | I'm almost done. |

**TABLE 4-1  Additional Approaches for Working with Students with AD/HD**

| Paradigm | Elementary School | Middle School | High School |
|---|---|---|---|
| Psychodynamic | Artwork; incomplete sentences; psycho-educational lessons/handouts on self-understanding; recognizing feelings and basic motivation; understanding of goals; mutual storytelling | Artwork; incomplete sentences; psycho-educational lessons/handouts on self-understanding; recognizing feelings, basic motivation, defense mechanisms, and goals; mutual storytelling | Artwork; incomplete sentences; psycho-educational lessons/handouts on self-understanding, defense mechanisms, and goals |
| Humanistic/Existential | Core therapeutic conditions; role play and "I" statements for social and behavioral issues | Core therapeutic conditions; exploration of values, purpose/meaning; role play and "I" statements for social and behavioral issues | Core therapeutic conditions; exploration of values, purpose/meaning; role play and "I" statements for social and behavioral issues |
| Behavioral/CBT | Positive reinforcement; token economy; Premack principle; behavior charts; behavior contracts; time-out, modeling; behavioral rehearsal in person or through play with toy figures; role playing; overcorrection; response cost; lessons and worksheets on disputing irrational beliefs; automatic thoughts; self-talk; visual imagery; "picture on paper" | Positive reinforcement; token economy; Premack principle; behavior charts; behavior contracts; time-out; modeling; behavioral rehearsal in person; role playing; overcorrection; response cost; lessons and worksheets on disputing irrational beliefs; automatic thoughts; self-talk; visual imagery | Positive reinforcement; token economy; Premack principle; behavior charts; behavior contracts; time-out; modeling; behavioral rehearsal in person; role playing; overcorrection; response cost; lessons and worksheets on disputing irrational beliefs; automatic thoughts; self-talk; visual imagery |
| Family Systems | Parent–student collaboration building and negotiating; training for dealing with relevant behavioral, academic, and social issues; understanding family–school–community dynamics | Parent–student collaboration building and negotiating; training for dealing with relevant behavioral, academic, and social issues; understanding family–school–community dynamics | Parent–student collaboration building and negotiating; training for dealing with relevant behavioral, academic, and social issues; understanding family–school–community dynamics |
| Emergent | Miracle question; sparkling moments; empowerment group; exploring interpersonal incidents; role playing; exceptions; flagging the minefield | Mutual storytelling; story writing and reading; journaling; deconstruct and externalize problems; miracle question; sparkling moments; empowerment group; communication analysis; interpersonal incidents; role playing exceptions; flagging the minefield | Story writing and reading; journaling; deconstruct and externalize problems; miracle question; sparkling moments; empowerment group; communication analysis; interpersonal incidents; role playing; exceptions; flagging the minefield |

| | |
|---|---|
| C: | OK, go ahead and take a minute to finish. Once you have your note card back, pick the solutions you think will work best for you. We are going to go around the circle; if you feel comfortable, you can share your problem and your favorite solution. Who wants to start? |
| LUPITA: | My problem is that I procrastinate doing my classwork and homework once I get stuck on a problem. My favorite piece of advice was to ask for help from my teacher, but I tried last week and the teacher said she was too busy and told me to sit down. Now, I'm afraid to talk with my teacher. |
| C: | Why don't we talk more about this after group but, perhaps, you and I can talk with your teacher together to break the ice [client–student advocacy]. |
| TOM: | My problem is that I sometimes forget important things I need to do. My favorite piece of advice was to carry a notebook with me and write down the things I need to do in one place. |
| SHIRONDA: | My problem is trying to find motivation to do my homework. My favorite piece of advice was not to think about not wanting to do it but instead focus on a goal or reward once I finish. |
| C: | You all have wonderful ideas to share with each other. |
| MARTIN: | That was really fun. Can we keep our cards and can we do this again? |
| C: | Yes. We are almost out of time today. Next week, we are going to spend some time organizing our backpacks and binders. Be sure to bring these in next week. Why don't you take a moment to add a reminder to your cell phone. We are going to be meeting with your parents today [school–community advocacy]. Thank you all for meeting today. We look forward to seeing you next week. |

## Outcome

When comparing two consecutive semesters, the data indicated that students who participated in the group demonstrated an improvement in school attendance, an increase in GPA and credits earned, and a decrease in the number of failing grades. The students reported that the group was most helpful in connecting them with peers who shared similar difficulties. Their favorite activity was receiving feedback from their peers on a problem they struggled with. The parents reported that their meetings were helpful. One parent suggested that a video be purchased or developed for a teacher in-service training to help teachers better understand students with AD/HD, their needs, and how to work more effectively with them (school–community systems advocacy). We received approval from the assistant principal to obtain and show a video on

AD/HD at an upcoming staff development day. We had planned to use the Conners 3 for pre- and postanalysis, but that was unfeasible because the composition of the group members changed over the course of the group. We may use a closed format for future groups in order to ensure that group members participate in all sessions and complete both pre- and posttests.

## Final Process Questions

- What does our data suggest that we continue doing, alter, or stop doing?
- What are the legal and ethical implications of identifying struggling students?
- Did our interventions empower students? If so, in what ways?
- Did our interventions address the three ACA levels of advocacy: client–student, school–community, and the public arena? How could we have advocated better?

## Resources

Alexander-Roberts, C. (1994). *The AD/HD parenting handbook*. Lanham, MD: Taylor Trade.

DeVoss, J. A., & Andrews, M. F. (2006). *School counselors as educational leaders*. Boston, MA: Houghton Mifflin.

Flick, G. L. (2002). *ADD/AD/HD behavior change resource kit*. West Nyack, NY: Center for Applied Research in Education.

Lewis, J., Arnold, M. S., House R., & Toporek, R. (2003). *Advocacy competencies*. Retrieved from http://www.counseling.org/resources/competencies/advocacy_competencies.pdf

Lougy, R. A., DeRuvo, S. L., & Rosenthal, D. (2009). *The school counselor's guide to AD/HD: What to know and do to help your students*. Thousand Oaks, CA: Corwin Press.

Quinn, P. O., & Stern, J. M. (1993). *The "putting on the brakes" activity book for young people with AD/HD*. New York, NY: Magination Press.

Reiff, M. I., & Tippins S. (2004). *AD/HD: A complete and authoritative guide for parents*. Elk Grove Village, IL: American Academy of Pediatrics.

Sklare, G. B. (2005). *Brief counseling that works: A solution-focused approach for school counselors and administrators* (2nd ed.). Thousand Oaks, CA: Corwin Press.

*Chapter 5*

# Multicultural Counseling in the Schools

LAURA BELL AND TAMMY DAVIS

## CASE BACKGROUND

Her homeroom teacher referred Jennifer, a 13-year-old Vietnamese American student, to the school counselor. She came to the school counseling office in tears and obvious distress. Her initial concern was related to not being able to stop crying. Jennifer described feelings of sadness and varying degrees of anger and rage. When questioned further, she explained her spiraling sadness had been going on for approximately two months. Recently she had also felt as though she did not want to live and had been contemplating how to take her own life.

Jennifer's father and mother had separated recently, which left Jennifer and her younger brother living with their mom. In terms of a parental relationship, Jennifer expressed that she feels closer to her father and misses him terribly. He lives with another family and his visits with Jennifer and her brother are rare. Jennifer's mom, a hairdresser in a local salon, immigrated to the United States in the early 1980s but speaks very little English. According to Jennifer, her mother has not assimilated into the culture found in many American homes. Although Jennifer respects her mom, she is embarrassed by her lack of knowledge of American culture and by what she views as "clinging to the old ways." Furthermore, her mom's standards are very high; Jennifer describes her mother's expectations as excessive and unreasonable. Although Jennifer achieves very high grades in school, her mom seems to fixate on any grade less than an A. Jennifer complains that in school her teachers are very pleased with her achievements, but at home she has peace from her mother's constant criticism only when she meets the highest standards. Never feeling as though she can measure up, Jennifer often thinks of running away to live with her father.

Jennifer's mom, through the use of a translator, explained that she does not believe in mental illness and would like her daughter to smile more often. Furthermore, her mom does not wish to have her daughter referred to an outside therapist because she does not have insurance and believes her daughter should just stop acting this way. She believes high standards are necessary for a child to be successful, and she does not want Jennifer to have to struggle, as she has, to survive.

Jennifer's teachers report she is an excellent student, scoring high in all subject areas and involved in the Gifted and Talented program. Her homeroom teacher expressed a fair level of concern for Jennifer's emotional state, indicating that Jennifer often has "meltdowns"

60

in class if she cannot understand the subject matter. Communication with Jennifer's parents has been nonexistent because of the language differences, but Jennifer's teacher recently has been contemplating how to overcome this barrier.

## INITIAL PROCESS QUESTIONS

- As a school counselor, what is my level of cultural competency regarding second-generation Asian American students? How does this affect the interventions Jennifer receives?
- What theory would be most appropriate to use with Jennifer? Is there more than one?
- How can this student be given the tools to function in school if she receives opposing messages about success from her mother and the school? How can these differing views become more aligned?
- How can a school counselor better understand the parent's cultural stigma about counseling or asking for help?
- As a school counselor, what are my own thoughts, feelings, and experiences concerning achievement and student success?
- Is the school counselor ethically obligated to seek further help for this child if her mother refuses outside care? If so, what options should the school counselor pursue?
- Which other professionals should be involved in Jennifer's treatment?

## ADDRESSING THE ISSUES

In examining the help-seeking barriers Jennifer's mom may be experiencing, it is necessary to understand that individuals of Asian American descent may have less favorable attitudes toward professional mental health providers for many reasons. The amount of exposure they have had to Western medical practices, their level of acculturation, and their language proficiency play major roles in their utilization of these services. For example, limited language proficiency, as in Jennifer's mom's case, may influence her decision to seek help for her daughter because she does not understand her daughter's condition and is apt to minimize her needs. As is the case with Jennifer, the younger, more acculturated student often serves as translator for the parent. Therefore, I knew from the beginning it was important to involve a Vietnamese translator. With help from my supervisor, I was able to achieve this goal and open the dialogue with Jennifer's mom almost immediately.

In working with Jennifer, I felt it was incredibly important to hear her story in her own words. I asked her very few questions; instead, through a humanistic, person-centered technique, I encouraged Jennifer to share with me what she felt was important about her situation. She selected the activities we engaged in in these client-centered sessions. Often, Jennifer simply wanted to vent her frustration with the ongoing situation at home. I used reflective questions to understand her outlook and perceptions, while being careful not to steer her into any particular area. This allowed me to establish a trusting and empathic relationship with her.

Soon after our first session, we discussed Jennifer's resources both in school and at home. This was to help her recognize her support systems and view her situation as hopeful rather than hopeless. I encouraged her to identify individuals she felt safe talking to. Furthermore, I gave her the crisis hotline number in case of emergency, as Jennifer had previously indicated some thoughts of self-harm. I explained that she should use this number immediately if she felt like hurting herself again, and Jennifer promised she would and would also call her aunt if she experienced these feelings again.

By our third session, Jennifer's mom had agreed to permit her to seek treatment and to allow me to continue working with Jennifer at school. This change occurred after several meetings with Jennifer and her mother. Through role play, Jennifer was able to practice asserting her needs without being aggressive toward her mom. At this point, I began to use a solution-focused approach that centered on Jennifer's strengths. I shared with her how amazing I believed she was not only for defining her personal goals but also for helping her family to understand her anxiety and fears. Using a lifeline exercise helped Jennifer share her story so she could understand her background and then to plan what she wanted for her future. This focus on strengths and a positive future helped Jennifer feel more in control over her life, especially her future.

By communicating with Jennifer's outside therapist, after gaining agreement from Jennifer's mom, I was able to apply some of the same cognitive-behavioral techniques used during their sessions. After learning Jennifer was using a journal, we began using drawings to illustrate feelings she wrote about in her journal. Jennifer's passion for art played a key role in all of our later sessions, as we both discovered this was a way for her to express her feelings and experience a sort of catharsis. Table 5-1 provides additional approaches for working with culturally diverse youth.

## IN SESSION

Jennifer is in the counseling office because report cards are going to be sent home today. In class, she discovered she would receive a letter grade of B in a course. All day, she has been crying in class and unable to focus. Her teacher sent an e-mail to the counselor indicating this type of emotional upset is common and she is concerned about Jennifer's reaction.

| | |
|---|---|
| JENNIFER (J): | She is going to go crazy!! The last thing my mom asked me this morning was if I was going to get all As. This B is going to make her so upset. |
| COUNSELOR (C): | What do you think will happen when she finds out? |
| J: | You don't understand. . . . My mom has standards NO ONE can live up to. The Japanese have high standards, the Vietnamese have even higher standards, and then there is my mom, whose standards are even higher than that. . . . |
| C: | I know it may seem like I can't understand, but I want to try. What do you think makes her have such high standards? |
| J: | I don't know. I guess because she wants us to do well. It feels like she wants me to be her perfect little Asian daughter, but I do not care for the life she wants for me. I have always loved school, but I am really starting to hate it because I am never good enough. |

**TABLE 5-1   Additional Approaches to Working with Culturally Diverse Students**

| Paradigm | Elementary School | Middle School | High School |
|---|---|---|---|
| Psychodynamic | Listening for issues of transference to counselor; addressing defense mechanisms; exploring parent–child relationship | Listening for issues of transference to counselor (anger, frustration); confronting defense mechanisms; exploring parent–child relationship; exploring issues around cultural identity | Listening for issues of transference to counselor; confronting defense mechanisms; exploring parent–child relationship; developing cultural identity |
| Humanistic/ Existential | Reflection of feeling; being nondirective; using active listening, immediacy; minimal encouragers and few questions | Reflection of feeling; being nondirective; using active listening, immediacy; gentle confrontation regarding cultural issues | Reflection of feeling; being nondirective; using active listening, immediacy; gentle confrontation; exploration of conflict regarding future plans |
| Behavioral/CBT | Positive feedback focusing on resources; reframing weaknesses into strengths; journaling or drawing about feelings | Positive feedback focusing on resources; reframing weaknesses into strengths; rehearsal or role play of conversations with family; journaling | Positive feedback focusing on strengths; reframing weaknesses into strengths; journaling; exploring future plans |
| Systems | Collaboration with parents about expectations; collaboration with school personnel to assist student | Collaboration with parents about expectations; assisting student in discussing feelings with parents; collaboration with school personnel to assist student | Collaboration with parents about expectations; assisting student in discussing feelings with parents; collaboration with school personnel to assist student |
| Emergent | Narrative telling of student's story encouraging student to self-advocate and be competent and confident | Narrative telling of student's story; encouraging student to self-advocate and be competent and confident; solution-focused techniques such as scaling and the miracle question | Narrative telling of student's story; encouraging student to self-advocate for postsecondary choices; solution-focused techniques such as scaling and the miracle question |

C:     What do you think would be good enough for her?

J:     I am not sure.

C:     So, you're feeling lots of pressure to be good enough. How do you manage these high expectations?

J:     I can't stop crying. . . . I cry all of the time. It's like I am never happy anymore and the darkness inside me won't let me see the light.

| | |
|---|---|
| C: | So, what would it be like for you to "see the light"? |
| J: | (*Sigh*) Well, my mom would just accept me as I am . . . no matter what grades I get. |
| C: | So, you'd like for her to just be happy with you as you are. |
| J: | Yes . . . I just am not sure I can live up to her expectations. |
| C: | I guess I would like to hear what YOU want, Jennifer. If you could wake up tomorrow and this pressure or problem were gone, what would that be like for you? |
| J: | (*Silent for a moment*) I don't know. . . . I guess it would mean I would get up and come to school, do my best, and whether I get a B or C or A, it wouldn't matter. |
| C: | Describe what it would be like with your mom if it didn't matter about your grades. |
| J: | I would come home and hand her my grades and she would just say, "Did you do your best?" and I would say, "Yes," and then she would say, "Then that's good enough for me." |
| C: | That would help you feel . . . |
| J: | Accepted. I just want to be who I am . . . not Vietnamese or anything . . . just me. |

## Outcome

Educating Jennifer's family about mental illness was one of the key factors in helping them to understand the necessity of treatment for Jennifer. Jennifer was diagnosed with major depressive disorder, put on medication, and received cognitive-behavioral therapy for the rest of the year. Her mom decided to undergo therapy as well because of her recent split with Jennifer's father.

Jennifer continued to receive support from school counselors and other school personnel as needed in the school setting. Providing collaborative support systems between school and home will assist Jennifer in achieving success throughout her school career. Counseling that addresses cultural conflict will help improve communication between Jennifer and her family as she plans for her future.

## Final Process Questions

- What cultural barriers might continue to trouble Jennifer as she continues through school?
- How intensive should the school interventions be, given Jennifer's involvement with an outside therapist?
- What support might be available to help Jennifer identify resources and support systems as she transitions to high school and beyond?
- As her school counselor, how can I ensure that Jennifer feels supported and makes a productive transition to high school?

# Resources

Adams, J. R., Benshoff, J. M., & Harrington, S. Y. (2007). An examination of referrals to the school counselor by race, gender, and family structure. *Professional School Counseling, 10,* 389–398.

Day-Vines, N. L., & Terriquez, V. (2008). A strengths-based approach to promoting prosocial behavior among African American and Latino students. *Professional School Counseling, 12,* 170–175.

Ellis, C. M., & Carlson, J. (Eds.). (2009). *Cross cultural awareness and social justice in counseling.* New York, NY: Taylor and Francis Group.

Schellenberg, R., & Grothaus, T. (2009). Promoting cultural responsiveness and closing the achievement gap with standards blending. *Professional School Counseling, 12,* 440–449.

Vela-Gude, L., Cavezos, J., Johnson, M. B., Fielding, C., Cavezos, A. G., Campos, L., & Rodriguez, I. (2009). "My counselors were never there": Perceptions from Latino college students. *Professional School Counseling, 12,* 272–279.

## Chapter 6

# Immigration

Miriam Eisenmenger

## CASE BACKGROUND

I met Mara during my first month as a beginning school counselor when she came into the office to schedule classes for her senior year. I took a quick look at her past records consisting of transcripts from six different school districts—one of which was not in English—her current report card, and her discipline record. These documents painted a picture of a bright and promising student who had a slew of discipline problems that seemed to have been brought under control by the end of her sophomore year. Her midterm grades had just been posted, and she wasn't surprised to see two failing grades in math and physics among five other grades in the 90s. When I inquired about the discrepancy, she told me that the night before those exams, her father sent her to stay with her aunt while he went away on business. Her aunt has three small children who become Mara's responsibility to care for when she stays in their small apartment. Mara also disclosed that her aunt's husband is incredibly strict and forces her to go to bed at the same time as the little ones—so she must forgo the time she usually sets aside for studying.

I was starting to get a better idea of why Mara had such a variety of discipline problems on her record. I observed from across the desk as her mood seemed to switch from pleasant to gloomy, then right back to pleasant—a darkness looming below the surface of her smile. There was a lot more going on in her life than most high school juniors deal with, and she reported that she just wanted to get on with her life. Mara confided that she was frustrated because she didn't have a say in her future. She had very few opportunities to properly express her anger and frustration with her circumstances, so she ended up lashing out at school where the consequences were short-lived and seemingly nonthreatening.

When we finally got to the reason she was called to the office, she was reticent to make a schedule for the following year because she was not entirely sure where she would be living. Her parents are divorced. Her mother lives in Florida with a new husband and two small children, and there was talk of Mara's moving there next year. Mara's grandmother, with whom she is very close, moved back to their homeland last year and has offered to have Mara move with her before college. Mara and her father live in the area, but he travels all the time, leaving Mara with her aunt. When asked what she would like to do if given the choice, Mara darkened slightly, sighed, and said, "I just want to finish school and go to college." She seemed tired of starting over. This was the longest she'd been in the same place since moving from her country of origin at 6 years old. She finally had a small group of trustworthy friends and wanted to start seriously planning her future.

With Mara's being naturally good at science and math, we discussed the possibilities of careers in engineering or perhaps teaching math or science. She remarked that she had thought about pursuing a career in engineering. However, as the only girl in a male-oriented household, she was unsure of how real those dreams could become before her priorities were set aside for her younger brother. Regardless, we set up her schedule, putting her into the advanced math and science classes just in case. I also provided her with some information on colleges that have good engineering programs, both in the area and in Florida.

## INITIAL PROCESS QUESTIONS

There were several questions running through my mind at the time of our first meeting that I needed to address before I saw Mara for our next session. Most of these questions focused on the ethical expectation that counselors need to be knowledgeable of in terms of multicultural issues—both about my own personal views and about my client's culture of origin. When working with students from different cultures, it is easy to assume that they want to be treated like every other American student. However, although part of them may want that, another part wants to preserve their cultural background. Also, often present is pressure from the immediate family and more distant relatives to stay centered on their culture of origin. Students still live with their parents and thus have to meet cultural obligations daily. As counselors, we need to be understanding, knowledgeable, and flexible enough to work with them from where they are, not from our own Western mind-set.

- What do I know about the student's history that can help me adequately interpret her current behavior? To what extent has this student become acculturated into American society?
- From what aspects of her culture of origin does she draw a sense of identity?
- What do I know about the student's cultural background that can help me understand her current circumstances?
- Who at home is acting as her support system? At school?
- Upon self-reflection, what biases, if any, may be detrimental to forming a productive relationship with the student and her family?
- What skills and talents does this student possess that can be used to empower her?
- What aspects of her culture of origin can be used to give her a sense of value and worth?
- What is the best way to blend an effective therapeutic process into her cultural belief system, without disrespecting her culture?

## ADDRESSING THE ISSUES

At all developmental ages, immigration has a unique effect. These students' lives have been affected in multiple ways: They are in a new place, living in a different home environment, often worrying about money and jobs (if they're old enough), missing family and friends, and not sure how long they will be staying in the specific school or town, or even in the country, due to visa/green card or political issues (Ellis, MacDonald, Lincoln, & Cabral, 2008). Additionally, in recent years there has been an influx of people into the United States from countries in political unrest or at war. Therefore, it is not unlikely that many of these students may be dealing with the ramifications of premigration trauma. Developmental age directly influences how a student may react to his or her circumstances (Ellis et al., 2008). Mara, for example, has been dealing with the implications of immigration through three developmental stages (early childhood, middle childhood, and adolescence). I believe that many of her current struggles could have been avoided had someone helped her process her transition to American life, and her parents' divorce, early on. Table 6-1 provides an outline of the types of techniques that would benefit students of all ages who are dealing with issues related to immigration.

**TABLE 6-1    Strategies and Interventions for Helping Students Adjust to Immigration**

| Paradigm | Elementary School | Middle School | High School |
|---|---|---|---|
| Psychodynamic | Analysis of transference and defense mechanisms; sibling relationships; acting as if | Analysis of transference and defense mechanisms; sibling relationships; acting as if | Analysis of transference and defense mechanisms; sibling relationships; acting as if |
| Humanistic/Existential | Therapeutic conditions; focus on the here and now; freedom, values, and responsibility; meaning in one's actions; self-disclosure; redirection of energy or actions | Therapeutic conditions; focus on the here and now; freedom, values, and responsibility; meaning in one's actions; self-disclosure; redirection of energy or actions | Therapeutic conditions; focus on the here and now; freedom, values, and responsibility; meaning in one's actions; self-disclosure; redirection of energy or actions |
| Behavioral/CBT | Positive reinforcement; modeling; behavioral rehearsal; role playing; flagging the minefield; exceptions/solutions; ABCDEs of REBT | Positive reinforcement; modeling; behavioral rehearsal; role playing; flagging the minefield; exceptions/solutions; ABCDEs of REBT | Positive reinforcement; modeling; behavioral rehearsal; role playing; flagging the minefield; exceptions/solutions; ABCDEs of REBT |
| Systems | Genogram; family sculpting | Differentiation of self; genogram; family sculpting | Differentiation of self; genogram; family sculpting |
| Emergent | Miracle question; empowerment; egalitarian relationship; therapeutic alliance; content and process affect; role playing; play therapy | Deconstruct problems; miracle question; gender role analysis; empowerment; sociocultural exploration of gender; egalitarian relationship; therapeutic alliance; content and process affect; role playing; play therapy | Deconstruct problems; miracle question; gender role analysis; empowerment; sociocultural exploration of gender; egalitarian relationship; therapeutic alliance; content and process affect; role playing; play therapy |

Even without premigration trauma, the effects of immigration transitions often resemble that of grief and loss in children as routines are altered, the whole family is anxious about the unknown, and familiar faces and scenes are no longer around (Kelly & Lamb, 2003). Children can become withdrawn, angry, aggressive, sad, or anxious at any age. Elementary age children tend to have an easier time adjusting once a new routine is set and the new faces become familiar, as consistency is key with this age group (Broderick & Blewitt, 2010). To help elementary students affected by immigration, it is important for counselors to be aware of the child's family system and work alongside parents to get the child back into a routine. In addition, it may be beneficial for elementary counselors to use play therapy to help those students who may be having a more difficult time processing the transition. Due to the constant moves in her life, Mara was not able to properly move out of that transition stage, and she could have benefited greatly from a counselor welcoming her to the school and helping her work through the instability in her life at an earlier age.

Middle school aged students have a little more loss associated with their transition, as they experience a longer history in their culture of origin (Vernberg, Greenhoot, & Biggs, 2006). They lose friends, family, and the comforts of the familiar. However, children in this age group are so thirsty to form an identity that they tend to pick up the customs of the new society more quickly. Then they have to learn how to balance the expectations of their parents with the expectations of the new culture (Broderick & Blewitt, 2010; Gelhaar et al., 2007). These are powerful years for identity formation, and students in this age group are going through significant physical changes and looking more to the outer world for a sense of identity (Broderick & Blewitt, 2010). During this time of her life, Mara attended two very different schools, one in New Jersey and one in Florida. In addition to having to transition between the two schools, Mara had to relearn how to live with her mother in Florida. By this time she had all but assimilated into U.S. culture. Mara spoke the language and wore the clothes, but she lacked a steady peer support group to help her with the other transitions in her life. Constantly being "the new kid" had taken its toll on her. She needed a consistent, welcoming, and knowledgeable adult in her life. I have come to believe that students who have immigrated at this age will often benefit from school counselors who help them focus on identity formation and resolving any transition issues. And, as with all middle school aged students, school counselors should address good decision making, taking responsibility for actions, and empowerment within the umbrella of transitioning.

As a high school junior, Mara had several issues that needed to be addressed, but I needed a better picture of what was going on in Mara's home life before continuing with counseling sessions. I had to understand the family system she grew up in and to find out whether anything had changed. So I sat down with her former school counselor and went over Mara's full case history. This school counselor had already worked with Mara, helping her to adjust to the new school system, ultimately helping her stop getting suspended for fighting and behaving disrespectfully toward teachers.

This is Mara's history: She moved to the United States with her father, grandmother, and brothers, at 6 years old; her parents had divorced not long before the move, and she had become very close to her grandmother. Mara has one older brother and one younger brother. The older brother was diagnosed with schizophrenia when Mara was a freshman, after he had a psychotic break in the principal's office. The younger brother is now starting to show mild signs of the same condition. The former school counselor added that the father also has the same tendencies at times and was referred for family counseling at a local counseling center. Having a genogram of the family was beneficial in understanding the family system and Mara as an individual.

Mara's behavioral problems seemed to have several causes, including lack of consistency due to multiple moves, varying parental figures, an absent mother, a limited and fluctuating peer support system, an unstable home life, and dependency (from years of decisions being made for her). As she got older, Mara tried to take control of what parts of her life she could, often becoming aggressive and argumentative to the point of getting suspended from school every other week. The former school counselor had helped Mara refocus her frustrations with not having a say in her own life by giving her the tools to take control of those parts of her life that she could: schoolwork, getting a job, making friends, setting her own schedule, etc. Even though Mara had come a long way already, certain issues still needed to be addressed, mainly her feelings of hopelessness about her future. Mara had a good grasp of the type of person she was becoming, had altered some of the negative aspects, and was now on the road to becoming someone about whom she could feel positive and admire. It was becoming evident that Mara would benefit from empowerment exercises, role play, role reversals (e.g., Mara playing the parts of her father, uncle, aunt, older brother), and a positive therapeutic alliance. It would also be beneficial to work through a sociocultural exploration of gender with Mara in order to help her better understand herself and her family.

## IN SESSION

Because Mara still struggles with transference issues—thus pinning her frustration with her father, brother, and aunt onto teachers and friends—Mara has become a regular in the office. She knows when she may react inappropriately, so she removes herself from the situation before she reacts. I introduced her to the empty chair technique to allow her to direct her feelings outward without harming anyone or anything. We have also incorporated role play into our routine. This is especially helpful when Mara is anxious about talking to her father about a topic that she doesn't feel he will receive well, such as going to college, career choice, getting a job. Mara's father believes all of these aren't necessary for a woman to pursue. In these cases, I take on Mara's role and she takes on her father's role, and we occasionally switch roles to give her different perspectives. These techniques not only help her to think through her issues but also empower her by allowing her to voice her feelings instead of keeping them bottled up. She has said on numerous occasions that she feels like a shadow in her house, as she is seldom heard by her father. Giving her a place to find her voice, and strengthen it, has proven most beneficial to Mara.

We have both benefited from her educating me on her culture, especially her role as the only woman in her home. We were able to work together to find a way to balance personal empowerment with respect for her father in his house. She responded well to the warm, egalitarian approach I offered. Giving her a chance to teach me boosted her confidence in herself, thus allowing her to feel that she was valued in the therapeutic relationship. This is something she doesn't often experience at home.

| | |
|---|---|
| Counselor (C): | So you've had the college and career talk with him? About the plans you have for after high school? |
| Student (S): | Well, not exactly. I've hinted. |

C:        What's holding you back?

S:        I'm afraid of how he will react.

C:        Do you know exactly how he'll react?

S:        Well, no.

C:        Have you ever pictured how the conversation might go?

S:        A million different times, and a million different ways. Always with the same outcome.

C:        The same outcome?

S:        Yeah. Him saying no.

C:        How about we play out one of these scenarios. I'll be you, and you be your dad.

S:        I guess. Seems kind of silly.

C:        Well, we'll work on that, but for right now, let's see how "your dad" is feeling today. Hi, Dad!

S:        What is it, Mara?

C:        I was wondering if we could talk.

S:        I'm very busy; make it quick.

C:        OK, well, I was hoping to talk to you about going to college.

S:        College? What for?

C:        Well, engineering. You see both my math and physics teachers think I'd be good at it.

S:        But that's a man's work.

C:        Well, there are a lot of women in the field now. And I really am good at those subjects. Just look at my report card!

S:        But I'm putting your older brother through college now, and your younger brother is not far behind.

C:        Well, there are a lot of colleges out there for people like me.

S:        No one will give you money. You should just go stay with your grandmother and find a husband to take care of you.

C:        But that's not what I want. I want to go to college.

S:        You don't want that. No self-respecting woman wants that.

C:        Wow. Let's stop there. Is that what you think he believes?

S:        Yes.

C:        Has he said these things before?

S:        Well, no. Not really.

C:        Not really?

S:        I guess it's what I expect him to say.

C:        Any particular reason for this expectation?

S:        Well, he has made some comments about the women he works with.

C:        Are you afraid he might think of you the same way?

S:          I don't know. He does seem proud when I show him my good grades.

C:          Proud?

S:          Yeah, he calls his brother to brag.

C:          To brag?

S:          Yes.

C:          Would you going to college be something that he could brag about too?

S:          I've never thought about it that way.

## Outcome

By the end of our time together, we had made a lot of progress. Mara now had the tools to cope with her fluctuating life. And although she still doesn't know when, or if, she will be moving, she has come to accept that no matter where she goes, she can make the best of it. Furthermore, she has been able to have some open discussions with her father about the options she has for life after high school, and he is beginning to understand that she has great potential here in America. Though he is not entirely comfortable with her newly found voice, he appreciates that she has started to open up to him, as her openness with him has had a direct effect on her discipline records. She has been suspension free for a year now.

## Final Process Questions

- How did the therapeutic techniques work within her cultural constraints?
- How will she benefit from this new sense of empowerment?
- If she moves to a different school for her senior year, what changes will make her transition smoother and allow her to continue to use the tools she has developed?
- How can we ensure that her father will continue to support her career choices when she doesn't have a personal advocate like a school counselor?

## Resources

Gelhaar, T., Seiffge-Krenke, I., Borge, A., Cicognani, E., Cunha, M., Loncaric, D., . . . Metzke, C. (2007). Adolescent coping with everyday stressors: A seven-nation study of youth from central, eastern, southern, and northern Europe. *European Journal of Developmental Psychology, 4,* 129–156. doi:10.1080/17405620600831564

Huan, V. S., See, Y., Ang, R. P., & Har, C. (2008). The impact of adolescent concerns on their academic stress. *Educational Review, 60,* 169–178. doi:10.1080/00131910801934045

Kelly, J. B., & Lamb, M. E. (2003). Developmental issues in relocation cases involving young children: When, whether, and how? *Journal of Family Psychology, 17,* 193–205.

McNair, R., & Johnson, H. (2009). Perceived school and home characteristics as predictors of school importance and academic performance in a diverse adolescent sample. *North American Journal of Psychology, 11*(1), 63–84.

Vernberg, E. M., Greenhoot, A. F., & Biggs, B. K. (2006). Intercommunity relocation and adolescent friendships: Who struggles and why? *Journal of Consulting and Clinical Psychology, 74,* 511–523.

*Chapter 7*

# Racism

HELEN RUNYAN

## CASE BACKGROUND

Jerome, an eighth-grade student, had been coming to see me off and on for about two years. Our initial visits were a bit challenging. He had been referred to me for "acting out in class," but it was actually more complicated than that. Jerome's sixth-grade science teacher sent him to the assistant principal, Ms. Whitehurst, several times because of his behavior during class. Ms. Whitehurst told Jerome's parents that she was going to suspend him if he got one more referral. His parents then contacted the principal, Mr. Stephenson, who asked me whether I would "have a chat" with Jerome. I called Jerome to my office and found him somewhat reluctant to speak with me. Our initial meeting consisted of my explaining what a school counselor does (which does not include discipline). Jerome agreed to return and talk with me again.

During our next meeting, he mentioned that other kids in his science class were "acting up" but not getting referrals. I observed this class and realized his observation seemed correct. The science teacher seemed to be a lot stricter with her Black students than with the others. Jerome and I had some individual counseling sessions and ended up forming a Multicultural Awareness Club. Everyone was invited to come to the bimonthly after-school meetings. Jerome amazed me with his persistence and imagination: He invited guest speakers from the community and made announcements about the club on the school news. By the end of the year, the turnout was amazing.

I believe that it was because of the relationship that Jerome and I had built through this process that he felt safe enough to share his thoughts about his eighth-grade math teacher with me. Jerome filled out an appointment request, so I wrote him a pass to come see me. When he came in for his appointment, he looked more worried than usual and immediately told me his issue: "Miss R, Mr. Jacobs is a racist." The words rang in my ears.

I already had my concerns about Mr. Jacobs, simply from the way he managed his classroom. Despite having a class of nearly all White students, 80% of his discipline referrals were for his Black students. When I consulted with him about students, he would call the White students by name. He referred to other students as "that Black student" or "that Asian" before he said their names, usually mispronouncing them in the process. He appeared to call on the White students with more frequency, praise their correct answers a little bit more, and crack inappropriate jokes. He did not even seem to know he was doing it.

So here I sat with Jerome, a student with whom I had bonded, who was affirming my gut feelings about Mr. Jacobs. My initial reaction was to protect Jerome. We had become so close, and I felt angry that he was hurting. He had worked so hard to conquer racist attitudes. It just seemed unfair.

My second reaction was both anxiety and disappointment: anxiety about having to deal with Mr. Jacobs and disappointment that the system that had been put into place over the past couple of years to address this issue had fallen short. I was also a little disappointed that I still had that feeling of anxiety at the thought of dealing with "the race issue." As a White, middle-aged, female school counselor, I matched the demographics of the teachers of my school. Even though I had a very different cultural background than most of the students, my deepest desire was to help them all whenever possible. I knew the students knew that. I believe my caring attitude is why we have been able to overcome our cultural differences. So, why did I still feel so insecure at the mere mention of the topic of race?

## INITIAL PROCESS QUESTIONS

- What is the best way to talk about this sensitive topic with Jerome, without revealing my thoughts about Mr. Jacobs?
- Should I already have broached the topic of race with Jerome even though we did not seem to have a problem with it within our relationship?
- How do I best support Jerome?
- What are some of Jerome's strengths, and how can he use them in this situation?
- How might Jerome's different cultural identities and roles in and out of school affect how I conceptualize his case?
- What are the ethical and legal issues specific to racism?

## ADDRESSING THE ISSUES

No matter the school population, prejudice and bias are commonplace issues. Anyone who claims racism is dead has failed to look at current research. Not only do students of color have challenges (Pachter, Bernstein, Szalacha, & Coll, 2010), but racism is experienced by teachers as well (Jay, 2009). Needless to say, I was dealing with Jerome's individual issue as well as a systemic problem.

To deal with the immediate situation, I simply had to take a deep breath. At this point, Jerome just wanted me to listen to him. Reflecting back on it, I think I was more upset about the situation than he was. In effect, while I was sitting there worrying about how to talk about this with him, Jerome was already solving his immediate crisis. He just wanted to be heard.

I allowed Jerome to tell me his story fully. By allowing him to be the expert on his own life (Sobhy & Cavallaro, 2010), I encouraged him toward self-empowerment (Holcomb-McCoy & Chen-Hayes, 2011). Jerome was further empowered when I asked him what he would like to see happen from this meeting instead of assuming the role of expert advisor. He stated that he just wanted to be treated like "the White kids." I asked him what being treated that way would look like. It took him a second to absorb the question. Jerome looked at me with a surprised expression and said he had never thought about it. Our time was almost up, so I invited Jerome to think about what that would look like so we knew what it would look like when we got there.

From our previous work together, I knew Jerome was driven. When he came up with a goal, he persisted relentlessly until he achieved it. I hoped to encourage and applaud this use of inner strength and perseverance. I planned to continue seeing Jerome at regular intervals while I went to work on the systemic concerns.

As for this bigger issue, I did what I was taught to do in counseling: When in doubt, consult. I consulted with others, without identifying individuals, of course. After consultation, further consideration, and more than a bit of consternation, I arranged a meeting with Mr. Jacobs. I told him what I had observed already and why I believed it was an issue. I then showed him the data: discipline rates disaggregated by teachers. Although he did not receive the information casually, it appeared by his demeanor that he was listening. When I informed him of an upcoming seminar concerning social justice, he told me, "I refuse to waste *my* free time dealing with *your* issues." I saw from his body language that the conversation was quickly spiraling downhill, so I offered to continue at some point in the future. When Mr. Jacobs said that he "didn't think it'd be necessary," I knew I had to talk to Mr. Stephenson, the principal.

Mr. Stephenson agreed that we had an issue and said he would "deal with Mr. Jacobs." Then he asked whether I would do an in-service training for the entire staff, including the teachers. I quickly agreed and went to work disaggregating current data for the school. I also attended the social justice seminar to which I had originally referred Mr. Jacobs. Then I started getting nervous. How was the staff going to take a White person lecturing on racism? Did I even know enough to appear knowledgeable on the topic? It turned out that the in-service training was quite successful. I was able to disseminate current information and best practices after overcoming the initial discomfort that always accompanies this topic (at least for me). Table 7-1 contains some other options for working against racism and for social justice.

**TABLE 7-1   Additional Approaches for Working with Students and within Systems Affected by Racism**

| Paradigm | Elementary School | Middle School | High School |
|---|---|---|---|
| Psychodynamic | Approaching teacher indirectly by employing parables or other modes of "theme interference reduction" (reducing generalized biases and prejudices; Dougherty, 2009) | Approaching teacher indirectly by employing parables or other modes of "theme interference reduction" (reducing generalized biases and prejudices; Dougherty, 2009); verbally exploring student's past and how this affects current thoughts and beliefs concerning oppression | Approaching teacher indirectly by employing parables or other modes of "theme interference reduction" (reducing generalized biases and prejudices; Dougherty, 2009); verbally exploring student's past and how this affects current thoughts and beliefs concerning oppression |

*(continued)*

**TABLE 7-1** *(continued)*

| Paradigm | Elementary School | Middle School | High School |
|---|---|---|---|
| Humanistic/ Existential | Avoidance of using a desk in counselor's office in order to be more personal than authoritative; being genuine; respecting the student, teacher, and/ or administrator; paying careful attention to avoid "blaming the victim" and/or ignoring systemic challenges | Avoidance of using a desk in counselor's office in order to be more personal than authoritative; being genuine; respecting the student, teacher, and/ or administrator; paying careful attention to avoid "blaming the victim" and/or ignoring systemic challenges | Avoidance of using a desk in counselor's office in order to be more personal than authoritative; being genuine; respecting the student, teacher, and/or administrator; paying careful attention to avoid "blaming the victim" and/or ignoring systemic challenges |
| Behavioral/CBT | Assessing and identifying irrational/dysfunctional beliefs, especially concerning power and oppression; postulating different points of view | Assessing and identifying irrational/dysfunctional beliefs, especially concerning power and oppression; postulating different points of view; helping students and teachers understand that people think (and therefore feel) differently; helping show how thoughts cause feelings; practicing overcoming negative thoughts and false assumptions | Assessing and identifying irrational/dysfunctional beliefs, especially concerning power and oppression; postulating different points of view; helping student and teachers understand that people think (and therefore feel) differently; helping show how thoughts cause feelings; practicing overcoming negative thoughts and false assumptions |
| Family Systems | Especially helpful when approaching the classroom from a systemic perspective; modeling effective, culturally competent classroom management skills when teaching classroom guidance lessons; teaching student about healthy boundaries | Especially helpful when approaching the classroom from a systemic perspective; modeling effective, culturally competent classroom management skills when teaching classroom guidance lessons; teaching student about healthy boundary setting and how that can help divert negative patterns | Especially helpful when approaching the classroom from a systemic perspective; modeling effective, culturally competent classroom management skills when teaching classroom guidance lessons; allowing student to problem solve, establish, and maintain healthy boundaries, especially in that classroom |
| Emergent | Building rapport; listening to student and teacher stories without blame; miracle question; pointing out sparkling moments; empowering student in healthy ways to decrease feelings of helplessness; identifying support system | Building rapport; listening to student and teacher stories without blame; miracle question; identifying healthy ways to obtain/retain power; identifying support system | Building rapport; listening to student story without blame; miracle question; encouraging identification of sparkling moments; identifying healthy ways to obtain/retain power, boundaries, and self-esteem; encouraging identification and expansion of support systems |

## IN SESSION

On one hand, I felt as though we were ahead of the game because Jerome and I had already developed a working relationship. On the other hand, I felt remiss in my duties because I had not broached the topic of culture with Jerome. It seemed that our whole relationship was about race and culture, yet I had never asked him how that affected our relationship. Although I had mixed feelings, I was happy that Jerome still felt comfortable enough to talk to me about his issues with his teacher. As opposed to the anxiety of that first session when Jerome approached me about Mr. Jacobs, I felt more prepared when Jerome returned a couple of weeks later. The beginning of our session follows.

| | |
|---|---|
| COUNSELOR (C): | Hi, Jerome. How are things going for you today? |
| JEROME (J): | Oh, about the same. |
| C: | Can you describe what you mean by "the same"? |
| J: | Mr. Jacobs is still prejudiced, not that I thought he wouldn't be. Just saying . . . it'd be easier in his class. . . . |
| C: | I can hear the disappointment in your voice. Remember when you came in a couple of weeks ago and said you just wanted to be treated like "the White kids"? I asked you what it would look like when you were being treated. . . . |
| J: | (*Interrupting*) Yeah . . . yeah. You're always giving me stuff to do, Miss R. [(*Smiling*)] |
| C: | (*Smiling*) What were you able to come up with? |
| J: | I gotta tell you, it was a real hard question. I'd never thought about what it would feel like to be treated like them. I just didn't want to be treated the way *I* was being treated. I knew *that* wasn't fair. So at first, all I could think of was stuff like not being yelled at for telling a joke, not being given that look that I always get when I get the answer wrong, and stuff like that. But, I couldn't really come up with a picture in my head for that. So I tried real hard and I did come up with something. When I'm being treated right, I will be looked at the same way as every other kid in the class. I will be called on when my hand is raised, not called out when my hand is down. You know, stuff like that. |
| C: | I see that you have put a lot of effort into "the stuff I gave you to do." I'm wondering how you can use some of your strengths to make that happen. |
| J: | Well, I've already used my imagination to make it happen. (*Laughs*) Nah, but really, I know I can't change Mr. Jacobs. . . . (*Voice trailing off as he looks down at the floor*) |
| C: | But I can think of a lot of inner resources you have used in the past to help yourself. Can you think of some that you can use to help in this situation? |

## Outcome

With a little more prompting, Jerome was able to identify and use his strengths to deflect the biased words and actions of Mr. Jacobs when in his class. Even though Jerome could not "change Mr. Jacobs," he learned how to change his reaction to Mr. Jacobs. We role-played healthy boundary setting in my office. He also used his new tool of boundary setting with his girlfriend. He was very excited that some of "the stuff I gave him to do" worked "in real life" and not just in school.

I was able to take another look at my cultural competence. Through my reaction to Jerome, my conversation with Mr. Jacobs, the social justice seminar, and some self-analysis, I realized that I had been treating social justice as an event, rather than a process. A few years ago, when I was fresh out of graduate school, social justice was so high on my agenda. Over time, I had forgotten how important it was to keep it a priority. Even when Jerome and I first started working together and built the Multicultural Awareness Club, I remember having the mindset of how good it was for "them." Even while writing this chapter, I am still dismayed by the amount I have to learn.

## Final Process Questions

- How might the school system have functioned differently if I had been more proactive in social justice concerns?
- Was it my place as the school counselor to speak with Mr. Jacobs? If so, how might I have led a more productive conversation with him?
- Who might I enlist for additional efforts in multicultural awareness and social justice?
- How might I better facilitate multicultural competence in the school?
- Which community and family resources foster multicultural citizenship? How can these be used within the school?
- What else might be done to advocate for Jerome?

## Resources

Khalifa, M. (2011). Teacher expectations and principal behavior: Responding to teacher acquiescence. *Urban Review, 43*, 702–727.

Russell, S., Sinclair, K., Poteat, V., & Koenig, B. (2012). Adolescent health and harassment based on discriminatory bias. *American Journal of Public Health, 102*, 493–495.

Theoharis, G., & Haddix, M. (2011). Undermining racism and a whiteness ideology: White principals living a commitment to equitable and excellent schools. *Urban Education, 46*, 1332–1351.

Ullucci, K. (2012). Knowing we are White: Narrative as critical praxis. *Teaching Education, 23*(1), 89–107.

Young, E. Y. (2011). The four personae of racism: Educators' (mis)understanding of individual vs. systemic racism. *Urban Education, 46*, 1433–1460.

*Chapter 8*

# Existential-Spirituality in School Counseling

MOLLY B. QUICK AND CHRISTOPHER A. SINK

## CASE BACKGROUND

Sally is an 18-year-old White European American female in her final year of a faith-based private high school (enrollment of approximately 450 students). She has been a student at this school since the sixth grade when she transferred from her local public elementary school. In addition to working toward state graduation requirements, Sally has participated in a Bible class every year and attended weekly chapels. Other than these two spiritual commitments, students attending the school are not required to profess a belief in Christianity; in fact, no formal data are collected regarding student spiritual beliefs.

At this private school there is no state-certified school counselor; rather two academic counselors* serve students as educational advisors, informal guides, and support staff. Specifically, the academic counselor involved in this case is charged with the academic advising of students. Part of her work is to act as a liaison between students, families, and teachers to support the success of all students, particularly those who are approaching graduation or are at risk for academic troubles. The academic counselor coordinates academic testing and the creation of individualized student plans for success, which outline diagnosed learning disabilities and necessary accommodations. Comparable to professional school counselors, the school's academic counselor offers short-term emotional/psychological support to students, but in cases in which students are in acute crises, they are referred to relevant support agencies and organizations. Unlike a professional school counselor who spreads out his or her student support across several developmental domains, this academic counselor mainly focuses her student time on improving educational outcomes.

The referring teacher met Sally almost three years ago when Sally was in two of her classes (sophomore-level English Literature and Creative Writing). Since that time, the teacher has had only informal contact with Sally in the hallway and around campus. However, during the spring of 2011, Sally stopped by to show the teacher one of her paintings: a black-and-white painting of a lone girl at a bus stop (see Figure 8-1). "It has a Chuck Palahnuik (1999) quote,"

---

*The academic counselor has a BA in education with an endorsement in Special Education and an MA in education administration; she is certified through the National Institute for Learning Disabilities (NILD). Further, she engages in ongoing training for issues relevant to high school students (e.g., bullying, classroom discipline, teen depression, eating disorders, etc.). She has worked in the present school system for 17 years.

**FIGURE 8-1**  Sally's drawing reflecting some spiritual confusion.

Sally said. The painting, which adapts words from Palahnuik's *Invisible Monsters*, states, "Give me detached existentialist ennui, baby." Feeling that she might want to talk, the teacher asked, "What has been going on lately?" A synopsis of Sally's narrative follows.

Sally informed the teacher that she had been very depressed for some months and had ignored it, calling it "teen angst." However, these feelings intensified around December, just after Sally suffered two relational losses that she felt were the catalysts to feelings of worthlessness. First, Sally had to abandon a friendship that she described as "very abusive," and second, her boyfriend broke up with her after she admitted to him that she was struggling with depression. Sally described a pattern of self-harm that had progressed in to hate and anger over the next months. Sally could not eat or sleep; felt lonely and isolated; cried a lot and felt powerless to explain or control her teary outbursts; scratched at her arm with paper clips; and gave herself chemical burns by using the "salt and ice method." Subsequently, Sally began to think about suicide "uncontrollably" and had visions of "cutting her arms and blood everywhere." Despite the severity of Sally's struggles, she continued to try to conceal her pain until, just before school started again in January, Sally attempted to stab herself.

A friend was present to stop her, and this attempted suicide served as a breaking point for Sally; she checked herself into an urgent care clinic, with her mom's help. Sally spent a week in a hospital receiving evaluation, diagnosis, and initial treatments. It was during her hospital stay that Sally's mom contacted the school counseling staff about Sally's situation.

# INITIAL PROCESS QUESTIONS

Undoubtedly, when a student is in immediate harm, there are several germane questions:

- Is she currently with a trustworthy ally?
- Is she seeking professional help?
- How can I aid this student and her family?
- Are there any ethnicity or cultural issues that need to be considered in this scenario?
- How does Sally's European heritage impact her personal values and understanding of self, family, and so on (see Lee, Blando, Mizelle, & Orozco, 2007, chapter 11 on counseling European Americans).

However, in the case of Sally, whose immediate safety was certain, the academic counselor asked questions whose answers might support Sally's successful reentry into school.

- What is the best way to assist Sally and her family during this time of need and crisis?
- Is a strengths-based approach a possible option?
- How can the school staff (counselors and teachers) foster Sally's spirituality as a protective factor?
- How can the school staff support Sally's academic goals, including on-time graduation?
- How can the school personnel help and support Sally to comfortably communicate her needs to her friends and teachers?
- What ethical and legal issues are at stake? Such relevant questions, among others, must be considered: Will Child Protective Services (CPS) need to be called due to the student's suicidal ideations? Given that she's 18 years old and no longer a minor, should parental consent and input be sought? Is a medical examination required? How can the staff maintain contact with an outside therapist, and what paperwork needs to be completed? Consult state law and review ethical codes published by the American Counseling Association (2005) and American School Counselor Association (2010) to determine which topics might apply.

# ADDRESSING THE ISSUES

As alluded to earlier, the academic counselor collaborates with pertinent teachers and the administration regarding any substantial student issue that may arise. Students in serious crisis are referred to mental health support services outside of the school. Because her existential concerns were closely related to her emerging spirituality (Buddhism) and potentially in conflict with the school's Christian orientation, in dealing with Sally before and throughout this recent crisis, one of the counselors attempted initially to use a humanistic/existential perspective among others (Jones-Smith, 2012; see Table 8-1). In particular, relational and strengths-based models were seen as being able to help Sally. For example, the academic counselor worked to create an affirming atmosphere in which Sally's unique style was valued and in which she could speak freely about her life outside of school. This support continued through Sally's crisis and reentry into school. When Sally first returned to school, she stopped by the counseling office twice a day to check in or to take a break from the social demands of her school day.

| TABLE 8-1    Sample Approaches to Addressing Spirituality Issues in Schools | |
|---|---|
| **Paradigm** | **Interventions and Approaches** |
| Humanistic/Existential | Therapeutic conditions; role play and "I" statements for social and behavioral issues; revise misapprehensions; focus on the "here and now"; redirect feelings and actions toward positive ends |
| Solution-Focused Brief Counseling | Short-term intervention targeting solutions in the here and now; clients desire a change in their school performance, behavior, etc.; value of the methods rests largely on counselor's ability to interact with students and others in ways that encourage change and solutions (see also Murphy, 2008) |
| Family Systems | Parent consultation for managing pertinent social, academic, and emotional issues; tentative exploration of family dynamics; potential referral to family therapist (see also Davis, 2011) |
| Emergent | Narrative counseling to reframe and redirect concerns, examine personal constructs, increase personal support systems; view of spirituality as a developmental asset or strength that can be utilized to encourage student healing and restoration; use of positive psychology tools to help assess current status of meaning in life, spirituality, connection to spiritual characteristics (e.g., hope, thanksgiving, forgiveness) |

In addressing Sally's academic needs during her hospital stay and upon return to school, the academic counselor used a solution-focused model (Jones-Smith, 2012) to facilitate Sally's academic support. The academic counselor held a meeting with all of Sally's teachers to explain the situation in general terms while maintaining confidentiality. Upon Sally's request, the academic counselor served as a collecting point for Sally's missed schoolwork while she was away. Upon Sally's return to school, the academic counselor helped Sally to change her schedule in order to include an art class, allowing her an outlet whereby she could express her emotions in healthy ways, as well as providing her with a class that reinforced her talents.

Additionally, the core values of the school indicate that any intervention on Sally's behalf use community support and spiritual guidance. Teachers were able to support Sally in a personal and meaningful way as she reentered school by offering understanding, notes and words of encouragement, as well as extended time on assignments. Sally indicated, "I have received an enormous amount of support from the faculty. If I was unable to attend classes because of my condition, my teachers would willingly fill me in on what I had missed and helped [*sic*] me catch up on assignments." Ways to address this student's issues are multifaceted, and Table 8-1 includes various integrative orientations and their associated interventions for addressing the spiritual issues of students, a number of which were suggested by Jones-Smith (2012).

## IN SESSION

Sally and the academic counselor met regularly just after Sally's return to school. The following mini-conversations were re-created from the counselor's notes of those meetings as well as from an interview with the student. They are presented chronologically from just after Sally's return to school until about two months after her return.

| | |
|---|---|
| SALLY (S): | [On the first day of return, Sally came in to report that she could not make it through the day as she was exhausted.] |
| COUNSELOR (C): | We want you to know that all of us, your teachers and I, believe that your first priority should be to keep yourself healthy, and secondarily we can worry about academics. It is OK to be tired and exhausted after having been through such emotional trauma; emotional work is tiring work. [Later, she called Sally's house to check on Sally and ask how Sally had felt at school.] |
| C: | How's it going today? |
| S: | I feel overwhelmed, too stressed and frustrated to stay at school today. And I'm tired. I don't know why I feel this way. |
| C: | Is it all of school or certain parts of school making you feel this way? |
| S: | It's a lot of parts, but one is Spanish class. It's too much work that I missed, and I'm still supposed to be learning new things and we keep getting more. |
| C: | How would it be if we could switch you out of Spanish and into an Independent Art class in the middle of the day? |
| S: | I think that would help a lot. That would be great. . . . <br> . . . |
| C: | What are you doing to cope with emotions and frustrations? |
| S: | My mom gave me a book that's about not letting situations control my emotions and that's helping a lot. Also, the medications help. But I miss the hyperactivity because I could get so much done then. |
| C: | What is the book called? |
| S: | It's called *Open Heart, Clear Mind* but I don't know who the author is. [The book was authored by Thubton Chodron in 1990.] Also, taking art in the middle of the day helps me feel more normal. |

|   |   |
|---|---|
| C: | Has your faith helped you cope in any way? |
| S: | I have taken Buddhist principles and applied them to my life, which has changed the way I look at things. If something goes wrong, I accept that the situation is not directly making me sad, it is just a situation. The only cause of my sadness is myself. |

## Outcome

Sally described that she is currently in the "denouement" phase of her crisis. She regularly attends classes and there is a noticeable upbeat quality to her demeanor. Recently, she wrote a note to the referring teacher mentioned previously to update the teacher on her life at the moment. Sally wrote, "Love has taught me about sacrifice, truth and strength. I've had so many great experiences, but also my share of pain, fear and anger. I've had to learn to accept life as it comes and use every situation as a Vehicle [sic] to grow into the strong woman I hope to become."

## Final Process Questions

- How should the staff "monitor" Sally's status without being too invasive?
- How can the school personnel continue to fortify Sally's resiliency and self-worth by encouraging her spiritual seeking?
- How can the staff continue to use a strengths-based orientation to support Sally's reentry into the school?
- Can the family's ethnicity and cultural background provide any spiritual and emotional support for Sally? Can they serve as a protective factor?
- How can Sally's story inform the school about how to improve practices for dealing with students in crisis?

## Resources

American Counseling Association. (2005). *ACA code of ethics.* Retrieved from http://www.counseling.org/resources/codeofethics/TP/home/ct2.aspx

American School Counselor Association. (2010). *The ethical standards for school counselors.* Retrieved from http://www.schoolcounselor.org/files/EthicalStandards2010.pdf

Cashwell, C. S., & Young, J. S. (2011). *Integrating spirituality and religion into counseling: A guide to competent practice* (2nd ed.). Alexandria, VA: American Counseling Association.

Gold, J. M. (2010). *Counseling and spirituality: Integrating spiritual and clinical orientations.* Columbus, OH: Merrill.

Good, M., & Willoughby, T. (2006). The role of spirituality versus religiosity in adolescent psychosocial adjustment. *Journal of Youth Adolescence, 3*(1), 41–55.

Lee, W. M. L., Blando, J. A., Mizelle, N. D., & Orozco, G. L. (2007). *Introduction to multicultural counseling for helping professionals* (2nd ed.). New York, NY: Routledge.

Sink, C. A., Cleveland, R., & Stern, J. (2007). Spiritual formation in Christian school counseling programs. *Journal of Research on Christian Education, 16*(1), 35–63.

Sink, C. A., & Devlin, J. (2011). Student spirituality and professional school counseling: Issues, opportunities, and challenges. *Counseling and Values, 85,* 130–148.

Sink, C. A., & Hyun, J. (2012). A comprehensive review of research on child and adolescent spirituality: Evidence for the inclusion of spirituality in school counseling. *Journal of Asia Pacific Counseling, 2*(1), 19–43.

Wong, P. T. P., & Wong, L. C. (2012). A meaning-centered approach to building youth resilience. In P. T. P. Wong (Ed.), *Human quest for meaning: Theories, research, and applications* (2nd ed., pp. 585–617). New York, NY: Routledge.

*Chapter 9*

# English Language Learners

TIM GROTHAUS, TORI STONE, AMY UPTON, AND KIE ANDERSON

## CASE BACKGROUND

As a professional school counselor, I first met Zeneb in October when she and her Uncle Hassan came to enroll her in our middle school. Although Zeneb's 11-year-old brother Samir started school at the beginning of the year at the elementary school, Hassan mentioned that Zeneb's parents had not previously registered her because they believed she was needed to care for her four younger siblings and to help in the household.

Zeneb and her family fled the war in Sudan more than two years earlier and landed in a refugee camp. They were allowed to move to the United States and join Hassan's family just a few weeks prior to the start of the academic year. Uncle Hassan and his family have lived here for several years and are active in the local community. Hassan was able to help Zeneb's father secure a job with a local cleaning company.

Several local Lutheran congregations have sponsored families from southern Sudan over the past few years, but Zeneb was the first young person from Sudan to enroll at my school. I was aware of some of the extraordinary and challenging circumstances many Sudanese families encountered before arriving in the United States, but I was not familiar with Sudan's educational system.

I learned that, although the 2005 Sudan Constitution recognized Arabic and English as official languages, Zeneb had limited exposure to English and initially recognized only a handful of English words orally and none in writing. In addition, even though schooling in Sudan is intended to be both compulsory and free for children aged 6 to 13 years (with Arabic as the primary language of instruction), between the ravages of the war and the slow evolution in attitudes toward the education of girls, 13-year-old Zeneb had attended school only sporadically over a 4-year period. According to her Uncle Hassan, Zeneb had mastered basic reading and writing in Arabic. No school records were available.

After Zeneb's first few weeks with us, her teachers reported that Zeneb appeared to be a quick study with most tasks that weren't heavily language dependent (e.g., math, school procedures, orienting herself to the building and her schedule). In addition, the number of spoken English words she understood seemed to be growing rapidly. Socially, she was very shy around males but would engage with female classmates to some degree when they interacted with her. Her physical education teacher reported some concern about bully-ing, having overheard remarks about Zeneb's being "a Muslim terrorist."

There are multiple factors to consider when working with non-native born stu-dents who are English language learners (ELLs). For example, research indicates that students may learn enough English to function "on the playground" in 1 to 2 years, but competence in the academic English needed for content mastery of school subjects usu-ally takes 4 to 7 years (Gollnick & Chinn, 2009). In addition, it appears that having ELL students learn academic content in their native language while learning the English language seems to be the best method of promoting success in both areas. ELL students are also designated to receive special education services at approximately twice the rate of the general population and are significantly underrepresented in programs for gifted students and advanced courses (Callahan, 2005; Dowling, 2008). The need for cultural sensitivity in the use of assessment instruments and placement rubrics seems clear yet may require some advocacy efforts. It is likewise important to ensure that all involved parties are aware of the legal mandates that establish ELL students' rights to an educa-tion that specifically addresses their unique learning needs. Finally, given the antipathy toward non-English-speaking immigrants, especially those who are Muslim, school and community climate issues must be assessed and addressed.

## INITIAL PROCESS QUESTIONS

Some questions to consider in a case like Zeneb's might be the following:

- For many Sudanese people, the prominence of family and having a communitar-ian perspective are strong values. How might I encourage Zeneb's family mem-bers and important community members to be involved in the life of the school community and in her education? In addition, how can this be done while being respectful and sensitive to their views about education and gender roles?
- Given the challenging circumstances many refugees experienced prior to and after arriving in the United States, how might I cultivate a trusting relationship with Zeneb and her family?
- How might I interact with, collaborate with, and assist Zeneb, given my inability to speak or read Arabic?
- With the likelihood that Zeneb experienced losses resulting from her family's reset-tlement and the possibility that she encountered war-related trauma(s), how might I address these issues either in school or through collaboration with outside resources?
- How might I assist in connecting Zeneb and her family members with organiza-tions offering support, language and literacy training, orientation to the United States (while respecting the maintenance of their own valued cultural practices and perspectives), and access to needed services and resources?
- With the absence of any previous school records, how might I ethically and effec-tively advocate for and assist with culturally alert assessment, placement, and aca-demic support and resources?
- Given the bias evident in the intolerant remarks mentioned previously (i.e., "Muslim terrorist"), how might I collaborate with school personnel and community mem-bers to assess and address the school and community climate, to enhance Zeneb's sense of safety and belonging, and to promote an appreciation of diversity?

- How might I encourage a focus on Zeneb's strengths and interests among the faculty and school community?
- How might I work with Zeneb to enhance her overall well-being and also promote her academic, career, and personal/social growth?

## ADDRESSING THE ISSUES

School counseling with English language learners differs from work with the general student population for several reasons, the most conspicuous being that we cannot easily communicate with ELLs using words. This renders use of traditional counseling approaches more difficult. When Zeneb and her Uncle Hassan arrived at my office, I used person-centered techniques, such as empathic listening, minimal encouragers, and positive regard to convey a welcoming sense of warmth and acceptance (Rogers, 1961). I also utilized a free "app" on my smart phone that translates multiple languages in spoken and written form. Although this was a bit clumsy initially, we were able to put together an action-based plan I call the *village approach* to help Zeneb. My goal was to unite a group of concerned adults to provide Zeneb and her family with a sense of community, support, and access to resources in the United States.

My first step was to educate myself about the norms and expectations of the Sudanese culture. Through some brief Internet research I learned that in the Sudan, female family members and community elders educate girls on the ways of the family and the role of women. Because many Sudanese girls are not formally educated, their mothers, aunts, and grandmothers are the primary source of knowledge in their lives. Hence, a supportive group of women with a shared cultural history would be essential to ease Zeneb's transition to life in the United States. To this end, I reached out to local community organizations, mosques, churches, and women's groups to find support services that had been established by or for Sudanese refugees.

My next step was to meet with Zeneb's team of teachers. I shared the little I knew about Zeneb's history, as well as general information on the difficulties refugee children face when transitioning to life in the United States. Though at that time I was not aware of the traumas that Zeneb had faced in the Sudan, I spent some time talking to the team about posttraumatic stress responses in adolescents and asked them to be mindful of Zeneb's emotional state. In addition, I worked with my colleagues, administrators, and faculty to heighten awareness of possible student hostility toward Zeneb. At the same time, I expanded efforts in the community and at the school, class, group, and individual levels to cultivate appreciation for diverse cultures, the gifts they bring, and the value students from diverse cultures can add to our community.

The team and I also discussed partnering Zeneb with Aiman, a student who had immigrated to the United States from Iraq about two years ago. Though the girls had different cultural backgrounds, they shared a basic knowledge of Arabic and the experience of immigrating to the United States from a war-torn country. The ELL teacher planned to have Aiman give Zeneb a tour of the building, escort her to her classes, and sit with her at lunch— basically show her the ropes of life in an American middle school. The team also discussed inviting Zeneb to join an after-school multicultural club in which ELL students can share information about their homeland and learn about other cultures. We hoped that joining this group might help Zeneb to feel a sense of community with her new classmates.

My final, immediate concern for Zeneb was her inevitable grief that the loss of her homeland and way of life would bring. This grief, coupled with the memories of past traumatic events, needed to be addressed in a way that was in harmony with the Sudanese culture, not American culture (Duany, 2001). Early on, I had referred Zeneb's Uncle Hassan to the local public counseling center, where Zeneb participated in counseling with a female therapist trained to help clients with posttraumatic stress responses. In addition to providing individual counseling, the therapist referred Zeneb and her mother to a support group whose membership included two other women who were Sudanese refugees.

During her first few months at school, I checked in with Zeneb regularly. My initial approach was person-centered; I gained her trust, established a relationship, and gave her unconditional acceptance each time we met. As our counseling relationship progressed and Zeneb's grasp of conversational English grew, I transitioned to using more of a constructivist approach, specifically employing a solution-focused approach. Through periodic conversations with her individual therapist, I was aware that Zeneb was dealing with the issues of loss and trauma in the individual sessions and in the support group. I chose to focus on the adjustments to life in America and to her experience and success at school, hoping to help enhance what she believed was working for her and to change what she saw as problematic (O'Connell, 2005). In the end, the restoration of a sense of community, as well as counseling support that was focused on forward progress, not on analysis of the past, helped Zeneb to create a new life in America. English language learners come to school with a variety of needs and concerns, so many theoretical counseling approaches can be used (see Table 9-1).

## IN SESSION

After establishing rapport in earlier sessions and continuing to attend to the needs already addressed, a brief example of a session, assisted by the translation app, follows:

| | |
|---|---|
| COUNSELOR (C): | I'm glad you are here, Zeneb. What would you like for us to do today? (*Pause as Zeneb looks uncertain*). . . Last time we met, you were speaking about how you were adjusting to being in school in America and also having family members with different expectations. . . . |
| ZENEB (Z): | Yes, I care for my sisters and brothers and help at home. I also have homework. |
| C: | I can imagine that having all of these responsibilities and expectations can be hard. |
| Z: | It is hard for my parents with all of the changes. |
| C: | I appreciate how you want to help your family and also take care of work for school. What do you believe is helping you and your family handle these changes and expectations? |
| Z: | There is my Uncle Hassan's family. They have been here in America for longer. Also families we know in our mosque are trying to teach my parents about how things are in the United States. They try to explain to my parents about school and why it is important for me. |

**TABLE 9-1** Additional Approaches to Working with English Language Learners

| Paradigm | Elementary School | Middle School | High School |
|---|---|---|---|
| Psychodynamic | Focus on helping the child become more self-aware through the use of pictures, stories, and metaphors; exploration of recurrent themes in the child's fantasies and play; use of play therapy techniques to understand the child's current emotional state | Emphasis on helping the early adolescent to achieve normal developmental milestones and handle associated stressors and issues associated with acculturation, developing language proficiency, and cultural identities; variation of activities between play and talking, e.g., play in a sand tray while talking or drawing; use of metaphor; exploration of developmental themes highlighted in movies, TV, and books | Continuing to explore transference, projection, defense mechanisms, private logic, and goals that drive behavior; helping the adolescent to accept responsibility for the life choices that come with becoming an adult and to avoid regression toward childhood, where decisions were made on his or her behalf; assisting with adult identity formation in a culturally sensitive fashion |
| Humanistic/ Existential | Focus on developing an authentic relationship with the child; counseling seen as a way of *being with*, rather than *doing to* the child; culturally sensitive play therapy techniques to give children the opportunity to *play out* rather than *talk out* feelings | Encouraging self-exploration and self-discovery through warm, supportive, affirming therapeutic relationship; adolescents learn to accept themselves and begin the journey toward self-actualization; techniques may include providing support for goal setting, handling stressors associated with language acquisition, and decision making | Actively seeking to understand the world-view of client and convey caring, unconditional acceptance, warmth, and empathy; helping client to work through the feelings of "stuckness' that can accompany adolescence |
| Behavioral/CBT | With children younger than 8 years old, focus on concrete skills such as problem solving and behavior rehearsal; with older children, therapeutic alliance essential to help the child "buy in" to the therapeutic process and establish goals for behavioral change; positive reinforcement; token economies; behavior charts; and behavior contracts using photos and pictures | Teaching young adolescents the Stages of Change with emphasis placed on timing and choice to modify behavior; focus on development of coping strategies, disputing self-defeating beliefs, exploration of automatic negative thoughts, role play, and aligning behavior with personal goals; building on perceived strengths; using culturally relevant examples | Focus on feelings and behavior modification through the development of coping strategies such as the ability to dispute automatic negative thoughts, controlling self-talk and "all or nothing" thinking; making situationally intelligent decisions based on the context and salient cultural factors; consideration of the consequences of behavior to manage and direct thinking and actions to meet personal goals |

*(continued)*

**TABLE 9-1** *(continued)*

| Paradigm | Elementary School | Middle School | High School |
|---|---|---|---|
| Family Systems | Helping child/family to understand behavioral, academic, and social issues of transitioning to a new cultural environment; focus on familial relationships and times when the family successfully overcame difficulty; emphasis on strengths, community, and resources | Helping client to differentiate between self and family and to develop mature peer relationships; when working with parents, reframing adolescent's misbehavior into a developmental and emotional context; helping ELL parent to understand American adolescent culture and behavior | Building on client's existing strengths, resources, and successes; supporting client through identity development; helping family to understand changing parent–child relationships and need for independence that defines adolescence; exploring family and community resources ELL student could access for support |
| Emergent | Empowering the child; focus on communication skills, building friendships, and development of personal goals; attending to development of identity and fluency in both mainstream and native cultures, if student and family so desire | Teaching problem-solving skills such as breaking problems down into chunks, visualizing what a better life would look like, and establishing better communication skills with peers and adults; attending to development of identity and fluency in both the mainstream and native cultures, if student and family so desire | Focus on becoming empowered, improving interpersonal relationships, and rehearsing behaviors to achieve desired goals; attending to development of identity and fluency in both the mainstream and native cultures, if student and family so desire |

C:  I'm glad that your family has people who are helping you with the many changes you are experiencing. Are there times when all of these changes seem a bit easier for you?

Z:  At home, when Fatima, the wife of Hassan, talks with my mother and when Hassan helps my father. In school, when Aiman and I are together, she helps me understand how to be an American and also helps me learn how to ask my teachers when I do not understand.

C:  It sounds like being with Aiman is very helpful to you and being with others is helpful to your parents. When do you spend time with Aiman?

Z:  She is in some of my classes and my lunch time, but I do not want to bother her.

C:  I am glad you care for your friend and want her to be happy. I may be wrong, but when I see you two together, Aiman seems to like being with you. What do you think?

Z:  She is helpful and friendly like my friends from before.

C:  If she is friendly and helpful and does not seem be bothered and you wish to spend more time with her, how might you try to make this happen more often?

## Outcome

Zeneb was excited about the opportunity to spend more time with Aiman and made efforts to approach her. Aiman came to me and suggested that I could help arrange meetings with the teachers weekly so that Zeneb could ask questions about the work and feel more confident that she was able to understand what was being asked of her. Periodically, the two girls chose to eat lunch in my office and talk with me and each other.

I continued my efforts to connect with Zeneb's family and to invite them and their support network to participate in school activities by making a home visit and connecting with the imam at the family's mosque. It was helpful to have a cultural informant, someone who was fluent in both mainstream U.S. culture and could help me understand the values and views of the members of the mosque.

Our school and community efforts to appreciate and educate about the richness of our diverse community are ongoing. Also our work continues with the district office regarding satisfying legal mandates and dealing with assessment and placement issues with ELL students in an equitable and culturally responsive fashion. Zeneb appears to be doing well overall, given all that she has experienced. Hopefully, her school and community are learning and growing also.

## Final Process Questions

- What additional community resources might I access to help this student?
- Were my actions in "good faith" supportive of the student and within appropriate professional boundaries, or did I overstep my role as a professional school counselor?
- How might I advocate both for Zeneb and for systemic change in order to enhance the likelihood of ELL students' success?
- What is my role in assisting Zeneb in dealing with issues of grief and transition?
- What else could be done to respect Zeneb's communitarian perspective and cultural values?
- How might the interventions described in this case scenario assist in building upon Zeneb's strengths?
- What is my role in attending to school climate and appreciation for diversity?
- What more can I do to support English language learners?

## Resources

Callahan, R. M. (2005). Tracking and high school English learners: Limiting opportunity to learn. *American Educational Research Journal, 42*, 305–328.

Dowling, E. (2008). *English language learners and special education issues.* Retrieved from http://www.planesllessons.com/2008/12/english-language-learners-and-special-education-issues/

Iowa Department of Education. (2008). *Identifying gifted and talented English language learners Grades K–12.* Des Moines, IA: Author. Retrieved from http://www.iowa.gov/pages/search?q=identifying+gifted+and+talented&=Search

Koelsch, N. (2006). *Improving literacy outcomes for English language learners in high school: Considerations for states and districts in developing a coherent policy framework.* Retrieved from http://www.better-highschools.org/docs/NHSC_AdolescentS_110806.pdf

Spinelli, C. G. (2008). Addressing the issue of cultural and linguistic diversity and assessment: Informal evaluation measures for English language learners. *Reading and Writing Quarterly, 24,* 101–118.

*Chapter 10*

# Lesbian, Gay, Bisexual, Transgender, and Questioning (LGBTQ) Issues in School Counseling

JEFFREY M. WARREN AND JENNA N. WARREN

## CASE BACKGROUND

I first met Tanya, a 14-year-old African American female, when she was in the seventh grade. As a school counselor, I began working with her after she sought my assistance to help her through a relationship issue. Initially, our sessions focused on relationship difficulties involving young men. Shortly thereafter, she identified herself as bisexual and began opening up about her feelings toward females.

Through my work with Tanya during seventh grade, I learned much about her home life. Tanya resided in an apartment in the suburbs with her mother and younger brother. Tanya's mother, while supportive of her daughter, was physically disabled, which hindered her ability to attend school functions and parent–teacher conferences. However, her mother remained involved in Tanya's education through phone conferences. Tanya's mother also struggled with mental health issues and substance abuse issues. Tanya's brother, a sixth grader, received exceptional children services due to a behavioral health disorder. Tanya did not have contact with her biological father.

Tanya appeared to have average ability, although she seemed to struggle academically. Tanya was socially driven and appeared to place much emphasis on her interactions with others. She was well-liked by her peers and had many friends. However, Tanya often had disagreements with others and occasionally got in trouble for not following classroom and school rules.

Tanya spent the fall semester of her seventh-grade year in a regular middle school setting. However, due to academic difficulties and failing grades, she was referred to an alternative school setting for the spring semester. While in the alternative setting, Tanya earned As and Bs and met promotion standards for eighth grade.

Tanya returned to a regular middle school setting at the beginning of the eighth grade. I immediately became reacquainted with Tanya and her difficulties pertaining to social-emotional issues. During one session, Tanya discussed an argument she was having with her girlfriend, Mariah. She was distraught that Mariah was jealous of her going to a party with another girl. Tanya expressed many thoughts and feelings related to her relationship with Mariah.

# INITIAL PROCESS QUESTIONS

It is estimated that lesbian, gay, bisexual, transgender, and questioning (LGBTQ) adolescents make up 10% of the population (Savage & Harley, 2009). Therefore, it is imperative that school counselors are attuned to their own biases, realize the negative impact of stereotyping, and affirm all sexual orientations (American School Counselor Association, 2007). The ability to identify and address the needs of LGBTQ youth is crucial. Although training in this area is valuable, it can never prepare school counselors for every situation or encounter with a student. Therefore, considering new or uncomfortable situations as learning experiences can be invaluable. Self-reflection and the ability to ask oneself and others difficult questions is a key in multicultural growth. Here are a few questions you may have about this case scenario:

- Does Tanya's family affirm her affectional/sexual orientation?
- In what ways may Tanya's affectional/sexual orientation affect her academic performance?
- How, if at all, would you identify Tanya (e.g., lesbian, bisexual, questioning)?
- What strategies and techniques would be most helpful in working with Tanya?
- What do school counselors need to know about the LGBTQ population?
- How should school counselors address LGBTQ-related issues?

# ADDRESSING THE ISSUES

Lesbian, gay, bisexual, transgender, and questioning (LGBTQ) youth face many societal challenges, including discrimination, lack of acceptance, violence, and feelings of isolation, to name a few (Head, 2010). The context (i.e., school, home, and community) in which LGBTQ youth interact has a significant impact on their growth and development (Head, 2010; Horn, Kosciw, & Russell, 2009). Kelleher (2009) found that the well-being of LGBTQ youth is negatively affected in social settings that have tendencies to promote sexual- and gender-related stigmas. Additionally, a study conducted by D'Augelli, Grossman, and Starks (2006) found a significant relationship between youth being shunned for gender atypical behavior and their degrees of affectional/sexual orientation victimization and mental health issues. Parents, family members, and peers often instigate the verbal and physical attacks. Significant numbers of LGBTQ students reported harassment and feeling unsafe at school (Kosciw, Greytak, Diaz, & Bartkiewicz, 2010). Although LGBTQ youth may lack parental and peer support, schools and school counselors specifically are in ideal positions to educate and support youth on affectional/sexual orientation and gender-related issues.

School counselors have an ethical obligation to work with and support all students regardless of affectional/sexual orientation (Satcher & Leggett, 2007). Therefore, one role of the professional school counselor is to provide support to LGBTQ students by fostering academic success and well-being (American School Counselor Association, 2007). School counselors who collaborate with and engage the LGBTQ community have a better understanding of their own biases and promote effective ways to address student needs (Goodrich & Luke, 2010; Satcher & Leggett, 2007). For example, school counselors can organize student-led clubs such as Gay–Straight Alliances (GSA) in efforts to improve school climate, educate students, and support LGBTQ youth (Gay, Lesbian, and Straight Education Network [GLSEN], 2007). Resources including *ThinkB4You-Speak: Educator's Guide* (Gay, Lesbian, and Straight Education Network [GLSEN], 2008) can also serve as invaluable tools for school counselors in creating safe spaces for LGBTQ students. Understanding a "coming out" model will better equip school counselors as well when they are working with LGBTQ youth (see Cass, 1979). Additionally, Goodrich and Luke (2009) suggested school counselors can implement LGBTQ responsive services to support students. This model of school counseling is designed to engage and support the LGBTQ student population individually and systemically. School counselors responsive to LGBTQ students ensure programming is inclusive, attempt to educate the larger school community on LGBTQ issues, and encourage inclusivity of the LGBTQ community in documents, language, and the overall climate of school. When necessary, school counselors should also secure appropriate referral sources for LGBTQ students.

In this case scenario, I provided LGBTQ responsive individual counseling to Tanya while integrating several theoretical approaches. During the counseling relationship, I found Tanya responded well to strategies rooted in humanistic/existential, behavioral/CBT, and emergent paradigms. Using a trans-theoretical approach allowed me to be sensitive to Tanya's situation and provide her with the support to which she was entitled. During this particular session and on many occasions, I used strategies congruent with rational emotive behavior therapy (REBT) and the person-centered approach.

From an REBT perspective, I incorporated several strategies and techniques during this session including unconditional acceptance, modeling, Socratic dialog, and homework negotiation. Through these strategies I assisted Tanya in developing both practical and elegant solutions to her dilemma. I demonstrated unconditional acceptance of Tanya throughout our relationship, which served to model how she could view herself, others, and life. The basis for unconditional acceptance aligns with unconditional positive regard, a concept of the person-centered approach (Ellis, 2005, 2007). I accepted Tanya regardless of this situation, past struggles, ethnicity, or affectional/sexual orientation. I also showed Tanya that I genuinely cared for her and empathized with her situation. By integrating these person-centered conditions and REBT, as suggested by Ellis (2007), my office became a safe, nonjudgmental space for discussing sensitive issues. Tanya knew that this session, just as previous ones had been, would be driven by her perspectives, experiences, values, and goals.

I thought it was important for Tanya and me to explore a practical solution to her dilemma. For this reason, I modeled how to logically and rationally work through an adverse situation. Modeling thinking and behaving is effective in helping clients develop healthy, functional thoughts and behaviors (Ellis & MacLaren, 2005). Modeling healthy communication and how to effectively problem solve provided Tanya with an avenue for moving forward in this and future scenarios. Tanya and I discussed possible reasons why her girlfriend, Mariah, might be upset with her. We also explored Tanya's thoughts that prevented her from speaking with Mariah on the phone.

Ellis (2005) suggested that an elegant solution involves a cognitive shift toward rationality. Socratic dialog was used to achieve an elegant solution to Tanya's dilemma. Socratic dialog, also referred to as Socratic questioning, is often used to direct clients toward discovering thoughts that impede goal attainment (Dryden, 2009a). I engaged Tanya in a Socratic dialog to help her process the situation, become aware of unhealthy thoughts, and develop alternative rational thoughts specific to the dilemma. The Socratic dialog served to place Tanya in an expert role concerning her life and empowered her to address her relationship with Mariah (Dryden, 2009b).

In many cases, students become involved in situations (i.e., arguments, fights) that occur outside of school. These situations can be brought to school where they impede students' academic performance. From working with Tanya in the past, I knew that it is often difficult for her to focus on schoolwork when she was involved in disagreements or arguments. Therefore, I thought it may be helpful if Tanya and Mariah work through the situation as soon as possible. Although Tanya declined, I offered a space for her and Mariah to meet to discuss their relationship. Tanya indicated that she would call Mariah after school. I then returned to what her thoughts would be during the planned phone call. Homework was negotiated so that Tanya could practice a rational thought specific to resolving the situation. Dryden and Neenan (2006) suggested negotiating homework instead of simply assigning it. Homework negotiation can be a powerful way for students to take ownership in achieving their goals.

During this case scenario, I largely implemented strategies from REBT and conditions from the person-centered approach. However, various approaches and paradigms may be effective when working with LGBTQ youth (see Table 10-1). Although use of an integrative approach is often most effective, school counselors should not overlook the importance of building healthy relationships.

## IN SESSION

| | |
|---|---|
| COUNSELOR (C): | Hi, Tanya. How are you today? |
| TANYA (T): | Hey, Ms. Warren. Pretty good. . . |
| C: | So what's going on today? |
| T: | Well, as you could probably guess, I'm still having relationship issues with Mariah. |

[Note: I used open-ended questions and Socratic dialog throughout the session to assist the client in developing practical and elegant solutions to her problem.]

| | |
|---|---|
| C: | Would you like to share what happened? |
| T: | So, I thought everything was good between us, but then after this weekend, it all broke out again. |
| C: | So what broke out? |
| T: | Well, we were at this party down the street and I was supposed to meet Mariah there. My friend, Stacy—well, you know Stacy—hangs with us and she wanted to go too. So she met me at my house and we showed up at the party together. Mariah came about 10 minutes later and people were telling Mariah that Stacy and I came together and that's where everything started. Mariah was so mad. |
| C: | OK, so the last time we talked you told me that you and Mariah were dating, right? |
| T: | Yeah. |

**TABLE 10-1    Additional Recommended Strategies for Addressing LBGTQ Issues**

| Paradigm | Elementary School | Middle School | High School |
|---|---|---|---|
| Psychodynamic | Determining how past experiences and relationships may affect current thoughts and behavior | Identifying themes related to past situations and relationships with others; exploring how these themes may be present in current relationship difficulties; exploring transference | Identifying themes related to past situations and relationships with others; exploring how these themes may be present in current relationship difficulties; exploring transference |
| Humanistic/ Existential | Demonstrating empathy, unconditional positive regard, and genuine interest in student's well-being; role play of social scenarios and encounters with peers and others | Demonstrating empathy, unconditional positive regard, and genuine interest in student's well-being; role play and reverse role play of social concerns and/or dilemmas; facilitating processing of experiences | Demonstrating empathy, unconditional positive regard, and genuine interest in student's well-being; role play and reverse role play of social concerns and/or dilemmas; empty chair technique; facilitating processing of experiences |
| Behavioral/CBT | Exploring thoughts and feelings related to the area of concern; encouraging unconditional self-acceptance; fostering self-worth; supporting parents in modeling healthy thoughts and feelings | Exploring thoughts and feelings related to the area of concern; challenging irrational beliefs; teaching positive self-talk strategies; encouraging unconditional self-acceptance; fostering self-worth | Exploring thoughts and feelings related to the area of concern; teaching the ABCDE model; encouraging unconditional self-acceptance; fostering self-worth |
| Family Systems | Providing parents with strategies for supporting their child's growth and development; normalizing and reframing child's development; determining whether family dynamics are impacting the situation | Determining whether family dynamics play a role in the situation; seeking parental involvement; providing the family with strategies for supporting their child's growth and development; normalizing and reframing child's development | Fostering familial growth; educating parents on ways they can support their child; normalizing and reframing child's development; providing encouragement to family and child |
| Emergent | Connecting student to the appropriate support network; helping student develop narratives of possible outcomes and process each | Connecting student to the appropriate support network; helping student develop narratives of possible outcomes and process each; organizing beliefs about self with a card sort | Connecting student to the appropriate support network; helping student develop narratives of possible outcomes and process each; organizing beliefs about self with a card sort |

C:        Were you still together this weekend at the party?

T:        Yeah, but I talked to Mariah on the phone earlier and I told her that Stacy wanted to go and she was cool with that, so I don't get it.

C:        So, you and Mariah were still dating this past weekend and you're not sure why Mariah is mad.

T:        Well, I know she was mad because she told me and then wouldn't talk to me for the rest of the night, so I just hung out with Stacy. But I don't get it because I told her that Stacy wanted to come earlier. Now, I could see why she'd be mad if I just showed up with Stacy and didn't tell her about it, but I did. The three of us hang out all the time, so it doesn't make sense.

C:        You know Mariah is mad because you went to the party with Stacy, but you don't understand why she's mad because you feel like you told her about it earlier and she seemed OK with it.

T:        Yeah, exactly.

C:        Let me make sure I'm clear. I've heard you talk about Stacy before now. Tell me about your relationship with her, now and in the past.

T:        We're just friends now, and we chill all the time, but we did date a while back.

C:        I'm wondering . . . (Interrupted by the client)

T:        I think Mariah is mad because I dated Stacy a while ago and then went to the party with her.

C:        That sounds like a possibility. It would probably be important to ask Mariah yourself though. Have you talked since the party?

T:        No, not really. I called her but hung up the phone when she answered.

[In the next few exchanges, I explored and challenged the thoughts that prevented Tanya from speaking to Mariah on the phone.]

C:        What were you thinking to yourself as you hung up the phone?

T:        I was thinking about Mariah breaking up with me . . . it would be terrible! I was too nervous to talk.

C:        Well, what do you expect will happen if you continue to avoid her at this point?

T:        She'll probably think that I don't care about her and I want to be with Stacy again. She will break up with me!

C:        Is thinking that it would be terrible if you two broke up and avoiding Mariah really helping you work things out with her?

T:   Good point. It's actually making things worse.

C:   What would be a more rational thought to have about this situation?

T:   Like we've talked about before . . . you know . . . I'd like for things to turn out the way I want, but I can handle it if it doesn't . . . something like that, right?

C:   Sounds like a great thought, one that can really help you move forward.

T:   They've worked in the past. . . . I hope it works this time too!

[During the next several exchanges I attempted to help Tanya develop a plan for moving forward. Per Tanya's request, the plan became homework.]

C:   What do you think would be best for you and Mariah at this point?

T:   I think I should try talking to Mariah and ask her if that is why she is mad.

C:   Do you really think this could be part of the reason why she's mad?

T:   Now that we've talked about it, yeah, probably . . .

C:   Sounds like it would be a good place to start your conversation then. If you don't talk to her and ask, you won't know. Now, there is a possibility that she may say something completely different is bothering her.

T:   Yeah, but this is probably a big part of it because we've talked about my relationship with Stacy before.

C:   Will you have the opportunity to talk to Mariah today or would you like to talk to her now in my office?

T:   I think I'll call her tonight. I really just wanted to talk to you about it and then . . . I can talk to her about it tonight.

C:   So what will you think when you hear the phone ringing?

T:   Oh, you know . . . I can handle it, even if it doesn't work out my way.

C:   Nice.

T:   Bet you'd like for me to practice that one the rest of the day, like the other time.

C:   Are you OK with that?

T:   Yeah.

C:   OK . . . you know where I am if you'd like to talk again.

T:   Sounds good. Thanks, Ms. Warren! I appreciate it.

C:   No problem. Keep me posted.

| T: | All right. |
|----|-----------|
| C: | See you later, Tanya. Have a good day. |
| T: | Thanks; you too. |

## Outcome

School counselors are charged with meeting the developmental and social-emotional needs of all students. Students, especially those in middle school and high school, typically grapple with issues related to dating, sexuality, and gender. Many developmentally appropriate outcomes emerge during this period of growth. As a result, students often require various levels of support.

Individual counseling appeared to be an effective way of providing Tanya with developmental and social-emotional support. Tanya typically responded favorably to our sessions and would leave eager to implement the plans discussed. This session was no exception. In a follow-up visit, Tanya reported rehearsing the rational thoughts and calling Mariah on the phone to discuss the situation as planned. Tanya indicated the rational thoughts seemed to help her stay focused during the conversation. Tanya did find out that Mariah was upset because of Tanya's past relationship with Stacy. During the phone conversation, Tanya used the problem-solving and communication strategies she and I had explored. As a result, Mariah and Tanya were able to work through this situation and remain together.

Throughout my work with Tanya, she appeared to remain comfortable with herself and her affectional/sexual orientation. She was often confident in interactions with others and did not allow peers to influence her decisions. She continued, however, to struggle with the relationships she had with her dating partners, both males and females. Tanya and I met regularly to discuss her struggles. I continued to demonstrate unconditional acceptance and support for Tanya. We explored both practical and elegant solutions to her dilemmas. As she exited the eighth grade, her relationships with her partners appeared to improve, as did her academic performance.

## Final Process Questions

- In what way(s), other than individual counseling, could I have supported Tanya?
- What theoretical approaches would you have used in working with Tanya?
- Did I respond appropriately to Tanya's needs?
- How can school counselors advocate for LGBTQ youth?

## Resources

Frank, D. A., II, & Cannon, E. P. (2009). Creative approaches to serving LGBTQ youth in schools. *Journal of School Counseling, 7*(35), 1–25.

Gay, Lesbian, and Straight Education Network (GLSEN). (2007). *Gay–straight alliances: Creating safer schools for LGBT students and their allies.* (GLSEN Research Brief). New York, NY: Author.

Goodrich, K. M., & Luke, M. (2009). LGBTQ responsive school counseling. *Journal of LGBT Issues in Counseling, 3*(2), 113–127. doi: 10.1080/15538600903005284

Lemoire, S. J., & Chen, C. P. (2005). Applying person-centered counseling to sexual minority adolescents. *Journal of Counseling & Development, 83*, 146–154.

## Chapter 11

# Motivating the Unmotivated Student

TRACY MACDONALD

## CASE BACKGROUND

Danita, a 12-year-old African American female, was referred by her teachers because she is in danger of failing the seventh grade. In counseling, Danita has a pleasant disposition as she always takes the time to ask how the counselor's day is going at the beginning of each session and is very open to discussing her home life. However, Danita presents as unmotivated and uninterested in improving her grades as evidenced by her failure to turn in any of her homework assignments, dismissal of the value in studying for tests, and refusal to accept extra help offered by her teachers. As far as her home situation, Danita lives in a low-income townhouse with her aunt, two older brothers, and one older sister. Danita's aunt is the matriarch of the family and the only employed adult in the household. Her aunt also is the only adult listed on her home contact information in the school record. Danita's mother has struggled with substance abuse issues for the past 10 years. Danita has had no relationship with her father and has not seen him since she was 3 years old.

In terms of behavior, Danita has never been referred to the office for breaking school rules. Although Danita surrounds herself with students who have a tendency to make poor decisions, she has never followed their lead and has remained respectful toward all school staff. Her teachers describe her as friendly and polite but unwilling to follow through with homework, school projects, and test preparation. During class, Danita will attempt class work assignments but does not seem too concerned if she hands them in incomplete. If she does not understand something, she will not advocate for herself and raise her hand to ask the teachers. Danita does not use her planner to write down homework assignments or make notes.

## INITIAL PROCESS QUESTIONS

- Who has legal custody of Danita?
- Who has the authority to grant permission to continue to see Danita in a counseling setting?
- What medical or psychiatric diagnoses, if any, are indicated in Danita's school record that may affect her ability to learn?
- What has been the pattern of Danita's grades over the last 3 years?

- What cultural factors will influence the counseling relationship (e.g., gender, race, economic class)?
- What motivates Danita in other areas of her life? What activities does she enjoy?

## ADDRESSING THE ISSUES

After completing an initial intake with Danita and taking the time to get to know her through informal interviewing, I determined there were four underlying issues contributing to her lack of academic motivation. First, Danita did not feel as though she had academic potential. For example, Danita did not believe that she was intelligent because she usually received Cs on her report cards. Second, Danita had low self-efficacy. She lacked the ability to independently complete her homework, and no one was at home in the evenings to assist her with her assignments. Danita reported, "When I get home from school, I go hang with my friends. I come home when I want to. No one really cares when I come home because no one is there most of the time at night until late." After speaking with Danita, I understood that her family members had other priorities that took attention away from her. Money seemed to be the main stressor. Her family members were either working late or out for the evening. It seemed as though Danita was not viewed as a child who needed parenting but rather as another adult. Danita reported that no one ever asked her about her school day. I wondered whether good grades were celebrated in her home.

Third, Danita did not feel that any adults really cared about her. During the first meeting, Danita mentioned that her birthday had passed and she did not receive any birthday gifts or cards. She explained that her family had told her that because her birthday was so close to Christmas, they would celebrate it later and combine her birthday and Christmas gifts. However, it really hurt Danita's feelings that no one made her a birthday cake or sang "Happy Birthday" to her on her actual birthday. Fourth, Danita was not able to envision her future—or at least not what she would call a "successful" future. Danita did discuss that she wanted to be able to pay her bills and have money but did not view graduating high school or going to college as a needed step to do so. According to Danita, no one from her family had graduated from high school.

I chose an integrated approach with Danita by combining reality therapy and family systems therapy. Danita's academic situation called for an intervention that would deal with the present as well as involve her family. The goal was to use this combination of therapies to address Danita's four underlying issues to help her become motivated and want to pass the seventh grade.

As mentioned, Danita reported that she did not feel there were many adults who cared about her at home and that no one there was making her accountable for her schoolwork. It was important to invite Danita's aunt into a counseling session with Danita to see how Danita interacted with her aunt and to learn more about what kinds of values were important within this family. A deeper understanding of how Danita's family functioned would offer some insight into Danita's emotional state. Further, this allowed an opportunity to bring Danita's family up to speed on her academic status. I also wanted to ask Danita's aunt for help at home so that things at school might improve for Danita.

One of the goals of family systems therapy is to work with the family as a team to help them address the presenting problems. This is especially important when working with school-aged children. Teachers and school counselors can help the student during the school day, but it is vital that the family support the student at home. Therefore, my goal was to develop an intervention plan with Danita's aunt, Danita, and me in which everyone had a role so that Danita would feel supported at home and school. Developing an academic intervention plan would help Danita become more accountable if it included me at school checking to see that her homework was written down correctly followed by her aunt's supervising her at home while she did her homework. An important aspect of this strategy was for Danita to see her aunt sitting in a school conference on her behalf and making a plan with the school to help her.

Reality therapy was used to address Danita's feelings of academic inadequacy, her inability to make plans for the future, and her lack of academic motivation. Reality therapy emphasizes the concept of having choices in life and developing a "picture in my mind" of the goal to be achieved. This picture then leads to the creation of a road map for success. Danita did not realize that her choices, not her inability to be successful in school, were the cause of her failing grades. Early adolescence is a time when individuals are just becoming aware that personal choices determine their status. Teaching Danita about choice theory was important to show her that she could choose to either pass or fail the seventh grade. Specifically, Danita needed to grasp that by choosing to do her homework and study for tests, she could raise her grades to a passing level. Once Danita's grades started to improve, she would believe she had academic potential and hopefully become more motivated to make plans for the future. This is a key aspect of improving anyone's self-efficacy: successful performance attainments. When students succeed at a task, they build confidence that they can achieve a future task. Table 11-1 presents additional strategies and techniques helpful in motivating the unmotivated student.

## IN SESSION

COUNSELOR (C): [January 3] Danita, in our last session, we identified some choices that you made that resulted in your receiving failing grades for this marking period. For example, you mentioned that you chose not to accept the extra help Mr. Dunn offered to you when you were struggling on your science project. You also mentioned that you failed your math benchmark because you did not take time to review the study guide. What are some choices you can make right now to help you bring your grades back up?

DANITA (D): I could ask Mr. Dunn if I could still hand in my science project late and then work on my project this week with my aunt. I could go to after-school tutoring on Wednesday to help me with my math test on Friday.

C: [January 5] Danita, you mentioned that you felt that you did not have any academic potential. I can help you show yourself that you do if you are willing to make some choices and some changes to your evening routine. Some of these choices include writing down your homework each night in your planner and committing to studying for 1 hour the night before each test.

**TABLE 11-1    Additional Approaches for Motivating the Unmotivated Student**

| Paradigm | Elementary School | Middle School | High School |
|---|---|---|---|
| Psychodynamic | Student draws a tree and makes a branch for each person in her life she feels she can trust | Listing some positive things about self to draw on strengths, encourage, and build self-esteem; student draws a tree and makes a branch for each person in her life she feels she can trust | Exploring the effects on student of mother's drug abuse |
| Humanistic/ Existential | Establishing therapeutic conditions; student shares what the past 2 years have been like for her | Establishing therapeutic conditions; exploring significant changes in her life, both good and bad | Establishing therapeutic conditions; exploring with student her elementary, middle, and high school experiences |
| Behavioral/CBT | Examining recent situation in which student may have made a bad choice, and asking what a better choice may have been; student completes a learning behaviors chart each day; setting up rewards system for completed class work and homework | Teaching student about choice theory and helping her list some of her good and poor choices that have contributed to her current academic situation; student checks in and out with counselor each day to determine whether she is writing down her homework and coming to school prepared | Teaching student about choice theory; collaborating with student to set up clear and tangible academic goals; student lists some possible choices she can apply to her future (e.g., college, community college, military) |
| Family Systems | Inviting aunt in to talk about student's current academic status; asking her to participate in developing an academic intervention plan | Inviting aunt in to talk about student's emotional and academic status; trying to learn what values are important to the family | Inviting aunt and mother in to talk about student's future plans beyond high school |
| Emergent | Student writes a short story about how she raised all of her grades by the end of the school year | What actions would student commit herself to if she woke up the next morning and decided she wanted to get all Bs on her next report card? | Asking student to identify someone in her life who would be the least surprised to see her planning for her future |

C:  [January 15] Thank you so much for coming, Ms. Fields. I wanted to invite you in to talk about Danita's current academic status and share with you some concerns we have about Danita as well as find out what your hopes are for Danita. Danita's teachers and I are concerned about Danita because she is currently failing the seventh grade. However, it is only the middle of the school year. I think if we all work together as a team we can help get her back on track. One of the suggestions I have is establishing a set time each evening that Danita does her homework. I can monitor her at school with a check-in and checkout system and make sure that she has correctly written her homework down in her planner. Could you commit half an hour each night to sit with her and supervise her to ensure that she gets her homework done correctly?

## Outcome

It was helpful to invite Danita's aunt, Ms. Fields, into one of the counseling sessions. Ms. Fields expressed that she did value education and had attended community college and received an associate's degree. This was the first time Danita had heard of her aunt's accomplishment. Ms. Fields explained to Danita that her degree was framed and hanging over the fireplace. It made an impact on Danita that her aunt had graduated from high school and gone on to postsecondary school. Ms. Fields was already feeling bad that she had not been supporting Danita at home with her schoolwork. She knew that Danita was not being successful in school but had been at a loss for how to help. Ms. Fields was grateful to be a part of the academic intervention plan.

One of the advantages of being a school counselor is the opportunity to be a part of the student's school day, if necessary. This is especially helpful when using reality therapy as an intervention technique because the counselor can be there for the "teachable moments" after a poor choice has been made. I was able to point out the incongruence in what Danita said she wanted and what she actually did. After Danita decided she did want to pass the seventh grade and was willing to follow through with the check-in/checkout plan, I was able to assist her on a daily basis. Through this process, I feel that Danita learned to be accountable at home and at school. At the end of each day I gave her a lot of praise (throwing in some candy as a reward also helped). A real moment of accomplishment occurred when Danita received a B on a math quiz, as it seemed to become a turning point in her self-efficacy development. Danita learned that her choices to study for tests really had paid off and that she did have academic potential. Danita began to do better in school and became more motivated to pass the seventh grade. Danita went from failing grades to passing grades in four of her six classes. She also joined one of the weekly academic success groups and has become a very important member of it. The other students in the academic success group really liked Danita, and she was delighted to point out when any other group member made a poor choice! Danita made substantial improvements in her self-perception that she could be a successful student, her academic self-efficacy development, her relationship with her aunt, and a creation of a vision of success for her future.

## Final Process Questions

- Did the integrated approach produce the desired results?
- What other approaches could have been used to help motivate Danita?
- How can the school counselor continue to support Danita's aunt so she is able to follow through with the strategies discussed?

- What are some other suggestions that can be made to Danita's aunt so Danita feels cared about at home?
- What are some suggestions that can be provided to Danita's teachers?

- How might the school climate be a barrier for diverse students?

## Resources

Corey, G. (2005). *Theory and practice of counseling and psychotherapy* (5th ed.). Belmont, CA: Brooks/Cole.

Glasser, W. (1998). *Choice theory: A new psychology of personal freedom*. New York, NY: HarperCollins.

Walter, S. M., Lambie, G. W., & Ngazimbi, E. E. (2008). A choice theory counseling group succeeds with middle school students who displayed disciplinary problems. *Middle School Journal, 40*, 4–12.

## Chapter 12

# Working With Gifted Children

Elisabeth Bennett and Mary Brown

## CASE BACKGROUND

Marin, a 15-year-old student in 11th grade attends our high school for two classes each day while also attending the local community college for three college courses each quarter. When Marin was 5 years old and ready to start kindergarten, she was assessed by the school psychologist. It was discovered that Marin was functioning at a much higher level than her 5-year-old peers. In addition to having mastered the normal entry tasks for kindergarten, Marin was reading at a fifth-grade level; could perform basic addition, subtraction, and multiplication; had an understanding of the scientific method; and was able to perform the daily functions of a 12-year-old. An assessment of her intelligence indicated performance in the very superior range. She appeared to be well adjusted and eager to attend school, and it was recommended that she begin school in at least the first grade. In consultation with her parents, the principal, her preschool teacher, the school counselor, and the kindergarten and first-grade teachers—and following the school district's promotion policy—it was determined that she would, indeed, begin her public education at the first-grade level. Her first-grade teacher reported at midyear that she believed Marin was struggling to find a position in the class and that she was under-stimulated academically.

By second grade it was evident not only that Marin had established herself as a "smart" kid but also that she was struggling to make and keep friends. Her teacher noted that Marin regularly corrected other students (and at times the teacher), which tended to put others off. Her classmates called her a show-off on more than one occasion. By third grade she had gravitated toward two other children who seemed to also struggle socially. These friendships appeared to come and go, although Marin's academic performance continued to be strong. In the fourth grade Marin had several visits with the school counselor. Once the teacher confronted Marin about not showing her work when completing math problems and sent her to the school counselor for being argumentative. Marin reported emphatically to the counselor that it made no sense to her to have to work through math problems step by step when she was able to complete them in her head. During a number of visits with the school counselor, Marin talked about what she deemed her "fate of the smart kid" and described herself as "weird" and "different" from her peers. At this time, Marin also began to participate in an after-school math program through which she seemed to experience a sense of accomplishment and belonging as the "math genius" of her group.

By all standards, Marin was successful in her core academics and the after-school math program, but junior high held the requirement of an art class that provided Marin with her first grade of less than a solid A. The art teacher reserved A grades for those students whose projects were truly outstanding, and although above average, Marin had underdeveloped technique and produced average products. The art projects required skills that did not come easily to Marin. Instead of focusing on the task at hand and learning the new skills, Marin was overcome by a sense of defeat. The resulting B grade was devastating to her, and she responded to the perceived failure with passive-aggressive disrespect for her teacher. She stopped doing her assigned tasks, sat in the back of the art room, and made belittling comments about the lack of value in an art class. The art teacher sent Marin to the office; there she was then seen by the school counselor to whom she confessed tearfully her perspective of herself as unable to do all things related to art, athletics, and friendships.

Marin's first year of high school was relatively quiet. She excelled in her courses, including her gym class in which she discovered a capacity to calculate and chart her diet and exercise, and experienced a sense of empowerment at her self-charted fitness. She also developed a set of Internet friends, other adolescents she met in chat rooms related to teen nutrition and weight loss. This virtual friendship group became very important to her as the first group of friends with whom she felt a connection and acceptance. Marin's sophomore year was not as pleasant. She began with a repeat of her junior high art experience because art was the only available elective given the remainder of her academic schedule. Her teacher struggled with Marin's attitude of defeat and attempted to motivate her with threats of poor grades and comparisons to Marin's older sister, who had excelled artistically the prior year. This began a downward spiral that resulted in depression and suicidal ideation by January of her sophomore year. February began with Marin making suicidal threats to one of her virtual friends, who alerted school officials. The vice principal and school counselor intervened immediately and partnered with a community mental health professional, who determined Marin to be severely depressed but not an imminent danger to herself. Marin completed her sophomore year without further incidence and with reported enthusiasm about spending her junior year of high school at the local community college.

## INITIAL PROCESS QUESTIONS

- How might the school counselor build a relationship with a gifted or talented student before any issues arise? What core conditions are critical to building that relationship?
- What challenges might the counselor have to face in providing the core conditions and building an effective counseling relationship with a gifted student?
- How might the school counselor assist teachers and the student in maximizing the gifted student's potential?
- How might the school counselor assist gifted or talented students in maximizing their potential?
- What is the school district's policy on promotion and retention? What are the pros and cons of promoting a gifted student? What factors might a school counselor consider when weighing in with a collaborative team about the promotion of a gifted student?

- What conditions in a school setting might contribute to a gifted student's sense of belonging and self-concept as an important part of the school community?
- What developmental issues might contribute to the gifted student's experiencing low self-esteem or negative self-concept?
- What resources are available for assisting the gifted student in achieving success academically, socially, personally, and in relation to career development?
- Who are the critical people with whom the school counselor should collaborate when planning for services and resources to be provided for the gifted student?
- What ethical concerns must be considered in relation to Marin's situation?

## ADDRESSING THE ISSUES

Although many gifted children navigate through elementary, middle, and high school without major problems, the issues that Marin experienced are not uncommon. Marin's struggles are addressed well by the *ASCA National Model*'s (American School Counselor Association, 2012) three domains defining the delivery of an effective school counseling program: academic, career and life planning, and personal/social. The following discussion depicts the interventions the school counselors facilitated to assist this gifted student through each of the three areas as she progressed through her school years.

### Academic

Marin's academic abilities stretched across several areas including math, each of the sciences, English language and composition, and foreign language. It seems a common myth of the gifted that their intellectual abilities make all academic areas easy. Marin's case demonstrates several of the academic challenges typical of the gifted. A short list of these includes frustrations with the pace and requirements of general education that can promote underachievement, lack of persistence with subjects or skills that require effort to accomplish, and a strong drive for perfectionism in areas the student deems important.

Each of these challenges produced situations that were met via a team approach including the school counselor, parents, teachers, a private practitioner, and Marin herself. During her elementary years Marin's parents provided supplementary study at home; learning opportunities in the community and online were employed; and the counselor and teachers worked together to assist in making Marin's learning environment and requirements fit her special needs and not be just additional busy work. For example, Marin spent a portion of each school day in a pullout advanced reading group where she and several other students of varying grade levels would read and discuss books that provided more of an intellectual challenge. Marin also left the regular classroom twice a week for an advanced math class taught by a retired high school math teacher.

By junior high school, Marin was experiencing some of the normal angst of young adolescence. Individual sessions with her school counselor focused primarily on the development of her self-concept as a student with great, moderate, and lesser strengths, all of which would require some attention and effort from Marin to make the most of her learning experience. The expectation that Marin would need to expend effort to excel was difficult for her. Her mind-set was that everything should come easily. If it did not, she did not see herself doing it at all.

Marin was encouraged to participate in extracurricular experiences, and the after-school math program provided an outstanding experience for her to develop a sense of belonging and an opportunity to work as a team player. Because math was a known strength, it was a great base for working on areas that came less easily for Marin. She was able to complete some of her high school math requirements in junior high through a program that transported junior high school students to the high school. Marin participated in a talent search through which she was honored for her strong PSAT scores and invited to take summer college courses during her high school years.

A private mental health practitioner was a great collaborator with the school's team and Marin's family, and assisted Marin in dealing with her struggles in her art courses and the self-doubt and depression that ensued. Other programs that helped to provide an academic base included the honors and advanced placement courses. Additionally, the school counselor was able to facilitate Marin's entrance into either a dual enrollment program (students enroll in select high school courses that can also count for college credit) or a program that allowed students to start taking courses at the community college at the beginning of their junior year. Marin was delighted to have the opportunity to earn an associate's degree while completing high school, and to be able to create a friendship base with other students from her own and other high schools by being in this program.

## Career and Life Planning

Difficulties for Marin related to her career development and life planning centered mainly on two issues. The first issue was that the school district's career and life planning programs did not have built-in contingencies for Marin, who had already developed and maintained a clear agenda for her career goals. Almost every assessment and planning requirement in the district career development program was redirected to align with Marin's goals. She was able to be very proactive in positioning herself for competitive college admission as well as activities and experiences that would contribute to her résumé for entry into her field of study. The second issue was addressing Marin's difficulties in developing a full and positive sense of self in addition to her academic gifts. Individual sessions with the school counselor involved career and personality assessments as well as techniques centered on self-awareness, increased perception of self as competent even when not perfect, and self-soothing techniques designed to assist in emotional regulation. Marin also participated in shadowing experiences with two medical doctors during school breaks that allowed exploration of her desired profession and conversation about its work activities and potential lifestyle. Each of these factors contributed to Marin's capacity to define her career path in relationship to her strengths and lifestyle, as well as fulfill requirements along that road in a competent and satisfying manner.

## Personal/Social

Marin's perfectionism, identity as a "brainiac" at the expense of other relational qualities, and difficulties handling frustrations adequately often left her isolated. Although she desired friendships all along, it was difficult for Marin to let her guard down long enough to develop the kinds of relationships with her peers that would be conducive to friendship. Elementary interventions included classroom guidance lessons on friendship building and maintenance, group counseling centered on the development of behaviors conducive to friendships, individual sessions that supported the building of more friendly behaviors and the self-confidence needed to practice them, and focus on a broadened identity of self as much more than a brainiac. Junior high school interventions involved ongoing supportive sessions, a focus on self-concept and self-efficacy development, and collaborative work with Marin's teachers and parents to develop a course of study most conducive to effective learning. Perhaps the best intervention for promoting social success and a sense of accomplishment and belonging was the promotion of Marin's involvement with the after-school math program. High school and the accompanying developmental tasks of adolescents merged to produce issues of depression for Marin that were assessed by the school counselor as severe enough to require the assistance of a counselor in the community. This mental health counselor worked collaboratively with the school counselor and other school personnel along with Marin and her family. The counseling appeared to be effective in reducing Marin's depressive symptoms and very helpful in building her sense of self as capable even when she found she was not exceptionally capable at the task at hand. Table 12-1 presents additional strategies and techniques for working with the intellectually gifted.

**TABLE 12-1   Strategies and Interventions for Helping Gifted Students**

| Paradigm | Elementary School | Middle School | High School |
|---|---|---|---|
| Psychodynamic | Analysis of ego development and immature defense mechanisms (acting out, projection, regression); assistance in psychosocial development (achieving initiative versus guilt and industry versus inferiority); free association | Analysis of ego and immature/neurotic defenses (projection, regression, acting out, splitting, devaluation); assistance in psychosocial development (industry versus inferiority and identity versus role confusion); analysis of transference via free association | Analysis of ego development and immature/neurotic defenses (projection, regression, acting out, splitting, devaluation, displacement, rationalization, intellectualization); assistance in psychosocial development (identity versus role confusion); processing transference issues |
| Humanistic/ Existential | Therapeutic conditions promoting the counseling relationship; role playing; emotions identification and appropriate expression; establishing a sense of self including a sense of belonging to classmates, classroom, school, and community; self-soothing/nurturing activities; mentoring relationships | Therapeutic conditions; role playing; active listening, reflection, and clarification; "I" statements; examination and expression of emotions and behavioral issues related to belonging, personal and global responsibility, and freedom; development of self-concept as a contributing community member; counseling relationship; mentoring relationships | Therapeutic conditions; role playing; active listening, reflection, and clarification; "I" statements; examination and expression of emotions and behavioral issues related to belonging, personal and global responsibility, and freedom as a contributing member of society; counseling relationship; mentoring relationships; developing accurate self-concept and self-worth |

| Paradigm | Elementary School | Middle School | High School |
|---|---|---|---|
| Behavioral/CBT | Learning rational coping thoughts; self-talk with positive affirmation; dismantling perfectionist thinking; modeling; role playing; miracle question; flagging the minefield; psycho-education groups regarding friendship building and emotional regulation; parent education regarding perfectionism, anxiety, low frustration tolerance, and emotional regulation | Examining thought patterns; disputing irrational beliefs; increasing self-talk with positive affirmations related to one's role in school and community; modeling; role playing; miracle question; bibliocounseling; psycho-education groups regarding friendship maintenance and emotional regulation | Examining thought patterns; disputing irrational beliefs; self-talk related to one's role as student, family, employee, and community member; modeling; role playing; miracle question; flagging the minefield; bibliocounseling; rational emotive imagery; assertiveness training; psycho-education regarding conflict resolution and emotional regulation |
| Family Systems | Coaching and collaborating with family in developing and maintaining boundaries, hierarchy, and reactions that support effective family structure and healthy emotional expression; looking for exceptions; miracle questions; educating parents, siblings, student regarding struggles and strengths of the gifted; building effective working models | Coaching and collaborating with family in developing and maintaining boundaries, hierarchy, and reactions that support effective family structure and healthy emotional expression; interrupting patterns, shifting positions, and looking for exceptions; miracle questions; educating parents and student regarding struggles and strengths of the gifted; challenging ineffective working models | Coaching and collaborating with family in developing and maintaining boundaries, hierarchy, and reactions that support effective family structure and healthy emotional expression, particularly for a family with a child preparing to leave home; looking for exceptions; miracle questions; challenging unhealthy working models while fortifying effective working models |
| Emergent | Sparkling moments; gender role analysis; therapeutic alliance; role playing; mentoring; identification and development of signature strengths | Sparkling moments; gender role analysis; therapeutic alliance; role playing; mentoring; identification and development of signature strengths | Deconstruct/externalize problems; sparkling moments; gender role analysis; therapeutic alliance; role playing; mentoring; support and development of signature strengths |

# IN SESSION

The following dialogue is from a typical session with Marin while assessing her current situation as a student in both high school courses and at the community college.

COUNSELOR (C): What I'm hoping we can accomplish today is to review your transcripts and be sure that you are on schedule to

|  |  |
|---|---|
|  | graduate with your class next year and that the direction you are taking is still in line with your goals. |
| MARIN (M): | Actually, I will have satisfied all requirements for high school and an AA degree by March. |
| C: | Wow, good for you. Walk me through your transcripts and your plans so I can see what you have put together and how you are going to accomplish that goal by March. |
| M: | Sure. I only have the equivalent to American Government and English 4 for here, both of which I will take in fall term at the college. I won't have classes here at all next year. The remainder of the credits I need for the AA will be finished in winter quarter. Here's my schedule and the plan. (*Shows completed worksheet*) |
| C: | That's got to feel good! Your planning and organization is impressive. How do you feel about all of this, Marin? |
| M: | Really good. I'm right on track. |
| C: | Indeed, those are the two courses you need for graduation. Now, what about advisory? |
| M: | I'm not going to be taking any classes here next year, so I won't be going to advisory. |
| C: | Probably you won't attend the advisory period. Still, you will need to complete the requirements of advisory including the senior project and the steps that lead up to the final presentation. |
| M: | That makes no sense. Why would I have to do that if I am not even going here for school? Besides, I know what I am going to do with my life. Advisory is for kids who have no clue. I haven't gotten anything out of it yet, and the whole senior year is about plotting after high school life. . . . It is a waste of time to research other careers when I know what I want to do already. |
| C: | Maybe we could look at the senior project as a stepping-stone to what you already know you want to do. Perhaps we could explore more about what you will need to do between now and medical school in order to move in that direction. |
| M: | Is there any way to just dismiss the requirement altogether? |
| C: | No, it's a requirement. I think we can work out something that is more helpful and maybe even fun for you to do so that your senior project really showcases what you have accomplished and the steps you are planning to take between here and your final goal. Are you still thinking of medicine? |
| M: | Yes. Medicine for sure, maybe surgery. |

C:   You know, I remember meeting with you your freshman year, and you told me the same thing then. Medicine it is?

M:   Yes. I took Anatomy and Physiology and Chem this year, and I am even more certain now.

C:   So, let's look toward the senior project as a way of discovering experiences that might be meaningful as you look toward medical school.

M:   You mean like getting certification as a nurse's assistant so I can do work in the field during college?

C:   Exactly! You could develop the steps you have taken and those yet to take for your senior project.

M:   Yes, I could do that. That would kill two birds with one stone because I need to check into that more thoroughly anyway.

C:   Any thoughts about where you will apply for college yet?

M:   I found an undergraduate program on the East Coast I like, but my parents won't let me go farther than one day's drive from here. It is ridiculous, but that's the way it is. So, I have six schools that will do.

C:   Could I be helpful to you in planning out what you need to do to make your applications?

M:   Thanks, but I think I have that covered. I would appreciate your completing the counselor parts of the applications. I'm doing both of the universal applications. I wish all six schools just used the common app.

C:   I would be happy to complete the counselor portion. Have you selected a teacher as a reference yet?

M:   Mrs. T. said she would complete one for me. She writes well and knows my strengths. I think it will go well.

C:   How about your SATs or ACTs?

M:   I already took them both. ACT is 35. SAT is 2380.

C:   Excellent. How does that feel to you to have done so well?

M:   My mother thinks I don't need to take them again. As usual, she thinks I stress out too much over my scores. I know what I missed on the SAT, so I am thinking about retaking it. Either way, I'm guessing I'll get into the schools where I am applying.

C:   Hey, I like that. You let your excellent scores be the excellent scores that they are!

M:   Yeah, don't go overboard with that. They are good.

C:   I'm just really tickled for you. Now, tell me how it's going at the college.

| | |
|---|---|
| M: | It's good. Actually, I really like it. There are a lot of people there who don't care about what they are doing, but there isn't any of the high school game-playing, either. I can't wait until next year when I don't have to come here at all. No offense intended. |
| C: | None taken. Tell me about the friends you are making. |
| M: | Made. I've made friends. One of the girls in my Chem class—we've studied together—is applying to four of the same schools as I am. If we both get into the same ones, we might room together freshman year. |
| C: | That sounds good. What do the two of you do besides Chem? |
| M: | I don't know. Oh, we went to a movie downtown to fill a requirement we both had. |
| C: | How was that? |
| M: | It was good. Fun. We ate before at a restaurant. That was really fun. No parents. She drives. |
| C: | You're smiling! |
| M: | Yes. I liked that. It was like we were already off to college. |

Typical of a gifted student, Marin is several steps ahead of her peers when it comes to academics and the planning of her path into her career. Still, she is right on track in experiencing the transition into independence.

## Outcome

Marin is currently finishing her junior year and reports that she is satisfied with her academics, her career plans, her friendships, and her potential for being a successful medical doctor. She has plotted out the remainder of both her high school and community college courses assuring graduation from each. She has explored her desired career path and is giving some attention to potential alternatives in the event she needs one (albeit reluctantly). Marin is discovering traits and talents aside from her academic prowess and has willingly begun music lessons to fulfill a required elective at the community college. She has made clear that she may well earn a B in this course, and she is equally clear that she is "good with that." Marin has entered a new social situation at the college that has provided more opportunity for connections with a variety of friends and has allowed her to more easily forge a new social identity, alleviating some of the pressures she has felt to identify herself primarily as a brainiac. Although she isn't delighted about the added requirements at the high school (such as advisory), she has found a way to make them meaningful for herself and still complete the required tasks. On the whole, Marin is a well-rounded and happy gifted student.

## Final Process Questions

- In addition to those used with Marin, what other services/opportunities might the school counselor employ at the elementary, middle, and high school levels to assist in providing the optimal learning environment for a gifted student?

- How does a school counselor recognize limits in his or her expertise or limits in this role that may necessitate a referral to another professional? What role might consultation play in the recognition of those limits? How might a school counselor assure an effective consultation resource for these discussions?
- What considerations would the school counselor make regarding exceptional students whose culture and/or ethnicity might be a factor in their academic achievement?
- What other types of giftedness exist, other than the academic giftedness of students such as Marin? How might these types of giftedness present different concerns? What special issues and appropriate interventions might best suit students with various types of giftedness?
- What kinds of collaborative efforts might the school counselor seek to assist in providing the best learning environment for gifted students such as Marin or students with other types of giftedness?

- How do the various developmental stages affect the needs and struggles of gifted students such as Marin?
- In addition to friendship, what other classroom guidance lesson topics might help all students work toward a peak learning environment in the academic, career and life planning, and personal/social domains?
- How might the existing required programs be adjusted to become a better fit for gifted students? How might the school counselor assist other school personnel in buying into the idea that gifted students may need creative accommodations made to requirements at all grade levels, and not simply added work?
- What are some ethical dilemmas likely to be presented by gifted students who have struggles similar to Marin's? What ethical guidelines and legal concerns might a school counselor want to keep at the forefront in assisting a gifted student such as Marin?

## Resources

Gifted Development Center, http://www.gifted-development.com

Johns Hopkins Center for Talented Youth, http://cty.jhu.edu/

Johns Hopkins magazine for kids: *Imagine*—big ideas for bright minds, http://cty.jhu.edu/imagine

Neag Center for Gifted Education and Talent Development, http://www.gifted.uconn.edu/

William & Mary School of Education Center for Gifted Education, http://education.wm.edu/centers/cfge/

# Chapter 13

# College Access

LINDSEY M. NICHOLS

## CASE BACKGROUND

Growing up in a rural, low-socioeconomic community, Samarium faced numerous barriers as she sat alongside her eighth-grade classmates with her high school schedule in hand. The oldest of four children, Samarium was entrusted with many parental responsibilities as her single mother, with only a high school education, worked two jobs trying to support the family. Samarium lived in an area historically divided by race issues. As a Black student attending a school of predominantly White students, Samarium was constantly trying to make sense of the various messages she received about her potential as a student while balancing attention issues in classes.

In my role as the school counselor, each spring semester I went into an eighth-grade elective class to assist students with planning their transition to high school after general information had been distributed to them in their homerooms. Samarium, like many others, was overwhelmed. But, she had been working hard in class, holding a 3.0 GPA, preparing for the demands of high school, and dreaming of college. Two minutes after starting to input her teacher-approved college-track schedule into the computer, which included plans for multiple advanced placement classes, her hand went up. As I approached her seat, she turned around, tears streaming down her face, "I can't do this. My family needs me. My mom says I am being selfish by putting time and money into school when I should get a job and help her. I've had to work so hard in middle school. I will never be smart enough for college anyway. I don't know why she signed this." My previous interactions with Samarium primarily focused on her attention and distractibility issues. I was surprised by the uncharacteristic self-doubt and anxiousness in her voice. With the hard copy of her schedule in her hand, I asked the homeroom teacher to keep an eye on the class as Samarium and I walked down the hall to my office.

## INITIAL PROCESSING QUESTIONS

- At this major transition point in the student's life, what other changes is the student experiencing that might be affecting future planning?
- What is the student's family situation and background, particularly surrounding education and career (e.g., job/military focused, negative educational experiences)?

- What are my personal biases toward traditional education, vocational, and military aspirations that might influence my interaction with students, families, and teachers?
- What cultural values and environmental influences might be affecting the student?
- What is my role and responsibility as the school counselor to help students explore colleges, application processes, and financing options?
- What are my ethical and legal obligations to involve the student's parent(s)/guardian(s) as we are developing a high school curriculum plan?

## ADDRESSING THE ISSUES

Preparation for college access, like a lot of topics centered on transition, is an important focus of school counselors' work with students. The transition from K through 12 education into postsecondary education needs to be attended to throughout the elementary, middle, and high school years (Hoyle & Kutka, 2008). Many factors specific to individual student needs at each level (e.g., developmental stage, cultural background, interests, aptitudes, accommodations based on IEP or 504 plan) should be considered when exploring college access and applying strategies guided by any of the five counseling paradigms (Niles & Harris-Bowlsbey, 2009).

For Samarium, her being overwhelmed that day was a result of the accumulation of many factors in her life, compounded by developing the first of many plans that will direct her educational and eventual career or work path. In Samarium's school district, students begin exploring careers in elementary school through career days, rigorous curriculum, and academic testing to help prepare them for college and as demanded by the *No Child Left Behind Act* of 2001 (NCLB, 2002). Many school counselors approach the topic of college access during high school through classroom guidance sessions, providing information to all students about the various academic, personal, financial, and social (e.g., volunteering, extracurricular activities) requirements of colleges. Small group experiences can also be important for students such as Samarium, who have special needs. Although they express a clear interest in going to college, they might not have the support at home due to a lack of experience in the family and could benefit from the support of other students experiencing similar problems by meeting in a smaller setting. Eighth-grade students in Samarium's school could also apply to a semester-long shadowing program or a one-time event organized by the school related to various career areas (e.g., medical professionals at local hospital). Students could identify their own opportunities or get assistance from the coordinating teacher at the school. The local Lions Clubs were active in collaborating with district schools to create shadowing and mentoring opportunities. Working with financial support from the Gates Foundation, the district also had an Early College High School where students could begin taking college-level courses in conjunction with completing their high school academic requirements.

For many families, especially those of lower income, college is not only an academic commitment but also a major financial investment that can be difficult to fathom and accomplish (Klungman & Butler, 2008; Wyner, Bridgeland, & Diiulio, 2007). As many school counselors have learned through their own college experiences, it can be challenging to manage both the initial and overall costs of college for tuition, room and board, books, and transportation. With the emergence of the Internet, students, parents/guardians, and school counselors have access to a great deal of information to help students navigate college access. Because sifting through the abundant information can be overwhelming, school counselors can help students process this information by using the different theoretical orientations.

At each level, school counselors can apply the various theoretical frameworks presented in this text to explore and address students' interests and concerns, as in Samarium's case, as they concentrate on college. As shown in Table 13-1, the paradigms can help guide school counselors toward specific approaches. Using a psychodynamic approach focuses school counselors on childhood experiences and/or uncovering unconscious messages potentially affecting students' current perspectives on college access. Using a systemic perspective allows school counselors to plan meetings with parents/guardians to gain insight into students' familial and cultural contexts that might have a student disrupting generational patterns by attending college. Although many strategies and techniques can be applied across paradigms, theoretical intention allows school counselors to develop goals and language to use within individual and group sessions.

After Samarium's reaction in the classroom, it was important for me to acknowledge my humanistic orientation and focus on Samarium's ability to understand herself and her current situation. Believing in the power of the counseling relationship, I also recognized that no one knows the intricacies of her situation better than she. My role was to help her navigate her present circumstances and the challenges of college and encourage her to discover the best path for her future.

**TABLE 13-1    Additional Strategies and Techniques to Address College Access**

| Paradigm | Elementary School | Middle School | High School |
|---|---|---|---|
| Psychodynamic | Identifying interests and behaviors and role in family and friendships using role play (e.g., use of puppets); exploration and interpretation of behaviors through drawings and play; parent consultation | Processing childhood interests and experiences; exploring how individual views family and self roles through art, short stories, and skits; free association to understand career and college interests; parent consultation | Processing childhood interests and experiences; exploring how individual views family and self roles in discussions and/or writing compared to desired future roles; free association to understand career and college interests; parent consultation |
| Humanistic/ Existential | Listening to and reflecting feelings; relationship building with play and art; providing support for interest exploration; role play of various occupations using puppets and other implements; genograms | Listening to and reflecting feelings; relationship building; providing support for interest exploration and how this relates to developing identity and educational needs; role play of various occupations focused on training/education needed; taking interest inventories; genograms | Listening to and reflecting feelings; relationship building; providing support for interest exploration and how this relates to current and future identity as well as educational needs; role play of various occupations; using Internet to explore colleges and take interest inventories; genograms |

| Paradigm | Elementary School | Middle School | High School |
|---|---|---|---|
| Behavioral/CBT | Understanding student thoughts/knowledge surrounding college; parent–teacher consultations; role playing; brainstorming career possibilities and relating to educational needs; identifying and practicing seven steps to decision making; miracle question; disputing irrational beliefs | Understanding student thoughts/knowledge surrounding college; parent–teacher consultations; role playing; brainstorming job possibilities and relating to educational needs; administering interest inventories; disputing irrational beliefs; classroom guidance focused on exploring colleges/financial aid; miracle question | Understanding student thoughts/knowledge surrounding college; parent–teacher consultations; role playing; brainstorming job possibilities and relating to educational needs; administering interest inventories; disputing irrational beliefs; behavioral rehearsal; presentations from college reps and assigning homework for students to explore colleges/financial aid; miracle question |
| Systems | Parent–teacher consultation; parent presentations on elementary support and involvement necessary for future success; community/family members' participation in career days; drawings/collages identifying future goals; teacher training on exposing all students to college | Parent–teacher consultation; education genograms; parent presentations on importance of requirements and involvement necessary for college admission and success; writing stories, making drawings/collages identifying future goals; community/family members' participation in career days; getting students involved in job shadowing programs; using online message boards for students to interact with professionals; teacher training on exposing all students to college | Parent–teacher consultation; education genograms; parent presentations on importance of requirements and involvement necessary for college admission and success; community/family members' participation in career days; college recruitment fairs at school/in region; getting students involved in job shadowing programs; using online message boards for students to interact with professionals; teacher training on exposing all students to college |
| Emergent | Reading stories about different careers; creating drawings to understand interests; storytelling; providing student with age-appropriate information about college; miracle question | Reading information about different careers; creating drawings about interests; storytelling about future career goals; providing student with age-appropriate information about college; miracle question | Writing stories or narratives about student's interests or what student wants in life; using Internet and other sources to learn about career and college options; sharing stories about people the student might be aware of, their learning process, and how they pursued their careers; miracle question |

In this particular case scenario, I was drawn to the cognitive-behavioral paradigm to process Samarium's thoughts and dispute some of the irrational messages she was saying to herself (and perhaps hearing from others), regarding her potential access to college. Yet I had to acknowledge that her background and identity did impact her choices (Grodsky & Riegle-Crumb, 2010). Considering her developmental level and being in a predominantly White school, it was important for me to recognize Samarium's exploration of her identity and need for belonging. Piaget identified adolescence as a time of formal operational cognitive development (i.e., being able to think abstractly and use deduction to answer questions; Berk, 2007). Many of Samarium's classmates considered college the definite, natural next step after high school. However, in Samarium's family and the Black community in the area, college was not widely understood or accessed. As a result, Samarium and other Black students sometimes felt as though they were not challenged or encouraged to strive for the same opportunities as their White peers.

School climate has many implications for students, and school counselors certainly need to take an active role with all stakeholders to create an equitable and supportive environment for all students (American School Counselor Association, 2012). When school counselors have included their school climate perceptions on the beginning-of-the-year needs assessments, they can then use this information to identify students who might need individual support as well as to plan student groups and classroom guidance activities. By creating an alliance with school administration and staff, school counselors can bring concerns to grade-level and school-wide meetings about any disparities and issues within the school. When this alliance facilitates student activities, such as the Peer Ambassador program in Samarium's school, such action supports student-driven efforts to raise awareness of and involvement in a positive school culture while continuing to support systemic change. School environment, particularly in high school, is an important issue for many reasons, including its effect on postsecondary decision making (Engberg & Wolniak, 2010). For Samarium, navigating her school climate was an added challenge to envisioning a future that went against what she had always known. She needed a great deal of information and support to begin getting her questions about college access answered.

## IN SESSION

After taking a brief walk down the hall in silence, I unlocked my office door and Samarium followed me in, immediately sitting on the couch. Still visibly upset, she sat quietly at the far end of the couch and stared at her schedule. I closed the door behind me and pulled my chair adjacent to where she chose to sit.

| | |
|---|---|
| COUNSELOR (C): | You were sounding pretty overwhelmed working on your high school schedule a few minutes ago. Tell me, what is going on? |
| SAMARIUM (S): | I don't know. I'm never going to get into college anyway so I should probably stop fighting with my mom about trying to go. |
| C: | Never going to get into college? There is no way that you will be able to get into college in 4 years? |

S:      It feels like it, but I guess that is why I have been talking to my mom so much about trying to figure out ways. College is something that I really want to do, but she just talks about all the negatives. Everyone else is being encouraged by their parents but me.

C:      That sounds like a tough situation to be in. I know you have been working hard in your classes. So you think everyone else is being supported to go to college but you?

S:      Yes . . . well, I guess a few other people have talked about their parents freaking out about how much it costs. I just know that my mom is working hard to support me, my brother, and sisters, but she only has a high school degree so she can't get better jobs. I don't want to have to take whatever job I can get like she has to . . . and I tell her that! We've been learning a ton about how school is really important to get a good job, and I want a good job!

C:      So seeing the limited jobs available to your mom because she didn't go to college, and you starting to notice careers that require going to college, has made you really focused on continuing school after high school.

S:      Yes! I know college is expensive, but you have already started talking to us about scholarships and those grant things, and I see commercials on TV all the time for students to borrow money. My mom says I'm the oldest and it's my responsibility to help her. Maybe I am being selfish because if I left, things at home would fall apart.

C:      I hear you starting to think about some options, but it sounds like you and your mom are looking at the situation differently. So college sounds like something that would make you have to leave home. But what does falling apart mean?

S:      Well, I don't know. I mean, I guess there are a few community colleges around here. I guess when I think of going to college, it means living somewhere else, but maybe it doesn't have to. Fall apart? I mean I do ALL the stuff around the house. Now that I think about it, I've been doing this for 3 years, and my sister is only 2 years younger than me. Maybe she needs to start doing more now to help me, like I help my mom while she's at work.

C:      And if your sister started to help you?

S:      Then when or if I leave, she'll know what to do, plus that would help give me more time now to do my own work! I don't know how I didn't think of this before!

C:      And how do you think your mom would react to this idea?

| | |
|---|---|
| S: | I'm not sure. It's frustrating. I don't want to disappoint my mom and not get a job, but I just want her to let me do what I want. I feel punished for working hard in school and wanting a good job. Being the first in my family to go to college should be a good thing, not bad, right? |
| C: | I can hear your frustration and confusion. College does come with a lot of opportunities, but also a lot of responsibilities like we've talked about in class. It sounds like you have some specific ideas about what college means to you and how you could get there. How about doing a role play with me so you can practice talking to your mom about this? |
| S: | Sure, that would be good! It makes me nervous just thinking of her reaction. |

After going through the role play, Samarium and I discussed that, although it was helpful for her to talk through some of her points, she knows that her mom has deep feelings about her not going to college. Although Samarium has 4 years until graduation, we talked about some of the issues she might encounter, such as high school classes that fulfill college requirements and applying for financial aid. We discussed the importance of involving her family in the decision, including some of her aunts and uncles in her extended family on whom she has relied for support. Particularly, Samarium decided that she would like to have her teachers, her mother, and me meet again to talk about her current academic progress and future plans so that hopefully her mom would gradually open up to the idea of college. Taking into consideration family systems, the family background, and the cultural context, I assured Samarium that I would do all I could to advocate for her by providing her mother with information about college options.

## Outcome

After our meeting, with Samarium's approval, I contacted her mother about scheduling a meeting to discuss Samarium's academic improvements and the plan to keep her on a positive track through high school. Her mother was happy to take proactive measures to continue her daughter's achievements. All except one of Samarium's teachers, as well as one of the high school counselors, agreed to participate as well. I also notified them that Samarium had a strong interest in discussing college as an option when we met. After hearing the recommendations and concerns from her teachers, I felt confident that the discussion could help Samarium's mother get a better sense of her daughter's potential.

I checked in with Samarium during lunch the following day. She had gone home the day before and talked to her mom about what had happened in school. The role play had helped her to think about the situation with more clarity. She said her mother was frustrated, but after getting a positive phone call from me, was willing to come in and meet with us, the teachers, and the high school counselor. At that meeting, Samarium's mother was reserved, but attentive. After everyone, including Samarium, had the opportunity to speak, the group decided that she should move forward with her college-track plan, knowing that she had a great deal of work ahead. Now connected with her high school counselor, Samarium and her mother felt supported by the school and more optimistic that she could be the first in her family to attend college.

After that interaction, I realized what a stressful process this was for many students and families regardless of the number of parent presentations or amount of curriculum pertinent to career exploration and college access the district provided. During one of our follow-up meetings, Samarium and I discussed what would have been helpful for her to try to prevent the "meltdown," as she called it, and what would be useful as she entered high school. She not only said being able to have more one-on-one time with the school counselor would help but also expressed the desire to speak with other students who are in a simi-

lar situation. With that, I added career/college exploration to the needs assessment survey I distributed to each homeroom every year. I also shared my experience with other school counselors in the county at the next district meeting so we could try to figure out ways to carve out more one-on-one time for students. Samarium has gone on to successfully negotiate high school, and although her career interest has changed, her focus on college has not. After working a part-time job after school and researching various grants and scholarships while in high school, Samarium and her mother agreed that her future was worth the investment. She has already started filling out applications to two local community colleges and three 4-year universities.

## Final Process Questions

- How effective was my rapport with this student, and did she feel heard?
- Did I acknowledge the student's concerns while providing her with information and tools to help her process and understand her situation and options?
- What other interventions could I have used to help Samarium, and what could I prepare for future students to become more multiculturally competent?
- Are school counselors focusing enough time and using effective approaches to demonstrate the

importance of career planning and preparing for educational requirements?

- After reading this case scenario and reflecting on your own transition to college, what has changed within the present-day K through 12 system (e.g., technology, school demographics and structure, demands of school counselor role), and how do you think current counselors can adapt to better assist students?
- How do these adaptations meet the needs of diverse students, families, and communities?

## Resources

It is important to have direct contact with community colleges and universities (including transition academies that can be helpful with students who are currently served with IEP or 504 accommodations) to learn more about ways to increase college access for all students. However, the Internet can provide much of the same material at your fingertips. Particularly, school counselors should become familiar with the resources of the U.S. Department of Education and the College Board. The website of the U.S. Department of Education, Office of Postsecondary Education (http://www2.ed.gov/about/offices/list/ope/index.html) connects counselors with such informa-

tion as financial aid options including policies and procedures pertinent to students and families. Additionally, school counselors can learn more about such programs as GEAR UP (Gaining Early Awareness and Readiness for Undergraduate Programs), which is specifically targeted at providing grant funding to support disadvantaged middle and high school students in reaching their goals of postsecondary education. The College Board website (http://www.collegeboard.org/) also directs school counselors, students, and families to helpful resources including specific topics related to preparing for college through each year in high school. The National Association for College Admission Counseling (NACAC) and National College Access Network (NCAN) also provide resources and insight specifically focused on college access; however, they do charge membership fees to access the majority of their information. The Internet has a wealth of the most up-to-date information, but always be cautious about the sources of the information.

American School Counselor Association. (2012). *The ASCA national model: A framework for school counseling programs* (3rd ed.). Alexandria, VA: Author.

Berk, L. E. (Ed.). (2007). *Development through the lifespan* (4th ed.). New York, NY: Pearson.

Engberg, M. E., & Wolniak, G. C. (2010). Examining the effects of high school contexts on postsecondary enrollment. *Research in Higher Education, 51,* 132–153. doi:10.1007/s11162-009-9150-y

Grodsky, E., & Riegle-Crumb, C. (2010). Those who choose and those who don't: Social background and college orientation. *The ANNALS of the American Academy of Political and Social Science, 627,* 14–25.

Klungman, J. R., & Butler, D. (2008). *Opening doors and paving the way: Increasing college access and success for talented low-income students.* White paper. Retrieved from http://www.princeton.edu/~tprep/pupp/forum/PUPP_GSF_White_Paper_Opening_Doors_02-09

Niles, S. G., & Harris-Bowlsbey, J. (2009). *Career development interventions in the 21st century* (3rd ed.). Upper Saddle River, NJ: Pearson.

Wyner, J. S., Bridgeland, J. M., & Diiulio, J. J., Jr. (2007). *Achievement trap: How America is failing millions of high-achieving students from lower-income families.* Retrieved from http://www.jkcf.org/assets/files/0000/0084/Achievement_Trap.pdf

## Chapter 14

# Counselors in Alternative Schools: The Last Line of Defense

KIMERE K. CORTHELL, LINDY K. PARKER, AND CATALINA MORILLAS

## CASE BACKGROUND

Alternative schools are often the last stop before expulsion for students who have behavioral and emotional issues in the public education system. As such, school counselors working in alternative schools could be considered the "last line of defense" for these students. Alternative schools are a growing presence in school districts across the nation; therefore, school counselors must be prepared to work effectively and efficiently both in and with these schools. The alternative school environment can present new and varied challenges that a school counselor may not encounter at a traditional school. The needs of the students as well as the demands from the administration and district can be uniquely challenging to a counselor new to the alternative school setting.

Additionally, school counselors not working in the alternative school should be prepared to work with students during their transition to and from alternative school. Just as the process of transferring a client from one counselor to another should be done with preparation and care, transferring a student from one school and its respective counselor to another should be done just as carefully and professionally. Traditional school counselors need to be familiar with the programs in place at the alternative school in their district, maintain contact with the counselor at that alternative school, and be prepared to facilitate the successful entry or reentry of a former alternative school student into the traditional school environment. Although counselors working in alternative schools could be considered the last line of defense for these students, traditional school counselors facilitate the continued and often ultimate success of these students when they return to their traditional schools.

Raywid (1994) categorized alternative schools into three typologies. Type I alternative schools use innovative curricula and programming, and provide an alternative for students who choose for various reasons to attend a nontraditional setting to better meet their educational needs. Type II schools are often referred to as "last-chance programs" or "soft jails." Type II schools differ from Type I schools in that their primary objective is to modify the behavior of students to avoid expulsion from the district. Finally, Raywid (1994) stated that Type III schools are "for students who are presumed to need remediation or rehabilitation—academic, social/emotional, or both" (p. 27) and who the school hopes to successfully treat. In this case scenario, we explore the work of school counselors in only Type II and Type III alternative schools.

Although the stakes are high for students attending Type II and III alternative schools (e.g., permanent expulsion, jail etc.), these schools offer a unique opportunity for both the students and the school counselors. When students are mandated to attend alternative schools, they are denied many of the benefits (e.g., sports, student government, and school clubs) offered in a traditional school setting. Conversely, students in alternative schools ideally gain access to much needed counseling resources and to staff who are uniquely trained to provide the appropriate interventions. Counselors working in alternative schools are charged with taking advantage of this opportunity and preparing students academically, socially, and emotionally for successful reintegration into traditional schools. The ultimate goal of this successful reintegration is based on the idea that traditional schools afford the students the greatest access to benefits the district can provide for the students' current development and their future success.

To illustrate the role of counselors in an alternative school setting, we present a case scenario of the process involved in helping one of our students, Julio. For context, the alternative school Julio attends is what Raywid (1994) refers to as a Type II alternative school setting, a last-chance program—the final stop before his permanent expulsion. This particular school also has some elements of a Type III school, including multiple counselors on campus as well as teachers and staff who are invested in the success of the students, all of whom use innovative approaches for remediation.

Julio, a 15-year-old Hispanic male currently in the eighth grade, is an undocumented citizen. He has lived in the United States since he was 3 years old, when his mother brought him and his 5-year-old sister into the United States. Julio reports that he does not have a relationship with his father, who still lives in Mexico. Julio's mother works at two different fast-food restaurants, but still has trouble paying the family's bills. Julio shared that he feels bad that his mother is under so much stress, and as the "man" in the family he believes that he has a responsibility to help support his family financially. Even though Julio's mother is opposed to drug use and selling, Julio stated that he began selling drugs in order to help support his family, but he does not use the drugs he sells. Julio's random drug testing, ordered and provided by the juvenile court system, supports this assertion. According to a school district evaluation, Julio tested with average intelligence, but he is reading on only a third-grade reading level, possibly in part because English is his second language.

Julio was arrested for the first time for marijuana possession when he was 14 years old. As a part of his subsequent probation, he was required to complete a substance abuse treatment program, which he did. The terms of his probation also required that he attend school regularly and not receive any disciplinary sanctions. So, when he got in a fight on the school campus with another student, he violated his probation and was remanded to a juvenile detention center. After completing his 6-month sentence at the detention center, he was ordered to complete an entire year of school in an alternative school before being allowed to return to his traditional school. He continues to receive random drug testing by the court.

The primary goals for working with Julio encompassed both academic and social skill development. More specifically, the treatment goals included the following: (1) developing better classroom behavior and study skills, (2) developing anger management skills, (3) developing effective social skills, (4) developing positive family relationships, and (5) increasing self-esteem. The overarching goal for Julio was to develop the skills needed for successful reintegration into a traditional school.

Certainly, we the authors of this chapter realize that traditional schools may not be for every student; some students have unique needs that may require a nontraditional form of school (Verdugo & Glenn, 2006). But taking into consideration both Julio's personal situation as well as the limitations of long-term nontraditional school options available to Julio within our own school district, we felt that ultimately his best option to experience success would be in a traditional school. Recognizing all the benefits a traditional school can offer Julio, we find ourselves as school counselors being social advocates, attempting to reconnect Julio and all of our alternative school students to those traditional school benefits, and encouraging them to remain connected to those benefits all the way through to graduation (Chang & Gnilka, 2014).

## INITIAL PROCESSING QUESTIONS

A counselor working at an alternative school with a student like Julio will want to process several questions, such as the following:

- What are some of the biases you have about alternative school students? About students with prior drug convictions?
- What are the implications of Julio's not receiving the resources of a traditional school?
- What are some of the social-cultural issues in this case?
- What do you think about the counselor acting as a social advocate?
- What are some assumptions you might make about Julio? His family? His traditional school?
- How does the climate of an alternative school help facilitate successful transition back into the student's traditional school?
- Do you think long-term nontraditional schools are needed? If so, what kind of students might require this type of school environment? How can school counselors advocate for more of these kinds of school alternatives?
- What are your immediate goals for Julio? What are your long-term goals? Does Julio share those goals?
- How are the goals that you have for Julio at the alternative school the same as or different from those goals for a comparable student in a more traditional school setting?

## ADDRESSING THE ISSUES

The mission of our Type II alternative school is to prepare students for successful reentry and sustainability in their traditional school setting. The greatest success is achieved in these circumstances: when the student is able to feel fully invested in the reentry process, has a good understanding of the purpose of his or her traditional school, has a newly developed or renewed sense of self-efficacy in his or her own ability to be successful in that traditional school, and, finally, has a feeling of support from the systems that surround him or her.

Regardless of our own personal theoretical orientations, we find it essential to integrate a systemic approach when conceptualizing the issues of students in an alternative school. We acknowledge that some theoretical orientations say it is students' own behaviors, thoughts, or choices that have led them to an alternative school setting; however, the actual placement of the student in a Type II or III alternative school setting is usually a result of the school system's design, and not the choice of the individual student or his or her guardians. Therefore, although Julio was immediately assigned to a counselor with whom he could have individual counseling sessions, we made sure that he met all the counselors in the school. Each one took a moment to express his or her interest in Julio and his story, making him feel welcome and comfortable within his new system. We also introduced him to the school principal, the assistant principals, the discipline coordinator, his teachers, the parent center coordinator, the school nurse, and the administrative assistants. It is certainly important to build a strong network of support for the student in any environment, and we were transparent in how we went about it so that we would be able to talk with Julio about how he could initiate those relationships with the teachers and staff at his traditional school in the future.

Keeping the systemic approach in mind, we also determined it necessary to communicate with Julio's mother, his parole officer, a substance abuse counselor (external to the alternative school), and current teachers at the alternative school as often as needed and possible. As part of student enrollment in our alternative school, most parents and guardians willingly agree to sign a release that allows us to communicate with these parties and others, and we allow the student to be involved in this release as well. (Other school counselors should follow the ethical and legal guidelines set by their unique school.) Julio and his mother liked this team-like approach and immediately agreed to the release. We provided psycho-education related to substance abuse, immigration issues, community resources, and adolescent development to his teachers, his mother, and his probation officer in order to confirm that all were focused on supporting Julio's successful reentry into traditional school. We also began updating his traditional school counselor on his progress when we met, either in person or over the phone, during Julio's monthly reintegration meetings. We felt it was important to include Julio in most of these meetings when it was therapeutically appropriate. His inclusion in these meetings allowed Julio to communicate his past experience with his traditional school and explain situations in which he felt misunderstood by that school's personnel. These open conversations allowed all parties to have a better understanding of and appreciation for one another's perspectives.

We also viewed the student from a multicultural counseling perspective. Julio is a unique individual with membership in various cultural groups (e.g., Hispanic, immigrant, Catholic, male), and all of the counselors who worked with him are also unique individuals representing various cultural groups. For example, Julio worked with Hispanic, African American, and Caucasian counselors, both male and female. A large proportion of students in alternative school settings identify with an ethnic minority group (Foley & Lan-Szo, 2006; Lehr & Lange, 2003; Raywid, 1994). We have found this to be true in our own alternative school setting where Julio is. Thus, in working with Julio, it was essential to be mindful of the Multicultural Counseling Competencies (Sue, Arredondo, & McDavis, 1992).

The last group with which Julio needed to interact in order to facilitate his transition was his peers. Julio participated in a student process group that gave him an opportunity to build relationships with his new peers in a healthy, controlled way and discuss issues of concern with them, specifically issues that might impede their success in alternative and traditional schools. The group environment allowed Julio a chance to tell his story, have his experiences and feelings validated, and make connections with students who have similar stories and experiences. He was also able to watch experienced group members set and achieve their goals, which encouraged him to identify and achieve some of his own personal goals. Julio was also paired with a mentor who had overcome challenges similar to Julio's and was currently finishing his first year at a university. This mentor was one of several college students solicited through an undergraduate counseling course offered at a nearby counseling program. After being prescreened by two of our counselors, he (and many of the other identified college students) willingly agreed to spend a few days each semester with a mentee at our alternative school. We found it surprisingly easy to locate great college mentors through undergraduate counseling courses.

Throughout the school year, Julio's teachers completed behavior reports that documented improvement in his ability to control his anger. His grades improved, and his mother reported increased positive family interactions. Also, the number of behavioral referrals decreased as the school year progressed. Julio's positive social and academic gains increased his confidence and self-efficacy and allowed him to see what success looks like.

As Julio neared his return to a traditional school, he participated in an exit group, which focuses on processing the changes the students have made and developing their plans for success. This is a crucial step in the transition process, as it reiterates to the students the reasons for striving to be successful in their traditional school. Some students find themselves actually preferring the alternative school environment, with its smaller staff-to-student ratio and the highly therapeutic and supportive focus. However, the alternative school simply does not have all the resources these students should have access to in order to receive the full school experience, including athletic teams, a journalism department, advanced courses, etc. The alternative school counselors remind students that all the lessons they learned in the alternative school can be applied to their time at a traditional school, hopefully making that traditional school experience just as enjoyable for them.

With the information they process in the exit groups, students construct an "exit letter." They state their reasons for coming to the alternative school, what they have learned at the alternative school, why they want to be successful in their traditional school, and their concrete plans to create that success for themselves. They present these letters to the administrators and discipline coordinators at both the alternative school and the traditional school. Presenting these letters publicly is a proud moment for students, and it increases their self-efficacy. Also, the letter is something tangible students can take with them into their traditional school, a physical reminder of their reasons for striving for success and their plans for how to attain it. Julio reported that he enjoyed showing his letter to others, including his mother, substance abuse counselor, and parole officer. He spoke of being proud that he was able to draft a formal letter and express himself. This excellent intervention activity facilitates a successful transition.

When deciding on interventions and approaches, as always, be conscious of the developmental age of the student. Middle school and high school students require different focus areas throughout their reintegration process. High school students seem to be more concerned about credit recovery, GED options, and the impact reintegrating will have on their career and educational paths. Middle school students seem to be more focused on gaining peer, teacher, and family acceptance during their transitions.

As a middle school student, Julio showed improvement while participating in activities that allowed him to develop positive peer relationships and opportunities to strengthen his self-efficacy at school. He also participated in activities that allowed him to discuss ways to better his relationships at home, thus further contributing to his feelings of self-efficacy. Table 14-1 presents additional strategies and techniques helpful when working with students at alternative schools.

## IN SESSION

The following is an example of a conversation one of the authors had while in a one-on-one counseling session with Julio late in his stay at the alternative school.

| | |
|---|---|
| COUNSELOR (C): | Hello, Julio. How are you doing today? |
| JULIO (J): | I'm good, I guess. I've been thinkin' about what we have been talking about in our group, about what I'm gonna do when I go back to my home school. |
| C: | Yes, you have a major transition coming up next week. Would you like to spend our time talking about that today? We could also finish working on your exit letter, if that is OK with you. |
| J: | Yeah, when I be workin' on the letter it got me thinkin' about lots of stuff. |
| C: | Oh, yeah, like what? |
| J: | When I was writing about the things I learned while I was here, I kept on thinkin' about how I have not gotten into any fights while I have been here. And I'm passing all of my classes! |
| C: | That's true! You've really worked hard while you've been here. What do you think has helped you achieve these things? |
| J: | Cuz when I felt angry or annoyed I knew there were people, Mr. Smith, you, Mrs. Johnson, and a few other teachers, that I could talk to about what was going on. I am afraid that when I go back to my home school I will not have as many people to talk to when I be gettin' mad. I felt like people really cared about me here and that people were not judging me for my past. |
| C: | It sounds like you are worried that people [at your traditional school] will judge you or treat you differently because of your past decisions. |
| J: | Yeah, when I was at my home school before I was different. I want them to give me a chance to prove that I am not the same person that I was. I don't want to go back to jail. I know that I have to do good in school and stay out of trouble. I don't want to leave this school though. I don't want to go back. |

**TABLE 14-1   Additional Strategies and Techniques Helpful When Working with Students at Alternative Schools**

| Paradigm | Middle School | High School |
|---|---|---|
| Psychodynamic | Play therapy; exploring and processing past events that student chooses to discuss; uncovering and processing attachment issues, childhood conflicts, and motivation for behavior; consultations with guardians/primary caretakers; observing the student with peers | Play therapy; exploring and processing past events that student chooses to discuss; uncovering and processing attachment issues, childhood conflicts, and motivation for behavior; consultations with guardians/primary caretakers; observing the student with peers |
| Humanistic/Existential | Play therapy; developing self-awareness; demonstrating respect for student's unique self; consultations with family members/guardians; encouraging authenticity; building relationships and being present | Play therapy; developing self-awareness; demonstrating respect for student's unique self; consultations with family members/guardians; encouraging authenticity; building relationships and being present |
| Behavioral/CBT | Uncovering beliefs that facilitate destructive behavior; teacher and guardian consultations to work toward a healthy, reinforcing environment; role playing; challenging irrational and maladaptive beliefs and behaviors; encouraging client motivation to seek healthy thoughts and behaviors; being supportive; practicing new behaviors with the client; play therapy; homework including psycho-educational worksheets | Uncovering beliefs that facilitate destructive behavior; teacher and guardian consultations to work toward a healthy, reinforcing environment; role playing; challenging irrational and maladaptive beliefs and behaviors; encouraging client motivation to seek healthy thoughts and behaviors; being supportive; practicing new behaviors with the client; play therapy; homework including psycho-educational worksheets |
| Systemic | Consultations with guardians, primary caretakers, parole officers, community counselors, traditional schoolteachers, and counselors; determining client's perceived and actual role in the family, school, and community; facilitating healthy peer relationships and connections with mentors; connecting client with opportunities and community resources; play therapy; family sculpting; genograms | Consultations with guardians, primary caretakers, parole officers, community counselors, traditional schoolteachers, and counselors; connection to career counselors and/or college admissions offices; determining client's perceived and actual role in the family, school, and community; facilitating healthy peer relationships and connections with mentors; connecting client with opportunities and community resources; play therapy; family sculpting; genograms |
| Emergent | Role playing meeting new teachers and students in traditional school; empowerment and encouragement; miracle question; expressive paintings; play therapy; sand tray; using music to express thoughts and feelings | Role playing meeting new teachers and students in traditional school; role playing job and college interviews; empowerment and encouragement; miracle question; expressive paintings; play therapy; sand tray; using music to express thoughts and feelings |

| | |
|---|---|
| C: | It sounds like you have learned a lot here and are proud of the changes you have made. And it sounds like you might be a little nervous about people at your home school not being able to see those changes. |
| J: | Yeah, I just don't want people messin' with me. I don't want to get into any fights. |
| C: | What are some of the things that you think would be helpful in keeping you on this path when you go back to your home school? |
| J: | I think getting to know my teachers and the counselors might help, so maybe they can get to know the new me. |
| C: | So, it sounds like you want them to get to know you before they judge you. |
| J: | Yeah! They judge people that go to this school. They think we are all bad. |
| C: | Feeling judged can be hurtful. I know one of the counselors at your school, so maybe we could set up a meeting to discuss your ideas and let her know what some of your concerns are. |
| J: | Yeah, that's cool. I just don't want people to judge me on my past. |
| C: | Not being judged sounds really important to you. What if people do judge you? How will you deal with it? |
| J: | I don't know. I guess I will just keep doing what I have been doing here—walk away, go practice my anger management skills in a corner or in the bathroom by myself. |
| C: | You have been through a lot in your life. You have such incredible strength and courage. I know you will get through this too! I know everyone here is going to miss the positive impact you have on the other students, and I am sad to be losing one of our student leaders, but I am so happy for you in all that you have accomplished. |

As the session continued I assisted Julio with his exit letter. For each concern Julio expressed, I asked him to write down at least one concrete strategy he can act on at his traditional school that would address or alleviate that concern. For example, when he said he was worried about making "positive" friends that would be a good influence, he wrote down that he would talk to the soccer coach within his first week back so that he can get involved in his traditional school's sports team.

## Outcome

Julio was able to transition out of our alternative school and back into a traditional school. Using his acquired and strengthened skills, his time at his traditional school has been successful thus far. The school counselor at his traditional school has continued the work we started at the alternative school and communicates with us about Julio's continued progress. Of course, Julio's traditional school counselor used her own interventions that Julio has benefited from and enjoyed.

The process is not yet complete for Julio, and our job is not yet done. Although each individual success matters and should be acknowledged, it is important not to spend too much time celebrating the success of just one of our students making it through the system, when there are so many students who do not have the

opportunity to experience the same successful outcome. Being mindful of our unique ability to internally affect the system motivates us to continue to act not only as counselors to individual students but also as social advocates for all students (Chang & Gnilka, 2014). Through our hope that all students have access to all the benefits the school systems have to offer, we strive to reintegrate our alternative school students into their traditional schools, where the most benefits are usually available to them.

## Final Process Questions

- What role do you see Julio's traditional school counselor playing in his transition?
- When working with students in alternative schools, when do you think the reintegration process begins?
- How can you help Julio identify that his successes can transfer to a traditional school setting?
- After reading this case scenario, what other types of training do you think would benefit school counselors working in alternative school settings?
- What additional interventions/strategies would you use with Julio?
- What else can alternative schools do to help their students succeed?
- Is there a better way than the alternative school to address the needs of these students?

- How can counselors act as social advocates on behalf of these students?
- If you were the traditional school counselor, what would you find helpful in the transfer process?
- If you were the traditional school counselor, how would you work with the alternative school throughout the year to support Julio and the alternative school counselor and staff?
- If you were the traditional school counselor, how would you work with students, teachers, other faculty, and staff to assist all students in the transfer process?
- If you were the traditional school counselor, how would you minimize the negative connotations associated with alternative schools and students attending them?

## Resources

Ferguson, A. A. (2001). *Bad boys: Public schools in the making of Black masculinity (Law, meaning, and violence).* Ann Arbor, MI: University of Michigan Press.

Mathews, J. (2009). *Work hard. Be nice: How two inspired teachers created the most promising schools in America.* Chapel Hill, NC: Algonquin Books of Chapel Hill.

Mottaz, C. (2002). *Breaking the cycle of failure: How to build and maintain quality alternative schools.* Lanham, MD: Scarecrow Press.

Verdugo, R. R., & Glenn, B. C. (2006). *Race and alternative schools* (NCJ No. 226234) [Abstract]. Retrieved from National Criminal Justice Reference Service Abstracts Database, https://www.ncjrs.gov/app/abstractdb/AbstractDBDetails.aspx?id=248222&SelectedRange=init&SelectedSearchItems=init

## Chapter 15

# Transitions and Student Attendance

LACEY L. WALLACE

## CASE BACKGROUND

I received an e-mail from a teacher expressing concern about the attendance of one of her students. As a member of our school's Attendance Committee, I have often received such e-mails. Making phone calls regarding attendance was not my favorite activity because I often felt as though I was asking for personal information when I called parents to see whether there was anything I could do to improve their child's attendance. Jerry was a new student to our school, having enrolled in second grade at the beginning of the school year. I wanted to gain sufficient information before I called Jerry's parents so I perused his cumulative folder to look for attendance records from previous schools, past report cards, and any other pertinent information I could find.

As I went through Jerry's folder, I began to find letters from Attendance Committees at his previous schools about frequent absences that were considered "unexcused" by law. His report cards from these schools showed that Jerry was a hard worker and extremely intelligent because he was still making straight As even while being excessively absent. I also noticed that he had report cards from two different schools in first grade and yet a different school for kindergarten. After acquiring a bit of background knowledge from reviewing his folder, I called home to see what the root of the problem was and what I could do to help.

Jerry's mother apologized profusely and explained that she knows the law. She admitted that Jerry has had difficulty each time he transitioned from one school to the next. His father was preparing to deploy in the following weeks, and Jerry was refusing to leave his father for fear of losing him. Jerry's mom also explained how many times Jerry had had to transition between schools and the difficulty they had trying to convince him to attend each new school. She shared that his last school was wonderful for him. There he was viewed as a "talented" student, he was the custodian's special helper, and everyone in the school knew him. I asked his mother to bring him into school the next morning to meet with me first thing so I could speak with Jerry and create a plan with him. She agreed and we hung up the phone.

## INITIAL PROCESS QUESTIONS

- How is this parent going to respond to me "prying" into her family's personal business?
- Is this a pattern that has been modeled by his parents, or is Jerry trying to avoid something?
- What does Jerry get by refusing to attend school? What is his goal?
- How can I instill hope when there have not been many positive experiences for this child in this setting?
- How can I help this child feel a part of the school community?
- How can I create an environment at our school that emulates the positive climate he had at his last school?
- In what ways can I encourage the parent to get the child involved in extracurricular activities so he may feel a sense of belonging and start to form relationships with his peers?
- How long will it take for him to feel comfortable and confident at our school?
- If I don't create a sense of hope for him right away, will he resist coming to school every day?

## ADDRESSING THE ISSUES

Jerry's avoidance of the school day was not a new behavior. However, it seemed that if I could collaborate with his classroom teacher, the health room staff, and our head custodian, we could put a plan in place to create a more exciting and positive environment for Jerry. As I began brainstorming strategies to meet Jerry's needs, I automatically thought of using an approach that consisted of strategies from the psychodynamic, emergent, cognitive-behavioral, and humanistic/existential paradigms.

During my first session with Jerry, we spoke a great deal about his previous school that he missed so much. We talked about the special jobs he had had there, the friends he had been so close to, the teachers he had known so well, and all of the sacrifices he has had to make during his last move. I started off by using the psychodynamic technique of catharsis. Jerry wrote a letter to the custodian at his previous school to express how much he missed everyone. We looked up his previous school's mailing address, put his letter in an envelope, and placed it in the school mailbox.

I also used an emergent approach in working with Jerry in order to reframe his thinking about his experiences at our school. I asked Jerry a "miracle question" about what his perfect school day would look like if he woke up the next morning and everything was wonderful. I also asked him to name "sparkling moments," or times that he can remember enjoying school this year.

In order to make Jerry feel as though he were a valued member of our school community, Jerry and I created a plan. We agreed that he would be one of my student helpers and the head custodian's helper. Jerry was to visit my office every morning before he went to his classroom so he could feed my fish and sharpen pencils. I explained how imperative his jobs were to my fish's well-being and students being able to write while they were in my office. We also planned to have informal "lunch bunches" where I would have lunch with Jerry and a couple of peers he had met so far this school year who he viewed as potential friends. Our lunch bunches would serve as a setting for him to create stronger relationships with his peers to reinforce his sense of belonging.

I collaborated with his classroom teacher, his mother, and the health room staff because Jerry had been frequenting the health room due to reoccurring stomachaches. We agreed that Jerry would continue to go to the health room if he complained of stomach pain. The health room assistant would then take his temperature, call his mother to inform her of what it was, and if it was lower than 100 degrees, Jerry would be sent back to class to remain in school. In order to encourage Jerry's improvements in attendance, we created a plan for positive reinforcement. If Jerry came to school every day and stayed the entire day, his mother would take him to do a fun activity in the community over the weekend (e.g., go to the park, go bowling, see a movie, get ice cream). Table 15-1 provides additional approaches for helping students who experience frequent school transitions.

## IN SESSION

During one of our sessions, we talked a great deal about what Jerry missed about his old school, along with his memories of the current school year to date.

COUNSELOR (C):    Tell me the wonderful things you remember about your last school.

JERRY (J):    It was the best. My best friend, Calvin, goes to school there. I always got to go with Mr. Davis and Ms. Norris.

**TABLE 15-1 Additional Techniques and Strategies for Helping Children Experiencing Frequent School Transitions**

| Paradigm | Elementary School | Middle School | High School |
|---|---|---|---|
| Psychodynamic | Analysis of avoidance (e.g., refusing to come to school); talking about the fears and worries over loss/separation | Analysis of relationship with father and mother throughout childhood; determining role of father in his life; evaluation of avoidance and other defense mechanisms | Analysis of relationship with father and mother throughout childhood; determining role of father in his life; evaluation of defense mechanisms |
| Humanistic/ Existential | Therapeutic conditions; role play and empty chair as if he is speaking to his friends at his old school; "I" statements to use when feeling worried, anxious, or upset; creating a job or role for him to feel a sense of meaning; informal "lunch bunches" with him and potential friends to foster relationships among peers and sense of accomplishment and connection | Therapeutic conditions; role play; empty chair; "I" statements for worries and concerns about deployed parent and changes within the home; helping to provide a sense of belonging by creating a special role for the student (e.g., mentor younger students, special job to complete daily) | Therapeutic conditions; role play and "I" statements; helping to provide a sense of belonging by creating a special role for the student (i.e., mentor younger students, special job to complete daily) |

| Paradigm | Elementary School | Middle School | High School |
|---|---|---|---|
| Behavioral/CBT | Positive reinforcement for coming to school; behavior charts to encourage willingness to come to school; assigning a job to foster a sense of belonging and responsibility; disputing irrational beliefs about school being scary and negative; cognitive restructuring of what the school day is like; self-talk during entry to the building; visual imagery of positive interactions and experiences; modeling positive self-talk; behavioral rehearsal; role playing; "picture in your mind" of coming to school and being happy to play with friends; exceptions; miracle question; overcorrection; response cost; flagging the minefield | Positive reinforcement; token economy; Premack principle; behavior contracts; disputing irrational beliefs; cognitive restructuring; specify automatic thoughts; self-talk; visual imagery; modeling; behavioral rehearsal; role playing; "picture in your mind"; exceptions; miracle question; overcorrection; response cost; flagging the minefield | Positive reinforcement; token economy; Premack principle; behavior contracts; disputing irrational beliefs; cognitive restructuring; specify automatic thoughts; self-talk; visual imagery; modeling; behavioral rehearsal; role playing; "picture in your mind"; exceptions; miracle question; overcorrection; response cost; flagging the minefield |
| Family Systems | Parent training for dealing with transitions and the effects on children; education on the change in family dynamics in transitional situations; link with community resources to support family stability and locate extracurricular activities | Parent training for dealing with transitions and the effects on children; education on the change in family dynamics in transitional situations; link with community resources to support family stability and locate extracurricular activities | Parent training for dealing with transitions and the effects on children; education on the change in family dynamics in transitional situations; link with community resources to support family stability and locate extracurricular activities |
| Emergent | Miracle question; sparkling moments—focus on the times that were fun at school; focus on positive relationships with peers and adults; empowerment; communication analysis; interpersonal incidents; role playing; bibliotherapy about other students' experiences with transiency | Deconstruct and externalize problems; miracle question; sparkling moments; empowerment; communication analysis; interpersonal incidents; role playing | Deconstruct and externalize problems; miracle question; sparkling moments; empowerment; communication analysis; interpersonal incidents; role playing |

C:    Tell me more about Mr. Davis and Ms. Norris.

J:    (*Giggles*) Mr. Davis was the custodian that I helped all of the time. After lunch, I would stay and help him clean up the cafeteria. Ms. Norris was the Gifted and Talented teacher who would take me for math and fun enrichment activities.

C:    Well, I can see why you miss your old school. It sounds like you had a lot of people who cared about you at that last school.

J:    Yeah, and they had awesome playground equipment.

C:    Wow, you have lots of great memories from that school. Tell me about a fun activity you have done here at our school.

J:    Well, there really hasn't been anything very much fun yet this school year. We used to have different lunches, like from Pizza Hut and stuff, at my last school. We don't have that stuff here at this school.

C:    You're right about that. We don't have food like that, but you do have a field trip coming up, Character Parade once a month, and Star Show and Field Day in the spring.

J:    Yeah, but that stuff is so far away.

C:    I know it can be difficult to wait when you are used to things being a bit different at your last school.

J:    Yeah, I just wish I could go back. I miss my friends so much. I don't even have friends at this school.

C:    Hmm, friends are important. Who are some of the kids you play with at recess? Or, kids who live in your neighborhood?

J:    Sometimes I play soccer with Markus out at recess. Jordan lives in my neighborhood, but he's in first grade so I don't see him much during the school day.

C:    It's tough that Jordan's in a different grade because you don't have the same schedule, but I'm hearing you say that you play with Markus sometimes.

J:    Yes, and Clyde.

C:    Oh! That's great! What do you like about Clyde and Markus?

J:    Well, we all like to play soccer and our dads are all in the army.

C:    Well, it sounds like you all have lots in common. Jerry, would it be OK if I invite you and a couple of friends to eat lunch in my office about once every other week so we can help you to keep making friends?

J:    Well, what if they don't want to come with us to eat in here when I ask them to?

C:    Then we will ask someone else that you think might be a good friend.

J:    OK. When can we have lunch with you then?

C:    Let's go look at my calendar. Tomorrow! How does that sound?

J:    That's fine.

C:    OK, Jerry. So tomorrow morning when you get to school, come straight to my office so you can feed my fish.

J:    OK. I won't forget.

C:    Then tomorrow afternoon we'll eat lunch with some boys from your class, so start thinking about whom you might invite to join us.

## Outcome

Jerry immediately began to come to school without a great deal of resistance. He quickly formed relationships with his peers, as his social skills were above average. Around the time that his father deployed, he missed some time from school, but his mother always kept me informed prior to Jerry's missing any school. I explained to her that one way the Military Interstate Compact protected military families was that their vacation time prior to his father deploying would be considered "excused" due to their right to spend time together prior to and post-deployment. Jerry's mother and I kept in close contact to be sure that we were aware of any concerns regarding Jerry's attendance and well-being at school so we could quickly address any issues that might arise. Jerry continued to feed my fish for the remainder of the school year. We had four informal lunch bunches before Jerry had formed friendships with some of his peers and preferred to go to the cafeteria to eat with his classmates. Jerry and I met from time to time to create items for his father's memory box and to check in, but he came to school every day and was excited about coming!

## Final Process Questions

- What proactive measures can I put into place for students who may be having difficulty transitioning from one school to the next?
- What role should a professional school counselor have in regard to attendance?
- What can I do to monitor attendance prior to its becoming a significant concern?
- How can I create a community resource guide for members of the community or military population who are transient, perhaps including web-based and international resources?
- Although I always hear that students are resilient, at what point does this constant adjustment to new school environments affect a child's well-being?
- How can these students feel a sense of belonging when they may only be in any one school for two to three years at the most?
- What proactive clubs and morale boosting activities can I implement next year to build a sense of community and school spirit?

## Resources

Kraus, J. R., & Beyl, C. (2006). *Annie's plan: Taking charge of school and homework*. Washington, DC: Magination Press.

Krivitzky, N. (2009). *Always late Nate*. Northville, MI: Ferne Press.

Ragona, S., & Weber, S., (2007). *Coming to school is really cool!* Chapin, SC: YouthLight.

U.S. Department of Defense Education Activity. (DoDEA), *"Be Here!" Toolkit that gives strategies and handouts for attendance concerns*. Retrieved from http://www.militaryk12partners.dodea.edu/behere.cfm

Whitney, B. (2008). *A guide to school attendance*. Abingdon, OX: David Fulton.

*Chapter 16*

# Bullying (Relational Aggression)

JASMINE GRAHAM

## CASE BACKGROUND

Maria, a sixth grader at Bear Run Middle School, was referred to me for bullying issues. She was new to the school, having arrived 4 months into the school year. Hispanic and petite in build, her personality was shy and demure. She was a C average student and her appearance was well kept and neat, yet conservative compared to the trendy fashions of her peers. She was the youngest of three children, but lived alone with her grandparents who had recently adopted her. Her other siblings lived together with their aunt and uncle across the country; she seldom saw them. Her biological parents abused substances and were constantly in and out of correctional facilities. They had abandoned her and her siblings in their apartment building when she was 4 years old. Emergency responders rescued them, and they were placed with family members through the foster care system. Although Maria didn't recall the incident, she was aware of the story and asked about her parents and siblings often.

Outside of her drug abuse, Maria's mother, who was diagnosed with bipolar disorder and depression, had frequent in-patient visits at mental health institutions. As their biological daughter, she stayed in her parents' (Maria's grandparents') home when released from correctional or mental health facilities. These stays never lasted long, as she was inevitably forced to leave because she would threaten to harm herself, would harm someone else, or was arrested again. Maria's relationship with her mother existed within a constant revolving door, which made for a vicious cycle of abandonment. As for her father, Maria had no recollection of him outside of photos and the phone calls he made to her grandparents, occasionally asking to use their address to receive his disability checks.

A student bystander referred Maria to the counseling office because she had witnessed multiple instances of Maria being harassed by the group of girls Maria thought were her friends. They exiled her from their lunch table, taunted and teased her in the hallways, and had launched a strategic campaign to exclude her from their peer social group. The most recent event entailed the students making a Facebook page titled, "Bear Run's Dumbest." Over 30 students had signed onto the page and made comments about Maria ranging from threatening to vulgar. Some comments referred to her parents, insulting them and suggesting they didn't love her. Typically a good-humored student, when asked about the web page, Maria's mood switched abruptly. Her face became red, her fists clenched, and tears began streaming down her face. Her posture became rigid, and she became verbally unresponsive, replying to questions with only a short shake or nod of her head. She was intensely angry and very hurt by the ongoing rejection and cruelty of her peers.

## INITIAL PROCESS QUESTIONS

Prior to addressing any bullying issues and well before the school year begins, all professional school counselors should ensure they are up-to-date with federal legislation pertaining to bullying. They also need to familiarize themselves with state laws, the school system's rules and policies, as well as any of their particular school's rules or programs that address bullying. Furthermore, they should specifically research their school system's definition of bullying, as well as their school's definition of bullying (which may vary slightly), and the consequences the school has in place to respond to bullying. This information will allow the school counselor to build effective anti-bullying programs and lessons that align with the culture of the school system, as well as effectively guide stakeholders through a bullying incident by providing accurate and valid information. Most states have laws pertaining to bullying, and as a result, most school systems have formal reporting systems in place for bullying. School counselors need to make certain they are familiar with what's required of them in this process and carry out those responsibilities with fidelity, as negligence can lead to litigation in bullying incidents.

Ensuring the students' safety is paramount in bullying situations. A bevy of emotions, irrational thoughts, and harmful behaviors can lead to life-threatening consequences. As such, the foremost concern of a professional school counselor should be to remove any threats to the students' safety. Emotionally charged dilemmas can create feelings of hopelessness and lead to irrational and impulsive resolutions. It is critical for the professional school counselor to explore such thoughts and feelings thoroughly and address them appropriately. While conducting the initial session, the counselor can informally assess the student's crisis level by listening for suggestions of self-harm, harm to others, and suicidal ideation. A statement as simple as "I just don't want to do this anymore" should be clarified. The counselor can respond by saying, "You sound overwhelmed; tell me what you mean by that," or "When you say *this*, I'm wondering whether you are referring to suicide." The counselor may pull from his or her standing knowledge of the student, being cognizant of any history of self-harm, a change in the student's affect or mood, or behaviors that may suggest that the student would harm himself or herself or others. If the student's responses lead the school counselor to believe there is intent to harm someone, he or she needs to follow the appropriate protocol, conduct a formal assessment, and pull in the required support systems.

It is equally important to collaborate with appropriate stakeholders in one's school. When confronted with a dilemma wherein a student may be harmed, it is imperative that the professional school counselor work with the administrative team, making them aware of the concern immediately. Prior to the beginning of the school year, the school counselor must be sure to have a discussion with his or her immediate supervisor about whom to notify should a bullying incident occur and how that notification should occur. Time is often of the essence in situations such as these, and working as a team affords the counselor time to address the situation efficiently and thoroughly, while an investigation is underway and parents are promptly notified. For example, in this case scenario, while I was assessing the student's emotional state and working toward a resolution, the administrator and school safety officer were investigating the website threats, identifying the bullies, and contacting parents, assigning consequences as necessary. I was able to work with the school safety officer to ensure the Facebook page was removed from the site. I also worked with the administrators, making certain that all parents were asked to come into the school to be made aware of the extreme nature of their students' behaviors. While the administrator and school resource officer spoke of school policy and legal consequences in the conference, I was able to guide the session—allowing the students to process the events—mediate their relationships, and educate all parties about bullying and the severity of its consequences. In addition, when confronted with a complex case, it is vital to reach out to one's colleagues for resources, collaborating with them to find the most effective intervention and response. Oftentimes, they will have helpful insights or offer appropriate resources.

## ADDRESSING THE ISSUE

Oftentimes, it's assumed that the bully victim is the only person in need of counseling. That is a fallacy. The counselor is responsible for all students, including the bullies and the bystanders. A school-wide anti-bullying or character building program allows counselors to provide learning opportunities and put preventative measures in place. Some of the best school-wide anti-bullying programs stem from the behavioral approach. For example, Positive Behavior Interventions & Supports (PBIS), a school-wide reward-based program offered in most Maryland schools, employs reinforcement and token economy techniques for kind and respectful behavior. Students are able to earn points toward incentives for behaving appropriately in school. There is a plethora of tools and techniques that can be employed from behavior therapy for relational aggression issues. Reinforcers and incentives garner a great deal of buy-in from students of all ages. Maintenance and extinction are particularly useful in the secondary school environment. Unlike elementary school, secondary school offers more independence and responsibility to the student. As such, reinforcement programs should follow suit. For example, a student beginning a daily behavior chart should be given a 6-week goal, in which time the student can earn his or her way to a weekly behavior chart. By the fourth week, the student should be able to self-evaluate, filling in the chart for the teacher to review and initial. Similar to a contingency contract, professional school counselors can also use anti-bullying contracts in individual, group, and school-wide sessions.

Due to its time sensitivity, solution-focused brief counseling is very appropriate for relational aggression counseling in the school setting. With increasing caseloads of 300 plus students, and limited time for individual counseling sessions, solution-focused brief counseling (SFBC) becomes a desirable and reasonable approach. It is also useful in that it can offer a bullied student immediate solutions.

An imbalance of power is one of the main components of bullying. Oftentimes, the victim has been bullied for an extended period of time, and by the time the counselor is made aware of the situation the student is frustrated and feels powerless. Locking a student in the janitor's closet, excluding a student from peer activities, or ostracizing someone from peer social groups are purposeful acts on the part of the bully to show that the bully is in control and has significant power and influence over another student. This imbalance of power is sustained by fear, not only from the student who is bullied but also from the bystanders who witness and sometimes indirectly encourage the bully's antics, leaving the bullied student feeling lonely, hopeless, and powerless.

Within the initial counseling session, it is imperative to begin introducing the client to the notion of taking ownership of the resolution process. You can start by allowing the student who has been bullied to influence the determination of goals and empower himself or herself to control the desired outcomes of both long-term and short-term objectives. It is equally important to let the student know that although the entire issue may not be resolved that day, certain measures can be executed immediately, and to allow them to have influence as to what those initial steps may be. The counselor must be careful not to seize control of the issue, resolving it without the student's influence or involvement, because doing so would validate the student's sense of helplessness and inability to maintain control over the events in his or her life. In her seminar "It's NOT Just Joking Around," anti-bullying activist and expert Jodee Blanco (2012) offers guidance on how to introduce the intervention phase in a way that empowers the student. As a national author of anti-bullying books, including the best-seller *Please Stop Laughing at Me* (Blanco, 2010), she shares that a common mistake made is telling the victim, "I know how you feel." Rather, Blanco suggests validating the student's feelings about the circumstances. A great start to SFBC for a bullying incident is the counselor's admitting that he or she could not possibly know how the student feels at that moment: "I don't know how you feel, and I can't imagine what you're going through." Then the counselor begins processing: "Let's talk about some steps we can take together to help you with this problem." From there, begin to establish an intervention that will chip away at the situation. A bullying issue is not going to be resolved within a 45-minute session, but the school counselor can introduce effective interventions to alleviate the client's anxiety and dejection.

With the emotional, physical, and mental safety of the student being the primary concern, the appropriateness of the intervention will be determined by the severity and danger imposed by the bullying; and there are numerous interventions that may be implemented. Many states have anti-bullying laws that evolve into policies and regulations within public school systems, ensuring bullying incidents are reported to the proper stakeholders, investigated, and addressed. Such a reporting system can be very helpful and effective when used with fidelity. In states with anti-bullying laws, parents also have the option of reporting the incident to the police. If the bully is found culpable in the incident, the bully may have to enroll in an anti-bullying program through the U.S. Justice Department. In the case of more severe incidents, the bully may have to take part in a mentoring program whereby he or she checks in with police officers or at a juvenile detention facility. On the other side of the spectrum, the school counselor may implement a lower level of intervention to reestablish peer support. For example, the counselor may allow the student who was bullied to invite two peers to have lunch in his or her office, or have them walk to class with a peer group that has been trained in how to be a good bystander. A mediation session or a schedule change may be the appropriate first step, along with making all parents aware of the issue. Time is very limited in a school setting, so one intervention may be all that can be put in place that day. Yet no matter how small the intervention may seem, it can make a world of difference to the student because the counselor has given the student a sense of hope and power; something he or she may not have felt for a while. When the student reports feeling relief from the intervention, praise the student and point out how his or her participation turned the situation around. Last, it is critical to ensure that whatever the counselor agrees to put in place gets done within the time frame that was agreed upon. Make sure any timelines are realistic. It takes a lot of courage for a student to finally tell an adult about bullying, and the school counselor needs to maintain that trust.

Aspects of the psychodynamic framework are also applicable to relational aggression events. Free association, releasing unconscious thoughts and emotions without restraint, is a very useful technique to use in counseling. When conventional verbal communication is inhibited, students may feel more comfortable expressing themselves through less threatening ways such as movement, writing, or drawing; such activities provide a gateway for the counselor to analyze and interpret submerged emotions and thoughts. In addition, empowering exercises are key techniques that should be employed in relational aggression circumstances. The Adlerian technique of developing a student-defined goal and working through the barriers to attain that goal is invaluable to a bully victim. Acting "as if" is also a helpful technique that can be used at the elementary age and when employing play therapy methods.

Although the humanistic/existential paradigm doesn't offer many defined techniques, several underlying beliefs are applicable to counseling sessions for relational aggression. The three essential conditions of the student–counselor relationship (i.e., genuineness, unconditional positive regard, and empathy) are key to most counseling sessions and are extremely appropriate for relational aggression counseling. Bullying issues can leave students feeling powerless and worthless, so the existential perspective that the student has control over life outcomes offers the empowerment needed to combat those thoughts and feelings. This approval maintains the students' locus of control, while encouraging their individuality, uniqueness, and authentic self. "I" statements promote awareness and authenticity with elementary aged students; and techniques such as empty chair, role reversal, and exaggerated body movements are helpful in processing emotions, especially when the bully is unable or unwilling to participate.

Last, elements of interpersonal psychotherapy are applicable to relational aggression issues as well. Relational aggression conflicts typically require that the student reexamine friendships and explore the distress caused by those relationships. Focusing on the here and now, students can explore their expectations of friendships and weigh them against reality. Negotiating the discrepancies between the two, the student can begin to sift out the salvageable parts of relationships and adjust to distress-causing friendships. Additional strategies for addressing relational aggression and other types of bullying are provided in Table 16-1.

## IN SESSION

This complex case scenario had many unresolved factors. Maria was encountering multiple major life transitions simultaneously: She was transitioning into a new family system, beginning her first year of middle school, being introduced to a new peer group, and transitioning into the developmental stage of identity creation. As with most counseling cases, her bullying concern wasn't an isolated issue; it was multifaceted and contained many underlying layers that made her more vulnerable to bullying behaviors.

**TABLE 16-1    Additional Strategies for Addressing Bullying (Relational Aggression)**

| Paradigm | Elementary School | Middle School | High School |
| --- | --- | --- | --- |
| Psychodynamic | Analysis of defense mechanisms; "as if"; free association | Analysis of transference and defense mechanisms; goal-driven behavior; free association | Analysis of transference and defense mechanisms; goal-driven behavior; free association |
| Humanistic/ Existential | Play therapy; unconditional regard; empathy; appreciation for uniqueness; "I" statements; role playing | Unconditional regard; empathy; appreciation for uniqueness; purpose seeking; empty chair; "I" statements; role playing | Unconditional regard; empathy; appreciation for uniqueness; purpose seeking; empty chair; "I" statements; role playing; exploring life scripts |
| Behavioral/CBT | Anti-bullying contracts behavior charts; self-talk; modeling; behavior rehearsal; miracle questions; response cost; token economy; positive reinforcement rational emotive behavior therapy (REBT) | Anti-bullying contracts; behavior charts; self-talk; modeling; behavior rehearsal; miracle questions; response cost; token economy; positive reinforcement; disputing irrational beliefs; rational emotive behavior therapy (REBT) | Anti-bullying contracts; behavior charts; self-talk; modeling; behavior rehearsal; miracle questions; response cost; token economy; positive reinforcement; disputing irrational beliefs; rational emotive behavior therapy (REBT) |
| Family Systems | Educating parents on bullying signs, process, and interventions | Educating parents on bullying signs, process, and interventions | Educating parents on bullying signs, process, and interventions |
| Emergent | Storytelling; examination of interpersonal relationships; communication and social support system analysis; role playing | Storytelling; examination of interpersonal relationships; communication and social support system analysis; role playing | Storytelling; examination of interpersonal relationships; communication and social support system analysis; role playing |

Because Maria was unable to verbalize her thoughts and feelings in our first session, we began with the use of free association techniques. As she was unable to speak though her tears and anger, I gave Maria one of the journal notepads that I keep stocked in my office. I explained that sometimes in bullying situations, we lose our desire to speak out because we feel that no one will listen to us, that no one will understand. Sometimes, I said, the anger and hurt has built up so much that it's like a wall, and it's hard for the words to get through that wall. I told Maria that I respected her feelings but thought it important for her to be heard, and that I would be available to listen. I explained that the notepad was hers and that she could express herself freely in it without fear of penalty or judgment.

Maria nodded her head, agreeing to participate, and I opened the notepad to the first page. I asked Maria to express what she was thinking and feeling about the bullying situation in her journal. I told her she could write, draw, or do whatever she needed to get her emotions out. She sat frozen in her seat, unable to move past her emotional block. I gave her a worksheet with a multitude of feeling words linked to facial expressions and asked her to point to whichever one she was feeling. She pointed to three illustrations: the angry, frustrated, and sad faces. I asked her to help me understand where those feelings come from by using her notepad. Maria drew a few kids playing and talking with a bunch of little dots surrounding them. She depicted a little girl standing off to the side, crying, with a piece of paper in her hand. Written on the piece of paper was the message, "I hate Maria." I began discussing the picture with her, checking with Maria for accuracy as I went along: "This looks like a little girl crying and there are a lot of students standing around her having fun. She looks sad and alone. I wonder if that's how you feel today; that you're all alone?" She nodded her head, affirming my statement. I asked a few more questions, and Maria affirmed or refuted my statements with head nods or shakes. As our session progressed, she began to open up and started responding verbally and clarifying her answers with longer explanations. "The dots are all the students in the school. I don't really care about what they think. My grandmom-mom tells me that everyone isn't going to be your friend. But the big circles are Paula, Stacie, Melissa and Angelica. They were my friends and. . . ." She began crying. I handed her a tissue and said, "It's OK, Maria; this can't be easy for you. Take your time." "I don't have a lot of friends, and I thought they were my friends. No one wants me!" she said.

Moving into reality therapy, I challenged Maria. "I wonder if real friends say things like this" I said, pointing toward the "I hate Maria" message she drew in her picture. We began processing the qualities of real friendships, defining the various levels—best friend, friend, and acquaintance—and exploring the various levels of trust and expectations for each. Comparing Maria's current friendships to those expectations, we discovered that her distress was caused by her assigning them the trust and expectations that they weren't worthy of, leading her to feelings of betrayal.

Maria and I came up with a short- and a long-term goal that would help her achieve the relationships she desired. Maria liked the bowl of written affirmations I had on my desk, so she decided that her short-term goal was to give herself a positive affirmation every day, confirming her self-worth. As a long-term goal, Maria wanted to develop new friendships. I also referred her to an in-school community counseling program specifically for adopted children, enabling her and her grandparents to work through their family transitions. Breaking her long-term goal into smaller, more manageable assignments, she began by surveying her classrooms and the lunchroom for students who had the friendship qualities she was looking for. Each week she was allowed to invite two friends to have lunch in the counseling office with her.

As her friendships progressed, we worked on the social skills needed to generate and maintain quality friendships. We spoke in depth about establishing reasonable expectations of trust and reciprocation, which aligned well with her counseling sessions with the adoption specialist. As we progressed toward her long-term goal of developing new friendships, we sorted through good friends and not-so-good friends, and worked on coping and conflict resolution skills. Although not to the same extent as her initial conflict, she did encounter other peer conflicts during the school year. We resolved those conflicts, settling them through peer mediation. Eventually, I noticed that Maria was expressing less and less desire to come to my office. She was eating lunch with a new group of girls and preferred to stay in class. She had more confidence and was expressing a desire to be more independent. Approximately three months from our initial meeting, we concluded our final individual session.

The formal bullying report and investigation determined three students were responsible for bullying Maria. The school resource officer reviewed the Facebook page, pulling student data from the site, and shut it down. All the parents, including Maria's grandparents, and the students were required to attend a conference the next morning with the school principal, the school officer, and the professional school counselor. The parents were made aware of the findings of the investigation, the school's policy regarding bullying, and the legal ramifications. The students were given the opportunity to tell their parents the extent of their involvement in the incident and make amends for their behavior. Two of the three girls expressed extreme remorse, but one, the student who started the Facebook page, was unapologetic. Concerned for Maria's safety, her grandparents requested that Maria's schedule be changed so she no longer had classes or lunch with the unapologetic student. All three girls were assigned school consequences, and Maria's grandparents decided to exercise their right to press charges, taking the unrepentant student to court. The court deemed that the student did bully Maria; consequently, that student had to enroll in a mandatory anti-bullying program that required her to check in with a mentor police officer weekly and attend anti-bullying classes twice a month for 6 months. I never had any other bullying issues from any of the three young girls for their remaining middle school years.

## Outcome

At the end of the third semester Maria returned to my office, requesting to speak with me. I still saw her every now and again when she reported to the counseling office for her weekly sessions with the adoption counselor, but she hadn't had a reoccurring bullying issue in a long time. She stepped in my office with four of her friends behind her and asked that I sponsor her anti-bullying group. She handed me a proposal, a piece of wrinkled paper with smeared ketchup in the upper right corner, outlining some ideas and goals the girls had for the group. Beaming with pride, I readily agreed. The student-run group facilitated and sponsored food drives, anti-bullying assemblies, and collaborated with the PBIS team to develop school-wide character building events. I could tell that Maria felt empowered, and she was sharing that power with her peers. She continued her counseling for her adoption-related concerns with her grandparents. At the end of the year, she told

me her grandparents were moving so they could be closer to her mother, who was incarcerated out of state. Her grandparents withdrew her during the summer, and she did not return the following year.

I never heard from Maria or her family again, although I have thought of her often. Having moved out of state, her transfer was listed simply as "out-of-state," impeding any attempt to check on her transition to her new school. Nonetheless, her anti-bullying group continued, meeting with me regularly. They established a group mission and vision statement, established rules, and recruited like-minded students. They implemented a few school-wide events that school year, such as collecting money for victims of an international disaster and food for victims of a national disaster and organizing an anti-bullying rally; and the group began a peer support group that mentored students throughout the school year.

## Final Process Questions

It's not uncommon to come across adults who do not take bullying seriously because they're of the mindset that "kids will be kids," and teasing and roughhousing are just a part of growing up. Some school communities may seem to be culturally infused with bullying behaviors that adult stakeholders perceive to be the norm. Consider a school that is serving a low socioeconomic community with high needs and limited access to community resources. The culture of the community may be primarily motivated by basic psychological and security needs, as mentioned in Maslow's hierarchy of needs, and therefore ranks anti-bullying behavior low on its list of priorities. An affluent school that fosters competitiveness and is motivated by the prestige that comes with an accomplished reputation may demonstrate extreme hesitation in assigning consequences to the school's trophy-winning quarterback who loves to physically and verbally taunt the smaller students, or the class valedictorian who relentlessly mocks the meeker and less affluent students.

Be prepared to counsel and educate teachers, administrators, and even parents about the importance of preventing bullying. I have found that even when stakeholders struggle to be empathetic to the intangible consequences that do not affect them directly (i.e., the mental, emotional, and physical effects of bullying), they are able to appreciate the sphere and reach of state laws, policies, and regulations to which they are held accountable. Last, before processing the intricacies of a case, it is important for counselors to check themselves for any cultural bias that may impede the counseling process. A good question to ask in this case may be, "Do I have any bias or strong emotions concerning relational aggression or bullying that may act as a barrier to my client or blur my analysis of this issue?" If one finds oneself with barriers, invest in attending speaking engagements, training seminars, and speak with students and family members who have experienced bullying to gain a better understanding of the issue.

Dan Olweus (1993), the founding father of bullying research and prevention, defined *bullying* as "A student is being bullied or victimized when he or she is exposed, repeatedly and over time, to negative actions on the part of one or more other students" (p. 9). Most definitions of bullying embrace the framework of this definition, expanding on the identifying behaviors of bullying. Forty-nine states have passed anti-bullying laws. School counselors must ensure that they are familiar with state laws and legislation regarding bullying (Policies & Laws, 2012). School counseling programs should have a clear definition of bullying that is aligned with their state's laws and their school district's definition of bullying.

Bullying issues seldom go away overnight. Students often bully in hopes of elevating their social status, so it is not uncommon for other students to impulsively join in. That being said, it is important to continue to monitor the situation even after a particular conflict has been resolved. Be sure to keep an eye out for self-isolating behavior, and assist the student in filling in those social gaps. Also, empowerment is the key. I cannot stress enough the usefulness of an effective school-wide anti-bullying or character building program at the primary and secondary school levels. Empower students to lead the change and take ownership of a positive school environment. The Olweus (1993) program integrates student participation in its program; and numerous programs, grants, and competitions encourage students to initiate, share, and take ownership of the anti-bullying revolution. Peer mentor programs, peer mediation groups, and service learning projects are wonderful opportunities for students to practice empathy and explore these issues; it will make a world of difference for everyone in the school.

- What are the components of an effective anti-bullying plan or program?
- Which stakeholders should be included in your program?

## Resources

Any good anti-bullying program will consist of the following five main components: an assessment to determine the needs and deficit areas of one's school; a clearly defined bullying definition; policies and rules structured around this definition; reoccurring education for stakeholders on a consistent basis; and opportunities for engagement by stakeholders, allowing them to take part in bullying prevention planning and intervention activities. A plethora of research, tools, programs, and resources related to bullying saturates the research and educational market. Deciding which resources will best serve a particular school and stakeholder community will greatly depend on the culture of the school and its needs.

A good place to start with any bullying program would be to assess one's school community. Olweus (1993) has researched and studied bullying behavior and interventions for over three decades. A leading expert in the field, he's considered the founding father of bullying research. His world-renowned book, *Bullying at School: What We Know and What We Can Do*, is respected in the fields of counseling and psychology. Passing its extensive litmus test, his Bullying Prevention Program has been accepted nationally as a model program by the U.S. Department of Justice and includes assessments for use in conducting research. Nonetheless, this program may not be for every school, as it is fairly expensive, costing thousands of dollars to implement with fidelity. It also requires dedicated participation from various stakeholders, including parents, multiple teachers, a counselor, nonteaching staff, the school resource officer, the school principal, and the playground supervisor.

Numerous other programs offer assessment tools, lesson plans, and program resources. Many school counseling supervisors and coordinators have programs that are purchased by the school system, making licenses and material available to schools that express the desire to use them. Consult with your site supervisor or school counseling coordinator to determine what is already available to you. Collaborating with other counselors in your school building and school system is also helpful, as many of them have probably implemented effective programs and lesson plans.

Last, bullying is a popular topic in education, and many educational and counseling associations have taken notice and now provide resources to educators. Search the websites of professional organizations of interest. I have found many useful bullying prevention research articles, resources, and lesson plans through the following websites:

American Counseling Association, http://www.counseling.org/

American School Counselor Association, http://www.schoolcounselor.org/

U.S. Department of Education, http://www.ed.gov/

*Chapter 17*

# Bullying (Physical Aggression)

Caron N. Coles

## CASE BACKGROUND

I recall my elementary years with fondness. I was an eager learner and enjoyed the small, as well as significant, events of the school day. "Reading Is Fundamental" was the mantra, and I looked forward to the free RIF books, the weekly Math Power drills, the bag lunches that we could eat outside, and the arguments with friends over the best song from the *Thriller* album. My experience as a professional school counselor has revealed that there are far more fundamental concerns that consume students' thoughts as they consider their school experience. For many elementary school students, bullying is all too familiar. Bullying, a form of aggression, has the potential to negatively affect student learning and cause lasting harm for bullies, victims, and bystanders. Professional school counselors share in the responsibility to promote an academic environment conducive to learning—for all students. Among the additional functions of professional school counselors is our role in advocating for students' academic, physical, emotional, and psychological well-being.

The mention of student welfare prompts me to reflect on the experience of an African American male student that I had the privilege of working with. Calvin was a kindergartner when I met him. During the week, he lived with his mother, stepfather, and older brother. At the time, Calvin's mother was pregnant and later gave birth to his little brother. Calvin also spent time with his grandfather during the week. Usually, Calvin spent weekends with his father, his father's girlfriend, and several children referred to as step-siblings.

Initially, Calvin was referred to me by his classroom teacher for school counseling services due to maladaptive behaviors such as verbal outbursts, refusal to complete work, destruction of school supplies and materials, and failure to comply with adult instructions. I contacted Calvin's mother to discuss the concerns identified by his teacher and explain the school counseling services offered. This was also an opportunity to obtain background information regarding her impressions of Calvin's behavior within his home environment. According to his mother, Calvin's actions at home were not aggressive and he complied with her instructions. However, she provided written consent allowing him to participate in individual and small group counseling. I scheduled meetings with Calvin individually and included him in a small group counseling experience. Sometimes, however, we had impromptu meetings as I worked with Calvin to assist in the current crisis. While still honoring confidentiality, which is essential to the counselor–client relationship, it was helpful to check in with Calvin's mother to report on the themes that surfaced. I also informed her of some of the activities that Calvin completed during our sessions.

Eventually, Calvin's behaviors escalated to the point that he was suspended for being physically aggressive toward peers and staff members. On several occasions, I met with Calvin's mother, and we discussed her preferred manner of handling his in-school behavior and consequences, both positive and negative, for his actions. We brainstormed ideas on how to demonstrate the home–school connection for Calvin, who seemed disconnected from the idea that behavior at school could be applied to privileges at home and that consequences may be positive or negative. Communication was maintained between Calvin's mother and teacher through his agenda notebook. In addition, we worked together to create a plan for how Calvin's mother could integrate a positive discipline approach in her home. This might include holding a family meeting to discuss the existing rules within their home and the rationale behind the establishment of each rule. She would then identify three to five "must-have" rules; explain the expectations underlying the rules; and invite feedback from all family members to create positive and negative consequences to apply when expectations were and were not met. As well, I offered information on birth order that could be helpful in understanding Calvin, as he would soon be a "middle child" in his mother's home once his little brother was born.

Following parent conferences, multiple suspensions, a child study meeting, and collaboration with district officials, Calvin's schedule was adjusted, and he attended school for half of the day rather than the full school day. Despite the shortened school day, Calvin continued to receive discipline referrals for attacking a classmate with a pencil, cursing, using threatening gestures, bullying, and intimidating students with his physical presence (he was bigger than many other kindergarteners and played sports). During one incident, Calvin targeted a first grader on the bus, yelled and screamed, moved in and out of his seat, and punched the student repeatedly. Following an administrative investigation, he was placed on long-term suspension.

## INITIAL PROCESS QUESTIONS

- What previous experience does Calvin have in an academic setting? Preschool experience?
- What triggers Calvin's outbursts?
- What happens after his outbursts?
- Which needs are not being met at school? At home?
- What is Calvin's role within his family? His school community?
- How might academic ability factor into Calvin's behavior?
- What evaluations have been completed inside or outside of school?
- What implications might suspension have?

## ADDRESSING THE ISSUES

In working with Calvin, it was important to use the core counseling skills (humanistic/ existential approach) emphasized during my graduate study: encouraging, paraphrasing, reflecting feelings, appropriate questioning, and summarizing. The theoretical backbone of the interventions I used with Calvin were primarily an integrative approach aligned with a cognitive-behavioral emphasis, such as solution-focused brief counseling and behavioral counseling, in addition to choice theory. I recognized that, in many ways, Calvin was doing what he knew to do in order to get what he wanted. At the same time, I recognized that by highlighting his positive behaviors, I could increase the likelihood of Calvin using more appropriate behaviors to meet his needs. The ultimate goal of my counseling interventions was to assist Calvin in thinking differently about his experiences of misbehavior: specifically, helping him think in different ways about the meaning he seems to assign to his experiences of misbehavior. I wanted him to learn more appropriate ways of getting his needs met.

During individual meetings with Calvin, I initially established rapport by using art therapy techniques. For example, I encouraged him to complete a family portrait and then identified themes in his drawing. In a later session, we used a sheet of paper from a large roll and drew a life-sized figure of Calvin. After he completed the drawing, we discussed a time when he felt angry and the bodily sensations he recalled. I wrote his thoughts as he dictated the feelings experienced in his hands, legs, chest, mouth, throat, and face. We later created a picture of a volcano and labeled it with situations that often triggered his anger. Another useful intervention was to discuss the importance of filtering speech. This concept was illustrated through the use of thought and speech bubbles. Using hypothetical situations mostly based on reality, Calvin was encouraged to share the first thought that popped into his head, and we wrote that in the thought bubble. We then explored how others might react to his thought if he spoke it aloud. After considering the consequences, Calvin crafted a more appropriate response, and we wrote that in the speech bubble.

A behavior plan was created to monitor Calvin's classroom behaviors. His teachers awarded his appropriate behavior with stickers, encouragement, and extra privileges. Initially, Calvin seemed eager to please. He sat up straight and gave me the thumbs up when I went to his classroom to observe his progress. He thrived on the positive recognition. He was also allowed to join me for Lunch Bunch as recognition for his efforts. We were diligent in acknowledging the exceptions to Calvin's misbehavior. We practiced relaxation techniques and retaught school and classroom expectations. Surprisingly, his unpredictable behavior continued. To explore further, we discussed the changes that were taking place within his family and considered the impact that these events had on him. Calvin attended a few small group meetings with me. During one group meeting, we simulated potential stress-inducing situations by playing board games. Prior to the game, we reviewed the rules and discussed appropriate ways to express anger and frustration, as well as the importance of being a good sport and supporting group members. Calvin experienced success at times, but was later removed from the group due to yelling and behaving aggressively by tossing chairs and yelling at group members.

There appeared to be constant communication between the school and Calvin's parents. I provided referrals for community-based resources that might assist his parents. I collaborated with administrators and teachers, along with the school social worker and school psychologist. The school's parent involvement specialist was brought in and visited Calvin's dad on his job during one of Calvin's suspensions. There was an outpouring of assistance, yet Calvin's mother appeared resistant. Ultimately, Calvin received a long-term suspension and began receiving home-based instruction. Listed in Table 17-1 are several additional ideas to consider when working with students who become physically aggressive.

| TABLE 17-1 | Additional Approaches for Working With Physically Aggressive Students | | |
| --- | --- | --- | --- |
| Paradigm | Elementary School | Middle School | High School |
| Psychodynamic | Empty chair; role playing | Empty chair; role playing; exploring unconscious themes through use of a timeline to chart significant life events | Empty chair; role playing; exploring unconscious themes through use of a timeline to chart significant life events; exploring unconscious through student's interpretation of dreams, thoughts, and self-talk |
| Humanistic/ Existential | Emphasizing the counselor–student relationship; focus on the person the student desires to be through art therapy techniques (mask activity) | Emphasizing the counselor–student relationship; focus on the person the student desires to be through art therapy techniques (mask activity); encouraging student to write a letter to his or her ideal self | Emphasizing the counselor–student relationship; focus on the person the student desires to be through art therapy techniques (mask activity); encouraging student to write a letter to his or her ideal self; allowing student to analyze ads for their messages; consideration of the ads' role in society and the meaning of his or her choices |
| Behavioral/CBT | Behavior intervention plans; scaling questions to address degree of catastrophizing; positive reframing to challenge negative predictions; miracle question | Behavior intervention plans; scaling questions to address degree of catastrophizing; positive reframing to challenge negative predictions; miracle question; exposure therapy; mentoring | Behavior intervention plans; scaling questions to address degree of catastrophizing; positive reframing to challenge negative predictions; miracle question; exposure therapy; mentoring; identifying assumptions; challenging irrational thinking |
| Family Systems | Genogram; analysis of family rules and expectations; evaluation of communication style; exploration of conflict management techniques; parent training | Genogram; analysis of family rules and expectations; evaluation of communication style; exploration of conflict management techniques; parent training | Genogram; analysis of family rules and expectations; evaluation of communication style; exploration of conflict management techniques; parent training |
| Emergent | Fill-in-the-blank exercises; sentence stems; free association; word sort activities; coat of arms | Fill-in-the-blank exercises; sentence stems; free association; word sort activities; coat of arms; writing an autobiography; practicing deconstructing beliefs; experimenting with perspective taking | Fill-in-the-blank exercises; sentence stems; free association; word sort activities; coat of arms; writing an autobiography; practicing deconstructing beliefs; experimenting with perspective taking |

## IN SESSION

| | |
|---|---|
| COUNSELOR (C): | Calvin, let's talk about the referral you got yesterday. |
| STUDENT (S): | For when I got mad? |
| C: | Right. You were very upset yesterday and made some choices that got you in trouble. Tell me about what happened. |
| S: | It wasn't my fault. I raised my hand but she never called on me. |
| C: | Sounds like you were disappointed because you wanted a chance to share and you didn't get to. So what did you decide to do when she didn't call on you? |
| S: | I got mad. |
| C: | Mad? And what happened? |
| S: | I just got mad. |
| C: | Imagine that you were the teacher yesterday and you saw a student doing what you did. How would you have known that the student was mad? |
| S: | I pushed my chair and pushed David. |
| C: | Uh-hmm. |
| S: | I had to sharpen my pencil. |
| C: | Let me make sure I have this right. You raised your hand to share, but when the teacher didn't call on you, you felt let down and then got angry. Your anger was bottled up inside and you decided to let it out by moving around. So you decided to sharpen your pencil and you pushed your chair and David on the way to the sharpener. |
| S: | Uh-hmm. |
| C: | What was the message you were sending? |
| S: | Hmm? |
| C: | What did you want people to know when you decided to do those things? |
| S: | That I was mad. |
| C: | Tell me about a time when you were mad but you didn't push your chair and you didn't push anyone. |
| S: | I don't know. |
| C: | Imagine other ways that you have been able to let people know how you were feeling. |
| S: | Tell them. |
| C: | Tell them? So what could you have said yesterday? |
| S: | I could tell my teacher that I was mad. |

| | |
|---|---|
| C: | And how would you explain the reason that you were mad? |
| S: | She never calls on me. |
| C: | Say that using your "I" message. |
| S: | Hmm? |
| C: | How would you say it if you wanted to tell her what happened, how you felt, and what you want to happen instead? |
| S: | I was mad because she didn't call on me and I want a turn too. |

## Outcome

There were behavior milestones and celebrations along the way. Unfortunately, however, Calvin's behaviors became so severe that the safety of those around him superseded his ability to continue in a mainstream setting. He never returned to our school following the conclusion of his long-term suspension, as his mother selected an alternative educational setting.

## Final Process Questions

- What limitations to intervention existed?
- How might the school's crisis management system be employed in this situation?
- How can schools foster positive relationships with parents?
- What advocacy measures were in place for Calvin?
- How might the professional school counselor's role have been expanded?
- In what ways might one's family of origin shape one's worldview?
- How might breaches of confidentiality influence counseling relationships with minors?

## Resources

Burk, L. R., Armstrong, J. M., Park, J., Zahn-Waxler, C., Klein, M. H., & Essex, M. J. (2011). Stability of early identified aggressive victim status in elementary school and associations with later mental health problems and functional impairments. *Journal of Abnormal Child Psychology, 39*, 225–238.

Joussemet, M., Vitaro, F., Barker, E. D., Cote, S., Nagin, D. S., Zoccolillo, M., & Tremblay, R. E. (2008). Controlling parenting and physical aggression during elementary school. *Child Development, 79*, 411–425.

Renouf, A., Brendgen, M., Seguin, J. R., Vitaro, F., Boivin, M., Dionne, G., & Perusse, D. (2010). Interactive links between theory of mind, peer victimization, and reactive and proactive aggression. *Journal of Abnormal Child Psychology, 38*, 1109–1123.

Snyder, J., Cramer, A., Afrank, J., & Patterson, G. R. (2005). The contributions of ineffective discipline and parental hostile attributions of child misbehavior to the development of conduct problems at home and school. *Developmental Psychology, 41*(1), 30–41.

*Chapter 18*

# Helping Students Who Are Lesbian, Gay, Bisexual, Transgender, and Questioning (LGBTQ)

Brandy K. Richeson and Rebekah Byrd

## CASE BACKGROUND

Christian was a 12-year-old, fifth-grade male student who had been at the school since third grade. We worked together on several issues throughout the school year including problems with other students, teachers, and his parents, as well as some personal issues. He was a little older and bigger than the other fifth-grade students, and he had problems fitting in. Also, because Christian and I had worked together previously, I knew that Christian had a great relationship with his mother (which is an important note for this particular case scenario), and I had also spoken with her many times as she was involved with the school and had come to counseling sessions in the past.

When Christian came to my office one morning, he was visibly shaken. As we sat down to talk, he confided in me that he'd had a dream that made him feel very "weird." He went on to tell me that he had dreamed about having a sexual encounter with another male. He also kept saying that he was worried about and feared that he was gay. He said, "There's nothing wrong with people who are gay, but I don't want to be like that." This was my second year working as a school counselor and the first time a student had shared a dream involving a sexual encounter. Although I was unsure of where to go with this conversation with a 12-year-old, I knew that he needed me at that moment. I think that it could be noted that I more clearly understood Christian's affectional/sexual orientation identity because of my previous conversations with Heather (Christian's mother). However, understanding Christian is my primary role and responsibility regardless of what a parent may be concerned with or tell me about his or her child. As school counselors we often face juggling the information and concerns of parents with seeking to understand the concerns of our students. And sometimes the two simply don't match up.

In this case scenario, it is imperative for a school counselor to note the importance of his or her own beliefs and biases related to affectional/sexual orientation. "Ethical counseling practice is dependent on the counselors' awareness of their attitudes toward individuals from minority groups" (Byrd & Hays, 2012, p. 1). Awareness of and understanding for the need of affirming attitudes are necessary for the therapeutic alliance and the counseling process. If these components are lacking, the relationships could be harmed (Matthews & Bieschke, 2001). School counselors must understand and be aware of the influence of their personal beliefs on lesbian, gay, bisexual, transgendered, and questioning (LGBTQ) individuals. In this case scenario, it would be important to determine whether one's discomfort in talking about a sexual dream was exacerbated by the same-gender component of the dream. If that factor did increase the discomfort, was attention paid so that the discomfort wasn't communicated to the client? Also, if there is discomfort regarding same-gender sexual contact, then we school counselors want to do our own work so we do not project any of our discomfort or confusion onto the client.

I was also struck by Christian's discussion of "gay." He stated that there was nothing wrong with being gay, but also noted that he didn't want to be gay. Such a remark seemed to note his acceptance of others being gay, but also indicated he would not accept himself as gay. This expression provided some information in terms of how Christian accepts differences because he could have stated that he worried about being gay because being gay was "wrong," which is a view he did not convey. School counselors should note how these conversations could have been different based on the student's understanding or views about being lesbian or gay. It seemed as though Christian was already somewhat nonjudgmental of diversity of affectional/sexual orientations. Many students who present with issues of affectional/sexual orientation identity may not have a well-developed understanding of biological sex, gender role, gender identity, and affectional/sexual orientation. It is necessary for school counselors to note the differences in similar cases and ponder what would have been different in this case if Christian were not as accepting of affectional/sexual orientation diversity.

In working with any adolescent, it is important for professional school counselors to keep in mind possible risk factors. Adolescents who are LGBTQ identified face particular risk factors that may include suicide ideations, psychological care, depression, substance abuse, and high-risk sexual behaviors (Stone, 2003; Vare & Norton, 1998; Weiler, 2004). In this case scenario, Christian was potentially presenting as a questioning youth. It would be imperative to approach this case with individualized care, as each case is different. A protective factor for LGBTQ youth is having a supportive adult present in the school (McCabe & Rubinson, 2008). Thus it is essential for professional school counselors to understand their roles and responsibilities in working with LGBTQ adolescents and to provide a safe atmosphere for all students. I understood my ethical codes and guidelines, was familiar with ASCA's position statement on LGBTQ youth (American School Counselor Association, 2007, 2010), and worked to provide a safe, supportive, and affirming atmosphere for Christian.

As we continued to talk, Christian told me that he had also shared this dream with a classmate, who then told the other students in his class. If Christian is gay, it is important to consider the notion that developmental concerns can be exacerbated by the individual's decision whether to hide or disclose his or her affectional/sexual orientation (Harrison, 2003). Further, by keeping affectional/sexual orientation and identities secret, youth who are LGTBQ are denied, and deny themselves, positive role models. Future school counselors should note the multiple concerns present for each individual with whom they are working. By being up-to-date on research, literature, and by understanding aspects of Christian's case that make it unique, I was better able to support him.

In Christian's case, the students started calling him "gay boy." However, it is also important to understand that bullying and victimization of peers includes homoprejudiced epithets directed at heterosexual individuals as well as youth who are LGBTQ (Espelage & Swearer, 2008; Swearer, Turner, Givens, & Pollack, 2008). Therefore, professional school counselors must not assume that a student is LGBTQ just because he or she is being called names. Fineran (2001) indicated that youth who are LGBTQ are more likely than heterosexual youth to be sexually harassed at school. Thus, students who are LGBTQ are victims of acts of school violence and sexual harassment, and nearly one-third of the students who reported assaults of harassment to a school official or staff member stated that school staff did nothing (Kosciw, Diaz, & Greytak, 2008). Many issues of assault and harassment go unreported as well. Key findings from the Gay, Lesbian, and Straight Education Network's (GLSEN; Kosciw et al., 2008, p. 41) most recent school climate study reported the following in reference to students' reporting of harassment and assault in school:

- The majority of students who were harassed or assaulted in school did not report the incident to either school staff or a family member.
- Among students who did not report being harassed or assaulted to school staff, the most common reasons given for not reporting were the beliefs (1) that staff would not effectively address the situation or (2) that reporting would make the situation worse in some way.
- Only about a third of students who reported incidents of victimization to school personnel said that staff effectively addressed the problem. In fact, when asked to describe how staff responded to reported incidents of victimization, students most commonly said that no action was taken.

I was reminded once more of the importance of being an advocate for Christian and others like him, and the need for bullying prevention programs that include LGBTQ information.

Given statistics that discuss the lack of reporting of bullying and the lack of intervention after a report was made, I was so humbled that Christian came to me. I knew how important it was to look at multiple aspects of this case as I considered ways to intervene. I was also reminded of the many students who may never come to see me or any other school personnel to discuss affectional/sexual orientation issues. Future school counselors should consider the fact that there may be individuals in their schools who are dealing with affectional/sexual orientation identity issues and yet may never seek an adult's assistance. It is obviously incorrect to assume that there are no LGBTQ students in one's school based on the fact that none have identified themselves as such to the school counselor.

Christian and I talked for a while longer. After listening to Christian tell about his feelings, his talk with his classmate, the name-calling (bullying), and the discussions he had already had with his mother, we both thought it would be a good idea to call his mom, Heather, with whom he was very close.

An important caution for future school counselors is to consider when it is necessary to contact parents/guardians regarding a confidential and trusted sharing by a client. It can be harmful to the student and damaging to the counseling relationship to contact a student's parents/guardians when he or she has come out to you or even shared his or her questioning regarding affectional/sexual orientation. Research notes that after a family member found out about affectional/sexual orientation or after the individual came out to family, 22% of gay and lesbian youth reported being sexually abused by a family member (Gonsiorek, 1988). Further, many LGBTQ adolescents may find themselves in unbearable home situations that result in running away or even being forced to leave home (Harrison, 2003; Weiler, 2004). Disclosure to an unsupportive family member or guardian can lead to adolescents resorting to any means of supporting themselves. For these reasons and more, the consideration of disclosure needs to be assessed *extensively* with the student, with colleagues in consultation, and with a trusted mentor before a call is made to parents/guardians. If school policies and procedures indicate otherwise, the school counselor should be a strong advocate for policy change. He or she needs to work hard to inform administrators, faculty, and staff of the sensitive nature of this and other issues; remind them of confidentiality expectations; and provide in-service training to all school personnel on LGBTQ issues and school liability related to this topic.

Possessing pertinent knowledge, awareness, and skills for working with LGBTQ individuals is ethically imperative given the detrimental consequences and risk factors discussed. Many issues warrant careful consideration for this population. For example, pressuring individuals to come out to others can be detrimental (Gagne, Tewksbury, & McGaughey, 1997; Lemoire & Chen, 2005). Possible repercussions such as familial and peer rejection, financial and emotional consequences because of rejections, violence, and other concerns are all issues related to the coming out process (Gagne et al., 1997; Harrison, 2003). A breach of confidentiality by counselors in regard to affectional/sexual orientation has led some LGBTQ individuals to complete suicides (Black & Underwood, 1998). A negative coming out experience can lead to heightened feelings of rejection, which may increase mental and emotional distress and risky behaviors (Lemoire & Chen, 2005). In regard to the coming out process, it is also important to consider that when adolescents are at this point, it is essential to provide them with a safe atmosphere. Given these consequences, understanding the needs of this population may equip counselors and educators to provide the necessary support system to promote success for these students (Callahan, 2001). These factors had already been considered with this particular case scenario, and Christian's mother was contacted, at Christian's request, in order to assist Christian and provide support. When Heather arrived, she informed me that Christian had been discussing this issue for quite a while. Heather was very supportive of her son and willing to assist him as needed.

## INITIAL PROCESS QUESTIONS

- What is my role as a school counselor in assisting students who might be questioning their affectional/sexual orientation?
- What is my role as a school counselor in assisting students who are seeking to understand LGBTQ-related concerns?
- What in-school issues facing students who are LGBTQ need to be addressed?
- Does Christian, and other students who are LGBTQ identified, feel safe in this school? At home? In the community?
- What can the school do to create a more positive atmosphere for all students?
- Which theoretical approaches would work best to serve students who are LGBTQ?
- How can schools infuse diversity training and promote affirmation of others?
- What is the best way to address those students who bully without making the situation worse for Christian or other students who are being bullied?
- What are the ethical and legal ramifications of NOT addressing affectional/sexual orientation with students?

## ADDRESSING THE ISSUES

There were several issues that needed to be addressed to assist Christian, and in my role as a professional school counselor I knew that I had to be very careful how I dealt with them. There were two primary issues of immediate concern. First, I believed that it was important to get Christian the help needed in his identity development journey for wherever that path may lead. Second, harassing and bullying behavior toward Christian needed to be confronted. I explained to Heather (his mother) that in addition to Christian having me as a resource at school it would be very helpful for him also to see a counselor in the community. I spoke with my director of counseling and guidance and several of my colleagues to get referrals for counselors who specialized in working with adolescents who are LGBTQ. After collecting several recommendations, I passed the information on to Heather, who worked very diligently to get an appointment for Christian.

Next I had to figure out how to address the bullying behaviors. I decided that the best way to do so without drawing additional attention to Christian, would be to speak to the entire grade level. I presented a classroom guidance lesson in every fifth-grade classroom about kindness and acceptance. The lesson emphasized the importance of being unique, glorified personal differences, and taught the students to be accepting of persons who are different. As a follow-up to the lesson, I also had the assistant principal speak about kindness and bullying on the school announcements. She communicated about the value of kindness and the consequences of bullying, while encouraging each student to do his or her part to make the school a fun and safe place for everyone. The intervention seemed to have made the students more aware of their actions and eased much of the taunting with which Christian had been dealing. Although I knew that it was just the beginning in terms of bullying prevention and creating an accepting, affirming school climate, it was a step in the right direction. From this experience, I learned how important it is to be proactive, so every year since, I have started the school year with similar lessons for each grade level school-wide.

To help Christian, I operated from an integrative approach. Even though I firmly believe that a humanistic approach often works best to show students genuineness and empathy, I knew that I would also need to incorporate other theories, such as constructivism, to honor Christian's own perspective/meaning and his reality. Further, because negative thoughts and beliefs can affect one's actions, it was important for me to work with Christian to identify and change his negative belief patterns. This does not mean that he would alter his belief that the dream might reflect an attraction to males; but instead, if that is the meaning, that he would examine how his identity as questioning or even gay identified might be affirmed.

Christian and I met weekly on a set schedule, and he could also come see me as needed. To challenge some of Christian's irrational beliefs and internalized homoprejudice, we used biblioguidance (Frank & Cannon, 2009). We reviewed books that I purchased by and about LGBTQ persons so that he could see the wonderful things being done by lesbian and gay individuals, that being "like that" was one part of one's identity, and that many lesbian and gay individuals were very self-affirming. He seemed to enjoy learning and hearing about different people, and I really began to see a difference in his attitude about gay individuals and about being gay. An important aspect of creating a safe school environment is having books, resources, and other information about

LGBTQ individuals readily available in the school library, on bulletin boards celebrating diversity, and infused in all classroom guidance lessons.

Christian and I spent time talking about his dream, the name-calling at school, and Christian's feelings toward girls and boys. I think having these discussions was helpful in showing Christian that one's affectional/sexual orientation is only a part of who someone is, and it doesn't exclusively define the person. I would like to believe that my nonjudgmental attitude and genuineness were helpful in successfully getting Christian through his fifth-grade year.

Whereas Christian happened to be a 12-year-old fifth grader, LGBTQ issues can and do occur often in middle and high school as well. Christian's level of understanding and development was not that of a typical middle or high school student, but many of the same strategies I used with him could also be effective with students in any grade level.

Biblioguidance is an effective approach because it challenges a heteronormative atmosphere by showing students that there are gay people who are positive role models in our communities. Although Christian's mother had told me that Christian was gay, he never directly expressed that to me, and I did not directly ask him or force him to define himself. As the school counselor, I believed it was my job to assist in countering any possible negative thoughts he may hold about people who are gay (although he indicated he doesn't have negative thoughts about others, only about himself as gay, I still felt this was an important aspect to address) and to present some opportunities for Christian to see people who are gay in a more positive light, regardless of his own affectional/sexual orientation. Further, it was my role to assist Christian in feeling safe and protected when coming to school, which I did by addressing and challenging the negative remarks coming from his classmates. I would follow the same steps for youth at the middle or high school levels, adjusting for maturity level. Table 18-1 provides alternative techniques and strategies for working with students dealing with affectional/sexual orientation issues at all grade levels.

## IN SESSION

The following is a portion of the session previously described in which Christian discusses his dream and his feelings about people who are gay.

| STUDENT: (CHRISTIAN) (S) | Last night I dreamed that I was with a male, touching him and he was touching me. |
|---|---|
| COUNSELOR (C): | How do you feel about that? |
| S: | Disgusted. I know there are nice people who are gay, but I don't want to be that way. |
| C: | What is "that way"? |
| S: | You know. Gay. |
| C: | You are thinking you don't want to be that way. I am curious to know, what does it mean for someone to be gay? |
| S: | It means boys like boys and girls like girls. |
| C: | Hmmm, so you are wondering what having a dream like that means for you. |

**TABLE 18-1  Approaches for Working With LGBTQ Students**

| Paradigm | Elementary School | Middle School | High School |
|---|---|---|---|
| Psychodynamic | Use of free association; relationship of events and current functioning; dream analysis | Use of free association; relationship of events and current functioning; dream analysis; interpretation | Use of free association; relationship of events and current functioning; dream analysis; interpretation |
| Humanistic/ Existential | Focus on the therapeutic relationship; use of role play, role reversal, and "I" statements; focus on freedom and responsibility | Focus on the therapeutic relationship; use of role play, role reversal, and "I" statements; focus on freedom and responsibility | Focus on the therapeutic relationship; use of role play, role reversal, and "I" statements; focus on freedom and responsibility |
| Behavioral/CBT | Disputing irrational beliefs through education (e.g., biblioguidance); cognitive restructuring; modeling; role play; developing coping strategies; self-talk | Disputing irrational beliefs through education (e.g., biblioguidance); cognitive restructuring; modeling; role play; developing coping strategies; self-talk; visual imagery | Disputing irrational beliefs through education (e.g., biblioguidance); cognitive restructuring; modeling, role play; developing coping strategies; self-talk; visual imagery |
| Family Systems | Teaching family strategies to address behavioral, academic, and/or social issues; questions; "I" positions; teaching individuality despite family pressure | Teaching family strategies to address behavioral, academic, and/or social issues; questions; "I" positions; teaching individuality despite family pressure | Teaching family strategies to address behavioral, academic, and/or social issues; questions; "I" positions; teaching individuality despite family pressure |
| Emergent | Therapeutic alliance; empowerment; focus on communication; role playing; exploring alternative explanations to problems; question and challenge | Therapeutic alliance; empowerment; focus on communication; role playing; exploring alternative explanations to problems; question and challenge | Therapeutic alliance; empowerment; focus on communication; role playing; exploring alternative explanations to problems; question and challenge |

| | |
|---|---|
| S: | Sean says it means I am gay and now everyone is calling me that. I don't want to be that way. |
| C: | I wonder if a dream can mean someone is gay or not. It seems as though you are worried about that. |
| S: | Yeah. |
| C: | Tell me more about that. |
| S: | I just don't want to be that way. I am afraid I am gay. |
| C: | You are worried and afraid and you aren't quite sure how you feel about all of this. |

| | |
|---|---|
| S: | Yeah. |
| C: | I want to address your classmates calling you names. They are just being unkind, and you and I can talk about how we should handle that a little bit later. Right now I wonder if it might be helpful for us to gather some information on what it means to be gay and explore that. We can also role-play about some things that you can say or do when you have problems with classmates calling you names. What do you think? |
| S: | OK. |

## Outcome

Christian and I gathered information about lesbians and gay men and about heterosexuality. This is not something that I would do in every situation concerning LGBTQ issues, because every situation and each individual is unique. Christian's mom, Heather, was very much on board and wanted Christian to be properly educated about sexuality. After going over the information that we had found, Christian and I role-played scenarios and things that he could say if his classmates began teasing him again. Heather immediately started Christian in outside counseling with a qualified counselor who specialized in working with clients with sexual identity and LGBTQ concerns. Christian and I met once a week for about a month and a half and then as needed for a couple more months.

## Final Process Questions

- How did I effectively assist the student and address his concerns?
- How did I intervene within the limits of my education and experience?
- How did I respect the student's right to privacy and confidentiality?
- How would I approach working with students whose parents were not as accepting or cooperative as Heather?
- How would I approach working with students who were not as accepting or understanding of diversity?
- How can I continue to advocate for students who might be questioning?
- How can I continue to advocate for all LGBTQ students (even the ones who might never show up in my office)?
- How can I continue to implement school-wide programs that promote a safe environment for all students?
- How should I document the intervention(s)?
- Did I maintain my professional integrity and advocate for social justice for all involved?

## Resources

Byrd, R., & Hays, D. (2012). School counselor competency and lesbian, gay, bisexual, transgender, and questioning (LGBTQ) youth. *Journal of School Counseling, 10*(3). Retrieved http://jsc.montana.edu/articles/v10n3.pdf

Carroll, L. (2010). *Counseling sexual and gender minorities.* Upper Saddle River, NJ: Pearson Education.

Gay, Lesbian, and Straight Education Network. (GLSEN). (2009). *The safe space kit: Guide to being an ally.* New York, NY: Author.

Goldman, L. (2008). *Coming out, coming in: Nurturing the well-being and inclusion of gay youth in mainstream society.* New York, NY: Routledge.

*Chapter 19*

# Dating and Relational Violence

Laurie A. Vargas and Hugh C. Crethar

## CASE BACKGROUND

Natalie is a 17-year-old Latina who is currently in the 12th grade and attends an urban high school. Natalie lives at home with her mom—a single mother who works two part-time jobs to support the family—and her 12-year-old brother. Oftentimes, Natalie is expected to help care for her younger brother. In school, Natalie has earned decent grades and participates in cheerleading. She has a steady group of friends with whom she spends time, and her younger brother is often included. She spends weekends with her mother and brother and attends church on a regular basis. Toward the end of her junior year of high school, Natalie began to date a 17-year-old friend in the neighborhood. To most people, the relationship appeared as most teen relationships would: The two were often spotted in the neighborhood with friends, eating out, or going to the movies. As summer progressed, Natalie spent increasingly more time exclusively with her boyfriend and stayed away from her friends and refused to care for her brother. What was not recognized by others was how the boyfriend had isolated Natalie from her family and friends and coerced her into sexual activity.

When her senior year began, Natalie started cutting classes and often would leave campus. It appeared that Natalie no longer enjoyed cheerleading and was asked to leave the squad. She left homework assignments incomplete and began to fail exams in her classes. A Student Success Team meeting was held with Natalie, her mother, her school counselor, and her teachers to address Natalie's attendance and decline in grades. Natalie's strengths were discussed, which set a positive tone for the meeting. Each teacher discussed how he or she had seen a dramatic drop in her grades and expressed concern about how she had cut class. Natalie's mother shared how Natalie's attitude at home had changed as well. Natalie spent all of her time with her new boyfriend and did not help out at home as she used to. Her mother mentioned that Natalie did not seem happy anymore and she could not figure out why. During this meeting, all the adults agreed that Natalie should begin to see the school counselor to help her get back on track academically, although Natalie was reluctant to do so.

## INITIAL PROCESSING QUESTIONS

As a school counselor working with Natalie, one will want to consider the following questions:

- What personal biases about gender and relationships do you have in general and specifically in working with Natalie?
- What is your initial reaction to hearing about Natalie's experiences with her boyfriend?
- What cultural considerations should you make in working with Natalie?
- How do you keep teachers and school staff informed of progress?
- How do different theoretical orientations drive the initial counseling sessions?

## ADDRESSING THE ISSUES

Although dating and relationships are a common component of the maturation process for many teenagers, it is not uncommon for them to form their first romantic relationships without a clear understanding of what might constitute "healthy" intimate relationships. Due to such relational naïveté, teens are more apt to become engaged in relationships that are verbally, sexually, or physically abusive. The 2009 Youth Risk Behavior Surveillance survey funded by the Centers for Disease Control and Prevention (2010) found that close to 10% of high school students reported having been hit, slapped, or physically hurt on purpose by their boyfriend or girlfriend in the previous 12 months. Furthermore, females report experience of physical violence significantly more often than their male counterparts (Hickman, Jaycox, & Aronoff, 2004).

Teen dating violence is comparable to domestic violence in that it commonly displays a clear pattern of three stages of repeated abuse: tension building, explosion, and the honeymoon (Walker, 1979). During the tension-building stage, the couple may argue a lot. It is not uncommon for abusers to yell for no reason and make false accusations about their significant others. The atmosphere between the couple is tense and the tension builds with each interaction resulting in relational violence: The tension explodes in a burst of verbal, emotional, physical, and/or sexual abuse. What commonly occurs afterward is the honeymoon stage, when abusers apologize and promise to not be abusive again. Unfortunately, these three stages often repeat in a cycle in abusive relationships.

### Prevention

Aside from rapport development, a key element of relational violence counseling is psycho-education. School counselors working with dating violence focus on teaching and exploring key elements of relational and domestic violence. One main issue that is covered is the aforementioned cycle of violence common in these relationships. Students may or may not notice how similar one abusive partner is to the next. Counselors work to help students recognize unhealthy behaviors. Another key element of the psycho-educational approach is teaching students the Power and Control Wheel (Domestic Abuse Intervention Project; Dutton & Starzomski, 1997; Graham-Kevan & Archer, 2008). This focus helps victimized students understand that they are not "crazy" at all, but instead that "crazy making" is a technique often used by abusers to gain and maintain control over another

**TABLE 19-1** Additional Techniques and Strategies for Helping Adolescents Who Have Experienced Teen Dating Violence

| Paradigm | All School Levels |
|---|---|
| Psychodynamic | Exploring and processing attachment issues, particularly with the male caregiver; parent consultations; encouragement |
| Humanistic/Existential | Active listening and reflecting feelings and meaning; demonstrating unconditional positive regard |
| Behavioral/CBT | Focus on avoiding and coping with anxiety triggers; behavioral rehearsal; role playing; bibliotherapy/books on empowerment of girls and women; disputing irrational beliefs |
| Family Systems | Focus on how this experience affects the client's perception of self in system; working on intergenerational transmission of relationship interactions; paying attention to homeostatic pressures that hinder client growth |
| Emergent | Creating drawings and writing or telling narrative stories about relationships; storytelling; providing student with age-appropriate information about various aspects of intimate relationships |

in abusive relationships. Another technique used by abusers is the manner in which they strive to isolate their significant others in order to increase the latter's dependence on them. Psycho-educational approaches that explore such destructive patterns and how they relate to their relationships help victimized students understand (1) that they are not alone in their feelings and experiences and (2) that they can experience healthier relationships. Thus, school counselors focus on empowering students to become and remain safe and unharmed as they develop interpersonal relationships. Table 19-1 provides additional techniques and strategies for dealing with dating violence.

Addressing teen dating violence from a prevention model is just as necessary as intervening in it. School counselors ought to work with their school administrators to develop a beneficial prevention program as part of the counseling possibilities. A well-designed program could be offered to all students within the same grade, with the understanding that the program would be repeated each year. Key lessons could include the following:

- Evaluating relationships (including friendships)
- Developing healthy forms of communication
- Understanding warning signs
- Learning how to get help (for you or a friend)

School counselors could either work with a local domestic violence agency or provide the lessons themselves in a classroom. In addition, school counselors can consult with classroom teachers and teach them how to provide appropriate lessons in the classroom. The benefit of consulting with teachers is that they are with students many hours throughout the day and often are first responders in these situations. Teachers are also able to continue the discussions throughout a student's academic career.

## IN SESSION

At the time of the following session, the school counselor and Natalie had met a few times to review confidentiality and the goals of the sessions. Parental consent was initially given during the Student Success Team meeting.

| | |
|---|---|
| COUNSELOR (C): | Hi, Natalie. Thank you so much for coming in today. I'm really glad that you're here. |
| NATALIE (N): | Yeah, well, I didn't really feel like I had a choice. My mom kept telling me I had to come, but there's nothing wrong with me. |
| C: | I understand where you're coming from. At the meeting we had a few weeks ago I could tell that your teachers and your mother were worried about changes they've seen in you. Can you tell me about those changes? |
| N: | Well, last year [in 11th grade], I guess they thought I was happier. I mean, I am still happy, just not as much. My grades were better and I went to class more. I was one of the lead cheerleaders and had lots of friends. I still have friends; it's just that I don't really talk to them anymore. |
| C: | Can you tell me more about your friends? What did you enjoy doing with them last year? How has that changed? |
| N: | We used to have so much fun. (*A faint smile appears*) After cheerleading practice we would pick up my brother from school and just hang out. Listen to music. Study. Eat. We didn't really make plans to do things, we just did it. It's like we all knew what we wanted to do. They were really good with my brother too. It's like he was their little brother! |
| C: | Wow, sounds like you used to have a lot of fun with them, hanging out, listening to music, and even studying. Can you think of anything that has changed since last year? I'm wondering why you don't spend as much time with them. |
| N: | Oh, well, over the summer I started going out with my boyfriend. And I guess we spent so much time together that my friends didn't want to be around us anymore. |
| C: | So your friends used to hang out with you and your boyfriend? |
| N: | Yeah, they did. But then my boyfriend would sometimes tell them that it was just going to be the two of us that night. He wanted it to be all special. It made me feel good that he wanted to spend so much time with just me. I didn't mind at first. He told me he loved me. |
| C: | It sounds like your friends enjoyed being around both you and your boyfriend, but that it was your boyfriend who |

didn't want to spend so much time with them. And at first, you didn't mind. When did that change?

N: *(Natalie's head drops and she looks at the floor. She is silent for a minute)* I don't really know. I just know that in the beginning he always wanted to be with me. He called me all the time. He texted me that he missed me when we weren't together. I thought that was the way it should be. He told me that he loved me and I believed him. Sometimes he'd get jealous when he saw me talking to other boys. I'd tell him that those were my brother's friends and he would laugh saying he was just kidding. I thought he was. But then . . . he started to tell me that I shouldn't be talking to other guys because then people would start rumors that I was cheating on him. Because we're from the same neighborhood I knew that he could easily find out if I was talking to other guys. So I figured it was easier for me to ignore people. I didn't take my brother anywhere or hang out with my friends anymore.

C: You mentioned that your boyfriend would get jealous. How did that make you feel when that happened?

N: At first I really liked it. I thought it meant he really liked me. And I would tell him that I would never cheat on him or do anything like that. But then, he started calling me names, telling me I was acting like a "whore" when I talked to other guys. I started to get really angry and scared. Sometimes he'd just stare at me. His eyes looked like they were on fire. I was afraid he was going to hit me. So I figured that if I didn't talk to other guys then he'd be fine. But then, he started blaming me that guys were talking to me. I don't get it. He wasn't like this when we were just friends. He tells me it's my fault he gets so mad or jealous. He doesn't even want me talking to my friends at church. He thinks they all talk about him and that they are trying to break us up.

C: Natalie, thank you for telling this to me. It seems as if you're carrying around a lot. On one hand, you liked it when your boyfriend wanted to spend a lot of time with you, but then on the other hand, you didn't like that he would get jealous of you talking to other guys.

N: Yeah, it was like dating two different people. He'd be sweet in front of people but when we were alone he started to get mean sometimes. As if I could never do anything right. And then, he started making moves faster than me. I wasn't ready to do some things. You know.

C: Sounds like a difficult situation. You've mentioned that at times you were afraid that he would hit you and that he began making moves faster than you were ready. I can imagine that you were scared during these times. . . . (*Natalie cuts in*)

N:  (*Natalie crying*) I was so scared. One time he told me that if I loved him I would do what he wanted. You know. So I did. I wanted him to know I loved him. But then he made me go further. He told me that he loved me so much and wanted to make "it" special. I didn't want to do it. And I told him to stop. He yelled at me, asking me if I didn't want to do "it" because I was already doing "it" with some other guy. He called me a "whore" and other things, told me that I better do it with him because he'd start rumors if I didn't. I didn't know what to do. I was so scared. I thought it was my fault that he thought I was with another guy. I told him that I was sorry and that I did love him and would never cheat on him. I was crying. He shushed me and told me he loved me and that's why he didn't want me talking to other guys—so that way he wouldn't suspect things. Then he told me how much he loved me and he began kissing me all over. It felt like my old boyfriend was back. I didn't want to do "it" but he kept telling me how much he loved me and that he would never hurt me. I don't know what to do now. I'm stuck. I love him sometimes and other times I want him to stay away forever. It hurts.

C:  Natalie, you are so brave for being willing to tell me all of this. I know how difficult it is to share this with anyone. As I mentioned in previous meetings, I am not here to tell you what to do but rather help you understand what the options are. I know that you were referred to me because of your grades, but after today's meeting I can tell that there is much more than that going on.

## Outcome

Natalie and her school counselor agreed to meet for several more sessions while a referral could be made to an appropriate mental health provider. Her school counselor called the local child abuse reporting agency for a consultation but has not been able to make any reports to the police because Natalie has not revealed the identity of the boyfriend. After meeting with the school counselor, Natalie is engaged in therapy with an on-site community-based organization that works with victims of teen dating violence.

At Natalie's request, the school counselor did not inform the teachers of the specifics but did let them know that Natalie was dealing with stress in her personal relationships.

An important aspect of school counseling is being able to maintain confidentiality as well as respecting the professionals on the school campus. Considerations must be made as to the information that will be shared. When issues directly affect academics, usually it is in the best interest of students to share information, taking into account the most appropriate way to share it as well as determining what would be done with that information. When discussing a situation such as Natalie's, the student's well-being must be considered. How would teachers and staff benefit from knowing the specifics of the situation? Could teachers and staff still provide empathy and understanding to Natalie if they were informed that Natalie was having a great deal of stress due to personal relationships, or would more detail be necessary? Another consideration to make is whether or not sharing the information could put Natalie in danger, either with her boyfriend or with her mother. Discussing with Natalie what will be shared allows her to feel a sense of control and allows teachers to be able to build and maintain a caring, trusting relationship with Natalie, thus increasing her support network.

## Final Process Questions

- What are the most important things to focus on when first discussing experiences of teen dating violence with your students? How does date rape differ?
- How can school counselors create an environment that is and feels safe and supportive of students who have relational experiences like Natalie's?
- How do local child abuse reporting laws affect the outcome of counseling?
- How do school counselors work with teachers and staff without breaching confidentiality?
- What does the local state education code state in regard to confidentiality of pupil information?
- How do school counselors maintain trust with school staff when they are not able to share specifics?
- At what point and for what reason(s) would the school counselor refer Natalie's case for counseling outside of the school? How would the counselor go about doing this while maintaining an effective client–counselor relationship?
- Imagine working with Natalie for the school year. Did you see any of your cultural biases coming out? If so, how would you address them?
- What different/additional approaches or interventions would you use with Natalie?
- What can be done at the primary prevention level when focusing on teen dating violence within your school?
- After reading this case scenario, what role do you think school counselors have in working with students who have experienced teen dating violence? Has your response changed from what it was at the beginning of the case scenario? Would your approach differ in an LGBTQ dating relationship? Why or why not?

## Resources

Dating Matters. (2012). *Understanding teen dating violence: Prevention.* Retrieved from http://www.vetoviolence.org/datingmatters

Moles, K. (2001). *The teen relationship workbook: For professionals helping to develop healthy relationships and prevent domestic violence.* Wilkes-Barre, PA: Wellness Reproductions & Publishing.

National Center of Domestic and Sexual Violence, http://www.ncdsv.org

Walker, L. E. A. (1979). *The battered woman.* New York, NY: Harper & Row.

### FOR IMMEDIATE ASSISTANCE

National Dating Abuse Helpline, http://www.loveisrespect.org, 1.866.331.9474, TTY: 1.866.331.8453

National Domestic Violence Hotline, http://www.thehotline.org, 1.800.799.SAFE

## Chapter 20

# Chronic Illness

Heather McCarthy and Tammy Davis

## CASE BACKGROUND

By all appearances, Damian was an upbeat, energetic third-grade student. Despite missing days of school somewhat regularly due to living with Type I diabetes, Damian has achieved academic success and attracted many friends; his teachers adored him. I was a bit saddened at the thought of such a young boy being weighed down by having to manage such an adult disease. However, it quickly became evident that this young student was not weighed down at all. In fact, it was much the opposite; he always seemed bubbly and positive.

One day, however, was different. Damian had just helped me clean up the game we had played, and he packed away his insulin kit. We headed toward the door, and, using the technique of positive feedback with words of affirmation and focusing on his strengths, I marveled (as I often would) about his self-knowledge, self-sufficiency, and confidence in caring for himself. He smiled as usual. But as I reached for the door handle to usher him out, Damian turned back and murmured softly, "I hate having diabetes."

My heart lurched, and as I looked down at him I realized that although he might have been as well-adjusted as anyone could imagine for someone with an incurable and lifelong illness, Damian hurt some days, too. I spent some time reflecting and validating his feelings on our walk back to his class, but after I dropped him off, I couldn't shake the feeling that that wasn't enough. Thoughtfully, I processed our conversations and decided to try group counseling as well as individual counseling to respond to Damian's unique needs.

## INITIAL PROCESS QUESTIONS

- What already exists to support Damian in school? A school health plan? A 504 plan? Is there anything else the school can do to remove barriers from Damian's school experience and social-emotional and academic success?

Special acknowledgment goes to Teresa Chapman, a professional school counselor at the elementary school level in Fairfax County Public Schools, who cofacilitated this small counseling group and continues to offer this group to students with chronic illnesses at her school. Also, thanks to Dr. Carol Kaffenberger who shared her chronic illness resources during the development of the group lessons.

- How can I support Damian's teacher(s) in working with Damian and his family? Are proper accommodations being made in the classroom and when he misses days of school due to his illness?
- Although Damian presents as positive and upbeat, will a classroom observation shed more light on his overall well-being in school?
- As a counselor, what are my own thoughts and feelings about and experiences with diabetes and chronic illness in general?
- What is my personal outlook on working with a student whose prognosis may not be positive?
- How is Damian's self-perception? Does he have an identity beyond his diabetes?
- What does the school perceive to be Damian's biggest concerns? What about what his family perceives?
- Is there anyone in Damian's family that has (or has had) a chronic illness?
- What does Damian see as his biggest concerns? Perhaps his concerns have nothing to do with having a chronic illness.
- How does Damian perceive having a chronic illness? How much does Damian actually want to talk about having a chronic illness?
- What kind of support system does Damian have at home? What kind of social supports and outlets does he have at school?
- How does Damian spend his time, aside from taking care of himself?
- What are my legal considerations as I am handling health and medical issues with students such as Damian? Am I involving and consulting with the appropriate experts so that I am dispensing relevant information and encouraging habits and self-care that are aligned with medical treatment plans, etc.?
- What ethical considerations do I have to consider in terms of confidentiality? Are there school personnel who need to be informed about his condition and, if so, how much do I tell them?

## ADDRESSING THE ISSUES

When working with students who have a chronic illness, a top priority is ensuring that the health issues interfere with academic access and achievement as little as possible. Many times, school counselors' interventions can be time consuming and intensive; yet they are limited to facilitating communication between home and school, developing and monitoring a school health plan, and serving as a point of contact for all parties involved. Understanding that a student with a chronic illness may be absent more frequently than other students, school counselors may try to keep the students in class for instruction as much as possible when they are present. This may limit the amount of time for counseling. Also, because of these absences, these students may have academic experiences that are quite different from those of their peers, as they might not have the opportunity to connect with their peers on a consistent basis.

Damian first came to my attention because the public health nurse mentioned that he might benefit from counseling. Damian did not always take care of himself. For example, it was reported that at times he would purposefully eat things he knew were off-limits for him, possibly because he felt that doing so gave him something he could control in a situation that was largely outside of his control. Immediately, I took the opportunity to form a relationship with him using integrative counseling techniques. Using the humanistic, person-centered technique of being nondirective, I began our sessions by allowing Damian to determine all aspects of our counseling activities. A natural conversationalist, Damian delighted in eating lunch with me for our first meeting together, and we enjoyed several subsequent sessions after that, eating lunch or playing games that he selected. I used active listening and reflective questions to establish rapport and trust.

Using the technique of immediacy, we focused on how Damian was feeling each time we met. Because he was well-educated about diabetes, Damian was quick to explain how his unique body functioned. Damian was self-sufficient in managing his illness. He proudly showed off his personal insulin self-monitoring system and taught me about how he checked and balanced his blood sugars. The whole process was so foreign to me that he would have to explain it again each time I saw him. Damian would laugh and gladly demonstrate it again and again.

In counseling Damian, it was clear that he was quite adept at maintaining conversations with adults, as this was probably the group he spent the most time with both in and out of school. Things seemed to be going so well for Damian that I sometimes wondered whether he really needed my support at all. He would politely leave his classmates and activities and march happily down the hall with me when I came to get him, and he always responded pleasantly to my questions. After several individual sessions, Damian had me convinced that he was totally adjusted. Yet after the comment he made that one day leaving my office, I knew he needed something more.

I collaborated with a couple of local university professors, and one directed me to *The Handbook for School Support Teams* (Kaffenberger, 2010), a comprehensive set of guidelines for serving students with chronic illnesses. I was particularly drawn to the five-step process for managing a chronic illness (Huegel, 1998): (1) Face your fears, (2) be good to yourself, (3) know your limits, (4) focus on what you *can* do, and (5) express your feelings. In a matter of weeks, I developed a small group counseling curriculum based on these five steps for chronic illness management and lobbied for Damian's buy-in to participate.

Over the course of a few weeks, Damian's excitement to share his experiences with other students that had chronic illnesses increased, and he was beside himself when we all gathered for the first time. The first session ran like any other first counseling group session: Students selected hand motions that represented themselves. For instance, when it was my turn, I clasped my hands and made them into a roller-coaster motion for "Ms. McCarrrrrr-thy!" Each week I challenged the students to remember each of the hand motions. We made a group name, group rules, and even a group sign. The students talked about interests that had nothing to do with their illnesses.

The public health nurse was thrilled to join our group as well, having been closely involved with almost every member of the group throughout the year. During the second session, each student received a colorful picture of the human body, and the school nurse assisted each student as he or she explained to the other group members about his or her chronic illness and which system of the body it affected the most. The students drew arrows to the parts of the body on their pictures and labeled the pictures with the names of their friends' illnesses. We made a session of "show and tell," and true to form, Damian gleefully showed off his insulin kit. The other students watched in awe as he explained how to use it. When he sat down, another student jumped up, lifting her shirt just slightly to show us the knob in her stomach that allowed her parents to insert a feeding tube for her at night. She admitted that she had never shown that to anyone before. Almost immediately, as students one by one shared about their experiences, they seemed to bond— nobody thought they were weird or that their contraptions were scary. They left gleaming and more reassured that they were not alone in their illnesses.

With each session, the students processed their feelings, fears, strengths, and strategies for self-care together. By using a solution-focused strategy of finding exceptions, students could think about times they had forgotten all about having an illness, and how they could have more of those moments. One activity they enjoyed was "roller-coaster check-ins." Discussion revolved around the fact that sometimes they would feel "up," sometimes "down," and sometimes they would feel all over the place—much like a roller coaster. At the beginning of each session after that, my "2-minute check-ins" with them would involve adding onto a roller coaster that they had started drawing during the "feelings" session. Finally, they drew themselves as superheroes; using the Adlerian technique of reframing, students were encouraged to think about themselves as strong and courageous rather than weak and sick. Most had never viewed themselves in that way before.

This five-step framework is easily adaptable for students at both the middle and high school levels, with developmentally appropriate activities substituted for those that better serve the elementary school population. At any level, students can be encouraged to prepare a presentation to educate their classmates about their conditions. Another option would be to run the small counseling group with "mentor pairs"—an older student that has either completed the group process successfully or is otherwise well-adjusted paired with a younger student who has the same illness or is just going through the group process for the first time—an option that did benefit Damian. Table 20-1 provides additional approaches, techniques, and strategies for use with students with chronic illnesses.

## IN SESSION

For the activity that requests students to draw themselves as superheroes and their illnesses as villains, the counselor works with students to create features that bring their daily struggles to life in narrative fashion. It may take focused energy on strengths-based counseling on the part of the counselor to assist students in drawing themselves as courageous and strong, especially if students are experiencing a more difficult time than usual at the time of this activity.

| | |
|---|---|
| DAMIAN (D): | I've been thinking about all the things that I can't do because of my diabetes. |
| COUNSELOR (C): | So you feel like there are things that your diabetes keeps you from doing? |
| D: | Yes . . . |
| C: | . . . and it makes you feel sad? |
| D: | Uh-huh. |
| C. | Let's talk about that. I'm wondering if we could change how you're thinking and feeling about that. |
| D: | I hope so. |
| C: | So, I want you to think about your diabetes and what it looks like if it was a person. Does it have a mean face? A sad face? A kind, smiling face? Is it ugly? Or scary? |
| D: | I think it is black with fire coming out of the top of its head. |
| C: | OK. Let's draw that. [Have student draw the "illness."] What can you tell me about your picture? |

**TABLE 20-1** Additional Approaches for Working With Students With Chronic Illnesses

| Paradigm | Elementary School | Middle School | High School |
|---|---|---|---|
| Psychodynamic | Listening for defense mechanisms and gently confronting; exploring feelings of inferiority | Listening for defense mechanisms and gently confronting; exploring feelings of inferiority; exploring ego strength and addressing issues of resistance | Listening for defense mechanisms and gently confronting; exploring feelings of inferiority; exploring ego strength and addressing issues of resistance |
| Humanistic/ Existential | Reflection of feeling; nondirective; using active listening; immediacy | Reflection of feeling; nondirective; using active listening; immediacy; gentle confrontation regarding illness | Reflection of feeling; nondirective; using active listening; immediacy; gentle confrontation regarding illness; exploring feelings regarding impact of illness on postsecondary plans |
| Behavioral/CBT | Positive feedback focusing on strengths; reframing weaknesses into strengths; understanding how student perceives the illness and how student feels and acts; "picture in your mind" what it would look like if . . . | Positive feedback focusing on strengths; reframing weaknesses into strengths | Positive feedback focusing on strengths; reframing weaknesses into strengths; exploring realities of impact of illness on future life plans (e.g., relationships, family planning) |
| Systems | Counseling for siblings and/or parents; parent education about school support systems available; education and collaboration for school personnel to assist student; examining school policies for any unintended impediments to student success | Counseling for siblings and/or parents; parent education about school support systems available; education and collaboration for school personnel to assist student; examining school policies for any unintended impediments to student success | Counseling for siblings and/or parents; parent education about school support systems available; connecting family to resources to support student in postsecondary options; examining school policies for any unintended impediments to student success |
| Emergent | Narrative telling of student's story; externalizing the illness from the student; empowerment to self-advocate and be competent and confident | Narrative telling of student's story; externalizing the illness from the student; empowerment to self-advocate and be competent and confident | Narrative telling of student's story; externalizing the illness from the student; empowerment to self-advocate and be competent and confident |

| D: | Well, it has black curly hair with fire and smoke coming out of the top of its head, and it has scary arms that reach out and say, "I'm diabetes and I'm going to get you!" |
| C: | Oh, that is scary! |
| D: | Yeah . . . and the fire won't go out and it's always there. |
| C: | Are you worried that your diabetes isn't going away? |
| D: | Sometimes. But my mom and my doctor say that the treatment will help control the symptoms. |
| C: | I see . . . |

## Outcome

This is one of the questions that appeared on the group work pretest and posttest instruments for students to answer: "There are some good things about my diagnosis (circle one): YES or NO." On the pretest, all students circled "NO" for this question. After participating in the group, processing their feelings, and learning about the positive attributes they had acquired due to living with their chronic health conditions on a daily basis (e.g., courage), the students answered the same question on the posttest. This time, three students wrote in, and circled, the word "MAYBE" in between the options "YES" and "NO." This was a profound opportunity for a group of young students to reframe their struggles in terms of strengths.

The students were sad when the group finally ended and begged for it to come together again the next year. Although I left the school, the counselor that remained brought back that same group of students the next year. In fact, making use of the emergent technique of empowerment, she encouraged Damian and one of the other older group members to help plan new activities for the next group, as they would have both new and returning participants. Seeming to feel a sense of purpose, Damian took his charge very seriously and proceeded to plan thorough activities for the next group.

During one of the following years, Damian paired up with an older student who had diabetes, but who managed his illness very responsibly. Through a modeling and peer-mentoring relationship, Damian matured in his approach to self-care and began to flourish even more with his growing desire and willingness to "be good to himself."

## Final Process Questions

- Have I connected this family/student with relevant resources and well-informed professionals in and outside of the school? Would Damian benefit from outside counseling, a support group, or even an online community (chat boards, etc.)?
- As a school counselor, how can I prepare myself to deal with the realities of an illness that unfolds over time (e.g., a student's condition worsening)?

In the event that this happens, how can I process this with students and staff?
- As students' awareness and insight increase (with maturity, age, time, etc.), how can I assist a student with a chronic illness face and work through realistic fears about the illness (e.g., prolonged or serious health risks and outcomes)?

## Resources

Clay, D. L. (2004). *Helping school children with chronic health conditions: A practical guide.* New York, NY: Guilford Press.

Geist, R., Grdisa, V., & Otley, A. (2003). Psychosocial issues in the child with chronic conditions. *Best Practice & Research: Clinical Gastroenterology, 17,* 141–152.

Kaffenberger, C. J. (2006). School reentry for students with a chronic illness: A role for professional school counselors. *Professional School Counseling, 9,* 223–230.

Shiu, S. (2001). Issues in the education of students with chronic illness. *International Journal of Disability, Development and Education, 48,* 269–281.

Webb, N. B. (2009). *Helping children and adolescents with chronic and serious medical conditions: A strengths-based approach.* Hoboken, NJ: Wiley.

*Chapter 21*

# Helping Students With Grief and Loss Experiences

STACY SOLSAA AND KELLY DUNCAN

## CASE BACKGROUND

Tina, an 18-year-old high school senior, lost her best friend in a car accident 2 weeks into her senior year. Tina and Beth had been best friends ever since Tina moved to our small Midwest community as a sophomore. Beth and Tina had spent the preceding summer making plans for their senior year and college to follow. After Beth's accident, the senior class shared in their grief, and then they moved forward with the excitement of their senior year. Most kept Beth in their thoughts, but Tina couldn't picture her senior year without her best friend.

One afternoon during homecoming week, Tina walked into my office with tears in her eyes. Her class was in the middle of planning the float for the homecoming parade. Three of Tina's classmates followed her, asking her to return to the classroom. She looked at me, her eyes filled with tears, and said, "I can't go back right now." I told her classmates that Tina just needed a few minutes and asked them to close the door on their way out.

## INITIAL PROCESS QUESTIONS

- What stages and tasks of grief has this student experienced?
- Where is the student in the grieving process?
- To what extent is the student's grief interfering with her daily functioning?
- When the student's grief is worst, what is she thinking and feeling?
- What has the student already tried to do to help herself move forward?
- How supportive are family and friends in her grieving process?
- What does the student know about the process of grief?
- What techniques might work in helping her cope with her grief?
- How might my feelings of loss regarding her friend affect my ability to help the student?
- What cultural or religious considerations need to be made when working with the student?
- Would this student benefit from a referral outside the school?

## ADDRESSING THE ISSUES

Grief is a unique and personal experience, and each individual will work through loss in a different way. Students who are grieving often show signs of grief at school. According to the American School Counselor Association (ASCA; 2012), school counselors can provide guidance by following several delivery methods outlined in the *ASCA National Model*. School counselors should educate teachers, administrators, and students about grief when necessary. School counselors can also help a student's parents understand what their child or teenager is going through. Most often school counselors work either with an individual or with groups of grieving students. There are also times when school counselors may refer students who are having difficulty working through grief to outside therapists.

The most common guide related to the grief process is the Kübler-Ross (1969) model. This model includes five stages of grief: denial, anger, bargaining, depression, and acceptance. It is believed that people can move back and forth from one stage to another depending on circumstances and situations. Some people move through every stage whereas others may experience only some of the stages. Normalizing the grieving process is important when working with individuals of all ages. Using the Kübler-Ross model can help students understand the process of grief. I have found that it is helpful to put the stages of grief on a ladder to provide a concrete visual for students of different ages. They understand that people can go up and down a ladder, even skipping steps at times. This helps them to see that it is OK to have a wide range of feelings (e.g., from sad to happy) and to feel these at different times while grieving.

Other factors to consider when working with grieving students are their age and stage of development. According to the National Cancer Institute (NCI; 2011), the developmental age of children affects how they understand grief. NCI also stated that at ages 3 to 6 years children do not grasp that death is final. Children at this age often think the person who died will come back. Further, children ages 6 to 9 years are often curious about death and want to know details such as what happens to the body when someone dies. Children over age 9 years generally understand death as adults do, as final and something that happens to everyone.

I used a cognitive-behavioral approach with Tina, also taking into consideration the need to educate her about the process of grief. I already had a strong relationship with her, as she had often stopped by my office to talk about life's challenges and her college planning. Because we knew each other well, we were able to begin working on Tina's grief issue immediately. I first discussed with Tina the extent to which her grief was interfering with her daily activities. She was having problems getting her homework done, concentrating in class, getting to work, and participating in anything that she previously had planned to do with Beth. We talked about the thoughts that she was having and the underlying belief that she was not the same person without Beth.

When working with lower elementary students who are experiencing grief, it is important to help them understand the process of grief, work through feelings, and realize that death is final. It is helpful for students at that age to be able to draw about their feelings. Often children's books about death are also useful. For example, I have used the book *When Someone Very Special Dies* by Marge Heegaard (1996), which is a combination of learning about grief and drawing that allows children to express their feelings. There are many other books and resources available as well. When working with upper elementary students ages 9 to 12 years, activities to process the death are helpful. Creating a memory box to hold special photos or items can help them keep the one they lost close. It is also important to help a child this age express thoughts, feelings, and questions that he or she might have about death. When working with Tina, I used techniques such as disputing irrational beliefs, cognitive restructuring, self-talk, and bibliotherapy. Additional strategies and techniques for working with students with grief and loss issues are included in Table 21-1.

**TABLE 21-1    Additional Strategies and Techniques for Working With Students With Grief and Loss Issues**

| Paradigm | Elementary School | Middle School | High School |
|---|---|---|---|
| Psychodynamic | Free association and interpretation | Analysis of defense mechanisms; free association and interpretation | Analysis of transference and defense mechanisms; free association and interpretation |
| Humanistic/ Existential | Therapeutic conditions; safe, comfortable, fun environment; role play; "I" statements; unconditional positive regard and empathy | Therapeutic conditions; "I" statements; empty chair; unconditional positive regard and empathy; respect; growing independence | Therapeutic conditions;; "I" statements; empty chair; unconditional positive regard and empathy through respect |
| Behavioral/CBT | Disputing irrational beliefs; cognitive restructuring using activities; self-talk; visual imagery through stories; modeling; role playing; miracle question; bibliotherapy through children's stories | Disputing irrational beliefs; cognitive restructuring using questions and activities; self-talk; visual imagery; modeling; exceptions; miracle question | Disputing irrational beliefs; cognitive restructuring using questioning; specifying automatic thoughts; self-talk; visual imagery; modeling; exceptions; miracle question; self-help bibliotherapy |
| Family Systems | Parent behavior training/education on grief process; signs of problematic grief at age level; behavioral, academic, and social issues; family dynamics | Parent and child behavior training/education on grief process; signs of problematic grief; behavioral, academic, and social issues; family dynamics | Teen and, when appropriate, parent behavior training/ education on grief process; signs of problematic grief; behavioral, academic, and social issues; family dynamics; social dynamics |
| Emergent | Miracle question; sparkling moments; empowerment; interpersonal incidents; role playing | Deconstruct and externalize problems; miracle question; sparkling moments; empowerment; interpersonal incidents | Deconstruct and externalize problems; miracle question; sparkling moments; empowerment; communication analysis; interpersonal incidents |

## IN SESSION

As Tina's friends closed the door, she sat down and cried. I asked her to let me know when she was ready to talk and sat in silence as she cried for a couple of minutes. When the tears slowed down, she began.

| | |
|---|---|
| TINA (T): | How am I going to make it through my senior year without Beth? I don't know who I am without her. We were Tina and Beth and now I am just Tina, and everyone thinks I should be happy because it is homecoming week. She is missing out on everything. How can I be happy about that? |
| COUNSELOR (C): | I know your whole world was turned upside down when Beth died and nothing can make it right. But are you sure she really isn't sharing all this with you in some way? (*Tina sat and thought about my question for a while as I waited in silence*) |
| T: | I never thought of it that way but I think she is sharing all this with me, but just not in the way I need her to be. |
| C: | I know this is not what you had planned for your senior year but sometimes life gives us surprises. If you were where Beth is and she was here, what would you like to see her doing right now? (*Tina paused again for a couple minutes before she spoke*) |
| T: | I would want her to find a way to be happy, to enjoy her senior year. I would want her to know that I was right there in her heart all the time. I would want her to do everything that we had planned to do this year and not to think of me as missing it, because I would really be there cheering her on in everything she did. |
| C: | Wow, what a good friend you are. I think Beth would feel the same way, don't you? |
| T: | I do, I really do. The problem is that I don't know how to be happy right now because everything I see and do makes me cry. |
| C: | I don't think that is too uncommon of a thing, when you lose a best friend. I think that with some counseling and some time, you can get through it. I know how strong you are, I have seen you overcome many things. You are welcome to come and talk to me and we can figure out together how to get you through this, or if you would prefer I can suggest a counselor outside of school, if you would like. |
| T: | I think you are right; I maybe just need a little help. I never had anyone so close to me die before; this is new to me. I think I just want to see you. I know you and I seem to cry a |

lot at school lately; can I just come in when I am having a difficult time?

C: I think that is a good idea. Let's set up a time, so I can check in for a while, but you can come in anytime you are having trouble, and we can try to figure out how to help get you back to the good old Tina I know is still there. Do you think you are ready to head back to the float discussion?

T: I do feel much better, but what if I start to cry again?

C: Try to think about the fact that Beth wants you to enjoy this week, and remind yourself that she is with you always.

T: OK, I think that might help. I will try that.

C: Go have some fun with your class and remember to try to use those thoughts we talked about.

## Outcome

At first Tina would come in once or twice a week depending on how she was doing. Tina continued to work on changing the way she thought about Beth's death. She also worked on trying to define who she was without Beth. Tina found the book *Teens, Loss, and Grief* by Edward Myers (2006) to be very helpful and returned it to me near the end of the school year. Tina and I discussed putting all her wonderful memories with Beth in a special place, so that she could always have these memories close. Tina enjoyed scrapbooking so she decided to create a scrapbook of all the great times that she had had with Beth. She worked on it throughout her senior year, and it turned out to be one of the most therapeutic activities she did throughout her grieving process.

Throughout the school year I saw Tina move up and down the ladder of grief. At times she was on the acceptance step for weeks or months and then an event would most often take her back to the sadness step. At times she also experienced anger, sometimes at her family, at her friends, and even at God. Tina developed coping skills to help her during times of anger and sadness, and journaling was one coping mechanism that Tina found useful. It

was also important for Tina to understand that the emotions she felt were normal and that everyone goes through the grieving process differently. Her family often pressured her to move through the grieving process faster than she was able to, and all of her friends and classmates had moved on, so providing her with the support she needed to continue working through her grief was imperative to her success.

Tina began to visit my office less and less, and eventually we met only when she came by with something specific she needed to talk about. There were a few difficult times, but because we had discussed what might be challenging, she was well prepared to cope at those times. Beth's birthday and prom were Tina's most difficult times after she had worked through most of her grief. Graduation came and she was at peace with Beth's death. Although graduation wasn't what she had planned, Tina said, "It is graduation. It is a time to be happy and excited about the future and a time to remember and cherish everything about high school." Throughout her grieving process, Tina learned skills that will help her through other difficult situations in life.

## Final Process Questions

- How well did Tina work through her grief?
- What additional approaches or interventions could have been used?
- How important was Tina's faith in working through her grief, and how comfortable was I in working with her faith?

- What other ways can a school counselor help students grieve?
- What help might Tina need while transitioning to college?

## Resources

Erford, B. T., & McKechnie, J. A. (2001). *Good grief.* Board game for children available through the American Counseling Association Bookstore

Humphrey, K. M. (2009). *Counseling strategies for loss and grief.* Alexandria, VA: American Counseling Association.

Leeuwenburgh, E., & Goldring, E. (2008). *Why did you die?: Activities to help children cope with grief and loss.* Oakland, CA: Instant Help Books.

Noel, B., & Blair, P. (2008). *I wasn't ready to say goodbye.* Naperville, IL: Sourcebooks.

*Chapter 22*

# Addressing Disruptive Behavior in the Classroom Using an Ecological Approach

ADRIA SHIPP AND TARA HILL

## CASE BACKGROUND

As a school counselor, I met Tyler during the first weeks of school the year he started kindergarten. He came to kindergarten orientation with both of his parents and his two brothers, one younger and one older. He had everyone's attention as soon as he walked into the room. Tyler knocked over buckets of toys, threw books on the ground, and did not share with other children. He did not participate in cooperative play, but preferred to work alone, doing non-directed activities away from other people. For example, he enjoyed building with Legos®, but yelled when asked to play a game or color a picture.

As the first months of kindergarten progressed, Tyler's behavior became increasingly problematic. Tyler often was sent to the office for disruptive behavior such as yelling profanities, refusing to follow directions, or hitting other children. He would "chill out" in the office for 5 minutes before being sent back to class, but would inevitably be chilling out in the office again a short while later. It became obvious that if this pattern continued, Tyler was going to learn to dislike school at a very early age. Typical classroom reward systems were not working with Tyler. Tyler's teacher referred him to the Response to Intervention (RTI) committee for behavior issues, and he quickly moved to Tier III, at which time a committee meeting was held to discuss Tyler's lack of progress on set behavior goals. Previously, meetings had been held with Tyler's parents and his teacher, but now that he was in Tier III, the entire committee met to discuss individualized interventions that might help Tyler. The committee consisted of the school psychologist, the school counselor, an administrator, and several classroom teachers.

Both of Tyler's parents attended the RTI committee meeting and reported experiencing similar behavior issues with Tyler at home. They believed he was overly aggressive with both of his brothers, had few friends, and struggled to complete homework assignments. Although they felt that most of Tyler's behaviors required discipline, they believed that there was another component of his behavior that warranted further evaluation by a professional and so were in the process of having a psychological evaluation conducted. Tyler had been in counseling since he was 3 years old, but was not currently seeing a therapist. His mother also discussed the variety of medications Tyler had been prescribed in the past, including those for AD/HD and mood disorder. They were in the process of switching psychiatrists.

As a result of this meeting, a behavior plan was put in place to address two sets of behaviors: aggression toward others and noncompliance. The plan focused on consequences for not making good choices, whereby Tyler was given three strikes (i.e., the first is chill out in the classroom, the second is chill out outside of the classroom with an adult, and the third is chill out in the office). After three strikes, Tyler could be sent home. In case of a crisis situation, in which Tyler becomes a threat to himself or others, Tyler's psychiatrist would be called, as would his parents.

## INITIAL PROCESS QUESTIONS

- Which individuals are potentially influencing Tyler's situation?
- How might a school counselor decide at which level to intervene using an ecological approach (i.e., the individual, micro system, or macro system)?
- Who would the school counselor wish to include when behavior plans and interventions are put in place?
- How might a school counselor decide where to focus to create change (i.e., behavior, attitudes, feelings, thoughts)?

## ADDRESSING THE ISSUES

I chose to use an ecological model to understand the factors affecting Tyler's behaviors at school. The ecological model (Bronfenbrenner, 1979) generally considers that Tyler's development is influenced by the surrounding environmental systems and the interactions he has within those systems. He may be struggling in his environment because of dysfunction in the environment, his individual issues, or the interaction of both (Banning, 1989; Wilson, 2003). According to the ecological model, it is not enough just to try to intervene with Tyler at the individual level to decrease behavior issues at school. Instead, this model directs school counselors to consider factors such as home environment, family dynamics, peer group (micro system); cultural values regarding education, broader societal factors (macro system); as well as interactions between these systems (meso system). Taking into consideration the individual, micro, and macro systems of this student, Tyler's behavior issues take on a new perspective. The ecological model suggests all of these factors impact Tyler's behavior. It is important, as his school counselor, that I consider each of the three levels (e.g., individual, micro system, and macro system) when designing interventions to facilitate academic success (Howard & Solberg, 2006).

When collaborating with Tyler, and the micro system impacting him as an individual, Smead (1982) offered four options for school counselors: (1) Make changes in the environment, (2) assist the student to fit in a new environment, (3) help the student gain the skills necessary to make changes in the environment, or (4) assist the student in making the necessary attitude and perspective changes to make the environment more bearable. These options are not mutually exclusive, so more than one level can be the focus of intervention at any given time. As this case scenario demonstrates, interventions at the individual and micro system levels were simultaneously implemented. I elected to intervene on behalf of the student at the micro system level by making changes in the environment through collaborating with the professionals involved (micro system intervention).

School counselors are in a unique position to use an ecological approach with students for several reasons. First, school counselors can provide interventions at an individual level and at the micro system level. For students, the micro system level may include relationships within the student's school environment (e.g., peers, teachers, specialists, administration). School counselors may develop relationships with parents and provide interventions in the student's home environment as well. In addition to being leaders in the school, school counselors have relationships with professionals outside of the school. These professionals may include workers at social service agencies, outside clinical counselors, physicians, or even probation officers. Although school counselors may not always have the power to make immediate macro system level changes to society in terms of racism, economic oppression, or a student's socioeconomic status, they often are able to influence students as individuals, as well as students' micro systems (e.g., family, peer group, school).

One of the benefits of the ecological model is that school counselors can use a variety of theoretical approaches and techniques. However, this model differs from an eclectic approach because the ecological counseling perspective offers counselors a "framework for identifying appropriate interventions in their work with students" (Abrams, Theberge, & Karan, 2005, p. 286). Thus, the ecological model is a philosophy or perspective of case conceptualization and intervention as opposed to being its own theoretical orientation complete with interventions such as those of solution-focused or psychoanalytic approaches. Table 22-1 provides strategies and techniques applicable to the individual and micro system levels of the ecological approach.

In following the ecological model, I must consider three levels: including Tyler as an individual, Tyler's micro system (e.g., family, peers, school, community), and Tyler's macro system (e.g., culture, societal factors). Often school counselors and school teams attempt to create change at the individual level first, sometimes forgetting to incorporate the other levels into their conceptualization of the issues. Each of the three levels will be addressed next, beginning with Tyler's macro system, then micro system, and finally, the individual.

## Macro System

Generally speaking, American public schools are structured so that all students begin kindergarten when they are 5 years old. Prior to age 5 years, educational opportunities are left up to families and so depend on the early childhood options available. Tyler's family has stated that they were unable to afford preschool for Tyler, but did not qualify for subsidized programs. Although they realized he would benefit from structured early education, they were unable to provide those opportunities for their son.

Furthermore, students who demonstrate disruptive behavior issues in classrooms (which often have 20 or more students) interrupt the learning of others and are therefore often handled as discipline problems and sent to the office. In the case of Tyler, after reaching the end of his behavior plan, he was often sent home three or more days per week. An individualistic culture tends to hold individuals, no matter what age, accountable for their own actions and punish those who are unable to exhibit self-control or follow rules.

**TABLE 22-1   Strategies and Techniques Applicable to the Individual and Micro System Levels of the Ecological Approach**

| Paradigm | Elementary School | Middle School | High School |
|---|---|---|---|
| Psychodynamic | *Individual:* Drawing of self to clarify perception of self<br><br>*Micro System:* Creating a family drawing to better understand family dynamics | *Individual:* Addressing externalizing behaviors (e.g., fighting)<br><br>*Micro System:* Asking student to choose a song that describes his or her place within the peer group | *Individual:* Addressing internalizing behaviors<br><br>*Micro System:* Conducting a needs assessment to identify common issues (e.g., lack of transportation) within the school community |
| Humanistic/ Existential | *Individual:* Creating a timeline of past, present, and future life events<br><br>*Micro System:* Helping parents and staff understand the student's perspective; helping school staff understand student's symptoms from a variety of perspectives in terms of manifestation of symptoms | *Individual:* Helping student understand his or her diagnosis<br><br>*Micro System:* Forming a group for students with similar behavior issues to help them make meaning of their diagnoses (e.g., AD/HD); helping school staff understand student's symptoms from a variety of perspectives in terms of manifestation of symptoms | *Individual:* Having student list personal expectations, hopes, and plans for the immediate and later future for comparison to assist student in making meaning of current life circumstances<br><br>*Micro System:* Initiating a support team with student's involved school professionals to provide student with additional coaching and mentoring; consultation with school administrators to facilitate a school-wide awareness program to decrease in negative stigma regarding AD/HD and other mental health issues of students |
| Behavioral/CBT | *Individual:* Conducting a functional behavior assessment and developing a behavior intervention plan<br><br>*Micro System:* Identifying school settings where behavior issues are not present; implementing Positive Behavior Interventions & Supports systems within the school | *Individual:* Creating a Boffey map to better understand student's feelings, thoughts, behaviors, and physiological reactions to the situation; creating a behavior plan including a token economy with short-term and long-term incentives<br><br>*Micro System:* Developing school-wide behavior incentives to reward positive behavior; collaborating with students' families to create similar behavior rewards for home and school | *Individual:* Examining similar behavior issues that have arisen in the past and exceptions to those behavior patterns<br><br>*Micro System:* Forming a school committee of students and teachers to address school-wide behavior issues |

| Paradigm | Elementary School | Middle School | High School |
|---|---|---|---|
| Family Systems | *Individual:* Creating a family sculpture with a group of peers to identify family influences<br><br>*Micro System:* Facilitating a book club for parents around a specific issue (e.g., raising a child with AD/HD); assessing basic needs of family | *Individual:* Creating a family genogram to identify familial patterns<br><br>*Micro System:* Identifying common familial patterns and needs within the school community; connecting with external agencies to provide resources | *Individual:* Using a genogram to identify the strong and weak bonds in the family system as well as other significant patterns as they contribute to the student's behavioral issues<br><br>*Micro System:* Consultation with the parents regarding past family patterns and roles that may be contributing to behavior issues |
| Emergent | *Individual:* Using the miracle question to identify what the student would like to change<br><br>*Micro System:* Having student and family members write a narrative of an incident that occurred and then helping them make sense of the differing perspectives | *Individual:* Helping students find exceptions to their own behavior patterns and helping them brainstorm possible reasons for these anomalies<br><br>*Micro System:* Helping the family retell a behavior incident together step by step to understand all factors influencing the outcome | *Individual:* Helping students create a collage of their ideal worlds<br><br>*Micro System:* Sharing student narratives about discipline at school anonymously with staff at a staff meeting to help them understand student perspectives of school incidents |

## Micro System

Tyler lives in a rural community where education is not necessarily a top priority for all families. Being respectful and living up to your family name, however, are very important to many families, including Tyler's family. His parents reported hitting Tyler with a belt when he was perceived as disrespectful. His father is the disciplinarian in the family, and his mother says she has difficulty "getting Tyler to mind." Interestingly, the male teachers at school do not indicate having such issues with Tyler in class. In accordance with the mandated reporting laws in my state, as the school counselor, I reported Tyler's father's disciplinary measures to the local child protection agency. An investigation ensued and the case was closed without incident.

The school that Tyler attends does not have a school-wide behavior plan, but leaves discipline up to individual classroom teachers. Tyler's teacher uses a system whereby students turn over their apples when they do not follow the rules. Students showing good behavior are rewarded with gold coins that can be cashed in for a visit to the class treasure box at the end of the day. Although these classroom systems have not worked for Tyler, they have been even less successful since his teacher has been out on maternity leave. The classroom now has a long-term substitute teacher for the rest of the year. Since this change, there have been three incident reports about Tyler (e.g., student pinched another student, student fell and broke wrist on the playground, student ran away from the teacher) filed per week. Tyler has been reaching the end of his behavior plan more frequently since his teacher left.

## Individual

Tyler has seen many medical professionals since beginning school. He has been on several different types of medication, some which have worked to control certain behaviors, but to which he has had side effects (i.e., rashes, enuresis, and lethargy). Tyler's reported IQ of 80 is below average. However, he was reportedly experiencing an increase in inattention and impulsivity at the time of testing, so this score should be interpreted with caution.

Tyler responds better to rewards than punishment and is especially motivated by technology (e.g., iPad, computer). He becomes frustrated when he is unable to complete a task or when other students are in his personal space. Tyler's moods can shift dramatically during a day. For example, he might be silly during math time, but can become angry and withdrawn 30 minutes later during reading.

As a first step toward gathering more information about what is actually occurring at the micro system and individual levels during the school day, the classroom teacher assistant was provided a video camera to record Tyler's behaviors at random times throughout the day (with parental consent). I also recorded Tyler, sometimes when he was aware of the camera and at other times when he was not. I then shared the video recordings with his mother, who wanted to show them to Tyler's psychiatrist to give him a better sense of the school's concerns. I closely evaluated the recordings, leading to identification of triggers and high-risk situations, which proved to be incredibly helpful in creating effective interventions for Tyler.

In addition, I called Tyler's psychiatrist (after a signed release of information form was obtained) to notify him of the following: Tyler was still struggling with behaviors at school, what steps the school had taken so far, and the possible next steps to take if Tyler's behavior did not start to improve. The possibility of transferring Tyler to an alternative school setting with day treatment capabilities was being discussed in order to decrease his class size and increase the therapeutic behavioral interventions for Tyler that could occur during the day. The psychiatrist then called Tyler's mother to inform her that he had scheduled an immediate checkup to adjust Tyler's medications. Tyler's mother took the video recordings to the psychiatrist along with the following letter I wrote.

*I am enclosing video of Tyler during a single school day. Periodically during the day he was recorded, sometimes knowing that the camera was on and sometimes unaware. On this particular day, Tyler had done two "chill outs" by 1:00 p.m. There are several instances in which Tyler is not participating in regular classroom activities (e.g., working with shapes instead of cutting, hiding under the loft in his classroom after an incident in the gym, sitting beside the teacher while reading a story). I am concerned that he is not able to access educational services at this point and that he is not able to demonstrate his knowledge because of his behavior.*

*Some of the other behaviors we are seeing at school include rapid mood shifts (i.e., one video shows him laughing and in the next he is huddled in a corner), aggression toward other students and himself (e.g., banging his cast against the table or wall), defiance toward adults, refusal to complete assignments, refusal to participate in classroom activities, and overall behavior issues. Tyler seems worn out at the end of the day, especially days in which he has had several "chill outs" and seems defeated because he does not seem to understand why he has gotten into trouble. We have been implementing a behavior plan at school to help him, but continue to see inconsistent results. Tyler receives services under the Individuals with Disabilities Education Act (IDEA) under Other Health Impaired for AD/HD.*

*We are hoping to collaborate with a team of professionals who can help Tyler be successful at school. If you have questions, or suggestions, please feel free to call. I am available Monday—Friday between the hours of 7:30 a.m.—3:30 p.m.*

Tyler's psychiatrist did adjust Tyler's medication (individual intervention). I called Tyler's mom the afternoon of the appointment to check in and get some information about what types of recommendations the psychiatrist made as a result of viewing the recordings. She passed along the psychiatrist's suggestions, and we decided to meet on the following day to revisit Tyler's behavior plan at school to include these suggestions. The school principal, special education teacher, classroom teacher, Tyler's mother, and I were present at the meeting (collaboration with professionals and important members of the micro system). At this meeting, I shared with the team and Tyler's mom the steps I had followed in collecting information on Tyler's behavior within the classroom, the collaboration with Tyler's psychiatrist, and educated the team on the process of using an ecological approach. In addition, I instructed the team on how a paradigm shift in their perception of Tyler's disruptive behavior and his interaction with the environment would increase positive behaviors. This intervention with the team and Tyler's mom allowed us to brainstorm and create a new behavior plan based on the factors in Tyler's individual and micro system levels.

## IN SESSION

A new behavior plan was created that focused on one behavior, included several types of rewards, created choices for Tyler, and integrated classroom systems already in place. In addition, a table of consequences was also made to provide direction for the classroom teachers regarding which behaviors resulted in which types of discipline, rather than focusing on the quantity (i.e., number of strikes) of incidents during the day. This intervention focused on two different levels: Tyler (individual level; change in individual) and the classroom (micro system level; change in the environment). Here is a transcript from a session in which the behavior plan was explained to Tyler.

| | |
|---|---|
| COUNSELOR (C): | OK, Tyler, tell me what you need to do to be able to get a sticker and put it on your chart? |
| TYLER (T): | I have to behave. |
| C: | Yes, you're right. So if your teacher asks you to do something, you will get a sticker if you do what? |
| T: | If I do it the first time and she doesn't have to ask me again. |
| C: | Very good. You have such a good memory. That's exactly right. Every time you do what your teacher asks you to do the first time, you will get a sticker. How many stickers do you need to get before you get to choose a reward? |
| T: | 1, 2, 3, 4, 5. I need 5. |

C:                  Yes, 5. So when you get 5 stickers, you will get to choose a reward. What kind of reward do you get to choose? Look at your chart.

T:                  Play on the iPad, Legos, the computer, or puzzles. (*Pointing to each picture*)

C:                  Wow! Those are all really great choices. Tell me what happens if you get all the way to the end of the chart with your stickers.

T:                  Treasure box! I go to the treasure box!

## Outcome

Since implementation of the behavioral intervention, Tyler has not had a single chill out in the classroom or the office. An intervention in the micro system of creating a classroom culture that focused on what he was doing well, rather than on what he was doing wrong, dramatically decreased the number of discipline referrals Tyler received. The combination of adjusting medication (change in the individual), involving Tyler's parents (micro system involvement), and creating a clear behavior plan (change in the environment) based on observations collected through the video recordings changed the discussions about Tyler from alternative school placement to identifying additional reward choices. This transformation took less than two weeks' time. The behavior plan has needed some tweaking over time, but continues to be successful.

## Ethical Considerations

Several ethical issues emerged throughout the course of my work with Tyler. The first ethical consideration was my obligation as a mandated reporter of child abuse. Although the disciplinary measures parents choose for their children is up to their discretion, in most circumstances, the use of an implement such as a belt, wooden spoon, or paddle for spanking approaches a gray area in terms of excessive force. It is not my job as a school counselor to investigate or make a determination as to whether a particular incident occurred, but it is ethically and legally my responsibility to report any suspicions to the authorities.

The second ethical consideration relates to the release of protected health information and educational records. It is important to understand that consent for releases of information must be given on both ends of the exchange. For instance, Tyler's mom needs to sign a consent form for the psychiatrist to share information with the school and school counselor, and she should likewise sign a consent form for the school and school counselor to share information with the psychiatrist prior to the exchange of information. In addition, I need to be thoughtful about with whom in the school community I share information about Tyler. Only the educational team working with Tyler should be involved in behavioral planning. It is my responsibility to remind each team member of the importance of confidentiality as it relates to Tyler's behavior, his school performance, and any other information shared in meetings and as part of consultation with his parents.

Finally, it is my ethical responsibility as a school counselor to be culturally competent. Approaching Tyler's disruptive behavior from an ecological counseling perspective assists me in keeping the culturally relevant aspects of his macro system and micro system in the foreground. Cultural considerations in this case included recognizing that Tyler is a White male growing up in a low-income family living in a rural community in the southeastern United States. My interventions would have been markedly different had Tyler's cultural background been different.

## Final Process Questions

- In what ways can the school counselor offer continued support for Tyler and his family?
- What can the school counselor do to ensure fidelity with the behavior plan that is in place while taking into consideration the advantages and disadvantages of being raised in a low-socioeconomic and economically depressed rural community?
- What are some changes that can be made if the behavior plan ceases to be effective?
- How can school counselors advocate at the macro system level for students such as Tyler?

## Resources

Abrams, L., Theberge, S. K., & Karan, O. C. (2005). Children and adolescents who are depressed: An ecological approach. *Professional School Counseling, 8,* 284–293.

Banning, J. H. (1989). *Ecotherapy: A life space application of the ecological perspective.* Retrieved from http://www.campusecologist.com/1989/01/05/volume-7-number-3-1989/

Bronfenbrenner, U. (1977). Toward an experimental ecology of human development. *American Psychologist, 32,* 513–531.

Bronfenbrenner, U. (1979). *The ecology of human development.* Cambridge, MA: Harvard University Press.

Conyne, R. K., & Cook, E. P. (2004). *Ecological counseling: An innovative approach to conceptualizing person–environment interaction.* Alexandria, VA: American Counseling Association.

Hawley, A. H. (1950). *Human ecology: A theory of community structure.* New York, NY: Ronald Press.

*Chapter 23*

# Social Isolation

MAEGAN VICK AND CHARLOTTE DAUGHHETEE

## CASE BACKGROUND

Kelly stood a good foot taller and weighed 50 pounds more than the other fifth-grade girls in her class. The first time I saw Kelly, her hair hung wildly around her face, her clothes were unkempt, and she had difficulty in spitting out a sentence to me, although over time she began to trust me and open up. Kelly also struggled to have a casual conversation with her peers and was often the target of bullying and jokes.

Even in her family she was teased. Kelly mentioned to me that her mother and a cousin teased her about her weight. Because both parents worked, the father in construction and the mother as a waitress, it was difficult for Kelly's parents to be present at school functions and so they rarely attended. The few times that I had met the parents, Kelly's father did not speak at all and the mother appeared to be shy.

Kelly was such a kindhearted girl, in many ways different from the other fifth-grade girls. She had more childish or innocent interests; for example, she showed little to no interest in the most recent pop culture icons like most "tweener" girls did. She was certainly not considered fashionable and often came to school looking disheveled. Because Kelly talked rather slowly and struggled to carry on a casual conversation, one might mistake her for being unintelligent. However, she was very intelligent and showed no signs of academic struggles in the classroom.

Whereas many fifth-grade girls delighted in getting a note or a passing glance from some of the boys in class, Kelly shied away and hoped not to be noticed, for fear of being ridiculed. It was for these reasons that Kelly isolated herself from peers, or perhaps the reasons that her peers isolated themselves from her. Yes, Kelly wanted to have friends; however, it seemed too much a risk for her to attempt. And it was too much of a risk for the other kids in her class to befriend her as well. Kelly needed help with establishing friendships and positive social interactions.

## INITIAL PROCESS QUESTIONS

- Children who are different are often targeted by bullies. In what ways does Kelly differ from her classmates?
- Are some of these differences actually strengths that could be used to help her with social interactions? If so, which ones, and how could they be used to Kelly's advantage?

- What impact might her family situation have on her social isolation?
- Kelly wants to have friends. Would you approach this case scenario differently if she had not expressed an interest in, or longing for, friendship?
- What are the best interventions/approaches to use in this case scenario?
- How might rapport building be more of a struggle with Kelly?
- How might Kelly's teacher be included in the intervention?
- What other people and systems could be used as resources in this case scenario?

## ADDRESSING THE ISSUES

Positive social development is essential to a healthy lifestyle. Children who lack social skills may develop a negative self-concept regarding their social and emotional selves; such a self-concept interferes with the development of interpersonal skills and fosters a sense of inferiority. Because Kelly's problem was interpersonal in nature, I decided it would help her to be in a small group for girls that would have a focus on friendship, self-esteem, and social skills. In creating this group, I recognized that care must be taken in group member selection in order to generate a supportive, safe environment for learning, risk taking, and skill practice.

I used a cognitive-behavioral group counseling intervention that allowed for a safe interface with others. Aspects of social cognitive theory, which focuses on rewards and modeling, were integrated into the group activities. The cognitive-behavioral approach allowed for the children to confront negative self-talk; Adlerian theory  assisted in understanding the mistaken beliefs upon which this self-talk was based and constructing new, more positive life-enhancing self-talk. I set up specific goals for each session to address the children's disordered thinking and help them create new outlooks. Each group session gave them opportunities to learn and practice new pro-social behaviors that I modeled and used stories to demonstrate. The group activities also identified existing strengths and positives that the children could build upon.

Additionally, the concept of empathy was stressed throughout the intervention, thereby addressing the humanistic/existential aspect of social isolation. I believed it was important for the girls to understand the thinking behind their behavior and feelings, learn new skills, and increase their understanding of others. I carefully chose girls who would benefit from this group as much as Kelly would, including those who had exhibited some tendency for bullying behavior and therefore needed to develop their sense of empathy.

Thus, the Fab Five was born: Kelly, Davita, Andrea, Rosa, and Mary. The logistics of a group are crucial. Even with careful planning and screening, it is still quite hard to know whether the group will blend well. This group did. A few of the girls in the group had very good social skills and regular, healthy interactions with peers, such as Mary, who had all the social graces and leadership qualities to befriend anyone. Mary had previously been getting into trouble at school due to hanging around a crowd of intimidating girls known for bullying and starting trouble. However, she had recently separated herself from that group and taken on more favorable leadership qualities. Mary was currently in a leadership program led by our school principal, which had positively affected her behavior, but she still had a lot of growth potential. She was insightful, positive, and truly cared about the other girls in the group.

Conversely, Rosa was rather quiet and subdued. She had baton twirling to keep her busy, yet Rosa was also a target of bullying due to her shyness and lack of name-brand clothes. She did not speak up much in the group and was willing to let others do the work. However, whenever Rosa did share her thoughts with the group, she showed great insight.

Andrea was still struggling to define herself as either a bully or a "good girl." Although she often talked of religion and expressed to me that she wanted to be a better person, Andrea would regularly find herself getting sucked into bullying behaviors, as she was easily influenced by peers. Many of these behaviors were a defense mechanism she used to shield herself from being targeted and bullied by others. I hoped this group would help Andrea to empathize with victims of bullying.

Last, Davita—sweet, quirky Davita—struggled as much as Kelly with peer interactions. She did well academically but poor socially. She was clingy in any friendship she encountered, which eventually pushed others away. She, too, had more innocent interests, mostly dogs and playing outdoors. She struggled to recognize any nonverbal communication. In addition, she did not know how to handle conflict appropriately. She and Kelly were quite the pair. They both would say whatever was on their minds and did not seem to relate to others. My Fab Five cried, laughed, and learned. I did too.

The group consisted of six sessions with the first meeting used to establish group rules and to get to know one another. A few sessions stood out as being particularly valuable. During one group activity, the girls each had a cutout flower with five petals. Each girl signed her name in the middle of her flower and then passed the flower around so that every other girl had a chance to write one compliment about her. The joy I saw on their faces when they read the comments was priceless. With widespread smiles, each girl tried to guess who had written each kind message on her flower. The girls needed to know that they were important to one another and special. Pointing out what is right with one another, rather than what is wrong, is a very powerful intervention.

During another group session, the girls took a self-esteem rating test; of course, none of them scored extremely high. We followed up that session with a positive self-talk activity. The girls had to practice turning negative statements into positive statements. This was followed by the girls identifying a few negative self-statements of their own, exploring the beliefs behind those thoughts, and constructing a rational positive alternative statement. Over the course of the group, I modeled positive social skills and other group members, such as Mary, served as role models for pro-social behaviors. Table 23-1 provides additional strategies that may help socially isolated students across elementary, middle, and high school levels.

## ADDITIONAL CONSIDERATIONS

Although the focus of this chapter is social isolation rather than bullying, it is important to address the issue of bullying when working with socially isolated children. Farmer, Hall, Estell, Leung, and Brooks (2011) note that the association between bullying and social isolation is more complex than one might assume. Bullies who have a high social status can create a school climate that is more aggressive and more perilous for all students, especially socially isolated students. School interventions with bullies and school-wide initiatives to address a bully culture are critically important. Thompson (2012) suggests the communication of clear-cut rules against bully behavior; integration

**TABLE 23-1   Additional Approaches for Working with Socially Isolated Students**

| Paradigm | Elementary School | Middle School | High School |
|---|---|---|---|
| Psychodynamic | Exploring transference, countertransference, and defense mechanisms; analysis of Adlerian goal of misbehavior (goal of inadequacy) and building social interest through group activities; teaching "I" statements and other skills | Exploring transference, countertransference, and defense mechanisms; encouraging insight into unconscious aspects of problems through creative processes; analysis of Adlerian goal of misbehavior (goal of inadequacy) and building social interest through group activities; teaching "I" statements and other skills | Exploring transference, countertransference, and defense mechanisms; encouraging insight into unconscious aspects of problems through creative processes; analysis of Adlerian goal of misbehavior (goal of inadequacy) and building social interest through group activities; teaching "I" statements and other skills |
| Humanistic/ Existential | Core conditions for therapeutic change; providing opportunity for empathy and safe exploration of thoughts, feelings, and behaviors; encouragement of self-awareness and choice leading to acceptance of self and others; confronting inconsistencies | Core conditions for therapeutic change; providing opportunity for empathy and safe exploration of thoughts, feelings, and behaviors; encouragement of self-awareness and choice leading to acceptance of self and others; confronting inconsistencies | Core conditions for therapeutic change; providing opportunity for empathy and safe exploration of thoughts, feelings, and behaviors; encouragement of self-awareness and choice leading to acceptance of self and others; confronting inconsistencies |
| Behavioral/CBT | Positive reinforcement for pro-social behaviors; role play of new behaviors; recognizing and disputing negative thoughts and beliefs, replacing with rational self-talk; thought stopping and cognitive restructuring; homework; development of action plans for change; identifying positive behaviors and exceptions to the problem and striving to do more of the positive behaviors; use of scaling, role play, and the miracle question to identify positives/exceptions and strengths and to set tasks; flagging the minefield | Positive reinforcement for pro-social behaviors; role play of new behaviors; recognizing and disputing negative thoughts and beliefs, replacing with rational self-talk; thought stopping and cognitive restructuring; homework; development of action plans for change; identifying positive behaviors and exceptions to the problem and striving to do more of the positive behaviors; use of scaling, role play, and the miracle question to identify positives/exceptions and strengths and to set tasks; flagging the minefield | Positive reinforcement for pro-social behaviors; role play of new behaviors; recognizing and disputing negative thoughts and beliefs, replacing with rational self-talk; thought stopping and cognitive restructuring; homework; development of action plans for change; identifying positive behaviors and exceptions to the problem and striving to do more of the positive behaviors; use of scaling, role play, and the miracle question to identify positives/exceptions and strengths and to set tasks; flagging the minefield |

*(continued)*

**TABLE 23-1** *(continued)*

| Paradigm | Elementary School | Middle School | High School |
|---|---|---|---|
| Family Systems | Reaching out to parents to engage them in school and offer parent training; exploring family system through a genogram to identify behaviors and patterns passed down; coaching; "I" position | Reaching out to parents to engage them in school and offer parent training; exploring family system through a genogram to identify behaviors and patterns passed down; coaching; "I" position; discussing triangulation and working toward de-triangulation | Reaching out to parents to engage them in school and offer parent training; exploring family system through a genogram to identify behaviors and patterns passed down; coaching; "I" position; discussing triangulation and working toward de-triangulation; encouraging adolescent to explore "going home again" and work on differentiation from emotional reactivity in family of origin |
| Emergent | Deconstruct the problem-laden story; identifying unique outcomes and helping student coauthor a new story that is strength based; externalizing the problem and working against the problem; celebrating success; addressing attachment issues; here-and-now focus; role play; working on communication skills and accessing social support | Deconstruct the problem-laden story; identifying unique outcomes and helping student coauthor a new story that is strength based; externalizing the problem and working against the problem; celebrating success; addressing attachment issues; here-and-now focus; role play; working on communication skills and accessing social support | Deconstruct the problem-laden story; identifying unique outcomes and helping student coauthor a new story that is strength based; externalizing the problem and working against the problem; celebrating success; addressing attachment issues; here-and-now focus; role play; working on communication skills and accessing social support |

of peer mediation, social skills, and positive school climate building into guidance curriculum; as well as friendship groups for children who suffer bullying and need social support.

School counselors in all settings address transition issues. Elementary and middle school counselors must help students prepare for the expectations of the next level of academics. High school counselors assist students as they transition to post-school life. For the socially isolated child, school transition can be especially difficult. Kingery, Erdley, and Marshall (2011) found that peer acceptance and friendship was an indicator of successful transition to middle school. Therefore, intervention directed at socially isolated students is important for their future success and adjustment. In addition to working with the socially isolated student to augment social skills and friendships, elementary counselors should also coordinate services with middle school counselors to ensure continued support for the student in transition.

# IN SESSION

Throughout our sessions, it became evident that Kelly did not understand the art of conversation or social nuances. She once randomly blurted out, in the middle of a session, that Andrea had bullied her on the bus when she was in third grade. Andrea looked as though lightning had hit; her eyes were frantic, searching my face to see whether I would cast judgment on Kelly. Andrea began to cry. Kelly, of course, did not see that reaction coming.

| | |
|---|---|
| KELLY (K): | One time, when I was in third grade, Andrea called me an elephant on the bus. |
| ANDREA (A): | What? I did not! (*Starts crying*) |
| COUNSELOR (C): | Andrea, can you share with us how you are feeling right now? |
| A: | I'm mad, because I don't remember saying that! |
| K: | I'm sorry. I didn't want to make you cry. |
| C: | It seems you don't remember that happening Andrea, but Kelly does. Kelly, why don't you share what you remember and how you felt that day? |
| K: | I remember Andrea sitting with some girls who were mean. She called me an elephant. It hurt my feelings. She was not always nice to me. Now she is. |
| C: | In the past Andrea said some hurtful comments to you, but now Andrea is different. That's what you want to say to her? She has changed, and you're glad you're friends now? |
| K: | Yes. I am happy we're friends. Andrea is nice to me now. She is different. |
| C: | Andrea, it seems you felt "called out" when Kelly said you once called her a name. Maybe you were worried I would think you are a bully, but I don't. I will never judge you. It seems Kelly wanted to say you have changed and are a good friend to her now. Kelly values your friendship. We have all, at some point, said something that hurt someone else's feelings. That's why we have to choose our words carefully. How are you feeling now? (*Andrea looked remorseful*) |
| A: | Sorry, because I know I used to be mean sometimes. I'm sorry, Kelly. |
| K: | That's OK. We're friends now. |
| C: | It seems both of you care about each other. Kelly, sometimes you have to be careful of the way you confront others. Sometimes it helps to start by saying something positive first, such as, "Andrea, I want you to know that I am happy we are friends now, but one time you said something hurtful to me." Also, sometimes, it is best to accept people for who they are today, not the person they used to be. |

K:  I am happy we are friends now, Andrea. I forgive you. I know you are not like that anymore.

I used this as a learning experience. Both girls were able to forgive each other and bond through this experience. Kelly learned how to regulate her thoughts and express her feelings appropriately, and Andrea learned the power of harsh words.

## Outcome

Though Kelly never became the socialite of the school, she formed meaningful relationships with the girls in the group. Kelly was able to practice socializing in a safe environment during group. She was able to take risks without fear. That was the most important part of group for all of the girls: It was safe. They could express thoughts and feelings without fear of rejection or ridicule. They built one another up instead of tearing one another down. They were all able to practice positive social interactions, self-affirmations, and positive thinking. Their self-confidence grew. Kelly and Davita grew closer with each other, and the last I heard, they were good buddies in the sixth grade. The girls signed a pact during our last group meeting stating they would always look out for one another and stand up for one another. They seemed to have kept that pact.

Mary requested to sing "Lean on Me" (a song she had learned in choir) as the group's farewell song, and she did so beautifully. Kelly, who was also in choir, actually wanted her shot in the spotlight too. In turn, Kelly did her own rendition of "Lean on Me," which was quite beautiful as well. The last group session required each girl to write one lesson they had learned from group. One of the most profound comments came from Kelly. She wrote, "I have learned I can trust others." That is exactly what she did, trust others and begin to risk relationship with others.

## Final Process Questions

- What issues might Kelly face in middle school?
- Would the school counselor intervention for social isolation differ at the middle school level?
- As Kelly enters adolescence, social media will become more a part of her community context.

What problems might Kelly encounter regarding social media? Could social media be helpful to Kelly?

## Resources

Martenez, A. (2007). *Groups to go: Small groups for counselors on the go.* Warminster, PA: MAR*CO Products.

Ragona, S., & Pentel, K. (2004). *Eliminating bullying: In grades PK–3.* Chapin, SC: YouthLight.

Senn, D. S. (2007). *Creative approaches for counseling children in the school setting.* Chapin, SC: YouthLight.

Sitsch, G., & Senn, S. (2005). *Puzzle pieces: The classroom connection.* Chapin, SC: YouthLight.

Stop Bullying website, http://www.stopbullying.gov/

Swearer, S. M. (2009). *Bullying prevention and intervention: Realistic strategies for schools.* New York, NY: Guilford Press.

*Chapter 24*

# Working With Students Displaying Defiant Behavior

REBECCA CHRISTIANSEN AND KELLY DUNCAN

## CASE BACKGROUND

I was consulting on a behavioral plan when the telephone rang. One of the teachers from our self-contained behavior classroom for students with emotional disturbances (ED) was having an issue with Jack, a student in the program. Jack was refusing to follow instructions, making inappropriate comments to other students, and refusing to leave the room when instructed to "take space." The teacher indicated Jack was not being physically aggressive, but he was disrupting the educational environment. I instructed the teacher to remove the other students from the classroom and have an educational assistant monitor Jack until I got to the classroom.

I mentally reviewed Jack's week in my head. I knew that he was unable to go to his job placement due to missing assignments in his Algebra class. I also knew that Jack's parents were in the middle of a divorce, which was causing high levels of stress in the family. In addition, Jack's records indicated a clinical diagnosis of AD/HD-NOS (not otherwise specified), oppositional defiant disorder, conduct disorder—unspecified onset, and intermittent explosive disorder. In the past, Jack had been physically and verbally aggressive toward adults. I knew that I had to go into the situation in a nonthreatening manner and avoid further escalation. So, I took a deep breath and headed to the classroom.

## INITIAL PROCESS QUESTIONS

- What is the safest course of action to take with the student?
- What theoretical approaches would work best when dealing with a defiant student?
- What is the best way to establish rapport with the student?
- What do I need to do to avoid further student escalation?
- What are the ethical and legal aspects involved when dealing with defiant behaviors?
- What are the multicultural considerations to be aware of when working with defiant students?
- What techniques are best for getting to the root of the problem?
- What techniques are best for assisting the student to plan for success?

## ADDRESSING THE ISSUES

When I entered the classroom, my initial goal was to get Jack out of the classroom and into my office. This would provide a change of environment for the student, which often helps with de-escalation. I was aware that Jack had identified the teacher as the target of his anger and thought that perhaps his behavior was coming from a desire to have control over the situation. I relied on the person-centered approach, which cuts to the core of therapeutic success: the relationship of the counselor and client (Rogers, 1980). I focused on conveying empathy and unconditional positive regard for Jack during our conversation. I also knew that I wanted to use the motivational interviewing strategy of rolling with resistance in order to convey to Jack that I valued his insights and ideas about this situation (Chang, Scott, & Decker, 2009). In addition, I monitored the rate, tone, and volume of my voice in order to avoid further escalation of the student. I asked Jack what was wrong and allowed him to express his frustrations with the teacher. I then used some choice theory and reality therapy techniques by having Jack tell me what it was he wanted and what he was doing in order to get his needs met. I knew that Jack was trying to fulfill his need for power and that he needed to come up with a better way to fulfill his need. Once Jack realized that I was there to listen to him rather than to give him a directive, he was open to the suggestion that we move out of the classroom and down to my office. Jack willingly followed me to my office where our session continued.

When we arrived at my office, Jack and I continued to discuss his challenges in the classroom. Jack admitted to being angry that he was not allowed to go to work due to missing assignments. Jack went on to say that he was not going to complete his work, he was not going to comply with his teacher, and that there was nothing that I could do about it. I continued to express empathy and understanding toward Jack and asked him to tell me what he wanted. Jack focused on wanting to return to work and maintained his refusal to comply with the teacher. I then asked Jack what he thought he needed to do in order to return to work. Jack and I continued the discussion and explored what choices he could make in order to meet his goal of returning to work. We then explored the outcomes of each of his suggestions. This process took over 90 minutes. During our discussion, it was important that Jack see me as a neutral party, not invested in who "won" the battle of Algebra completion, Jack or the teacher. When Jack would become agitated or refuse to open up to the idea of complying with requests, I would point out the physiological changes in him, such as a red face or increased breathing. At that time, I would provide reassurance of the safety of my office and then give him a few minutes before continuing the discussion. When we started talking again, I would begin the conversation with something very nonthreatening, such as asking him about his job first, before transitioning into the topic of Algebra. Throughout the discussion, I continued to show unconditional positive regard, empathy, and monitored my own nonverbal methods of communication. I was careful to monitor the rate, tone, and volume of my own voice to assist in setting the tone of the session. Table 24-1 contains additional strategies and techniques for helping students displaying defiant behavior.

**TABLE 24-1   Additional Strategies and Techniques for Helping Students Displaying Defiant Behavior**

| Paradigm | Elementary School | Middle School | High School |
|---|---|---|---|
| Psychodynamic | Play therapy techniques to explore the child's life and value system; search for underlying goals of behavior; exploration of logical consequences; encouragement | Identifying and disclosing the goal of behavior through play therapy and role playing; identification of defense mechanisms; exploration of natural and logical consequences; providing encouragement | Identifying and disclosing the goal of behavior; exploration of reasons behind defense mechanisms; exploration of natural and logical consequences of behavior; encouragement |
| Humanistic/ Existential | Focus on therapeutic relationship; listening to and reflecting feelings via unconditional positive regard; incorporating self-esteem–building exercises; focus on choice; taking responsibility for one's actions | Focus on therapeutic relationship; active listening and reflecting feelings; encouragement; focus on choice; taking responsibility for one's thoughts, actions, and feelings and exploring how these also affect others | Focus on therapeutic relationship; active listening and reflecting feelings; encouragement; focus on choices open to the student; taking responsibility for one's thoughts, actions, and feelings and exploring how these also affect others |
| Behavioral/CBT | Play therapy; role play; focus on behavior modification through contracts with logical consequences child can understand; development of coping strategies; time-out | Role play of social situations; brainstorming solutions for change; focus on behavior modification through contracts; development of positive coping strategies; disputing irrational beliefs; time-out; exceptions; miracle question | Role play of social situations; brainstorming solutions for change; focus on behavior modification through contracts; development of positive coping strategies; disputing irrational beliefs; exceptions; miracle question |
| Family Systems | Teaching parent(s) strategies for dealing with behavioral, academic, and social issues; focus on interpersonal relationships and family dynamics; working with parents to give clear messages and increase family members' self-esteem | Teaching parent(s) strategies for dealing with behavioral, academic, and social issues; focus on interpersonal relationships and family dynamics; increasing communication; focusing on healthy patterns of communication | Teaching parent(s) strategies for dealing with behavioral, academic, and social issues; focus on interpersonal relationships and family dynamics; increasing communication; focusing on healthy patterns of communication |
| Emergent | Working with family to break problems down into pieces; empowerment; focus on communication; interpersonal relationships | Breaking problems down into pieces; miracle question; empowerment; focus on communication; interpersonal relationships | Breaking problems down into pieces; miracle question; empowerment; focus on communication; interpersonal relationships |

## IN SESSION

| | |
|---|---|
| COUNSELOR (C): | Thank you so much, Jack, for coming down to my office with me. |
| JACK (J): | No problem. It got me out of that stupid classroom and away from that dumb teacher. |
| C: | Tell me again what was frustrating you in the classroom. |
| J: | The teacher wanted me to do my missing math. She can't make me do my math and neither can you. |
| C: | Jack, you are absolutely correct. No one can make you complete your math assignments, and I am not here to tell you that you have to do your math. I am more worried about you. You seem really frustrated and I think you are frustrated about more than just your math. |
| J: | I am. I cannot go to my job placement until my assignments are done and that pisses me off. It's not fair. School is stupid and I am not going to college so I might as well work. |
| C: | It sounds like you really enjoy your job. |
| J: | I do. I can wear what I want to the bowling alley and everyone is very easygoing. No one tells me what to do like they do here. |
| C: | That does sound like a nice place to work. I bet you cannot wait to go back. |
| J: | That stupid teacher will never let me go back though. I am not doing those dumb math assignments and you cannot trick me into doing them. |
| C: | Jack, I am not worried about your math assignments. Why don't we go get a drink? Your face is really red and your hands are clenched, so I think we need to walk around a bit. |
| J: | OK. |
| C: | Thanks, Jack. I don't know about you, but I needed to move around for a minute. Now, tell me, how long have you been at your job? |
| J: | I have been at my job for 2 months. |
| C: | That is great, Jack! I am so proud of you! If I remember correctly, your last job only lasted a few weeks. It sounds like this job is a great fit. I understand why it is so important to return to work. |
| J: | Yeah, but I cannot go back to work until all of my math assignments are turned in. I just wish they were done. Then I could go back to work. |
| C: | Wow, Jack, you are in a tough spot. If I am hearing you right, you get to return to work as soon as your math assignments are completed. So, let's come up with a plan to get you back. |

Jack and I discussed a plan to meet his goal of returning to work. I got out a large piece of paper and had Jack write down the positives and negatives of each option employing a solution-focused technique of having the client focus on the goal and immediate courses of action toward getting the goal met (de Shazer, 1991). When we developed the plan, I had him concentrate his efforts on how to get his Algebra done outside of the self-contained classroom. I did not address his defiance with the teacher at this time as it was important to keep him focused on getting his need for control met first. Jack admitted it was reasonable to get his homework completed before going to his job. He also knew that completing it at home was not a good plan as he does not have a lot of structure at home. Jack developed a plan to attend Algebra tutoring during his study hall time and offered to give up part of his PE class in order to catch up. We discussed the positive outcomes of his decision and identified a target date of Jack returning to work.

I then turned my attention to the relationship between Jack and his teacher. Although the counselor–client relationship is important, so is the student–teacher relationship. In order to increase the probability of Jack's success in the classroom, it was vital to rebuild the relationship between Jack and his teacher before he returned to the classroom. I asked Jack to tell me how he had gotten along with the teacher before the incident in the classroom. We then explored the positive things that had happened to Jack in school since forming the relationship with the teacher. This was difficult as Jack was still fixated on the negative interaction in the classroom. I pointed out his past good grades, the role the teacher had played in his securing his job, and the positive reports that his teacher had been sending home. Rather than dwelling on the recent negative interaction between the teacher and Jack, I focused his attention on the positives of the whole relationship. Once Jack had made a few positive comments, we talked about what Jack perceived as the teacher's goals for him. After a few minutes, Jack identified that the teacher wanted him to be back at work as well. Once Jack saw that his quality world was aligned with the goals of the teacher, he was open to apologizing and returning to the classroom.

## Outcome

Jack did successfully return to the classroom. Before he spoke with the teacher, I pulled the teacher out privately to prep her for what I wanted to have happen. My goal was to reintegrate Jack into the classroom in a positive manner, rather than focusing on the negative interaction that led to his removal, which could inadvertently start the cycle of negative behaviors over again. I had worked closely with this teacher in the past, so she was open to my suggestions. Jack apologized to the teacher and then shared some of his ideas with her. The teacher followed my suggestions by accepting his apology, providing Jack with positive feedback, and allowing him to pick a spot in the classroom where he thought he could best get started on his Algebra assignments. In addition, we worked out a plan with the teacher to allow Jack to check out to a designated area when frustrated, allowing him to have control rather than waiting for a teacher to direct him out.

Jack and I continued to meet weekly to follow up on his assignment completion for his Algebra class. During our sessions, it was important that I allowed Jack to be in control of our conversations. He was more open to the idea of change when he was empowered to take the lead rather than have the adult "tell" him what he needed to do and how he needed to do it.

I kept the sheet of pros and cons that we had completed at the initial session and would bring that out every once in a while to remind Jack of his options. Jack could then add ideas or remove ideas that were not working for him. The weekly check-in provided Jack with some accountability in his assignment completion and also assisted him in staying on task with his homework to avoid having his job suspended again.

Following each of our meetings, including our initial interaction, I made sure to document a brief summary of our conversation, highlighting major themes, noting anything that I may have done or said that visibly upset Jack, and making note of what direction I wanted our conversation to go the next time. I also continued to follow up with the teacher, providing her with both emotional support and suggestions about how to positively manage Jack when he would become frustrated or overwhelmed. I then documented a brief summary of the teacher meeting in my notes for future reference. Both my documentation and follow-up with the teacher were helpful in assisting Jack in achieving a positive outcome.

## Final Process Questions

- What different approaches or interventions would you use with Jack?
- What would you have done if Jack had refused to leave the classroom?
- Where could you go from here with Jack? What are some other issues you could address to avoid a similar reaction in the future?
- After reading this case scenario, what role do you think school counselors have in working with defiant students?
- What differences exist in the way a school counselor works with a student with an emotional disability and with a student who just refuses to follow directions?

## Resources

DeJong, P., & Berg, I. K. (2002). *Interviewing for solutions* (2nd ed.). Pacific Grove, CA: Brooks/Cole.

de Shazer, S. (1991). *Putting differences to work.* New York, NY: Norton.

Glasser, W. (1998). *Choice theory.* New York, NY: HarperCollins.

Parsons, R. D. (2009). *Thinking and acting like a behavioral school counselor.* Thousand Oaks, CA: Sage.

Rogers, C. R. (1980). *A way of being.* Boston, MA: Houghton Mifflin.

Sklare, G. B. (2005). *Brief counseling that works: A solution-focused approach for school counselors and administrators* (2nd ed.). Thousand Oaks, CA: Corwin Press.

## Chapter 25

# Helping Students With Anxiety

NADINE E. GARNER AND BRIELLE E. VALLE

## CASE BACKGROUND

Renee, a bright, 18-year-old who was a high-achieving senior, came to see me for her ongoing issues with anxiety. She wanted to develop a healthy separation from her mother as she prepared to go to college out of town and to feel less guilty and anxious about disappointing her mother. Although she was still months away from her high school graduation and transition to college, Renee said her mother was already "making me feel guilty," by pressuring Renee to agree to come home from college every weekend and stay with her.

Renee has shared that as far back as first grade, she thought of herself as a "worrier." She perseverated over school subjects by checking over assignments numerous times, even when she knew her work was correct. Renee discussed how it was difficult for her to go to sleep because she had to review her to-do list dozens of times. No one in her family knew about this situation, and Renee's anxious thoughts and behaviors continued through the years. In middle school, she participated in dance and basketball but "never felt good enough." In high school Renee joined the Student Council, vocal ensemble, and got parts in school musicals, trying to be "confident, bubbly, and busy." In reality, she was an "anxious mess, and did not want to wake up" in the morning. Renee described herself as having "disordered eating" from the ages of 12 to 16 years; she would tell herself that she was "fat" and ate only salads for lunch at school. During her sophomore year at the age of 16 years, Renee "snapped" and "couldn't handle the pressure anymore." She quit dance and other activities, saying that she felt "sad but relieved."

Renee's first experience with counselors was at the age of 11 years when her parents separated. The school counselor was made aware of her parents' situation and asked to speak with her about the separation. Renee was upset during the whole meeting because the counselor did not disclose how she knew of the parents' separation. Renee did not ask her counselor how she had heard about it, feeling too embarrassed and shocked that the counselor knew and wondering whether the whole school might be gossiping about her. (Renee later found out her mother had called the counselor.) Renee reported feeling blindsided by being pulled out of class and that the counselor was "fixated on problems." When Renee refused to talk further with the school counselor, her mother forced her to see a counselor in private practice, believing that Renee needed to process her parents' separation and impending divorce. Without first discussing this with Renee or asking for her feedback or permission,

207

the private counselor broke confidentiality by disclosing to Renee's mother what Renee had shared in the sessions. When her mother confronted Renee about some of the content of the sessions, Renee said she felt betrayed by the counselor, angry with her mother, and so she quit counseling altogether. During the summer and fall of Renee's junior year, she recognized that she needed help with her overwhelming issues of anxiety. She then worked with a holistic counselor in private practice and found that experience to be very helpful. The counselor taught her meditation techniques, helping her become aware of her thought patterns and mindful of the present moment.

Although she had become more aware of her anxious thoughts and behaviors through counseling, Renee realized that she was still dwelling excessively on many different types of things during the day. Ongoing family issues between herself, her sister, and her mother also added to her anxious thoughts. Renee did not want to take prescription medication for anxiety, but when she turned 18 years old she decided that she needed to try it. She first took Paxil, which she did not find effective and which resulted in weight gain. She then switched to Zoloft and was on Zoloft during the time we worked together. Renee described the medication as "taking the edge off and giving me the chance to think rationally."

## INITIAL PROCESS QUESTIONS

- What are Renee's primary challenges at this point in her development?
- What is my assessment regarding Renee's current level of functioning?
- What else would be helpful to know about this student?
- What concerns do I have about Renee's past negative experiences with counselors?
- What personal strengths does Renee possess that may help in her struggles with anxiety?
- Which counseling approaches and interventions could be used in this case scenario?
- What multicultural issues might I need to consider with Renee, so that I could serve her in the most culturally sensitive manner?

## ADDRESSING THE ISSUES

I thought that Renee could benefit greatly from the rational emotive behavior therapy (REBT) approach. Although she had developed a habit of overthinking situations to the point of anxiety, I felt encouraged that she might be able not only to use her thoughtful nature to dispute the irrational beliefs that kept her stuck and anxious but also to channel some of her thinking energy into developing rational beliefs for herself.

Knowing that Renee had felt alienated by her first two counselors, I established rapport with her in several ways. I assured her that our conversations would remain confidential unless there was a threat of harm to self or others. I told Renee that I would encourage her to be an active participant in counseling, so that counseling would not just be an experience that happened *to* her. I also asked Renee whether she would like to learn the components of REBT on an intellectual level as well as a personal one, so that she would understand what I was doing in our sessions every step of the way. Renee really appreciated our talking about what the therapeutic alliance would look like. She eagerly jumped at the chance to discuss Ellis (n.d.) and his work, and she enjoyed having me explicitly teach her the model during our sessions. I gave Renee a book on counseling theories so that she could read the text for herself. Renee loved the idea and even took notes on the REBT chapter.

In Ellis's theory, students create happier and more fulfilling lives for themselves when they change the illogical ideas that they have been using to interpret events (Shostrom, 1965). REBT can help students acknowledge that they have been making themselves mentally unhealthy by the way they interpret events. Ellis (n.d.) wrote, "It is not only the event, but also our *attitudes and beliefs* about it, that cause our emotional reaction" (p. 3). The REBT counselor's techniques for change include helping students to challenge the irrational beliefs and irrational self-talk. Students then need to be willing to surrender their irrational/illogical thinking and the self-defeating phrases that accompany these beliefs and replace them with healthier ones (Shostrom, 1965). Ellis called this replacement the re-indoctrination of self using simple, declarative sentences.

Ellis's ABCDE model of emotional–behavioral disturbance is a straightforward approach, making it appealing for students to use. Counselors guide students through the process of understanding how the activating event (A) contributes to their emotional or behavioral disturbance or consequence (C) mainly because of the irrational/illogical belief (B) the students have been using to interpret the event (A) (Ellis, n.d.). Counselors then help students to analyze the irrational beliefs and dispute them (D) so that they can progress to a new emotional consequence or effect (E), where they formulate a new set of more rational beliefs. REBT is just one approach to helping students with anxiety, and Table 25-1 provides a variety of strategies that counselors can use when applying other theoretical perspectives to working with students with anxiety issues, most of which can be found in Henderson and Thompson (2011).

## IN SESSION

In the following conversation, we relate Ellis's ABCDE model to Renee's current situation. I drew a diagram of the model as we talked.

COUNSELOR (C): So what happens? What is the activating event?

RENEE (R): My mom pressuring me to come home on weekends, because she wants the most time with me. She asks me, "Will you be staying here for the weekends?" She always wants me to come home and wants to see me, and I feel sorry for her.

**TABLE 25-1  Approaches to Working with Students With Anxiety Issues**

| Paradigm | Elementary School | Middle School | High School |
|---|---|---|---|
| Psychodynamic | Adlerian play therapy to discover student's lifestyle and private logic; family constellation and family atmosphere; lifestyle; striving for significance and belonging; natural and logical consequences; modeling encouragement for student; teaching parents techniques for encouraging student | Early recollections to understand student's behavior patterns; lifestyle; striving for significance and belonging; natural and logical consequences; modeling encouragement for student; teaching parents techniques for encouraging student | Teaching student to identify mistaken goals; lifestyle; encouragement; striving for significance and belonging; natural and logical consequences |

*(continued)*

**TABLE 25-1** *(continued)*

| Paradigm | Elementary School | Middle School | High School |
|---|---|---|---|
| Humanistic/ Existential | Teaching student to (1) focus on here and now, (2) take responsibility for one's own thoughts, actions, feelings, and sensations, and (3) accept personal responsibility for change; teaching student to substitute the use of *won't* for *can't* and the use of *what* and *how* for *why*; teaching parents to use self-esteem–building activities with child; modeling active listening, congruence, unconditional positive regard, and empathy with student | Teaching student to (1) focus on here and now, (2) take responsibility for one's own thoughts, actions, feelings, and sensations, and (3) accept personal responsibility for change; teaching student to substitute the use of *won't* for *can't* and the use of *what* and *how* for *why*; teaching parents to use self-esteem–building activities with child; modeling active listening, congruence, unconditional positive regard, and empathy with student | Teaching student to (1) focus on here and now, (2) take responsibility for one's own thoughts, actions, feelings, and sensations, and (3) accept personal responsibility for change; teaching student to substitute the use of *won't* for *can't* and the use of *what* and *how* for *why*; modeling active listening, congruence, unconditional positive regard, and empathy with student |
| Behavioral/CBT | Teaching student about basic needs; control; quality world; choice; responsibility; total behavior; engaging in modeling and role playing with student; teaching student visualization and problem solving | Teaching student about basic needs; control; quality world; choice; responsibility; total behavior; engaging in modeling and role playing with student; teaching self-monitoring, decentering, de-catastrophizing, and stress inoculation to student | Teaching student about basic needs; control; quality world; choice; responsibility; total behavior; engaging in modeling and role playing with student; teaching self-monitoring, decentering, de-catastrophizing, and stress inoculation to student |
| Family Systems | Teaching student to recognize harmful communication patterns; assisting in building student's self-esteem; teaching student differentiation by modeling "I" statements | Teaching student to recognize harmful communication patterns; assisting in building student's self-esteem; teaching student differentiation by modeling "I" statements | Teaching student to recognize harmful communication patterns; assisting in building student's self-esteem; teaching student differentiation by modeling "I" statements |
| Emergent | Process of change results from dialogue between counselor and student (Anderson, 1993); empowering student to re-author a more successful story (White & Epston, 1990) | Process of change results from dialogue between counselor and student (Anderson, 1993); empowering student to re-author a more successful story (White & Epston, 1990) | Process of change results from dialogue between counselor and student (Anderson, 1993); empowering student to re-author a more successful story (White & Epston, 1990) |

C:    It is feeling stressful for you. . . .

R:    Because I am allowing myself to feel guilty.

C:    Feeling guilty is C, the consequence of what you tell your-self to believe at B; your mom pressuring you to come home on the weekends and be with her is A, the activating event. People think that A causes C, that "of course, because my mom pressures me, I feel guilty." But it is your belief at B that leads you to feel guilty.

R:    That she would be disappointed if I don't see her as much as she would like.

C:    How bad would that be for you, if your mom was disap-pointed?

R:    I would feel so guilty.

C:    And would her feeling disappointed really be so awful?

R:    I always thought that it would.

C:    Whatever you believe at B will guide what you feel at C. If you believe at point B, "That would be really bad if I disap-pointed my mom; it would be such an awful thing, and I am a bad daughter for not doing precisely what she wants all the time," you will likely end up feeling guilty.

R:    And angry.

C:    Oh, and angry— tell me about angry.

R:    Because I end up doing what other people want. But then I get annoyed about spending so much energy giving other people what they want, so that I can feel like a good person and not disappoint them. I am a "people pleaser." But I don't get to live my life the way I want to, so I get angry with them and with myself. So, should I just not care about how my mom feels?

C:    It's *not* that you are not supposed to care; but perhaps through seeking to understand this, you could find a more functional and healthy belief about the situation. Being aware of your beliefs at B about the activating events at A may help to understand what is irrational and what is not. A great thing that you worked on with your previous coun-selor is that you are now aware of how you feel at C, instead of wondering why you are feeling anxious about your relationships with people.

R:    I think that the only part I am aware of is that I don't like the feeling of being guilty. But I don't know what to do about it.

C:    OK, let's take a look at D, the disputing argument you use to attack the irrational belief at B. At D you can say, "OK,

Renee, wait a minute, is that a little irrational? Is it *really* that awful that my mom is disappointed? How bad is that really?" You can't change what the person did at A, but you can change the belief you have come up with to interpret the event. You can change the story that you tell about yourself. The new healthy phrases that you develop to describe a rational belief will become E, the new emotional consequence or effect. What do you want to feel?

R:  (*Pausing*) I don't know. Not a bad or negative emotion.

C:  You can decide what it is you want, what phrase at B the next time your mom brings this situation up would give you the desired result at C, so that you could leave this event that your mom started, not blaming her and not feeling guilty. Ellis would say that when you say to yourself at D, "How bad is this really that my mom will be disappointed?" you could go back up to B and replace the irrational belief with a more rational one. If at B you now say, "Yes, she is going to be disappointed if I don't give her what she wants, but it is not going to crush her; she will be disappointed, and I will be OK, and I will be clear with her, and fair, and schedule a time to see her."

R:  So it's like the logical thing to say to myself. I could see thinking of a compromise where I design a schedule to come and see her.

C:  Right. It's not that you never want to see your mom, you just don't want to be railroaded into giving her the schedule she desires at your expense; a rational statement at B is like, "Well, it's OK to see her as it works for me." And if she is still pressuring you, a rational statement could be, "Well, my answer to her about a schedule is reasonable even if she doesn't like it."

R:  This makes sense to me, but I just didn't know it.

C:  Most people don't know that B exists. They go from what someone said to them to how they feel about it.

R:  They go straight to C.

C:  When someone says, "You made me angry" they don't realize that no one can make you angry without your consent. No one can make you guilty without your consent.But in reality, we don't go right to C. Your brain just doesn't catch that you are at B first. But the more that you use this method, the more you can pause to reflect on your belief at B. That will give you a chance to change your belief to a more rational one.

R:  I have been saying to myself, "the terrible part is that she would be upset," so I have to decide, "how terrible is it that she would be upset?" and "how healthy is it for me to give her what she wants, knowing that I will be angry about it later?"

C:  Exactly.

R:  For B, what you say to yourself changes depending on the situation. Yeah, I get that, and I can become creative with the rational statements. This is definitely a process; this is all new to me. It's really helpful that you wrote the steps down. Why don't I think about it and try to wrap my head around it a little more.

## Outcome

Renee responded positively to our work together and applied REBT techniques to several areas of her life. Renee noticed that she was more aware of her feelings and the anxious phrases that she had habitually used. She found it very helpful to understand that she could dispute an irrational belief and that she was capable of changing her belief to a more rational one. Renee started keeping an organized planner so that it was obvious to her that she was on top of her tasks, which led to less perseverating throughout the day and less ruminating before bedtime. As she practiced creating rational beliefs, she separated herself more from the "toxic people" within her family and friends. Renee started to create healthy boundaries with the people who were very demanding of her, reminding herself of the phrase that we discussed in counseling: "your control ends where someone else's begins."

Renee was also able to reflect on patterns of interaction with her family that have kept her stuck:

At the age of 11, from the time my dad moved out of the house, I felt that I had to clean my mom's house, wake her and my sister up, and make them lunch, even though I was the youngest person there. I would say irrational things like, "I need to fix other people and control the situation," and then I would get angry about it. Now I am better at controlling myself and saying phrases like, "They're messed up, but I'm not going to fix it," and "I will not be abused or manipulated."

Renee reported another event in which she was able to cope with her anxiety using REBT techniques. She was driving alone in her car and realized that she was lost. She went 20 miles the wrong way and ended up paying a toll to go over a bridge. As she started to feel herself getting stressed, she noticed that instead of responding to the situation with anxiety, she was able to catch herself and calmly ask herself, "How bad is this really?" She was very proud of herself for this accomplishment and noticed what a difference it made in her overall functioning.

Renee came back to visit me after she had begun college to let me know that she was still using the REBT techniques and telling herself frequently that "A does not cause C." She mentioned that she had even just used it on the train ride home, when a passenger asked her to be quiet on the quiet car—she had been talking on her cell phone and did not realize that she was on the quiet car. She said that in the past she "would have felt mortified by being corrected and then perseverated about doing something wrong." However, this time she was able to make a rational statement to herself and say, "I really didn't know it was the quiet car, and I can let it go." Renee turned down going on a vacation with her mother and sister, so that she could go away by herself. She said, "They may be disappointed that I am not joining them, but it is more important that I have the solitude." As Renee considered her progress, she said, "In the moment I am getting better and I can accomplish a lot."

## Final Process Questions

- What are additional thoughts about supporting Renee in her positive changes?
- What can I do to help Renee seek counseling after high school?
- As a school counselor, what can I do to encourage students to be more willing to speak with me?
- What are some interventions that could have been done with Renee prior to high school that might have been effective?

- From a multicultural perspective, what will I need to consider in Renee's relationship with her mother, if Renee's culture values parental authority, even for children who are now young adults?
- What multicultural issues will I need to consider in Renee's relationship with both her mother and sister, if Renee is from a culture that emphasizes collectivism?

## Ethical/Legal Considerations

A dominant theme in two of Renee's three prior counseling experiences had been the lack of trust in the counselor. The first counselor who worked with Renee when her parents separated could have told Renee that her mother was the one who had called the counselor to arrange a counseling session, instead of leaving Renee to wonder how the counselor had learned of her parents' separation. The second counselor breached confidentiality by sharing Renee's disclosures with her mother, although there was no threat of harm to self or others in what Renee had shared. When I first began to meet with Renee, my primary intention was to foster a more trusting relationship by keeping the ethical guidelines regarding confidentiality at the forefront of my interactions with her. The Ethical Standards for School Counselors (American School Counselor Association, 2010) state that the counselor should secure the student's informed consent about what is likely to happen in counseling, which includes the purposes, goals, techniques, and rules of the relationship. To this end, I made Renee well aware that our conversations would remain confidential unless there was a threat of harm to self or others. I also secured Renee's permission in using REBT as our primary counseling theory and technique, giving her a book on REBT so that she would feel prepared to enter counseling as an engaged client.

## Resources

DiGiuseppe, R. (2007). Rational emotive behavioral approaches. In H. T. Prout & D. T. Brown (Eds.), *Counseling and psychotherapy with children and adolescents: Theory and practice for school and clinical settings* (4th ed., pp. 279–331). Hoboken, NJ: Wiley.

Ellis, A. (1998). *How to control your anxiety— before it controls you.* New York, NY: Citadel Press.

Ellis, A., & Harper, R. A. (1961). *A new guide to rational living.* Chatsworth, CA: Wilshire Book Company.

*Chapter 26*

# Helping Students With Depression

Tricia Uppercue

## CASE BACKGROUND

Graduation day had arrived. For most students, this day represents years of dedication, hard work, and overcoming obstacles. As the ceremony was underway, the wheelchair lift connected to the stage rose and delivered Chad to the top of the stage to receive his high school diploma. As Chad's school counselor, I felt a strong sense of pride as I reflected on the first time I had met him, 4 years earlier.

Upon first meeting Chad as a ninth grader, his grades were average and he seemed to be adjusting to high school fairly well. He came to see me about his classes, and we developed a positive relationship. I learned that he had been using a wheelchair since sixth grade, he was depressed, and there was strife within his family. Over the course of the next couple of years, Chad came to trust me as an adult who cared about him and his well-being and who supported him through his struggles, both in and out of school. It was in his third year of high school when things quickly began to worsen.

One day, Chad came to my office and confided that he was having thoughts of hurting himself. He was feeling very anxious and apprehensive about anyone else knowing how he was feeling. I reminded Chad of the guidelines that I explained to him previously, specifically about exceptions to confidentiality and the fact that I had to report three things: (1) if there was harm done to him; (2) if he had thoughts of harming himself; and (3) if he had thoughts of harming others. During this particular session, I determined that he was at high risk of harming himself because he had determined a plan, a method, and access to means. He was also engaging in some reckless behaviors outside of the school setting. Because we had a positive rapport and he trusted me, I was able to get him to agree to talk with a counselor from the county crisis mobile team. Once his guardian and the crisis counselor arrived at the school and began asking questions, Chad became angry and uncooperative, so our school resource officer was brought into the meeting. Chad was taken to the emergency room, but returned to school the next day, despite no change in his mood. Within the next couple of weeks, he began seeing a psychiatrist, who put him on medication, and he began seeing a school-based therapist on a regular basis. The guardian and student signed a release so that I could communicate with the therapist as needed. Chad and I continued to meet.

## INITIAL PROCESS QUESTIONS

In the months to follow, Chad came to see me when he was feeling depressed and hopeless. One day, he came to my office and said he felt very sad, did not care about anything, and wanted to drop out of school. The following are some questions I considered before Chad entered this session:

- Does he feel like he wants to hurt himself or others?
- On a scale of 1 to 10, how sad is he feeling right now?
- Does he want to call his therapist? Should I call his therapist?
- Did anything happen recently that is bothering him (in or out of school)?
- Why does he want to drop out of school? How are his classes going? What are his goals?

## ADDRESSING THE ISSUES

Chad had many different issues occurring at the time of his visit to my office. He was diagnosed with depression and struggled with limitations of being in a wheelchair. There were custody issues within his family, and Chad had feelings of resentment toward family members. He had seemingly given up on his academics and was failing all of his classes. His belief in himself and his abilities was low, and he often referred to himself as "stupid." He also reported not seeing graduation as a desirable or likely possibility. Getting through the school day became difficult for Chad. He began to visit me on a regular basis.

In an effort to help Chad, I used an integrative approach. A very important approach to working with Chad was person-centered counseling within the humanistic/ existential paradigm. Techniques such as genuineness, unconditional positive regard, and empathy were crucial in creating a trusting relationship and establishing a safe environment for Chad.

Oftentimes, school counselors are the first to recognize students in need of help. They make referrals to outside agencies, but sometimes families turn to school counselors for immediate help. As an advocate for students, I do whatever I can to help them achieve personal and academic success. Because Chad had so many matters to address, it was possible for me to use several counseling frameworks and techniques. His family issues and physical and mental health conditions were all contributing to his difficulty in successfully navigating the school setting.

Chad's past family history had a significant influence on his current feelings toward various family members. For me to fully understand the family dynamics, we created a genogram. There were legal and guardianship issues; and with the full support of Chad and his legal guardian, I became involved in discussions with the school-based therapist, family members, social services, an appointed mentor, and our local coordinating committee to get Chad more outside services.

When Chad was having a bad day, he would come see me, and we would use creative arts techniques, such as journal writing or drawing, to help him express himself. On days when the weather was nice, we would go out to the track for a short time so that Chad could listen to music as he wheeled a few laps around the track to clear his mind.

Cognitive-behavioral theories were also effective with Chad. I used techniques such as restructuring thoughts, positive reinforcement, self-talk, visual imagery, and developing coping strategies to help him. We focused on what he could do rather than what he could not do. We set realistic goals ranging from personal safety to doing well in his classes, graduating from high school, and planning activities that he could look forward to and participate in, despite his physical limitations.

I also used goals of interpersonal psychotherapy to help Chad focus on the present and see that there are many people who currently support him. We spent time working on communication skills and analyzing interpersonal events. Chad learned to use "I" statements (from a humanistic/existential perspective) to communicate his feelings. I facilitated meetings with his teachers to discuss his struggles and set up times for him to stay after school for extra help. Once Chad's grades began to improve, his goal of graduating became more realistic and attainable to him. He even signed up for and successfully completed two summer classes so that he would be eligible to graduate his fourth year of high school. Table 26-1 provides some additional strategies and techniques for working with students with depression.

## IN SESSION

One day during his junior year, Chad came to my office and expressed his feelings of sadness and his desire to drop out of school. Given his history of suicidal thoughts and depression, I felt it necessary to assess his current ideation. After I determined that he did not want to hurt himself, the session progressed. I asked Chad what was on his mind, and he responded that he did not want to go to his classes. He was failing them all, and he did not see the point of finishing high school. I then asked whether he had talked with his teachers, to which he responded that they—just like everyone else—did not care about him.

At this point, we made a list of all the people in Chad's life who do care for him and who would be willing to help him reach his goals. We then focused on his goals, for both the short and the long term. He did want to graduate and pursue a trade after high school. We then discussed the importance of his current academic performance in reaching his long-term goals. I also felt it was important to get him connected to something he liked in the school. Chad enjoyed sports, but could not participate due to his physical limitations. I talked with one of the coaches, who was able to offer him the job of managing one of the school's sports teams. This activity helped create a connection to school and other people and provided an incentive to improve his grades. We also arranged to have a meeting with all of his teachers.

Chad said that he had a lot on his mind, so he spent some time writing in his journal. After he put his thoughts on paper, he shared his writing with me. He enjoyed writing, so I suggested that he take a creative writing class next year. Chad seemed excited about this idea, which motivated him to take two summer classes so he would have room in his schedule the following year. At this point, he had things to look forward to as a reminder of his goals. He was ready to go back to class with his journal so that he could review his goals whenever he lost sight of them. Before Chad returned to class, we briefly reviewed the session.

| | |
|---|---|
| COUNSELOR: | How do you feel about the decision that you made to go to your classes and work to reach your goal of graduating? |
| CHAD: | I feel better. I feel like there is some time to bring up my grades and do some cool things that I like. |

**TABLE 26-1** Additional Approaches for Working with Students with Depression

| Paradigm | Elementary School | Middle School | High School |
|---|---|---|---|
| Psychodynamic | Analysis of transference; defense mechanisms; goals that drive behavior; how childhood/family events influence current behavior | Analysis of transference; defense mechanisms; goals that drive behavior; how childhood/family events influence current behavior | Analysis of transference; defense mechanisms; goals that drive behavior; how childhood/family events influence current behavior |
| Humanistic/Existential | Therapeutic relationship; role playing; "I" statements; identifying unique characteristics and meaning in life; promoting decision making | Therapeutic relationship; role playing; "I" statements; identifying unique characteristics and meaning in life; promoting decision making | Therapeutic relationship; role playing; "I" statements; identifying unique characteristics and meaning in life; promoting decision making |
| Behavioral/CBT | Positive reinforcement; token economy; behavior charts; behavior contracts; cognitive restructuring; disputing irrational beliefs; specifying automatic thoughts; modeling; role playing; behavioral rehearsal; miracle question; self-talk; visual imagery; exceptions | Positive reinforcement; token economy; behavior charts; behavior contracts; cognitive restructuring; disputing irrational beliefs; specifying automatic thoughts; modeling; role playing; behavioral rehearsal; miracle question; self-talk; visual imagery; exceptions | Positive reinforcement; token economy; behavior charts; behavior contracts; cognitive restructuring; disputing irrational beliefs; specifying automatic thoughts; modeling; role playing; behavioral rehearsal; miracle question; self-talk; visual imagery; exceptions |
| Family Systems | Parent/guardian training for dealing with behavioral, academic, and social issues; family dynamics; differentiation of self; genogram | Parent/guardian training for dealing with behavioral, academic, and social issues; family dynamics; differentiation of self; genogram | Parent/guardian training for dealing with behavioral, academic, and social issues; family dynamics; differentiation of self; genogram |
| Emergent | Miracle question; sparkling moments; communication analysis; interpersonal incidents; role playing | Miracle question; sparkling moments; deconstruct and externalize problems; communication analysis; interpersonal incidents; content and process affect; role playing | Miracle question; sparkling moments; deconstruct and externalize problems; communication analysis; interpersonal incidents; content and process affect; role playing |

COUNSELOR: What things are you looking forward to doing?

CHAD: I can't wait to take a creative writing class. Maybe I can work on my story that I started to write a couple of months ago.

COUNSELOR: That sounds great. I would love to read what you wrote so far and then read it again after you finish it.

| CHAD: | Cool. I am also going to look into some of those trade schools that we talked about earlier. |
| COUNSELOR: | So in the future, if you have a bad day, what are some things that you can do to help yourself? |
| CHAD: | I will think about the positive things in my life and talk to some of the people who care about me, like my therapist. I will also look back at my journal to review my goals. |
| COUNSELOR: | We will touch base in the next couple of days and see how things are going. |

## Outcome

Chad made it through his junior year earning half of his credits. He took two classes in summer school, and during his senior year, he took two online classes in addition to his full course load. Two major events occurred outside of school that seemed to have a positive effect on Chad: changes in his living arrangements and continuation in therapy. Chad's grades improved and he continued his involvement with school activities. Chad's visits to my office became less frequent, and talk of dropping out of school stopped altogether. As graduation day got closer, I could see Chad's sense of pride and excitement rise. A picture of him in his cap and gown on graduation day hangs proudly in my office.

## Final Process Questions

- What else could I have done as a school counselor to help Chad with his personal and academic growth, his educational and career decisions, and his interactions with others?
- What personal and family resources might aid Chad after he graduates from high school?

- What coping mechanisms and techniques did Chad learn that he can continue to use?
- Did I complete all of the documentation of measures taken with Chad?

## Resources

Capuzzi, D. (1994). *Suicide prevention in the schools: Guidelines for middle and high school settings.* Alexandria, VA: American Counseling Association.

Copeland, M. E., & Copans, S. (2002). *Recovering from depression: A workbook for teens.* Baltimore, MD: Paul Brookes.

Irwin, C., Evans, D. L., & Andrews, L. W. (2007). *Monochrome days: A firsthand account of one teenager's experience with depression.* New York, NY: Oxford Press.

Schab, L. (2008). *Beyond the blues: A workbook to help teens overcome depression.* Oakland, CA: New Harbinger Publications.

Strom, D., Randall, K., & Bowman, S. (2007). *102 creative strategies for working with depressed children and adolescents: A practical resource for teachers, counselors, and parents.* Chapin, SC: YouthLight.

## Chapter 27

# Self-Injury

AUDREY NEUSCHAFER

## CASE BACKGROUND

One day this past spring, Mr. Smith came into my office and shut my door. "I have a student I'm concerned about," he told me. As we talked, I learned that earlier that day Jessica, a 10th grader, had come to him and told him that her friend Michelle, a ninth grader, was cutting her arms and legs, and that Jessica was really worried about her. According to Jessica, Michelle had been cutting herself for the past few months and had begged Jessica and other friends not to tell anyone. Coincidentally, Michelle was the daughter of my secretary/registrar yet was not a student I had visited with in the past. In my conversations with Michelle's mother over the 2 years she and I had worked together, I had learned that Michelle did not have much "use" for counseling. Michelle's mother had occasionally talked with me about minor concerns she had with Michelle over the years. She said that she had suggested to Michelle that she come visit with me in the past, but that Michelle did not want to be seen as "weak" and wanted to handle things herself.

During the past year I taught a weekly character education session in a portion of the ninth graders' Health/PE class, so I knew Michelle in that capacity. Also as her mother's supervisor, Michelle and I had chatted one-on-one before, but never formally in my office. Michelle was a captain of the volleyball team, active in the band, liked by all her classmates, and an all-around good student with a great, albeit dry sense of humor. Michelle was also a leader in an after-school association. Being aware of Michelle's desire for privacy and not knowing whether the alleged behaviors were actually occurring, I took an opportunity when my secretary/registrar was out on an errand to walk down and get Michelle from her final class of the day. As Michelle and I walked to my office, we made a little bit of small talk while she eyed me suspiciously. She didn't ask directly but seemed to know that her secret was out.

## INITIAL PROCESS QUESTIONS

- Does Michelle know her rights with regard to confidentiality?
- Are the allegations of self-injury true?
- If so, are there concerns of suicidal ideation?
- How do I establish rapport with Michelle, especially in light of her negative perception of counseling?

220

- What are my ethical and legal obligations if Michelle is engaging in self-injurious behaviors?
- How should I introduce the solution-focused method I use without turning Michelle off to the "counseling process"?

## ADDRESSING THE ISSUES

Self-injury is not considered a suicide attempt. There are many different motivations and intents behind self-injurious behaviors, and I've kept current with research and professional development opportunities on the topic. Still, even with this knowledge in mind, I struggled, as I always do when working with a student who self-injures, with my ethical and legal obligation to report this behavior. In my years as a school counselor, I have encountered multiple cases of self-injury and have not always felt that the situation obligated me to report this behavior to parents/guardians or other authorities.

First, I wanted to make sure that Michelle felt comfortable with me and that she knew right off the bat her rights and expectations of confidentiality. As I went through my regular "what happens in the counselor's office, stays in the counselor's office EXCEPT . . . " speech, Michelle nodded but didn't look me in the eye. I really wanted to make sure Michelle understood my position. Specifically in this case, Michelle needed to know that I was not going to tell her mother what we talked about unless I was concerned for her safety or for the safety of other students. Michelle, after a slightly rocky start, admitted that occasionally she did engage in cutting behaviors by taking the tip of a mechanical pencil (without the lead) and scratching her left arm and legs. She showed me the inside of her left arm and tops of her thighs where there were some visible, healed over scratch marks. My next line of questioning was to assess whether or not Michelle was suicidal. After an emphatic, "NO! I'm not crazy," I felt reassured that Michelle was not contemplating suicide. We talked very briefly about the cutting behavior, and I made sure she knew that it is not a symptom of being "crazy" to feel overwhelmed and like you want to hurt yourself. As we talked, Michelle warmed up and seemed to open up to the idea of talking about herself more quickly than had I thought she would. She talked openly about feeling "stressed out" in school and in her extracurricular activities. It seemed Michelle was putting a lot of pressure on herself to get things done right and didn't know how to cope with her drive for perfectionism.

In order to help Michelle find more acceptable and appropriate ways to cope with stress, I used a solution-focused brief counseling (SFBC) approach. Before I started the SFBC process, I told her that I would like the opportunity to help her identify some more appropriate coping skills and that I would be asking her some questions that might seem strange. I also told her that I believed she already had the skills she needed and that I'd bet we could identify other things she had done in the past to cope with stress besides cutting. She was open to beginning the conversation, so I started the process with scaling by asking her to rate herself on a scale of 1 to 10 in regard to how stressed and compelled to cut she currently felt. I praised her on her relatively low self-rating of 4 and then moved on to the "miracle question," which I like not only for the information it reveals but also because the question itself seems to lighten tense moods in a counseling situation. It has been my experience that high school and middle school students find it amusing to think about a miracle happening while they slept that solved their "problem!" Through "What else?" probing on my part, she identified a few tangible, visible things that would be different after the miracle: some "exceptions" to her problem times.

My next line of questioning had to do with identifying times that the exceptions to her problems were already occurring and what skills she already possessed that led to times when the exceptions occurred. Michelle seemed to respond very well to this line of questioning, partly because I think she just enjoyed opening up about herself (something she didn't do very often), but also because I think it was so different from what she had expected. I did not probe into her past or ask a lot of intrusive questions. Michelle is very straightforward and logical and so I think SFBC appealed to her in that way. First we identified several things that Michelle was already doing that helped her cope with stress and pressures besides cutting (e.g., going for a jog, riding her horse, using her web camera to record a funny video). Then we examined things she could do proactively that would prevent her from getting to the point that she felt stress and pressure (e.g., putting her appointments, games, and homework on her new phone so she would get reminders; not putting off large projects; breaking down big assignments into smaller ones). Next I did some "flagging the minefield" by asking her to tell me concretely the things she was going to do if she felt herself stressed or under pressure in the future. Michelle certainly had a history of putting pressure on herself, and I knew this would not be the last time she struggled with that inclination.

As we closed our meeting, I asked Michelle to please consider telling her mother about her cutting behaviors and told her that I would be glad to be with her when she did. Michelle declined and said she didn't want to cause her mother stress. She stated that she wanted to "handle it" on her own. Michelle appeared worried that I was going to break her trust by telling her "secret." I reassured her that I was not going to tell her mother unless the cutting was something she could not stop. Then I told her that I wanted to check in with her the following week to see how she was doing in regard to the cutting behavior. She agreed.

My response to an incident such as this one would likely be the same for a middle school student. However, if the student (middle or high school) disclosed suicidal ideation, I would not have hesitated to tell the student of my obligation to keep him or her safe by involving a parent/guardian. If the self-injury was so severe that it was possibly life-threatening, I would also not have hesitated to consider it an exception to confidentiality. If it were an elementary student demonstrating the cutting behavior, I would be more inclined to discuss the issue of telling a parent/guardian while seeking to maintain confidentiality; I would perhaps be more concerned about a more serious underlying mental health issue. Also, my SFBC approach would vary slightly at the elementary level. I regularly use a 12-inch ruler when scaling with older elementary students (1 on ruler says AWFUL and 12 on ruler says AWESOME) and a scale with three faces (very sad, neutral, very happy) with very young elementary students. Also, when asking the miracle question, some elementary students with less verbal ability do well when they draw a picture of what happens after the miracle. Sometimes, I ask the miracle question couched in different terms that are more appropriate to their age range and more familiar to them: a genie's lamp grants them a wish, a fairy godmother waves her wand. Table 27-1 provides additional strategies and techniques useful in addressing self-injurious behaviors.

## IN SESSION

Michelle was not self-referred and was reticent about counseling. After I made some initial small talk to establish rapport and made sure she understood her expectations for confidentiality and exceptions to that confidentiality, that first meeting went something like this:

**TABLE 27-1    Additional Strategies and Techniques Useful in Addressing Self-Injurious Behaviors**

| Paradigm | Elementary School | Middle School | High School |
|---|---|---|---|
| Psychodynamic | Exploring transference, countertransference, and defense mechanisms; introducing that the past influences present behavior; sand tray | Exploring transference, countertransference, and defense mechanisms; understanding how the past influences present behavior; sand tray | Exploring transference, countertransference, and defense mechanisms; understanding how the past influences present behavior |
| Humanistic/Existential | Positive regard and focus on building rapport; role play; simple "I" statements for social and behavioral issues; bibliotherapy | Positive regard and focus on the therapeutic relationship; role play; more complex "I" statements for social and behavioral issues; bibliotherapy | Positive regard and focus on the therapeutic relationship; role play; "I" statements for social and behavioral issues |
| Behavioral/CBT | Positive reinforcement; token economy; behavior charts; behavior contracts; disputing irrational beliefs; self-talk; visual imagery; modeling; role play; time-out; use of puppets or other props to externalize the problem | Positive reinforcement; token economy; behavior charts; behavior contracts; disputing irrational beliefs; cognitive restructuring; specifying automatic thoughts; self-talk; visual imagery; modeling; behavioral rehearsal; role playing; time-out; some use of puppets or other props to externalize the problem | Positive reinforcement; token economy; behavior charts; behavior contracts; disputing irrational beliefs; cognitive restructuring; specifying automatic thoughts; self-talk; visual imagery; modeling; behavioral rehearsal; role playing; time-out; guided imagery for relaxation |
| Family Systems | Parent behavior training for dealing with relevant behavioral, academic, and social issues and family dynamics | Parent behavior training for dealing with relevant behavioral, academic, and social issues and family dynamics | Parent behavior training for dealing with relevant behavioral, academic, and social issues and family dynamics |
| Emergent | Breaking problem down into pieces; miracle question; empowerment; scaling; identifying exceptions; flagging the minefield; interpersonal incidents; role play; sand tray; puppets or other props | Deconstruct and externalize problems; scaling; miracle question; identifying exceptions; flagging the minefield; positive notes; empowerment; communication analysis; role play; sand tray; puppets or other props | Deconstruct and externalize problems; scaling; miracle question; identifying exceptions; flagging the minefield; positive notes; empowerment; communication analysis; role play; brainstorming |

COUNSELOR (C):    Michelle, one of your friends has told me that she is concerned about you. Do you know why she might say that?

MICHELLE (M):    (*Shrugs*)

C:    She says that she's concerned that sometimes you do things to hurt yourself. Do you know what she is talking about?

M:    (*Nods slightly*)

| | |
|---|---|
| C: | Tell me about what she might have been talking about? |
| M: | (*Mumbles*) I scratch at my arm with my pencil. I told them not to tell anybody. . . . |
| C: | Do you think she might have been worried about you? |
| M: | (*Nods*) |

[Later in session]

| | |
|---|---|
| C: | You told me you are at a 4 on my scale. I think that's great! Being a 4 tells me that some things are already going right. I am wondering, what keeps you from being worse—say at a 5 or 6? |
| M: | Mostly because I don't have any tests this week and spring break is coming up so I'm glad I'll get a break from school. |
| C: | I've got a crazy question for you: Suppose a miracle happened last night while you were sleeping so that when you woke up, the problem that brought you here to me today was solved! (*Michelle smiles*) What kinds of things would you notice that would tell you that the miracle had solved your problems? |
| M: | I guess I'd feel calm and not sick to my stomach. |
| C: | What else? |
| M: | I would probably wake up knowing what I needed to do that day— like have it stuck on my door or something. |
| C: | What else? |
| M: | Uhhh . . . I don't know— maybe I'd be smiling at my mom and she would smile back at me and I wouldn't fight with my brother and sisters? |
| C: | So, you would feel calm, know what it was you needed to do because it was written down somewhere, and you'd be smiling at your mom and siblings, right? (*Michelle nods*) Great! Tell me about the last time any of that was happening for you. |

[Later in session]

| | |
|---|---|
| C: | Michelle, based on what we talked about today, I wonder if I can throw a couple of things at you? (*Michelle nods*) The next time you feel like you are at an 8 or 9 on that scale we started out with, what are some things you think you can do besides cutting that would help you feel less stressed? |
| M: | I really need to put all my stuff that I do in my phone. |
| C: | What else? What about when you are already feeling stressed? What are some of the things you already told me you do that make you feel calm and smile at your mom and brother and sisters? |
| M: | If I keep the stuff I need to do written down, I'll be able to do it better. I really need to start riding my horse again because that really makes me feel better. Oh, also when I call Becca and we do our show, that makes me laugh and feel better. |

## Outcome

I checked in with Michelle twice more over the next 2 weeks leading up to spring break. She had not cut at all in that time. At the end of spring break, Michelle and some other students attended a retreat where Michelle opened up to her retreat camp counselor about her cutting behaviors. I received an e-mail from Michelle after that camp thanking me for my "intervention" and telling me about the help she was also getting through her interactions with her retreat camp counselor. She asked if she could "end counseling" and just e-mail me if she needed anything. I agreed but told her I'd be checking in on her from time to time. As we ended the school year, Michelle appeared to have stopped her cutting behavior. I was not concerned about her over the summer because her stress and worry, while part of her nature, did appear to have a lot to do with obligations at school, and Michelle told me via e-mail that she was looking forward to summer.

As self-injury cases go, my experience with this young lady had a very positive out-come. In my years as a school counselor, I can think of other students I have counseled who did not have such a quick, positive response to gaining control of their cutting. On at least one occasion, the self-injurious behavior precipitated a suicide attempt. Others have stopped cutting, only to relapse. In dealing with self-injury, ongoing follow-up is essential to ensuring that the student is maintaining alternative healthy stress responses and not turning to cutting or other unhealthy behaviors. I believe school counselors can be incredibly effective in helping students break self-injury patterns of behavior. Often school counselors are the first to know and the first to respond to such behaviors. However, school counselors always need to remember that if they are ever in a situation that they know is outside of their comfort level or expertise, they should never hesitate to either ask a more experienced colleague for advice or refer the student to a mental health professional.

## Final Process Questions

- Did I handle this situation to the best of my professional ability?
- What went well in this case?
- What didn't go well, and how can I make improvements for future cases?
- Will e-mail be enough of a touchstone for Michelle? Should I check in with her first thing next year?

- Would my response to Michelle have been different if she had been a different gender? Or of a different race/ethnicity?
- If her cutting continues to be a problem, at what point do I involve her parents?

## Resources

Bowman, S., & Randall, K. (2004). *See my pain! Creative strategies and activities for helping young people who self-injure.* Chapin, SC: YouthLight.

Levenkron, S. (1998). *Cutting: Understanding and overcoming self-mutilation.* New York, NY: Norton.

Strong, M. (1999). *A bright red scream: Self-mutilation and the language of pain.* New York, NY: Penguin Putnam.

To Write Love on Her Arms website, www.twloha.com

## Chapter 28

# Working With Families

DENISE B. EBERSOLE AND NADINE E. GARNER

## CASE BACKGROUND

Amanda, a 16-year-old student, was repeating ninth grade because she had passed only two classes the previous school year. Of even more concern to me was Amanda's increasingly flat affect, avoidance of eye contact, and constant referrals for counseling by school personnel. Although her learning support and regular education teachers made ongoing attempts to reach out to her, Amanda refused their redirection, prompts, and attempts to build a relationship with her. Amanda openly denounced school and proclaimed that she wanted to attend cyber-school, but could not convince her divorced parents to sign the paperwork. Almost daily, Amanda either skipped her least favorite classes by hiding in a bathroom or left the school grounds to meet friends who had dropped out of school. On the days Amanda remained in school, she vehemently harassed other students by throwing sharp objects, threatening to fight, and starting pregnancy rumors about peers because she said, "It makes school more fun." Despite her refusal to converse with most staff members, Amanda responded to me, her school counselor. During one counseling session, Amanda declared, "I hate this place, I hate every teacher here, and I am quitting school as soon as I turn 17 since I can't attend cyber-school. I don't know why everyone is wasting their time trying to help me because I am not going to change."

Amanda's academic progress steadily declined, and her disruptive behaviors escalated to the point that she was becoming a danger to others. I made repeated attempts to contact both parents. Because Amanda's parents shared physical custody, they had to communicate on a regular basis in order to maintain Amanda's living arrangements between the two households. Unfortunately, it was nearly impossible to collaborate with either parent. Amanda's father did not return my phone calls. Amanda proudly shared with me that her dad said he was not going to accept calls from the school because he was "sick of hearing the same thing." Amanda's mother did return my calls and seemed agreeable to the school's interventions, but she frequently missed the mutually agreed-upon meetings.

Both parents avoided contact with the school and reportedly allowed Amanda to skip school. After the maximum number of unexcused days had been reached, the school issued fines and took Amanda's family to court. Upon receiving the subpoena, both of Amanda's parents contacted the school and requested a meeting.

## INITIAL PROCESS QUESTIONS

- What are your primary concerns about Amanda?
- What are your initial thoughts about Amanda's current level of functioning?
- Is there anything else you would like to know about the student or her family?
- What approach do you think is best for improving this situation?
- How will you involve Amanda's parents so that they will collaborate with the school to help Amanda?
- What information will you share?
- Are there any ethical concerns that stand out to you?
- How will you respond if her dad refuses contact with the school?
- What interventions are you considering?
- What issues would you need to consider, and what strategies would you contemplate using, if Amanda's parents either did not speak English or did not speak English comfortably?

## ADDRESSING THE ISSUES

When students present with concerns, it is often necessary to communicate and collaborate with parents in order to help students obtain success and appropriately meet their needs. As a result, it is essential that professional school counselors develop the skill of working with families early in their careers. A student's family may consist of a broad range of people in addition to parents; for example, other relatives, guardians, caretakers, and close friends. Regardless of whether the school counselor is working at the elementary, middle, or high school level, he or she will need to be highly skilled in several family intervention areas, including interpersonal interactions, ability to observe verbal and nonverbal communication, and ability to diplomatically share difficult information with parents. The school counselor is often the first person that parents contact when they are concerned about their child but are not sure what to do. At other times the school counselor initiates the process by calling home to share concerns with parents. In either scenario, professional school counselors are often in the position of sharing difficult information, resolving conflict, clarifying confusion, and providing resources to families when necessary. During these conversations, it is essential to show professionalism, genuineness, patience, and commitment to student advocacy. Although there will definitely be some exceptions, the majority of parents will respect and appreciate the school counselor's role, and they will respond positively to the counselor's efforts to assist their child in becoming successful.

I approached this case scenario from a solution-focused brief counseling perspective, which focuses on the present and future. The family counseling session excerpt in this case scenario is consistent with LaFountain and Garner's (2008) process of facilitating a solution-focused conference, in which the counselor engages both student and parents in a positive, empowering dialogue that seeks to discover their strengths. Solution-focused counselors often ask students and their parents, "What would you like to change or do differently?" to set the expectation that each family member must take some responsibility for the change, think creatively, and allow the process to focus on solutions instead of problems (Garner & Valle, 2008). Solution-focused counselors listen to the language that students and their parents use, especially the usage of labels and absolutes, in order to identify exceptions. For example, Amanda shared that she "hated everyone in the school" so she just wanted to drop out. During our conversation, I looked for exceptions to her absolute language by asking, "Is there anyone here that you consider a friend?" Amanda immediately shared the names of several of her close friends and then smiled when she realized why using the term *everyone* was not really accurate.

Solution-focused counselors assist students and their parents in identifying skeleton keys, which are solutions that may transfer to other areas. "Instead of focusing on the difficulty (the lock), solution-focused counselors attend to the key that opens the lock" (Garner & Valle, 2008, p. 163). Table 28-1 provides a variety of strategies that counselors can use when working with families.

**TABLE 28-1   Additional Approaches for Working with Families**

| Paradigm | Elementary School | Middle School | High School |
|---|---|---|---|
| Psychodynamic (Henderson & Thompson, 2011) | Adlerian play therapy to discover the child's lifestyle and private logic; teaching parents techniques for encouraging the child; family constellation and family atmosphere; goals of misbehavior; lifestyle; striving for significance and belonging; natural and logical consequences | Early recollections to understand child's behavior patterns; Adlerian family counseling for family to learn to operate cooperatively; teaching parents techniques for encouraging the child; goals of misbehavior; lifestyle; encouragement; striving for significance and belonging; natural and logical consequences | Teaching parents and child that misbehaving children are discouraged children trying to find their place; teaching parents techniques for encouraging the child; goals of misbehavior; lifestyle; encouragement; striving for significance and belonging; natural and logical consequences |
| Humanistic/ Existential (Henderson & Thompson, 2011) | Teaching family members to (1) focus on the here and now, (2) take responsibility for their own thoughts, actions, feelings, and sensations, and (3) accept personal responsibility for change; teaching family members to substitute the use of *won't* for *can't* and the use of *what* and *how* for *why*; teaching parents to use self-esteem–building activities with child; modeling active listening, congruence, unconditional positive regard, and empathy with family | Teaching family members to (1) focus on the here and now, (2) take responsibility for their own thoughts, actions, feelings, and sensations, and (3) accept personal responsibility for change; teaching family members to substitute the use of *won't* for *can't* and the use of *what* and *how* for *why*; teaching parents to use self-esteem–building activities with child; modeling active listening, congruence, unconditional positive regard, and empathy with family | Teaching family members to (1) focus on the here and now, (2) take responsibility for their own thoughts, actions, feelings, and sensations, and (3) accept personal responsibility for change; teaching family members to substitute the use of *won't* for *can't* and the use of *what* and *how* for *why*; teaching parents to use self-esteem–building activities with child; modeling active listening, congruence, unconditional positive regard, and empathy with family |

| Paradigm | Elementary School | Middle School | High School |
|---|---|---|---|
| Behavioral/ CBT (Henderson & Thompson, 2011) | Teaching family about basic needs, control, choice, responsibility, total behavior; teaching parents about common irrational beliefs of children and parents; ABCDE model; "shoulds," "oughts," "musts"; catastrophizing; awfulizing | Teaching family about basic needs, control, choice, responsibility, total behavior; teaching parents about common irrational beliefs of children and parents; ABCDE model; "shoulds," "oughts," "musts"; catastrophizing; awfulizing | Teaching family about basic needs, control, choice, responsibility, total behavior; teaching parents about common irrational beliefs of adolescents and parents; ABCDE model; "shoulds," "oughts," "musts"; catastrophizing; awfulizing |
| Family Systems (Henderson & Thompson, 2011) | Teaching family members to recognize harmful communication patterns; assistance in building each family member's self-esteem; teaching family members differentiation by modeling "I" statements | Teaching family members to recognize harmful communication patterns; assistance in building each family member's self-esteem; teaching family members differentiation by modeling "I" statements | Teaching family members to recognize harmful communication patterns; assistance in building each family member's self-esteem; teaching family members differentiation by modeling "I" statements |
| Emergent (Anderson, 1993; White & Epston, 1990) | Process of change results from dialogue between counselor and family members; empowering each family member to re-author a more successful story | Process of change results from dialogue between counselor and family members; empowering each family member to re-author a more successful story | Process of change results from dialogue between counselor and family members; empowering each family member to re-author a more successful story |

## IN SESSION

The following conversation is a portion of the conference that took place between Amanda, her mother and father, and me. Examples of the solution-focused interventions that were utilized appear within brackets.

COUNSELOR (C): We're all here today to talk about how we can best support Amanda, and I'm wondering what it is that we want to change or do differently in order to make positive changes. [Setting the expectation for a positive result and that the parties involved will need to take responsibility for the change to happen]

MOTHER (M): We'd love for Amanda to do what other students naturally do every day . . . we want her to come to school, do her work, and make good choices so that we don't continue to receive fines or phone calls about her every day.

C: I'm really pleased to hear what you are saying because at school we are in total agreement with you. We want to see

Amanda make these changes; we don't want to keep sending discipline letters home, and we'd rather only call to provide you with positive updates. At home you have been trying different things, and at school we've been trying various interventions, but what it comes down to is that Amanda is the only one who can make this change. Let's focus today's discussion on how we can all work together to help her set herself up for a successful future. [Focusing on the present and future; focusing on solutions and not on problems; setting the expectation that positive change is possible]

M:      Amanda has become such a problem at home and at school that the only conversations we ever have are arguments, because there is nothing else to talk about.

C:      Can you recall a time when you and Amanda had a conversation that was enjoyable for the two of you? [Focusing on exceptions; attempting to identify a small change that can lead to bigger changes]

M:      Last summer, before this school year started and before she started getting in trouble, Amanda had just downloaded her favorite music album, and I asked her if I could hear what she was listening to. Amanda was surprised that I expressed interest in her music and just told me that I probably wouldn't like it. I told her that I really wanted to learn about the things she enjoys, so she gave in and let me hear it. We ended up listening to music and talking for hours that night. I'd love to do that again and really show Amanda how interested I am in her.

FATHER (F):      (*To counselor*) Don't pretend you care about Amanda. You don't care about her at all and that is why we're here. You are just trying to get rid of her and send her to another school. No wonder she is such a failure. It is too late for her to change so I don't know why we are even here.

C:      We all care very much about Amanda. We believe that she is a student who has several great qualities. She is assertive, determined, independent, and she is willing to accomplish goals that she has set for herself. Unfortunately, her current goal is to quit school and we don't want to see that happen, so we have recommended that she attend an adventure-based school that will offer her the ability to be more independent and have a hands-on learning approach. We don't believe that she is a failure. We believe this is a more appropriate setting because they can tailor her learning to accommodate her personal strengths. Our hope is that she will thrive in this setting once she realizes how different school can be for her. Let's work together to encourage her in this transition and show her that we all believe she isn't a failure.

[Shifting the conversation to Amanda's strengths by reframing the father's negative beliefs, language, and labels]

Amanda, I know that when you have refused to meet expectations at home and at school, that you have been called "stubborn," and I know that you have also given yourself that label. However, has anyone ever told you how "determined" you are? You've promised yourself that you won't do what the teachers want, and you've really followed through on your own promise, haven't you? I wonder what would happen if you used your determination to work toward another possible outcome that would be more effective for you. It is clear that you are a student who can follow through with the goals you set for yourself. [Empowering the student to tell a different story about herself; helping the student to see that she can redirect her label of "stubbornness" into behavioral descriptions that show her "determination"; encouraging the student to see that she can use a personal characteristic to her betterment instead of her detriment, allowing her to redirect it into a strength]

AMANDA (A): I never really looked at it that way.

C: (*To Amanda's father*) What have you noticed is effective in motivating Amanda?

F: The only thing I've noticed so far is that Amanda doesn't want us to continue receiving fines. That is the only reason we are here today, and this is the first time we've seen her willing to come into school for a meeting.

C: I think we are onto something here. It seems evident that a goal that all three of you share is avoiding additional fines. I would like to point out that the whole family coming to this meeting today shows that you are not only working together to avoid fines, but to help Amanda get her schooling back on track. I would like to recognize that attending today is a big change that you all have been willing to make. [Recognizing strengths and exceptions; identifying the family skeleton key of a shared goal]

## Outcome

Focusing the conversation on Amanda's strengths rather than her weaknesses and helping the family to see that Amanda was capable of achieving a goal when she set her mind to it, were major components of the solution-focused approach, which resulted in positive change for her and her parents. Prior to her counseling sessions with me and her attendance at the family meeting, Amanda had been extremely apathetic and emotionally numb to the adults in her life who lectured her about her mistakes. Because Amanda had a tendency to shut down around anyone who tried to convince her to change her behavior, she immediately noticed a difference in our conversations. Instead of talking *at* her, I talked *with* her and asked her solution-focused questions such as, "What do you want to change or do differently?" and "How motivated are you to make this change?" The meeting openly addressed her strengths.

As a result of the family meeting, everyone agreed that Amanda's placement at an adventure-based alternative school was the most appropriate way to assist her in getting back on track. Even though her parents initially disagreed with the idea, they understood the reason for it and agreed with the school's recommendation after seeing that it was a more appropriate setting for her. Shifting the focus off of Amanda's negative behaviors and onto her strengths was a paradigm shift for her parents as well as for Amanda. Prior to the meeting, her mother had focused on her weak relationship with Amanda, and her father had irrationally believed that it was too late for Amanda to turn her life around. Concentrating on Amanda's strengths, pointing out the exceptions, identifying a skeleton key, and emphasizing the future rather than the past were instrumental strategies in facilitating an effective meeting and accomplishing Amanda's eventual placement at another school.

Since the meeting, Amanda has transitioned to her new school environment and allowed herself to get to know her peers. I also have received reports that Amanda was sporadically doing her homework, which was actually a significant improvement compared with her previous refusal to complete any homework. Her parents have contacted me on several occasions not only to share positive updates about Amanda's progress but also to say that their new shared goal includes Amanda's graduation from high school. After inviting Amanda's parents to make positive changes in their family's functioning, they followed through by taking meaningful steps to create a healthier style of interaction. My efforts to establish a collaborative and empowering relationship with Amanda's parents—by meeting with them in person, supporting their role in their daughter's devel-

opment, and focusing on the positive changes that they were willing to make in their interactions with Amanda—played a key role in the improvement of their family dynamic. Working with families is often a very encouraging aspect of the school counselor's role. One can witness the profound changes that families are willing to make when they are open to (1) accepting the counselor's participation and support in their lives and (2) examining and changing their own family dynamics.

Working with Amanda's family highlights several areas of ethical considerations. Regarding confidentiality, and in keeping with the Ethical Standards for School Counselors (American School Counselor Association [ASCA], 2010), it was important to communicate with both Amanda and her parents that I would maintain confidentiality in our meetings unless there was a threat of harm to self or others. Being clear that I might have to breach confidentiality was a particularly salient topic in Amanda's case, because she had demonstrated behaviors that were a danger to others, such as threatening to fight, throwing sharp objects, and verbally harassing students. In my interactions with Amanda prior to working with her parents, I already had to act on my duty to warn and protect, as well as participate on a team of school personnel to assess Amanda's level of threat to the well-being of others at school. Although the Ethical Standards for School Counselors (ASCA, 2010) emphasize that the school counselor's primary responsibility is to the student, they also address the family's part in the process by stating that counselors "endeavor to establish, as appropriate, a collaborative relationship with parents/guardians to facilitate students' maximum development" (p. 4). In a proactive school counseling program, the counselor can create a climate of collaboration with families before the counselor ever needs to contact the family regarding a problem that the student is having at school. To cultivate positive school–family relationships, the counselor can initiate a number of strategies to help families feel connected to the school and their student's education. For example, the counselor may hold evening workshops on various topics, such as understanding the school counselor's role in their child's development; how to create optimal learning and studying environments at home; and parenting workshops and discussion groups. The counselor may invite parents to sit in on their children's classroom guidance lessons, so that parents may meet the counselor in person and also reinforce some of the counselor's lessons at home. Any way that a counselor can increase the ratio of positive to negative communications about students with their families lays a foundation for a more collaborative relationship between home and school. Some counselors find creative ways to inform parents about the successes and positive behaviors that students are having by using electronic newsletters or websites.

## Final Process Questions

- What multicultural issues might you need to consider with Amanda and her parents, so that you could serve this family in the most culturally sensitive manner?
- What further interventions could assist Amanda in her positive changes?
- What additional interventions could assist Amanda's parents?
- What can you do as a school counselor to prevent situations like this one?
- What are some interventions that might have been effective had they been implemented prior to high school?

- How would you handle the same scenario if Amanda had more supportive parents?
- Would you do anything differently if Amanda had a younger sibling living in the home?
- How will you decide which information is appropriate to share with Amanda's teachers?
- What could you do to increase positive communication with Amanda's parents?
- How soon will you follow up with Amanda's parents?

## Resources

Capuzzi, D., & Gross, D. R. (Eds.). (2008). *Youth at risk: A prevention resource for counselors, teachers, and parents* (5th ed.). Alexandria, VA: American Counseling Association.

McKay, G. D., & Maybell, S. A. (2005). *Calming the family storm: Anger management for moms, dads, and all the kids*. Atascadero, CA: Impact.

Somers-Flanagan, J., & Somers-Flanagan, R. (2011). *How to listen so parents will talk and talk so parents will listen*. Hoboken, NJ: Wiley.

*Chapter 29*

# Children of Deployed Parents

Lacey L. Wallace

## CASE BACKGROUND

One morning during my first month as a professional school counselor, I was floating around the school during arrival to greet and get to know the students. A staff member came to find me to assist Nyaja's mother in persuading Nyaja to come into the building. Nyaja was just starting kindergarten this school year, so I assumed that this hesitancy was due to Nyaja's attachment to her mom and not being used to going to school for a full day. I went out to the car and introduced myself to Nyaja's mother. I reached out my hand to Nyaja, hoping that she would feel safe enough to come with me, but instead she looked away. Being my first year as a professional school counselor, I did not have much confidence in talking to parents about their parenting strategies or suggesting different approaches. I quietly asked Nyaja's mother whether she would walk her to the door of the school and let me take it from there. I warned her that Nyaja would probably cry and try to hold on to her mother, but that I would not let her run out of the building. We did just as planned. As expected, Nyaja tried her hardest to hold on to her mother. Nyaja's mother pried Nyaja's fingers off of her clothing and quickly escaped through the door.

I hugged Nyaja and told her it would be OK and that I was going to be there for her. I asked whether we could go to my office to draw a picture before she went to class, and she nodded. During this first impromptu session, Nyaja did not speak one word. She reluctantly drew me a picture of her family and portrayed her father in his military uniform. I began asking a couple of questions about her father and then realized it might be too early for these questions. I asked Nyaja to show me where her dad was on the map in my office and she was able to identify the country. After assuring Nyaja that I would see her again at the end of the school day to play a game, we began to walk to her classroom.

After Nyaja returned to class, I called her mother to let her know that she had successfully gone to class. Her mother began explaining to me that her husband had recently been deployed and that they were new to the area.

## INITIAL PROCESS QUESTIONS

- If her mother cannot persuade the student to come into the building, how am I going to do so?
- Is this attachment to her mother, or is there another issue?

- Where do I begin to intervene—with the child or the parent?
- How can I help Nyaja understand her thoughts, behaviors, or feelings in hopes of increasing her willingness to enter the school?
- How can I incorporate other techniques to work with a child who is silent during our session?
- How can I help fill such a large void from her father being away at war?
- How can I help her family fill a similarly large void?
- Can I "treat" or help her family, or is the student my only concern?
- What resources are available for families of soldiers who are at war?

## ADDRESSING THE ISSUES

It was apparent that Nyaja's difficulty with her father's deployment was multifaceted, and I would have to use an integrative approach in working with her. In order to encourage Nyaja to come to school, I started by working with her classroom teacher using behavioral techniques to create a positive reinforcement chart for coming to school without resistance. I also included a humanistic/existential approach by creating a memory box with her to help her find meaning and purpose in her father's absence. This memory box would serve as a gift for her father when he returned. For each day that Nyaja would come to school willingly, she was able to spend time that morning creating pictures or crafts to put in the memory box. Her teacher also gave her the job of feeding the class pet to encourage her to come straight to class in the morning and to increase her sense of importance and belonging in the classroom. As Nyaja received positive reinforcement, she began to enter the building independently. She began to become excited to come to school to create projects for her father and to feed the class pet. As this occurred, Nyaja started to form relationships with other students and to have a sense of belonging.

As I continued to meet with Nyaja, we created items to keep in her memory box for her father. We would trace her hands and feet and write the date so her father could see how much she had grown during the time he was gone. She would save papers and art projects that she was especially proud of to put in the memory box. Her mother printed pictures to include when they did something as a family. Some days Nyaja would just write her dad a note to tell him how her day was going or something she was upset about.

I used techniques from family systems theory by working with her mother in finding appropriate resources to assist their family such as support groups for children and spouses of deployed soldiers. I found a number of resources through the Military Child Education Coalition (MCEC) to give to her mother, including information on keeping the household as normal as possible throughout deployment, activities to do with her daughters, and expectations for her husband's return home.

Nyaja's mom expressed that she would like Nyaja to meet other children at the same developmental level who are experiencing similar concerns. I sent home a needs assessment with parents and teachers to find out how many students had a parent who was deployed. The response was enthusiastic from all stakeholders, so I asked support personnel from Walter Reed National Military Medical Center (WRNMMC) whether they would be able to provide group therapy for the spouses of the deployed soldiers and sailors while I facilitated group counseling for the children. Our group met biweekly in the evenings for 6 months. Parents were able to receive psycho-education, counseling, and connect with resources in the community. Nyaja and the other children had the opportunity to process their thoughts and feelings about their parent's deployment and the changes within their family dynamic.

I also met with my principal and our school's leadership team to determine what additional professional development was needed at our school. Because most of the staff has worked with this population for a period of time, it had been a while since the current staff had had any professional development opportunities. To ensure that proper training was provided, our school liaison officer referred us to the appropriate community resources. Additional techniques and strategies for helping children and families of deployed parents are listed in Table 29-1.

## IN SESSION

During one of our sessions, Nyaja and I began talking about her father and all of the things she missed about him, along with her fears and worries.

| | |
|---|---|
| Counselor (C): | If you could see your dad, what would you tell him? |
| Nyaja (N): | That I miss him a lot and want him to come home. |
| C: | OK. Let's pretend Dad is sitting in this chair right here. Can you picture him? |
| N: | (*Giggled*) No. |
| C: | Just try your best; let's pretend Dad is sitting in this chair. Tell him anything you want. |
| N: | Dad, I miss you so much. Why can't you come home? Ally misses you too. We want to come where you are. |
| C: | I bet it makes you feel very sad when you see your sister getting upset about missing your dad too. |
| N: | Yeah, sometimes she cries a lot and says she misses Daddy. |
| C: | How often do you get to Skype with Dad? |
| N: | I did last night. |
| C: | Great! Tell me something special your dad said to you. |
| N: | He told me he got our box we sent him and that he loved the picture I drew him. |
| C: | I bet it meant a lot to him to be able to show his soldier friends all of the things his daughters made for him. Do you know when Daddy comes home? |
| N: | After my birthday. |
| C: | When is your birthday? |
| N: | July. |
| C: | Have you ever made a paper chain to count down the days before Christmas? |
| N: | Yes, I did it with my mommy and daddy this year. |

**TABLE 29-1**  **Additional Techniques and Strategies for Helping Children and Families of Deployed Parents**

| Paradigm | Elementary School | Middle School | High School |
|---|---|---|---|
| Psychodynamic | Analysis of avoidance (i.e., refusing to come to school), loss of father and its effect on current functioning; talking about possible unconscious fears and worries | Analysis of relationship with father and mother throughout childhood; determination of father's role in her life; evaluation of avoidance and other defense mechanisms | Analysis of relationship with father and mother throughout childhood; determination of father's role in her life; evaluation of defense mechanisms |
| Humanistic/ Existential | Therapeutic conditions; role play and empty chair as if speaking to her father; "I" statements when feeling worried, anxious, or upset; creating job or role for student to feel a sense of meaning; creating memory box to feel a sense of accomplishment and connection when student adds to the box | Therapeutic conditions; role play; empty chair; "I" statements for worries and concerns about deployed parent and changes within home; helping to find meaning in parent's deployment by having student work with even younger students whose parents are deployed | Therapeutic conditions; role play and "I" statements for talking to deployed parent; helping to find meaning in parent's deployment by having student work with even younger students whose parents are deployed |
| Behavioral/CBT | Positive reinforcement for coming to school; behavior charts to encourage willingness to come to school; behavior contracts to determine rewards for making it through the school day; disputing irrational beliefs about school being scary or Dad being hurt; cognitive restructuring of what the school day is like; self-talk during entry of the building; visual imagery of father walking her to school; modeling positive self-talk; behavioral rehearsal; role playing; "picture in your mind" coming into school and being happy to play with friends; exceptions; miracle question; overcorrection; response cost; flagging the minefield | Positive reinforcement; token economy; Premack principle; behavior contracts; disputing irrational beliefs; cognitive restructuring; specifying automatic thoughts; self-talk; visual imagery; modeling; behavioral rehearsal; role playing; "picture in your mind"; exceptions; miracle question; overcorrection; response cost; flagging the minefield | Positive reinforcement; token economy; Premack principle; behavior contracts; disputing irrational beliefs; cognitive restructuring; specifying automatic thoughts; self-talk; visual imagery; modeling; behavioral rehearsal; role playing; "picture in your mind"; exceptions; miracle question; overcorrection; response cost; flagging the minefield |

*(continued)*

**TABLE 29-1** *(continued)*

| Paradigm | Elementary School | Middle School | High School |
|---|---|---|---|
| Family Systems | Parent behavior training for dealing with deployment and its effects on children; education on change in family dynamic when one family member is temporarily away from home; education about return from war and its effects on family system; providing resources in community to support the family | Parent behavior training for dealing with deployment and its effects on children; education on change in family dynamic when one family member is temporarily away from home; education about return from war and its effects on family system; providing resources in community to support the family | Parent behavior training for dealing with deployment and its effects on children; education on change in family dynamic when one family member is temporarily away from home; education about return from war and its effects on family system; providing resources in community to support the family |
| Emergent | Miracle question; sparkling moments—focus on the times student has made contact with deployed parent; focus on parent return; empowerment; communication analysis; interpersonal incidents; role playing; bibliotherapy about other students' experiences that are similar | Deconstruct and externalize problems; miracle question; sparkling moments; empowerment; communication analysis; interpersonal incidents; role playing | Deconstruct and externalize problems; miracle question; sparkling moments; empowerment; communication analysis; interpersonal incidents; role playing |

C:    Let's make a paper chain, but instead of counting down we are going to count up. We are going to make a paper link for each day that Dad is gone and when he comes home you can use it to decorate your house for his welcome back party.

N:    His favorite colors are red and blue. Can we use those colors?

C:    Absolutely! Let's get started and we can cut out links to bring home so you can do this every day with your mom and sister.

## Outcome

Nyaja continued to come to school independently. She would often take extra time by the cubbies while she was unpacking her backpack, but always made it to her desk by the time the announcements started. Although I continued to check in and work with Nyaja as needed throughout the rest of the school year, I also felt that Nyaja and her family needed more support than what I was able to offer during the school day. I referred Nyaja and her family to work with the psychiatric nurse-practitioner for Walter Reed National Military Medical Center (WRNMMC). Nyaja and her mother continued to work with WRNMMC throughout the remainder of the school year and through the summer. At the start of the next school year, Nyaja's father received orders to move out of the country, and her family began preparing to meet him there.

## Final Process Questions

- What proactive measures can I put into place for members of the military population?
- How does the stress on the family affect a child's well-being?
- What understanding does a child at this age have of war and the dangers to her parent?

- What resources are available to families of soldiers at war that I am unaware of?
- In what ways can I support the parents whose spouses are deployed?
- Should I have referred Nyaja to outside services earlier in the school year?

## Resources

Andrews, B., & Wright, H. (2007). *I miss you: A military kids book about deployment*. Amherst, NY: Prometheus Books.

Kennedy Krieger Institute, Eagle Project: Military Children's Behavioral Health Clinic, http://www.kennedykrieger.org/patient-care/patient-care-programs/outpatient-programs/eagle-project

McElroy, L. T., & Paterson, D. (2005). *Love, Lizzie: Letters to a military mom*. Morton Grove, IL: Albert Whitman.

Military Child Education Coalition (MCEC) website, www.militarychild.org

Scillian, D., & Juhasz, V. (2011). *H is for honor: A military family alphabet*. Ann Arbor, MI: Sleeping Bear Press.

# Chapter 30

# Children of Divorce

NATALIE GRUBBS AND CATHERINE Y. CHANG

## CASE BACKGROUND

Callie is a 9-year-old White fourth-grade student attending a private elementary school. Her father is the sole financial provider for her upper-middle-class family. As an executive for a Fortune 500 company, Callie's father works long hours and travels frequently for work. Callie's mother does not work outside the home, is very involved with the school Callie attends, is active in the classroom and in the school parent–teacher association, and has a large social network of friends among other parents and families at Callie's school.

As a straight-A student, Callie is frequently recognized in school for her academic achievements. She is a very outgoing student and has many friends in the fourth grade. Callie always has enjoyed coming to school, but recently began to experience frequent headaches and stomachaches while getting ready for school in the mornings. Her mother brought her into the school clinic one morning to see the nurse about the aches Callie had experienced on the car ride to school. The nurse hypothesized that Callie's aches were related to anxiety about coming to school and asked her mother about possible sources of anxiety. Callie's mother then announced that she and Callie's father planned to divorce and that they had told Callie and her younger sister the night before. Callie's father informed the girls that he planned to move into his own apartment 5 miles from the family home at the end of the month. The nurse notified the teacher, who then consulted with me, the school counselor, to request that I meet with Callie. Callie's academics and peer relationships have not been affected by her parents' separation or divorce. Her main presenting issue, therefore, is the somatic symptoms (i.e., aches and pains) she experiences as well as her anxiety in the mornings.

## INITIAL PROCESSING QUESTIONS

A school counselor working with Callie will want to consider the following questions:

- What personal biases about divorce do you have in general and specifically in working with Callie?
- What is your initial reaction to hearing that Callie's parents are divorcing?
- What cultural considerations should you make in working with Callie?

- What assumptions might you make upon hearing about Callie's background and her parents' newly announced divorce?
- What role do school counselors have in working with students who are experiencing divorce in their family?

## ADDRESSING THE ISSUES

School counselors can work with children experiencing divorce either individually or in small groups. Specific interventions used can be rooted in any of the five counseling paradigms summarized in Chapter 1. When working with children at various school levels (elementary, middle, and high), age, maturity, and cultural background must be considered as school counselors seek out effective and culturally relevant interventions to implement with their student populations.

The school nurse, Callie's teacher, and I are taking a proactive, multidisciplinary approach in Callie's case. Many times when a family has chosen not to inform school personnel of an impending separation or divorce, teachers will notice that the children involved begin to experience a decline in academics, affect, or behavior, which is then brought to the school counselor's attention, usually by the children's teachers. It is always preferable for parents and school faculty to take a more proactive approach when facing a divorce situation as opposed to reacting to academic or behavior problems as they manifest. Taking such an approach is consistent with the developmental approach of the *ASCA National Model* for comprehensive school counseling programs (American School Counselor Association [ASCA], 2012).

In general, my approach with Callie was based on the person-centered or child-centered theoretical approach to counseling. Taking this approach, I allowed Callie to lead the conversation, being careful not to impose my own "agenda" in our session or allow my biases about divorce or my prior experiences with divorce, for that matter, to affect my conversation with Callie. I permitted Callie to initiate any discussions related to divorce instead of deciding for us that our conversation would be about the divorce. I did not have specific treatment goals for our session. Instead, consistent with my child-centered theoretical approach, my intention was to provide a safe, supportive environment for Callie to talk to me about whatever she felt was most "pressing" for her in the moment. I focused on establishing our relationship and reflected Callie's feelings about the concerns she shared with me. I also used interventions from a more emergent theoretical orientation—such as reading storybooks about divorce, drawing pictures, role playing, and providing information (i.e., psycho-education about divorce)—when I felt the topic was relevant and when Callie was open to the information or if she directly asked for some specific information. Play therapy is suggested as an appropriate intervention for elementary school aged children, because younger children have not yet mastered abstract reasoning and may not be able to comprehend or verbalize their feelings about mature themes such as divorce (Landreth, Baggerly, & Tyndall-Lind, 1999). As Landreth (2002, p. 132) points out, "toys are children's words and play is their language." Toys can be used with young children of divorce along with other materials such as art materials and picture books to provide them with alternative ways to express their feelings about what is happening in their lives.

Small groups are effective with children because they provide a safe and accepting environment to receive the support of others, and they are a natural medium for playing and learning. Additionally, groups teach children how to trust and how to share ideas in an environment of respect, tolerance, and empathy (Smead, 1994). Small groups are a developmentally appropriate approach for elementary and middle school children. Older middle school and high school students can also benefit from small groups, but some counselors may choose to refer to them as "workshops" or "lunch bunches" instead of small counseling groups to offer a greater appeal to adolescents. Many school counselors choose to offer groups at all three levels that might include children of divorce along with children experiencing other family changes such as moving, death, birth of a sibling, or remarriage. Conversely, other school counselors may choose to focus the group strictly on divorce and include only those children who are experiencing or have experienced a divorce.

The information presented in Table 30-1 provides various interventions school counselors can use when working with children of divorce. These techniques and strategies can be used in a group setting or in individual work with children.

Divorce is a situation that evokes strong emotional reactions from children of *all* ages. Thus, school counselors working at every grade level should take a proactive approach in caring for students at their school experiencing divorce in their families. Elementary school children may be more forthcoming about the details of their family's divorce than, say, an adolescent boy. However, school counseling interventions can be effective with children of all ages. Callie, an elementary school aged child, responded very well to one-on-one sessions using "talk therapy" interventions as well as play and art interventions such as drawing. She also enjoyed small group interventions such as role plays and group stories. Many interventions that are appropriate for elementary aged children can also be effective with middle and high school students. Art interventions and role plays can be used with older children, and middle school students could benefit greatly from small groups. With older students, school counselors could use "workshops" instead of small groups, or have students write a short story about their family's divorce as opposed to drawing a picture about it. As students get older, especially if their parents divorced when they were younger, school counselors should look out for students' reactions to family changes that may result from divorce, such as a parent moving or remarrying, or starting to date. In ideal cases in which school counselors have access to the same students over the course of several years, it is a good idea to check in with the student and parents periodically to continue to care for children through the various possible stages of divorce (separation, divorce, remarriage, blending families, etc.).

## IN SESSION

| | |
|---|---|
| Counselor (C): | Hi, Callie! How are you today? |
| Callie: | OK, but my mom and dad told me last night that they are getting a divorce and so I am really sad. |
| C: | I am really sorry to hear that, and I'm sorry that you are feeling sad. Sometimes moms and dads decide to get a divorce and it's very normal for kids to be sad when they hear that. |
| Callie: | My dad is moving to an apartment, and I'm sad because I've never lived away from my dad before. I'm used to seeing him every day and now I don't know when I'll be able to see him. |

**TABLE 30-1  Additional Techniques and Strategies for Helping Children of Divorce**

| Paradigm | Elementary School | Middle School | High School |
|---|---|---|---|
| Psychodynamic | Play therapy; exploring and processing attachment issues; identifying and disclosing goal of behavior; parent consultations; encouragement | Exploring and processing attachment issues; identifying and disclosing goal of behavior; parent consultations; encouragement | Exploring and processing attachment issues; identifying and disclosing goal of behavior; parent consultations; encouragement |
| Humanistic/ Existential | Play therapy; listening and reflecting feelings; encouraging; building relationship | Listening and reflecting feelings; encouraging; building relationship | Listening and reflecting feelings; encouraging; building relationship |
| Behavioral/CBT | Play therapy; parent–teacher consultations; role playing; brainstorming; bibliotherapy/books on divorce; disputing irrational beliefs; behavioral rehearsal | Role playing; brainstorming; parent–teacher consultations; bibliotherapy/ books on divorce; disputing irrational beliefs; behavioral rehearsal | Role playing; brainstorming; parent–teacher consultations; disputing irrational beliefs (it's my fault); behavioral rehearsal |
| Family Systems | Play therapy; parent–teacher consultations; parent training on helping children with divorce; teacher training on helping children cope with divorce | Parent–teacher consultations; parent training on helping children with divorce; teacher training on helping children cope with divorce | Parent–teacher consultations; parent training on helping children with divorce; teacher training on helping children cope with divorce |
| Emergent | Reading stories about divorce; creating drawings about divorce; storytelling; providing student with age-appropriate information about various aspects of divorce; role playing common divorce-related scenarios; miracle question | Creating drawings about divorce; storytelling; providing student with age-appropriate information about various aspects of divorce; role playing common divorce-related scenarios; miracle question | Writing stories or narratives about divorce; storytelling; providing student with age-appropriate information about various aspects of divorce; role playing common divorce-related scenarios; miracle question |

C: Do you know where your dad's new apartment will be?

CALLIE: He's moving into an apartment near our house. He said it was about 5 miles from our house now.

C: Have your parents talked to you about how often you will be able to visit your dad?

CALLIE: No.

C: So you're wondering how things will be different now that your dad is living in a different house.

CALLIE: Yes.

| | |
|---|---|
| C: | Well, I understand that you're feeling worried because you're not sure what all of this is going to mean for your family. When parents divorce, things do change for families, but lots of times moms and dads work really hard to make sure that everything stays as normal as possible for the kids. |
| CALLIE: | I am also worried because my mom and dad fight about money a lot. My mom said that we might have to move, and me and my sister may have to change schools. |
| C: | So you are feeling like there might be a lot of changes that you and your sister will have to deal with. How do you feel about moving to a new house and maybe a new school? |
| CALLIE: | Sad. I don't want to leave my friends. |
| C: | Yeah, so some of the changes that may happen for you are sad changes. |
| CALLIE: | Yeah. |

As our conversation continued, Callie worked very hard to "sort out" the family's new financial circumstances. Realizing that Callie was apparently trying to deal with her parents' divorce by "thinking it through," I allowed her to brainstorm and asked questions where appropriate. When I asked Callie how she knew so much about the family's finances, she said that her dad tells her and complains a lot about how much money her mom spends. She said she wishes her dad wouldn't complain to her about her mom. I talked to Callie about how she feels when her dad complains to her about her mom, and we role-played ways she could handle the situation differently in the future (e.g., change the subject, let Dad know she feels sad when he talks about Mom).

In terms of the divorce, Callie acknowledged that divorce is "sort of" a good thing because her mom and dad weren't fighting anymore, but she said that she and her sister had actually been having more arguments. With her sister being 2 years younger than she, Callie and her sister always have had a close relationship and never really fought. But now, Callie said they argue often, and she felt the increase in arguments was due to her parents' divorce. I asked Callie whether she could think of some ways she could work on her friendship with her sister. Callie suggested writing her sister a letter, drawing her a picture, talking with her about their feelings, and spending more time playing with her sister. I congratulated Callie for coming up with so many different ways she could get along better with her sister.

Callie and I talked for about 30 minutes before I wrapped up our conversation and walked her back to her classroom. Before we left my office, I set up a next appointment with Callie by asking her, "Would you like to come back and talk more next week?" Callie consented, and I let her know that I would work with her teacher to schedule a good time. When Callie went back to class, her demeanor was noticeably more cheerful and she seemed to have enjoyed talking with me.

## Outcome

Callie visited with me regularly over the course of the school year. I continued to focus on building rapport with her and both of her parents. I also consulted with Callie's teacher and with the school nurse (while maintaining confidentiality) about the aches Callie had been experiencing.

The nurse and the teacher both reported that her aches declined as the year progressed. I met with Callie's parents both individually and together with the teacher to discuss Callie's progress and provide strategies and tips on ways Callie's parents could help her adjust to their two homes. Callie would be living half the week at her mom's house and the other half at her dad's. Some plans we came up with included helping Callie work on a monthly calendar, marking all of her school and extracurricular events and including big school projects and tests. On her calendar each month, Callie would mark significant dates "at mom's" or "at dad's" to help her keep up with her schedule. Another strategy the parents adopted was for Callie to establish homework stations at each house equipped with study materials to cut down on the possibility of forgetting materials at one house or the other.

In the middle of the school year, I invited Callie to participate in a small group with other children whose parents had divorced or were divorcing. Callie was in a group with three other girls her age, and all four girls really enjoyed talking and listening to each other's stories. Callie benefited from the small group, and her parents were very grateful that she had such a strong support system at school. Callie's improvement was monitored by both her teachers and the school counselor based on her academic performance and her increased social interactions with her peers. Additionally, at the termination of the group, the school counselor asked the group members to identify what was beneficial about the group and what skills the group members will take away from the group. The school counselor also ended the group with a scaling question: "From a scale of 1 to 10, how do you feel about your ability to cope with your parents' divorce? This was the same scaling question that the school counselor had asked when the group first started meeting. Callie indicated that she felt she could better handle her stress (e.g., breathing exercises, journal writing, and asking for support) and that she no longer felt alone because she knew other students who were experiencing the same thing she was.

## Final Process Questions

- In cases of divorce at your school, what are additional things you can do to be proactive?
- How can you anticipate helping Callie transition through her parents' divorce as well as prepare for other changes in her life (transitioning to middle school, new school, new home)?
- How can you help Callie continue to connect with other kids, including her younger sister?
- Imagine working with Callie for the school year. Did you see any of your cultural biases coming out? If so, how would you address them?
- What different/additional approaches or interventions would you use with Callie?
- After reading this case scenario, what role do you think school counselors have in working with students who are experiencing divorce in their family? Has your response changed from before you read the case scenario?

## Resources

Brown, L., & Brown, M. (1988). *Dinosaurs divorce: A guide for changing families.* New York, NY: Little Brown Books for Young Readers.

Lowenstein, L. (2006). *Creative interventions for children of divorce.* Toronto, Canada: Pharma Plus.

Spencer, A., & Shapiro, R. (1993). *Helping students cope with divorce: A complete group education counseling program for grades 7–12.* New York, NY: Center for Applied Research in Education.

Winchester, K., & Beyer, R. (2001). *What in the world do you do when your parents divorce? A survival guide for kids.* Minneapolis, MN: Free Spirit.

*Chapter 31*

# Helping Children of Incarcerated Parents

ELISABETH BENNETT AND TOM O'CONNOR

## CASE BACKGROUND

Marcus first enrolled in our Title I elementary school as a 5-year-old kindergartener living with his paternal grandmother. Both his mother and father had been incarcerated due to illegal drug-related activities. His one sister was a middle school student at that time. Marcus's sister reported having tried to hold and comfort Marcus early in Marcus's life when their mother was absent or dealing with seemingly insurmountable personal problems. Common for many children with parents with multiple incarcerations, Marcus's life was often disrupted by his unstable circumstances. It was reported that Marcus had experienced early childhood trauma while in his mother's care in relation to her drug and criminal activity. Partway through his kindergarten year, Marcus moved to a second elementary school where he completed the remainder of kindergarten and first grade. He was then sent back to live with his grandmother with that school's recommendation that he repeat first grade, which he did. During that time, Marcus was assessed for special education assistance and qualified as learning disabled. He completed first and second grade while living with his grandmother and attending our school. During much of that time his sister and an aunt also lived with Marcus and his grandmother.

At the beginning of third grade, he moved back with his mother and maternal grandfather and attended yet a third elementary school. At the beginning of fourth grade, his mother was re-incarcerated, and Marcus returned to live with his grandmother, aunt, and sister. Marcus attended our elementary school again where he was promoted, in large part due to the added support from his teachers and other school personnel. At the beginning of sixth grade, Marcus returned to his mother's care, yet continued to attend our elementary school. Both parents were released from incarceration and were working diligently on both their own issues and their concerns for their son.

Marcus was not unscathed throughout his parents' incarcerations. Marcus exhibited difficulties throughout his elementary education in both his behaviors and negative comments to others. He had trouble regulating his emotions and had frequent anger outbursts. Marcus identified as a major issue his perception of being different because of his special education status. Transitions between his regular classroom and the resource room were met with resistance and refusal; and once in the resource room, he would occasionally shut down and refuse to work. His anger also seemed related to the absence of his mother and her care for him. As he grew, his behaviors at home with his grandmother became more difficult for her to handle as his resentment for her expectations became more a focus of his complaints. Marcus displayed an increasing sense of blame of others for his poor choices and seemed unwilling to take responsibility for his actions. Marcus's aggressive actions and words were his primary mode of communicating his issues and frustrations, and he seemed unable to label his needs or feelings in a more effective manner.

## INITIAL PROCESS QUESTIONS

- From a humanistic perspective, what core conditions must the school counselor hold and present to Marcus when entering Marcus's world? What challenges might exist in maintaining those core conditions?
- What ethical considerations for safety and confidentiality might be of concern when dealing with Marcus and his situation?
- How can the professional school counselor discover and highlight this student's strengths and resiliency so that learning is optimized?
- What developmental challenges might a professional school counselor consider given the disruptions in Marcus's life during his early elementary school experience? How might those challenges be evidenced (e.g., in attentiveness, adherence to classroom and school rules and norms, and interactions with peers, teachers, and staff)?
- What strategies and techniques would be helpful for a school counselor to consider implementing to help Marcus improve his behavior, shape his expressions of his feelings, and better communicate with his peers, teachers, and staff? What techniques might not be effective?
- What kinds of outside resources would be useful for referral of Marcus and his family?

## ADDRESSING THE ISSUES

Marcus's case scenario is in many ways typical when considering children of incarcerated parents; however, there are certainly variations and every child is unique. Many children in this situation do not have learning disabilities or qualify for resource room services. Certain children are able to maintain placement with the non-incarcerated parent, which results in greater stability in caregiver and home life. Many children of incarcerated parents do not have behavioral disturbances and usually possess effective coping skills. Still other children in this situation are even more heavily involved in state care; they may be moved a number of times including into and out of foster placement with nonrelatives. Some children will have learning disruptions, including and beyond the difficulties of this case scenario, as well as behavioral disruptions that rise to the level of delinquent activities. It is critical for the professional school counselor to note that each child's situation and accompanying conditions must be considered individually. A number of important considerations are common among children of incarcerated parents, including trauma, unstable home base and caregivers, identification of self as "different," emotional dysregulation, psychosocial development, and academic struggles. The school counselor must address these considerations to implement a comprehensive intervention plan.

## Trauma

The experience of professional school counselors indicates that children of incarcerated parents will possibly have undergone the following: neglect due to parental drug activity, being left alone during criminal activity, or even being abandoned when a parent was arrested if it was not known that the child existed or was in parent's care upon arrest. Furthermore, children of incarcerated parents sometimes witness their parents' criminal activity (e.g., drug manufacture, use, distribution) and may even be exposed to other individuals who have no interest in the child's well-being and may abuse the child. Issues of trauma may affect learning. A solid referral, partnership, or follow-up with a community mental health agency for assessment and counseling can be critical to the child's success in school. The school counselor worked as closely as possible with a local agency until Marcus's sixth-grade year when Marcus became resistant to continuing with outside counseling. The counselor continues to attempt to get this process restarted.

## Unstable Home Base/Caregiver

Like Marcus, many children of incarcerated parents experience multiple living environments and may even move several times within the school year. This necessitates consultation with personnel from other schools in order to assist in providing transitional support and to orient the student to the new school. Consultation is critical and should be ongoing with those caring for the child in each home situation. It is vital to support the stability of those such as Marcus's grandmother. Consultation with parents can be invaluable when possible, even when they are incarcerated and especially between their incarcerations. Furthermore, it is vital for the school counselor to create or support a means whereby the child remains in contact with the incarcerated parents. This can take many forms including direct contact within the rules of the incarceration, letters written even if not sent, and empty chair exercises that allow the child to, at a minimum, express his thoughts and feelings about his situation and his parents.

Within the boundaries of confidentiality, in this case scenario each consultation was aimed at creating as much stability and consistency as possible. Teachers were regularly and delicately informed (without breaking confidentiality) of the critical parts of Marcus's background. It was our hope as school counselors that the teachers would reflect on this knowledge and be continually aware of the implications of Marcus's background, with the result of demonstrating patience, kindness, and structure in response to his emotional outbursts and attempts to self-regulate. Consultations were also held with the mental health therapist. Ongoing family case management and counseling were aimed at increasing the stability of Marcus's home life.

Finally, due to shared concerns between school personnel and his grandmother, the school counselor connected Marcus to a local program run by an agency that partners children of incarcerated parents with gender-matched mentors. Initially, there was a plethora of male mentors in this program, so Marcus was rather quickly assigned a mentor. This immediately seemed to be very valuable. The mentor was active with Marcus and would frequently stop by the school to visit with school personnel and have lunch with Marcus. Planned outings were reported by Marcus as being fun. Marcus was eager to connect with his mentor and shared many positive comments regarding this experience.

Common to children in Marcus's situation, a move ensued back to his mother's care where the maternal grandfather was present. Following this move, the mentor's visits declined until they stopped altogether. Whether this was due to the presence of another male figure, declining interest on the part of the mentor, or other factors, the loss of the mentor appeared to be devastating for Marcus. Both Marcus and his grandmother experienced the loss as abandonment by the mentor, and Marcus was left with the reaffirmation that adults are not dependable and would not be there consistently over time. No closure was achieved with the mentor, which might have made a difference in how Marcus was affected by that loss. Finally, it is noted that in some cases, the school counselor is the one stable factor the child experiences, not just in his school life, but overall. Hence, the counselor's capacity and willingness to be consistent, understanding, empathetic, well-structured, and present with the child are critical.

## Identification of Self as "Different"

It is not uncommon for children of incarcerated parents to feel a sense of isolation from others. Ordinarily, this is due to the child's belief that the parents' crimes, arrests, and incarceration—as well as the child's unstable home conditions—make the child unacceptable, unusual, unlike others, and unlikeable by their peers. Marcus experienced an exacerbation of this sense of difference given his identification as learning disabled and his spending one to two hours per day in the resource room. Regarding this exacerbation, consultation with the school psychologist was invaluable in assisting school personnel in understanding Marcus's assessment and its impact on his academic performance and behavioral issues. To further address Marcus's concerns of being different, every attempt was made to assist Marcus in identifying himself as part of a group or system. This meant that group work became a central modality for assisting in conflict resolution, skill building, friendship work, owning personal responsibility for his own actions, and identifying strengths and solutions that empowered each student. Group work was instituted in second grade with five other second-grade students over six sessions.

Posttest data of this group work indicated that the students (including Marcus) understood their poor behavior choices and could identify appropriate ways of responding. It is also helpful to have students who share similar issues meet together to establish a sense of universality (e.g., Marcus is not alone; several of his classmates have parents who are incarcerated), to provide a forum for sharing the worries and events that may be unique to this situation, and to offer hope as children further along in the process of their parents' incarceration can share how they "made it through" the difficult times. Indeed, one clear example is that Marcus rarely mentioned his mother and father throughout his early years, only occasionally referring to them and their whereabouts. In a group setting, it was more likely that Marcus would hear others mentioning their parents' incarceration and therefore be more ready to discuss his own parents' positions and impact on his life. Group work can help children identify emotions, take healthy actions to soothe or regulate emotions, and talk appropriately about emotions. Classroom guidance regarding emotional regulation can benefit all students and can lead the children of incarcerated parents to feel more "normal" by recognizing that classmates experience similar emotions.

## Emotional Regulation

It is common for children of incarcerated parents to have difficulties with emotional regulation. Some display overregulation, and others are seemingly unable to regulate emotions. Marcus had frequent angry outbursts with an inability or unwillingness to control his behavior. Addressing this issue required a fair amount of attention in individual counseling by the school counselor. Once removed from the classroom, Marcus was usually able to calm himself relatively quickly, but not without directing a significant number of negative comments toward the teacher and classmates. He frequently perceived that everyone else was being unfair.

Triadic work with Marcus, another student, and me was aimed at working out problems by using "I" statements and other conflict resolution strategies. Marcus sometimes required attention when moving from his classroom to the resource room due to his angry resolution not to go to the resource room. Coaching Marcus individually in the resource room was usually effective in motivating Marcus to engage in his work once there, rather than persist in his negative spin and emotions, which limit his learning. Where possible, it may be beneficial to consider models of resource education that do not require the child to leave the regular classroom, such as through the inclusion model.

## Psychosocial Development and Friendships

Frequently moving, changing neighborhoods and schools, feeling "different," and having difficulties regulating emotions set up the child of incarcerated parents for struggles in building and maintaining friendships. Marcus had additional complications in that he had been held back a year, was markedly physically bigger than classmates, and was identified as learning disabled. Classroom guidance lessons can assist in building an environment more conducive to acceptance of differences and to friendly activity on the part of all students. For Marcus's class, the school counselor's guidance lessons focused on areas deemed helpful to Marcus: conflict resolution, emotional regulation, anger management, character traits modeling, bullying, and communication strategies.

Individual work on self-soothing, an ever-growing acceptance of self, and identification of personal strengths can assist the child to perceive self as friendship material. Group work involving children with similar life struggles builds a sense of universality and belonging, which can open the doors to friendship and success in social developmental tasks. Particular attention at times of entry or reentry to the school and classroom are merited.

## Academic Struggles

Although some students of incarcerated parents may do well academically, many struggle. It is helpful for the professional school counselor to seek consultation and assessment regarding potential academic limitations and strengths, to be an active participant in building individualized educational plans, and to provide individual support in assisting the child to fulfill the social and behavioral goals of that plan in and outside of the classroom. Attending to the child's self-esteem, sense of personal adequacy, perceptions of the school climate, and his or her relationships with the teacher and classmates is important because each facet contributes to the learning environment for the identified student and the entire class. Furthermore, consultation with the caregiver (Marcus's grandmother primarily) is invaluable in seeking to ensure that the student's home life supports his academic pursuits as helpfully as possible.

The issues that children of incarcerated parents experience appear to be similar across the various developmental levels. Table 31-1 provides additional techniques and strategies given the five major paradigms across various academic levels.

**TABLE 31-1   Additional Techniques and Strategies for Helping Children of Incarcerated Parents**

| Paradigm | Elementary School | Middle School | High School |
|---|---|---|---|
| Psychodynamic | Analysis of ego development and immature defense mechanisms (projection, regression, acting out) and transference with focus on effective structures; providing assistance in achieving industry versus inferiority; free association; attachment; assessment/building | Analysis of ego development and immature/neurotic defense mechanisms (projection, regression, acting out, splitting, devaluation); providing assistance in achieving industry versus inferiority and/or identity versus role confusion; analysis of transference via free association to develop healthier attachment processes | Ego development (fragile ego, under-/overdeveloped superego); immature/neurotic defenses (projection, regression, acting out, splitting, devaluation, displacement, rationalization, intellectualization); providing assistance in achieving identity versus role confusion; analysis of transference via free association with support of an effective attachment figure |
| Humanistic/ Existential | Therapeutic conditions; role play; emotions identification and appropriate expression; examination of anxiety and behavioral issues and a sense of belonging to classmates, classroom, school, and community; counseling relationship; mentoring relationships | Therapeutic conditions; role play; "I" statements; examination of anxiety and behavioral issues related to safety, belonging, and personal and global responsibility and freedom; development of self as contributing community member; counseling relationship; mentoring relationship | Therapeutic conditions; role play; "I" statements; examination of anxiety and behavioral issues related to safety, belonging, and personal and global responsibility and freedom as contributing law-abiding member of society; counseling relationship; mentoring relationship |
| Behavioral/CBT | Disputing irrational beliefs; self-talk; modeling; role playing; miracle question; flagging the minefield; psycho-education groups regarding friendship building, conflict resolution, and emotional regulation | Disputing irrational beliefs; self-talk, modeling; role-playing; miracle question; flagging the minefield; psycho-education groups regarding friendship building, conflict resolution, and emotional regulation | Disputing irrational beliefs; self-talk; modeling; role playing; miracle question; flagging the minefield; psycho-education regarding conflict resolution and emotional regulation |

*(continued)*

**TABLE 31-1**    *(continued)*

| Paradigm | Elementary School | Middle School | High School |
|---|---|---|---|
| Family Systems | Caregiver training for identifying and assisting with behavioral, academic, and social issues, loss, unpredictability, and the process of navigating the incarceration process; clarification of parent, child, and caregiver roles | Caregiver training for identifying and assisting with behavioral, academic, and social issues, loss, unpredictability, and the process of navigating the incarceration process; clarification of family and caregiver roles | Caregiver training for identifying and assisting with behavioral, academic, and social issues, loss, unpredictability, and the process of navigating the incarceration process; clarification of all member roles; strengthening working models |
| Emergent | Deconstruct/externalize problems; identifying strengths, sparkling moments; resiliency focus; therapeutic alliance; mentoring | Deconstruct/externalize problems; identifying strengths; sparkling moments; resiliency focus; gender role analysis; therapeutic alliance; mentoring | Deconstruct/externalize problems; identifying strengths; sparkling moments; resiliency focus; gender role analysis; therapeutic alliance; mentoring |

## IN SESSION

The following dialogue is part of a typical session with a child whose parent is incarcerated. Notice Marcus's lack of attention to the details of his home life—particularly his parents and their place in his world. An exception is made to provide limited but important clarification about his parents' whereabouts. Aside from his clarification regarding this, Marcus's greatest focus of worry is on being "different" and feeling like he does not belong.

COUNSELOR (C):   Marcus, I am so glad you are back with us. I was really glad to get a call from your grandma telling me you would be here this year. How is it for you to be back?

MARCUS (M):   I might not be here all year. My dad will come home, and I might move.

C:   He might get out of prison soon?

M:   (*Emphatically*) He's not in prison. He's in jail. My dad would never go to prison.

C:   So, your dad might get released from jail soon.

M:   He might. If he does, I might not go to this school then.

C:   You have moved before, and I know that meant going to another school. I hope that while you are here, we can make this school a good place for you to be and to learn.

M:   Yeah, but I am not going to resource.

C:   You are worried about going to resource.

M:   I hate it.

| C: | Suppose we had a wand that could make your experience just the way you'd like it to be. What would that look like? |
|---|---|
| M: | I want to stay in my class. It isn't fair that I'm the only one who goes there in my class. |
| C: | You would stay in your classroom. Tell me more about how things would be different. |
| M: | I wouldn't be dumb. |
| C: | Marcus, you are very smart in so many ways. . . . |
| M: | (*Interrupting*) Then don't make me go to resource. |
| C: | Let's see if you and I and your resource teacher can work together to find ways to help you catch up and learn all you can in ways that do not make you feel badly. |
| M: | Really? |
| C: | Yes, Marcus. I know you and I and your resource teacher and classroom teacher; we're all a team that cares about you. |
| M: | I'm not a part of that team. You guys just tell me what to do. |
| C: | Marcus, you are front and center on the team. We all want to put our heads together and make sure you get an education so you can be what you want to be. What do you want to be? |
| M: | I dunno. Maybe a fireman. |
| C: | A firefighter. That's a great job. Firefighters are so important. You are strong, and last year in our group you really showed me that you can keep your cool when things get hard. You would be a good firefighter. Let's work together to make sure you are learning what you will need to learn to become a firefighter or whatever you decide you'll be. |

Notice the effort expended in making the relationship a safe place for Marcus while yet clarifying the struggles (miracle question) and working toward an inclusive stance with a focus on validation of Marcus's perception and strengths even if he is unsure about them. The relationship between the school counselor and Marcus is, indeed, the most critical base to all the work a school counselor orchestrates throughout the year and across all students in implementing a comprehensive program. When working with a child of incarcerated parents, this relationship is particularly important for providing a stable and safe place for the child to work out issues that impede learning in the school setting.

## Outcome

We would prefer to conclude that Marcus is still a work in progress rather than assume his current issues are to be summed up as less than successful. Marcus is currently living with his mother. Though both parents are working diligently on their own issues, each is very concerned with their son's struggles. As a sixth grader, Marcus's behavioral problems and anger outbursts remain relatively common. He struggles with school in many ways—particularly in his use of the resource room and in making and keeping a positive social network. He still does not share much regarding his parents or his struggles within or outside of school; and his behavior and general mood remain indicative of his sense of not belonging, not seeing himself as

a part of a social network, and not seeing himself as responsible for his own valuable education. He will transition at the end of the school year to the middle school where we hope he continues to receive the care and services of his school counselor, teachers, and others invested in seeing Marcus into adulthood with a sound education and a sense of self as a contributing citizen.

## Final Process Questions

- As the student matures, what are different strategies and techniques that will fit his new strengths and limitations?
- What are gaps in terms of your expertise/ability to assist your student? Where and how can you gain education and training or partner with an expert who can better meet your student's needs?
- Have all systems that interact with the student been brought to the table to work together to promote the best interests of his family, school, and community?

- Specifically, what classroom guidance might intentionally be implemented to benefit each student as well as this student's needs (e.g., acceptance of difference, inclusion, bullying prevention)?
- How might the student be included and engaged in meaningful participation in the development and implementation of his learning plan and in his participation in his learning community as a contributing member?
- Are there any other safety concerns or needs that must be addressed?

## Resources

Children of Prisoners Library, http://www.fcnetwork.org/cpl/cplindex.html

State of Washington, Office of Superintendent of Public Instruction (OSPI), Children of Incarcerated Parents, http://k12.wa.us/Incarceratedparents/default.aspx

Washington State Department of Corrections, Family and Friends Services, http://www.doc.wa.gov/family/default.asp

*Chapter 32*

# Children of Parents Who Abuse Substances

Nadine Hartig, Sandy Kay, and Fran Steigerwald

## CASE BACKGROUND

The Lewis-Stanley family, a well-known family in the school system, has five children. As the elementary school counselor, I have worked with the three oldest children. April Lewis is 15 years old, attends high school, and has some absenteeism and truancy issues. James Lewis is 14 years old, attends middle school, and is academically at risk. He has been suspended several times for behavioral issues. Jocelyn Lewis is 8 years old and in third grade. Jocelyn's classroom teacher is concerned about her and has referred her to me for counseling.

Grace Lewis-Stanley, their mother, has struggled with her addiction to pain medications and alcohol since she was 16 years old. She had her first child when she was 19 years old and has financially struggled since. Al Lewis—April, James, and Jocelyn's father—left when Jocelyn was a baby and has had very minimal contact with the children. Grace and Al had a difficult marriage and divorce. Grace is currently remarried to Alex Stanley, and they have a 5-year-old daughter and 3-year-old son together. Alex and Grace met during a period of mutual sobriety. Alex reports that he is recovering from alcoholism. He wants Grace to stop using as well, stating that he is at the "end of his rope and can't keep living like this." Grace has made numerous attempts to stop using alcohol and drugs, including two inpatient rehabilitation stays and many outpatient efforts. Currently, she reports that she occasionally uses alcohol, but "has it under control."

Jocelyn is a bright and intelligent child who does very well academically, but struggles socially to make friends and connect with her peers. She is shy and withdrawn in school, yet enjoys being with her teacher. She often becomes tearful and anxious during the day, particularly when she does not do well on a test or assignment. She is very worried about getting a perfect score on the Standard of Learning Assessments. Her teacher is very concerned that Jocelyn puts too much pressure on herself; for example, she became almost inconsolable after receiving a B on a handwriting assignment. Another issue relates to her physical education (PE) class. Jocelyn faked an injury to avoid participating in class; when confronted about her motive for faking, Jocelyn reported that she hates PE. She said that she gets picked on and that she really likes to stay and help her teacher in the classroom during this time. The teacher reported that she lets Jocelyn read or clean up the room during PE time.

Some of Jocelyn's basic needs appear to be met, whereas others are neglected. For example, she appears well nourished, but does not have a winter coat for when it gets cold. In addition to her apprehension about her grades, Jocelyn also experiences anxiety about her mother. For example, she is sometimes very sleepy in school because the previous night she was worried about her mom and awoke "to check on her to make sure she is still breathing." When asked further about this, Jocelyn states, "My mom has had trouble breathing in her sleep before." Her mother has also shared that the children may have witnessed domestic violence when their birth father was in the home. It is difficult to get the parents to come in to the school, but once they are there, they are open about their family's struggles. Yet the severity of their issues still remains unclear.

## INITIAL PROCESS QUESTIONS

- How has Grace's substance abuse affected the children, specifically Jocelyn?
- What coping strategies does Jocelyn employ to deal with her struggles?
- How does the school counselor assess whether Jocelyn is being neglected?
- What ethical considerations need to be addressed before reporting child neglect?
- How does the school counselor provide support and interventions for Jocelyn while holding her accountable academically?
- How could the school counselor help Jocelyn with her test and performance anxiety?
- How might socioeconomic status play a role in Jocelyn's struggles?
- How do gender issues play a role in Jocelyn and her mother's issues?

## ADDRESSING THE ISSUES

### Practical Interventions

As the school counselor, I have a variety of tasks to conduct with Jocelyn to ensure her needs are being met at home and in the school. First and foremost, it is important to assess whether she is experiencing neglect at home. Financial resources are at a premium in this family, and not having a winter coat may be a manifestation. However, it may also indicate that Jocelyn's needs go unnoticed. I would talk directly to Jocelyn and ask her about various parts of her day and the people that help her with different needs in her day. For example, who helps her get ready for school in the morning and when she gets off the bus in the afternoon? Is there an adult present at home for supervision and help with her homework? I would want to talk to the parents to discuss the concerns that we at the school have for Jocelyn and further assess the family's needs.

Second, I would begin putting some support structures in place for Jocelyn during the school day. I would include her in a "lunch bunch" or lunch friendship group to work on connecting with peers. During the beginning stage of this group, I would facilitate the group and teach social skills. Eventually, once the group had learned how to interact with one another and how to read others' behavioral cues, I would remove myself from the group and give them a chance to interact alone. Hopefully, through this experience, Jocelyn would be able to connect with at least two other peers in the school, and she would develop skills that she could use with others in her peer group.

Third, I would rule in or out an anxiety diagnosis. Depending on the school policy, this might require a referral to a school-based therapist, school psychologist, or outside source. Jocelyn exhibits some symptomology of an anxiety disorder (test anxiety, withdrawn behavior, and avoidance of physical education class). Although these symptoms all seem related to wanting to be the perfect child and avoid situations that have negative social consequences, they could also be manifestations of an anxiety disorder. If she were diagnosed with an anxiety disorder, the school would develop a 504 plan to provide accommodations to help ease that test anxiety (e.g., build in breaks, test in a quiet place, present assignments in chunks to lower anxiety).

Fourth, I would also conduct a meeting with the PE teacher and the nurse to address fake injuries and work on helping Jocelyn build a relationship with the PE teacher. I would work with Jocelyn and the PE teacher to find an effective method for Jocelyn to report whether she is being teased. I would work with the classroom teacher to set boundaries, specifically that PE time is not the time to have her help in the classroom. By creating a consistent plan with a reward system, Jocelyn hopefully will feel reinforced to participate in her scheduled daily academic and specialty courses.

Fifth, there is a variety of appropriate referrals that should be considered, depending on the school district, location of the school, and parental consent to allow the student and/or family to participate in the interventions. Referral to a children of alcoholics (COA) peer counseling group conducted during or after school hours may provide Jocelyn with additional support and education. Jocelyn may be able to connect with other children who are struggling with some of the same issues. This could assist in Jocelyn's feeling that she is not alone and could assist in her building supportive relationships. In-home services would be a potential referral if the parents were receptive to additional support for the family.

As the school counselor, I would hold a child study meeting using the team that has been working with Jocelyn and her family. This could include the principal, social worker, psychologist, intervention specialists (RTI), teacher, nurse, specialty teacher, in-home counselor, and parents. Our team's purpose would be to share what has been put in place, what data have been collected (the incentive plans should have a data collection process), and what has been effective and ineffective, at both school and home. From that process we can modify our plans and put into place more support structures (peer and professional) that will assist Jocelyn and her family in making needed changes. It will be important to collect specific information on the effectiveness of these plans. With parental consent the school psychologist may administer a functional behavioral assessment (FBA), which can assist the team in the selection of interventions. Substance abuse is often a prevalent behavior among children of alcoholics. Even though Jocelyn is young, it would be advisable to rule out substance use or abuse for Jocelyn and her siblings. If the number of in-home counseling visits is limited and if it is determined that additional counseling is necessary for Jocelyn to meet her emotional and psychological needs, an outpatient therapist referral can be made.

## Counseling Therapeutic Interventions

In addition to the practical interventions, one-on-one counseling is very important in working with Jocelyn's needs and feelings about her family's substance abuse issues. Due to their brevity and ease, I would focus on solution-focused (emergent) and cognitive-behavioral interventions in the school. Specifically, I would implement a behavioral reward system for Jocelyn when she attends PE class, as well as when she appropriately interacts with her peers. I would also use solution-focused scaling to determine how well her needs are met at home and her levels of anxiety dealing with academic and familial struggles. Expressive therapies often engage children to tell their stories, so I would have available art media, music, and toys to assist Jocelyn in expressing herself.

Even though the family may not change, continued support is essential for Jocelyn. This support includes continued counseling and peer support groups (friendship and COA) whereby she can process her emotions and learn that she cannot control others, but can indeed control herself. Connecting Jocelyn with a trusted adult in her family, school, or neighborhood, or with a professional will help build her resiliency; and this person can be there for her when times get tough. Helping Jocelyn understand the roles that she takes on in her family may help her gain the insight of her thinking and behaviors, and desire to change them. The National Association for Children of Alcoholics (NACoA; 2001) has created the seven Cs to teach children of addicts: You didn't CAUSE it. You can't CURE it. You can't CONTROL it. You can CARE for yourself by COMMUNICATING your feelings, making healthy CHOICES, and by CELEBRATING yourself. By helping Jocelyn internalize these simple statements, the seeds may get planted for her own recovery and freedom from blame and guilt.

It is my goal that, with continued support and intervention, Jocelyn may become a healthy individual, with little emotional dysfunction. Continuing to address the whole family's issues is essential. However, one in five children growing up in the United States lives with a parent who abuses alcohol and therefore is at greater risk for emotional and behavioral problems due to the lack of available and persistent parenting (Johnson, 2002). The emotional problems these children present may be among the following: guilt from thinking they may be the cause of the problem; anxiety from worrying about the parent and fearing family fights; embarrassment from having to keep a secret about their family; confusion from lack of an available and predictive family; loneliness from an inability to connect or reaction to peer social interactions; and depression from the sadness and isolation. It is estimated that between 13% and 25% of all children of alcoholics will struggle with alcoholism themselves (National Association for Children of Alcoholics [NACoA], 1995). Therefore, continued support and education are vital. Jocelyn shows signs of coping through working to become controlled and a successful "overachiever" in school, isolating herself from other children and social interactions. Her emotional problems may continue into adulthood as stress-related difficulties. Implementing educational, emotional, and behavioral coping skills as a child may better equip Jocelyn to reach healthier adult functioning. Table 32-1 outlines additional strategies and techniques for working with children of alcoholics.

## IN SESSION

The following transcription is an example of how I used a combination of scaling and art therapy to identify and assess Jocelyn's anxiety and her struggles with her mother's addiction.

COUNSELOR (C):  Jocelyn, your teacher wanted me to talk to you about your feelings that came up today in your spelling test. She was concerned that you were upset and worried.

**TABLE 32-1 Additional Strategies and Techniques for Working with Children of Alcoholics (COAs)**

| Paradigm | Elementary School | Middle School | High School |
|---|---|---|---|
| Psychodynamic | Analysis of anxiety and defense mechanisms (especially avoidance); use of sand tray and symbolic play to better understand conscious and unconscious struggles | Analysis of anxiety and defense mechanisms (especially avoidance); expressive techniques in uncovering unconscious struggles | Analysis of anxiety and defense mechanisms; expressive techniques in uncovering unconscious struggles |
| Humanistic/ Existential | Therapeutic core conditions; acceptance and trust; puppets and expressive art therapies for social issues and familial issues; reflective play therapy to process anxiety and substance abuse | Therapeutic core conditions; acceptance and trust; role play; "I" statements for social and familial issues | Therapeutic core conditions; acceptance and trust; role play; "I" statements for social and familial issues |
| Behavioral/CBT | Positive reinforcement; token economy; behavior charts for social anxiety and general anxiety; disputing irrational beliefs; modeling; behavioral rehearsal for social skills; uncovering automatic thoughts and feelings about substance abuse | Positive reinforcement; token economy; behavior charts for social anxiety and general anxiety; disputing irrational beliefs; modeling; behavioral rehearsal for social skills; uncovering automatic thoughts and feelings about substance abuse; thought stopping; journaling | Positive reinforcement; token economy; behavior charts for social anxiety and general anxiety; disputing irrational beliefs; modeling; behavioral rehearsal for social skills; uncovering automatic thoughts and feelings about substance abuse; thought stopping; journaling |
| Family Systems | Assessing family needs; parenting to support developmental needs of children; parenting to teach consistency and availability for the children; support for family members enmeshed in the addiction (e.g., enabling and role discovery); autobiography/timeline of family events through sand, art, or play; family sculpting | Assessing family needs; parenting to support developmental needs of children; parenting to teach consistency and availability for the children; support for family members enmeshed in the addiction (e.g., enabling and role discovery); autobiography/timeline of family events; family genograms; family sculpting | Assessing family needs; parenting to support developmental needs of children; parenting to teach consistency and availability for the children; support for family members enmeshed in the addiction (e.g., enabling and role discovery); autobiography/timeline of family events; family genograms; family sculpting |

*(continued)*

**TABLE 32-1** *(continued)*

| Paradigm | Elementary School | Middle School | High School |
|---|---|---|---|
| Emergent | Scaling to determine needs and levels of anxiety; miracle question; narrative therapy (envisioning a future without substance abuse); role playing; expressive therapies—art, music, or play to tell life stories; stress reduction and mindfulness; psycho-educational and support groups to construct new realities | Scaling to determine needs and levels of anxiety; miracle question; narrative therapy (envisioning a future without substance abuse); role playing; expressive therapies—art, music, or play to tell life stories; stress reduction and mindfulness; psycho-educational and support groups to construct new realities | Scaling to determine needs and levels of anxiety; miracle question; narrative therapy (envisioning a future without substance abuse); role playing; expressive therapies—art, music, or play to tell life stories; stress reduction and mindfulness; psycho-educational and support groups to construct new realities |

JOCELYN (J): (*Visibly upset*) Yes, I think I got one wrong and I couldn't remember how to spell *shield*.

C: That is a tricky word and I know that you want to get all of the answers correct. We have been working on this worry about tests, but today I can tell how worried you feel.

J: Yes, today I just got really upset. I don't know why but it is really bad today.

C: On a scale of 1 to 10 with 10 being awful, how bad is your worry today?

J: A 7.

(*Jocelyn looks at the art supplies, and I place them in arm's length for her to use if she chooses. I nod my head so she knows she can use them if she wants. Jocelyn begins to draw*)

C: OK, a 7. How do you know that it is a 7 and not a 9?

J: Because I can stop crying, but my stomach hurts.

C: You are telling me ways that you know your feelings. Let's talk about how we can get the 7 down to a 6.

J: Coming here helps and I am starting to feel better.

C: Being out of the classroom and talking to me is helping you calm down.

J: Yes, I was upset before my test and then when I couldn't figure out the answer it just made it worse.

C: Tell me about being upset before the test.

(*Jocelyn shuts down and stammers a bit and focuses more on her drawing. Her drawing depicts a tornado with birds flying above the tornado*)

| | |
|---|---|
| C: | You are pressing very hard, making a very dark tornado. |
| J: | (*Continues to draw*) Hmm, it is a very strong tornado. |
| C: | That tornado can do a lot of damage. |
| J: | Yes, you don't want to be in the way of a tornado. |
| C: | I wonder if you sometimes feel like you are in the way of the tornado. |
| J: | Sometimes. |
| C: | Now you are focusing on the birds and they are flying away, escaping the tornado. |
| J: | The birds get away—they don't get stuck. |
| C: | You want to be like the birds, able to feel free and able to fly away. |
| J: | Yes. |
| C: | Would you like to talk about some ways that you can feel less stuck? |

## Outcome

Jocelyn has made progress with consistent and supportive interventions. She has stopped faking an injury to avoid PE class. The PE teacher has been more responsive to her in class and has been more vigilant in making sure the other students are treating her kindly. Jocelyn is still shy, but has made two friends that she has lunch with and plays with during recess. An anxiety disorder was ruled out, but I continue to watch those symptoms because they are still present and occasionally debilitating. I delicately approached Grace and Alex about having Jocelyn participate in a children of alcoholics (COA) group by explaining that children with parents in different stages of recovery participate, and it is designed to provide support to students, not blame parents. Both of them had been to 12-step programs and were familiar with the format. Grace consented to Jocelyn's participation, and Jocelyn began attending the COA support group once a week. Since then, Jocelyn has begun opening up about how she believes that the better behaved she is, the less her mother has to worry, and the less her mother will drink.

The family initially declined in-home services, but did allow for the school social worker

and me to do a home visit. We worked with the family to get a coat for Jocelyn and provided some parenting suggestions to the parents, based on what we saw in the home. Specifically, Jocelyn is so concerned about being perfect that she is easy to ignore, whereas the older adolescents in the family tend to be more emotionally volatile and the younger children are more physically demanding. Parental availability and predictability are important. We suggested that her parents spend one-on-one time with Jocelyn twice a week, even if it is for just 20 minutes. We also recommended ways that Grace and Alex can discuss the struggles each has had with substances in a way that is non-blaming for both the parents and for Jocelyn (e.g., Mommy and Alex have had to deal with an illness; part of this illness is that we have a hard time not drinking too much, but we want you to know that it is not your fault). We shared our behavioral reinforcement schedule for PE, making friends, and being less shy. The family is going to use our same system at home when Jocelyn asks for what she needs and interacts with her family.

It became apparent how overwhelmed Grace is with raising five children and trying to maintain sobriety. Once she saw that I was invested in helping her, rather than chastising her, she became receptive to my suggestions. After 3 months, she contacted me wondering whether the referral for in-home services could still be made. I quickly made the referral and after a brief wait the family has begun receiving services. Grace has had a major relapse during this period and has begun outpatient therapy for her addiction and depression. Despite the relapse, Jocelyn continues to make progress and is able to articulate her feelings about her mother's addiction.

## Final Process Questions

- What would you do if Jocelyn began regressing?
- How do you support children in a family system that is not likely to change?
- How do you envision Jocelyn will be as an adolescent?
- Ethically, how do you support a child such as Jocelyn if her parents do not consent to additional treatment or support?

## Resources

Adger, H., Macdonald, D. I., & Wenger, S. (1999). Core competencies for involvement of health care providers in the care of children and adolescents in families affected by substance abuse. *Pediatrics, 103*, 1083–1084.

Arman, J. F. (2000). A small group model for working with elementary school children of alcoholics. *Professional School Counseling, 3*, 290–294.

Black, C. (2004). *COA support groups.* National Association for Children of Alcoholics. Retrieved from http://www.nacoa.net/coasupp.htm

Emshoff, J. G., & Price, A. W. (1999). Prevention and intervention strategies with children of alcoholics. *Pediatrics, 13*, 112–1121.

Hussong, A. M., Bauer, D. J., Huang, W., Chassin, L., Sher, K. J., & Zucker, R. A. (2008). Characterizing life stressors of children of alcoholic parents. *Journal of Family Psychology, 22*, 819–832. doi: 10.1037/a0013704

Lambie, G. W. (2005). Children of alcoholics: Implications for professional school counseling. *Professional School Counseling, 8*, 266–273.

Moe, J., Johnson, J. L., & Wade, W. (2007). Resilience in children of substance users: In their own words. *Substance Use and Misuse, 42*, 381–398. doi: 10.1080/10826080601142147

Rice, C. E., Dandreaux, D., Handley, E. D., & Chassin, L. (2006). Children of alcoholics: Risk and resilience. *The Prevention Researcher, 13*(4), 3–6.

Webb, W. (1993). Cognitive behavior therapy with children of alcoholics. *School Counselor, 40*, 170–178.

# Chapter 33

# Physical Abuse

LATISHA WALKER NELSON

## CASE BACKGROUND

Sean, a 14-year-old African American boy, enrolled as a seventh-grade student during the last 6 weeks of the academic year. Our school serves a mostly affluent population and is situated in pristine suburbs of a Maryland county. Sean had relocated from a large urban city, and despite standing almost 6 feet tall, he was initially shell-shocked by his new surroundings. Yet, with his physical stature, gregarious personality, and the fact that he was from a big city, his peers gravitated toward him immediately. Nevertheless, his apprehension about being in a new environment led to daily visits to the counseling office. Being that I am actually from the same town as Sean, we quickly bonded over similar interests. This connection fostered an immediate, trusting counselor–student relationship that would soon serve the therapeutic alliance well. Before long Sean discussed events that led to his move so late in the academic year.

Sean wrote a paragraph in his reading class that revealed that while living in his previous home, his mother had suffered violence from her partner. Upon reviewing the paragraph, I called Sean to my office to discuss the assignment. He confirmed that his mother had been physically abused on a regular basis, which is what precipitated their move to Maryland. At the time, Sean did not disclose that he had also been abused, yet he expressed contempt for his mother's abuser and relief that the family was now safe from harm. Sean continued counseling until the end of the school year. I welcomed his visits as they allowed time to monitor his well-being and lay the groundwork for a therapeutic relationship.

When Sean returned for the start of the next school year, within one month it was clear that he was a different student than he had been. The air of confidence that once characterized him was no longer apparent, his grades were on the decline, and his teachers had begun to inundate me with messages regarding Sean's inappropriate behavior toward adults and peers.

As Sean's behavior continued to deteriorate, I immediately suspected that the mother's abuser had contacted them over the summer. Unfortunately, my hunch was correct. The mother's abuser was now living in Maryland with Sean's family. Furthermore, if the abuse had previously been limited to Sean's mother, it was no longer. Sean recounted that within the first 3 months of the new academic year, both he and his mother had been the victims of physical abuse and mental injury.

## INITIAL PROCESS QUESTIONS

- Although I am legally bound to report the abuse of my student Sean to the appropriate state agency, am I obligated to report the abuse of Sean's mother as well?
- Given Sean's cultural background and possible history of abuse, which counseling theories or techniques should be employed now and in future counseling sessions?
- Is this abuse affecting Sean's academic progress? If so, how do I solicit the assistance of his instructors while maintaining Sean's confidentiality?

## ADDRESSING THE ISSUES

Upon hearing Sean's abuse accusations, I immediately began to gather the information I would need to make a state-mandated report of abuse to Child Protective Services (CPS). Therefore, my first step was to obtain the name of every person involved in Sean's alleged abuse. This typically includes the aggressor, the victim, and any witnesses to the abuse. Then I asked Sean to describe the abuse in detail. As Sean recounted his story, I made certain to ask clarifying questions to be sure I could accurately relay the incident verbally to the CPS caseworker via telephone and in the written incident report required by the school system and the county. Last, I asked Sean whether this was the first time he had been abused and whether there was anything else he wanted to share with me. I often end with these questions in cases of abuse because students end up revealing salient evidence that spurs CPS to investigate the case.

All reporting and documentation of abuse should be handled as soon as the school counselor has ended the session or whenever the session comes to a suitable stopping point given the information that has been collected. In dealing with middle and high school students, I always remind students that I am obligated to make a report to CPS any time I believe they are being physically or emotionally harmed. I then give them the option of staying in my office as I make the report to CPS so they know exactly what was said and may be shared with their parents or guardians.

Much of the information the school counselor needs to collect in order to make a state-mandated abuse report can be obtained through the counselor's choice of counseling paradigm. With such a multifaceted case at hand, I used a multi-paradigm approach to address Sean's abuse accusations. The first paradigm I employed was the humanistic/existential approach, specifically, person-centered counseling, because it is often effective in dealing with issues of abuse. In my experience, students who are victims of abuse ultimately feel devalued and insignificant. Sean was no different. Therefore, engaging him in an empathic manner and showing unconditional positive regard created an environment in which he felt comfortable revealing the details of his abuse, both past and present.

There are merits to using portions of existential theory if there is a well-established counselor–student relationship. For instance, given my numerous counseling sessions with Sean over the course of 4 months, he had shown himself to be sensitive, trustworthy, and insightful. These personal characteristics helped facilitate the use of cautious self-disclosure on my part. Revealing that I knew what it was like to endure verbal abuse gave Sean a glimpse of the possibility of perseverance and survival. Overcoming his current situation was now a viable option. Because existential counseling requires a certain level of reasoning and insight, I believe it is better suited for middle and high school students, whereas person-centered counseling is useful with students from various cultural backgrounds and across the life span.

I segued from the humanistic/existential paradigm to the cognitive-behavioral paradigm with an emphasis on rational emotive behavior therapy (REBT). Let me preface here that in cases of abuse in which I have no prior history with the student, I would not rely heavily on cognitive-behavioral techniques. I say this because when encountering an accusation of abuse in the school setting, more often than not, there is simply not enough time to create an emotionally safe environment, gather the necessary information to make the state-mandated report to the local agency, and practice and model cognitive-behavioral techniques for the student in question. The school counselor's first obligation will always be to collect information from the student and report the abuse to the proper local agency in a timely manner. That being said, if a counselor–student relationship has already been forged, then incorporating cognitive-behavioral techniques into a counseling session can assist the student in coping with his or her abuse independently.

In Sean's case, after months of regular counseling sessions, we had built a strong therapeutic alliance. Having previously broached the topic of his perception versus the reality of various situations, I felt this would be an appropriate juncture to reinforce REBT techniques. I guided Sean through the ABCDE model. He was able to identify the *Activating Event* (physical assault and mental injury from abuser), *Belief* about the situation (believes he is weak and feels stupid), and the *Consequence*, or emotional reaction to the belief (extreme anger and verbal outbursts). I then worked with Sean to *Dispute* the irrational beliefs ("Are you stupid? I'd bet you could come up with evidence to dispute this") and *Evaluate* or practice a new, more effective response when faced with similar situations ("Let's come up with things you can say in your head to fight off negative thoughts). REBT works well with elementary, middle, and high school students alike. The theory's focus on unveiling a student's beliefs and its structured steps make it culturally accessible. What the counselor may discover with elementary students and those students with lower cognitive functioning is that more time may be needed in helping the student make the connection between the *Belief* and the *Consequence* portions of the ABCDE model.

In later counseling sessions with Sean, I used traditional cognitive-behavioral therapy (CBT) techniques such as addressing negative distortions, magnification, and overgeneralizations in conjunction with practicing thought stopping and self-talk. I chose these particular methods because, collectively, they work to give him a sense of control. This is important because from Sean's perspective, many of the occurrences in his home life are out of his control. With the proper cognitive-behavioral skills, he may soon feel empowered.

Cognitive-behavioral therapy can be effective across cultures with students in grades K through 12. Practicing skills is well suited to the school environment and increases the likelihood of students being able to recall and use a particular technique in times of stress. Although I used two paradigms in my counseling session with Sean, there are various methods and techniques that would have been appropriate to use. Table 33-1 outlines a sampling of strategies and techniques for working with children of abuse.

**TABLE 33-1 Additional Strategies and Techniques for Working with Children of Abuse**

| Paradigm | Elementary School | Middle School | High School |
| --- | --- | --- | --- |
| Psychodynamic | Identifying damaging defense mechanisms; understanding goals by pinpointing specific behaviors | Analysis of transference; identifying damaging defense mechanisms; understanding goals by pinpointing specific behaviors; examining impact of past experiences on present behavior | Analysis of transference; identifying damaging defense mechanisms; understanding goals by pinpointing specific behaviors; examining impact of past experiences on present behavior |
| Humanistic/Existential | Establishing relationship; role playing conflict resolution; unconditional positive regard | Establish relationship; role playing conflict resolution; unconditional positive regard; cautious self-disclosure | Establishing relationship; role playing conflict resolution; unconditional positive regard; cautious self-disclosure |
| Behavioral/CBT | Disputing irrational beliefs; self-talk; thought stopping; addressing negative predictions; scaling; miracle question; flagging the minefield; behavioral rehearsal; practicing skills | Disputing irrational beliefs; self-talk; thought stopping; addressing negative predictions; scaling; miracle question; flagging the minefield; behavioral rehearsal; practicing skills; ABCDE model | Disputing irrational beliefs; self-talk; thought stopping; addressing negative predictions; scaling; miracle question; flagging the minefield; behavioral rehearsal; practicing skills; ABCDE model |
| Family Systems | Referral to local agency for family intervention; objective counseling posture; questioning; identifying triggers; coaching | Referral to local agency for family intervention; objective counseling posture; questioning; identifying triggers; coaching | Referral to local agency for family intervention; objective counseling posture; questioning; identifying triggers; coaching |
| Emergent | Storytelling; sparkling moments; communication analysis; interpersonal incidents; role playing | Storytelling; sparkling moments; communication analysis; interpersonal incidents; role playing | Storytelling; sparkling moments; communication analysis; interpersonal incidents; role playing |

## IN SESSION

The following section contains an actual portion of my session with Sean. This excerpt is taken from the early part of the session in which Sean is giving a detailed description of his abuse. My goal was to display unconditional positive regard.

COUNSELOR (C): Sean, I'm concerned. What's going on? Did something happen at home?

SEAN (S): Of course! I swear I hate him. I should have punched him, yo.

C: OK, start from the beginning and tell me what happened.

S: I was in my room after getting out of the shower and he comes in my room calling me [unrepeatable slurs].

C: Who is he, Sean?

S: You know who he is, my mother's boyfriend!

C: OK, I just wanted to be certain. Go ahead.

S: So then he grabbed me by the wrist and my arms, and he starts saying he will kill me if I say that shit to him again. So, I bumped him off me and told him not to f—ing touch me again.

C: It sounds like things got pretty heated. I am sorry you went through that, Sean. (*Silence*) Was that the end of the fight?

S: I mean, he got in my face again and kept threatening me, saying he would f— me up in front of my little brother so we could see how much of a bitch his big brother is.

C: Did he place his hands on you again?

S: He pushed me and was in my face. Then my mom came in the room and told us to stop it 'cause I had to get ready for school.

C: So all this happened this morning when you were getting ready for school?

S: Yeah.

C: Wow! When you say he was in your face, what exactly was he doing? Describe it to me.

S: He was yelling right in my face. . . .

C: Did you guys stop once your mother came in the room?

S: Yeah.

C: Sean, I am sorry you had to deal with that madness right before school. You don't deserve to be physically or verbally assaulted. Frankly, given the circumstances, I am surprised to see you in school today. You are a strong young man.

S: I know I am, that is why he better be lucky my little brother was in the room or he woulda' been . . .

C: No, Sean, I meant emotionally strong. If it were me, I don't know if I could've made it to school today. But, you did and that says a lot.

## Outcome

Child Protective Services accepted my report of abuse and mental injury. The case was investigated and the caseworker suggested counseling resources for Sean's family. Eventually, the abuser did leave the home and the state. However, according to Sean, he still comes back from time to time. Sean's behavior in school and his grades continued to be a concern. As a result he was placed in a special elective class to address the academic concerns. In order to curb his inappropriate interactions with peers and adults (resulting from trauma), Sean was placed on a behavior contract and in a coping skills counseling group. Sean continues to meet with me weekly to review his behavior goals. This is when he has the opportunity to practice the ABCDE model and other cognitive-behavioral techniques.

## Final Process Questions

As I continue to work with Sean, I will monitor his emotional and academic progress.

- At what point should I follow up with Sean's mother regarding a referral for outside counseling or family counseling? He is currently receiving numerous services from the school. However, his emotionality continues to be a concern.

- The paradigm I continue to use with Sean is primarily cognitive-behavioral therapy. Should I consider shifting my approach to focus on a different paradigm? Will a shift set back Sean's progress?
- If Sean's emotional response to his hardship continues to affect his learning, what steps should I take to make sure he has the academic support he needs?

## Resources

Child Welfare Information Gateway, www.childwelfare.gov

Corey, G. (2012). *Theory and practice of counseling and psychotherapy* (9th ed.). Belmont, CA: Brooks/Cole Cengage.

Dahir, C. A., & Stone, C. B. (2011). *The transformed school counselor* (2nd ed.). Belmont, CA: Brooks/Cole Cengage.

*Chapter 34*

# Helping Students Living in Poverty

JASMINE GRAHAM

## CASE BACKGROUND

A quiet student in secondary school, Elizabeth entered our building with immense problems. She struggled with all of her classes, but particularly with courses that required reading and reading comprehension skills. Within the past 2 weeks Elizabeth had become withdrawn as evidenced by putting her head down on the desk and refusing to attempt to complete her work or participate in class. On her worst days, when prompted to participate, Elizabeth would begin crying inconsolably, her sobs sometimes lasting for hours. She was arriving to school late, her hygiene was deteriorating considerably, and she was not eating lunch. When asked why she wasn't eating lunch, she would respond angrily, "I'm just not hungry."

Her father worked for a department store, earning minimum wage, although he was well within retirement age. He cared for Elizabeth a great deal, occasionally bringing her a bag of potato chips during lunchtime and attending every requested meeting and all school events and performances. Elizabeth loved him dearly and would typically greet him by running down the hallway and jumping into his arms. The youngest child of three, she lived alone with her father, as her older siblings were adults and lived on their own.

Concerned with her increasingly disheveled appearance and growing isolation, I called Elizabeth to the counseling office after lunch. It was November, and Elizabeth wore a short-sleeved shirt riddled with stains that carried an unpleasant odor and tattered khaki pants. Petite in stature and fair skinned, her blue eyes were shadowed by the dark circles beneath them. Her posture was solemn, her eyes often downward cast, never making eye contact unless it was requested of her. Her responses were brief, limited to head nods, shakes, and shoulder shrugs. She sat, hunched over, shrinking into the chair. It was obvious that she didn't want to talk. I offered her one of the Pop Tarts I kept in my office; she gorged down the two in the package. "Would you like some juice?" I asked. "No, but can I have another Pop Tart?" she inquired. I began looking through my cabinet for another snack. Shrugging her shoulders she said, "That's OK. I have this." She pulled out half of an unwrapped sandwich from her pocket. Soggy and bitten into, it appeared as though it was scrap from the trash. "Where did you get that from," I asked. Looking down, she sat back in the chair and shrugged her shoulders. I repeated the question. "From the trash," she whispered, tears welling up in her eyes.

# INITIAL PROCESS QUESTIONS

As with most school counseling issues, the safety of the student is foremost. When dealing with poverty, the counselor should be cognizant of signs of abuse and neglect. Tangible indications of abuse or neglect should be documented and reported in accordance with the ethical and legal requirements of one's school system and state. If a case lands right on an ethical line, not falling completely within neglect, it is important to err on the side of caution and call the local child protection agency for guidance and advice. The goal of most child protection agencies is to keep families intact, so counselors should not be swayed by feelings of fear or guilt, putting them in a position that may jeopardize their license, employment, or morals.

Second, poverty is not defined by fixed lines. It swims fluidly throughout the various systems of the ecological model. Cultural evaluations can be vastly influential in the development of a student's "emotional template" by fortifying the student's beliefs about the world and his or her role in it, establishing standards for behavior, and setting beliefs of limitations to opportunities for *people like them* (Howard & Solberg, 2006). Cultural, contextual forces in the macro, exo, and micro systems vastly influence a student's development and need to be seriously considered by the professional school counselor. Macro system factors such as cultural history and "societal beliefs regarding diversity issues," exo system factors such as socioeconomic status and community safety, and micro system factors such as parent attachment and cultural identity all play an important role in defining that student's identity and belief systems. The student does not live in isolation with poverty; rather, the student lives within these systems, and the causes and effects of poverty touch many levels and factors within his or her ecological system. As such, it's crucial that the depth and reach of these factors is respected and recognized when developing interventions. An effective intervention for children cannot be ascertained simply by treating the barriers and causes of poverty; rather, understanding that the consequences of poverty have influenced the development of their identity, are sewn throughout many aspects of their day-to-day lives, and flow throughout the various systems of the ecological system model is imperative when engaging in best practices.

Furthermore, it's important that counselors do not allow their assumptions about poverty to drive the counseling and resolution processes. Poverty has a multitude of causes and appearances; it can reach all races, genders, and ethnicities, and it has many levels and layers. Poverty can be generational as easily as it can be circumstantial. It can strike a rich single father who's going through a divorce, as quickly as it can attack a two-parent household living paycheck to paycheck. It is important to thoroughly examine the student's individual circumstances and barriers before putting interventions in place; do not assume to know what the student needs. Not all students who are impoverished are hungry and malnourished. Some students simply need assistance with clothing, a place to do their homework after school, or resources to assist with utility bills.

While processing through the session, the professional school counselor should listen for symptoms that will enable triage of the student's needs and determine how dire the circumstances are. A student whose family is at risk of being homeless requires more urgent care and resources than one whose parents' hours were cut at work and needs assistance buying school supplies. The approach the school counselor takes in

dealing with a family in which poverty is a generational way of life will be very different from how the counselor handles a family experiencing a short-term setback. Look
for concerning behaviors such as hiding and storing food, soiled clothing, and an
increase in absences and tardiness. Last, inspect how the parents are dealing with the
financial hardship. Are they aware of the student's concerns, and how receptive are
they in getting help to meet them? In terms of priorities in the home, where does education rank? The answers to these questions will guide the session, offer direction on how
the counselor should approach the parent, and greatly influence the interventions put
in place. It is imperative that the counselor explore the circumstances surrounding the
financial hardship prior to offering solutions; if this is not done, the counselor may take
on an approach that is insulting or inappropriate.

Poverty can be an extremely sensitive subject to broach with parents. Whereas a
student may be forthcoming with fears and concerns surrounding the family's financial
hardship, parents can often feel ashamed and embarrassed, preferring that their circumstances not be shared with anyone outside of the family. It is important to approach
this topic with tact. Instead of hastily calling the student's parents and saying, "I noticed
your child didn't have anything to eat, and she told me you can't afford to buy her
lunch; so I'm going to send a food basket home with her today," the counselor should
ask the student's permission to speak with the parents first, inquiring how the student
thinks the parents would respond to the assistance. If the student is hesitant, work
toward a solution with the student. When speaking with a parent, a less direct approach
such as, "The school was fortunate enough to receive food baskets for the holiday sea-
son. I was hoping I could send one home with your daughter. You can keep it for yourself or offer the gift to someone else you feel may need it. If you don't mind I'd like to
send it home with her today," is often met with less resistance. Poverty can touch on a
person's pride, so a skilled and gentle approach can mean the difference between
whether or not an intervention can be put in place.

When dealing with poverty barriers, it is important to collaborate with appropriate stakeholders, keeping privileged information confidential. Details pertaining to
financial strain and homelessness are privileged information; they should not be shared
with staff members unless they are critical to putting the intervention in place. That
said, there are staff members who may need to be made aware of the student's hardship. It is not uncommon to need to collaborate with stakeholders in your school such
as the school psychologist, social worker, nurse, attendance team, administration, cafeteria worker, and other counselors to intervene in effective ways. Aspire to find the
right balance of pulling in the appropriate stakeholders, while ensuring that appropriate boundaries for confidential information are maintained.

Last, before processing the particulars of a poverty case, it is important for the
school counselor to check himself or herself for any cultural bias or judgments that may
impede the counseling process. It is not uncommon for people to have a visual image of
what poverty looks like, but in reality poverty has many faces and even more origins. It
would be a mistake to label parents who can't afford to feed their children, provide reliable housing, or be home after school, as bad parents. A colleague of mine often says of
parents, "If they had better, they would send better. Every day, parents send us the best
they have." Although the circumstances may not be ideal, this statement is often true;
parents send the school the best they have to offer and sometimes that falls short of
ideal. The school counselor needs to be cognizant of his or her perceptions and work

toward being a blank slate, absent of judgment. If the counselor's preconceived notions are weighing heavily, collaborate with a colleague who can offer a balanced perception of the case. Poverty issues seldom have one-day solutions, so throughout the process it is critical to repeatedly check oneself for any bias or strong emotions that may act as a barrier to the client, or blur one's analysis of the issue.

## ADDRESSING THE ISSUE

Perhaps the most applicable theoretical framework to apply to poverty issues is Maslow's humanistic approach known as the hierarchy of needs. Primary needs must be met before higher level needs can be considered. The education system often struggles with understanding the intricacies of getting a disadvantaged student to appreciate the benefits of education. However, when confronted with the task of prioritizing food, shelter, safety, and geometry, few would put geometry at the top of the list. Basic life elements that most people feel entitled to, such as sustenance, shelter, security, and love, are not guaranteed components of everyone's life. Before we can push a child toward academic success or excellence, we must first work toward filling the gaps in his or her primary needs.

Although a school cannot replace a reliable and nourishing home, it can provide for some of the needs typically fulfilled in one. A school can ensure that a child receives two good meals a day: breakfast and lunch. With a little extra effort, the school community can offer three good meals a day if it works to establish reliable community partnerships. The McKinney-Vento Homeless Education Assistance Improvements Act of 2001 is a federal statute that entitles homeless students to a wide range of services meant to remove barriers to learning (U.S. Department of Education, 2006). As this act is structured with the goal of strengthening access to education, students protected under it have access to special provisions to ensure they have a stable educational environment. As such, the school counselor may initiate the process of qualifying students for these services, giving them access to out-of-zone transportation, free breakfast and lunch, expedited registration processing, and educational support from their school system such as fee waivers for uniforms, field trips, and books. In addition, the school can offer safety by implementing character education and PBIS (Positive Behavior Interventions & Supports system) programs. The school can fill the relational parenting gaps made when parents are not able to parent because they work two jobs, by promoting after-school homework clubs, sport teams, and mentoring programs. Bridging these gaps clears the passage toward academic success, allowing students to move up the pyramid toward higher level needs.

The issues attached to poverty extend beyond the confines of the school building. Although a school counselor's clientele typically consists of students, it is difficult to intervene on poverty challenges in a durable way without establishing interventions that will affect the family household as well. As such, having a strong pool of community resources to pull from is essential. Although most utility companies offer hardship programs that assist low-income families, and there are state subsidy programs that aid in paying rent and purchasing food, these programs are in high demand. They are useful, but do run out of funding at times, which then causes interim suspension of the programs or makes the programs unavailable to new applicants. Therefore, it is important to build a strong network of partnerships able to fill in the gaps during those times by providing financial support and donations. Partnerships with local religious organizations, health agencies, shelters, food banks, and hotels and motels come in handy.

Aspects of the psychodynamic framework are also applicable to poverty issues. As poverty is a topic riddled with feelings of shame and anxiety, it can be difficult for students to find the words to express what they are experiencing and feeling. Often the topic is not even spoken about in the home for fear of offending or hurting someone's feelings. Using techniques such as free association allows students to release repressed thoughts and emotions openly without fear. Tasks involving movement, writing, or drawing provide a gateway for the counselor to delve into submerged emotions and thoughts.

In situations such as poverty, the student can be left feeling powerless. Adlerian and humanistic/existential techniques are helpful in combating such emotions. Establishing a student-defined goal, creating interventions, and processing through the barriers can evoke feelings of empowerment, giving the student license to influence the intervention process. Genuineness, unconditional positive regard, and empathy are keys to most counseling sessions because they are extremely appropriate for the sensitive nature of poverty issues—not only when dealing with the student but also when working with the family. Once primary needs are met, counselors should work to build the student's self-esteem by employing the existential perspective. Promoting an internalized locus of control, the school counselor can guide the student toward higher hierarchical levels in the Maslow pyramid, pushing the student toward individuality and self-actualization. Additional strategies for addressing relational poverty are provided in Table 34-1.

## IN SESSION

I went to the cafeteria and purchased a lunch, two milks, and a juice for Elizabeth. She ate it all. I gave her a piece of paper with an empty house drawn on it.

COUNSELOR (C): Show me what it's like inside your home. Make sure you include everyone you live with and every room in the house.

[Elizabeth drew one room and a bathroom. In the drawing, she was playing on the bed, and her father was sleeping in a chair. There were five suitcases in the corner of the room. We chatted about general details as she explained her picture.]

C: I see you have your suitcases out? Are you going somewhere?

ELIZABETH (E): No, that's where we keep all our stuff in case we have to move again.

C: Where did you move?

E: We moved to a motel in the city 2 weeks ago. I don't like living there.

C: Moving can be very stressful. I wonder how you're handling this change.

E: It's hard because I wasn't able to take most of my clothes and toys with me, and I can't play outside because bad people hang out there.

**TABLE 34-1   Additional Strategies for Addressing Poverty**

| Paradigm | Elementary School | Middle School | High School |
|---|---|---|---|
| Psychodynamic | Free association; writing; drawing; bibliotherapy; movement; music; tracking; restatement | Free association; writing; drawing; bibliotherapy; movement; music | Free association; writing; drawing; bibliotherapy; movement; music; metaphoric expression |
| Humanistic/ Existential | Community partnerships, after-school programs, and mentoring programs; unconditional regard; empathy; appreciation for uniqueness; "I" statements; role play | Community partnerships, after-school programs, and peer mentoring programs; unconditional regard; empathy; expression of uniqueness; "I" statements; role play | Community partnerships, after-school programs, and mentoring programs; unconditional regard; empathy; expression of uniqueness; role model |
| Behavioral/CBT | Functional behavior assessment; academic/ behavior progress charts; role play; sentence completion; behavior rehearsal; miracle question; token economy; positive reinforcement | Functional behavior assessment; scaling; academic/behavior progress charts; self-talk; modeling; sentence completion; mind mapping; cheerleading; miracle question; response cost; token economy; positive reinforcement; identifying exceptions | Functional behavior assessment; scaling, academic/behavior progress charts; self-talk; modeling; behavior rehearsal; mind mapping; cheerleading; miracle question; response cost; token economy; positive reinforcement; identifying exceptions |
| Family Systems | Working toward a collaborative relationship with family system; educating parents on parenting skills, developmental needs, and community resources | Working toward a collaborative relationship with family system; narrative-focused interventions; educating parents on parenting skills, developmental needs, and community resources | Working toward a collaborative relationship with family system; solution-focused interventions; educating parents on parenting skills, developmental needs, and community resources |
| Emergent | Storytelling; role play | Examination of interpersonal relationships; communication and social support system analysis | Examination of interpersonal relationships; communication and social support system analysis |

C:   What makes you believe they're bad people?

E:   There's always yelling and fights, and I see them selling drugs. This one guy has a gun; I saw it! The police are called almost every night so I try to stay awake as long as I can because I'm afraid they may hurt me or my dad.

[I took another piece of paper and asked Elizabeth to imagine that she had a magic wand and to write down three things she would wish for. She wrote home, clothing, Dad to get better.]

C:    Elizabeth, tell me a little bit about what you wrote.

E:    Well, my dad went to the doctor's a few months ago, and the doctor told him that he's really, really sick, and that if he doesn't take his medicine. . . . (*She began to cry*)

C:    It's OK, Elizabeth; take your time.

E:    The medicine makes him tired all of the time, so he can't go to work. I think he's going to die like my mom did, and I'm going to be all alone!

      [Empathetic to her situation, I comforted her, giving her time to flush out her emotions. She didn't know details about her father's illness, so I tabled the issue, hoping to get more information later.]

C:    Tell me about what you meant when you wrote "clothing"?

E:    They're ugly and everyone knows it! They have stains because my dad can't afford to wash them—and he's always tired anyways. Some of them are too small and they have holes in them. I wanted new school clothes this year, but I knew my dad couldn't afford them and I didn't want to hurt his feelings . . . so I didn't even ask.

C:    If we could start working on a plan to make one of these things better, which one would you choose.

E:    The motel; I hate it there!

C:    Well, I may be able to help, but in order for me to do that, I'm going to need to ask some of my coworkers to help. I won't share anything I don't have to, but would you mind if I told them about a few things we've spoken about?

E:    What would you share?

C:    Well, I'd share that you're living in an unsafe environment and that it's affecting your ability to perform well in school. I'd share your concerns about your dad's health as well, because I have resources that may get him the medical help he needs, and give him support with things like food and clothing. Is that OK with you?

E:    I guess so.

C:    I'd also like your permission to speak with Dad about what we've discussed. How do you feel about that? How do you think your dad would respond to me offering to help?

      (*She paused, a look of concern spreading across her face*)

C:    Elizabeth, I help a lot of students who are in positions similar to yours, and I know that is typically considered a private issue for most families. If you give me permission to speak with your dad, I promise to do it respectfully, and I'll do it in a way that won't suggest that you told me. How do you feel about that?

*(She processed the question for a minute, and looked up suddenly)*

E:        I don't think he wants other people to know, but we need help!

C:        Wonderful! Once I've spoken to a few people, I'll be sure to let you know so you know what's going on, OK? *(She smiled)*

I allowed her to return to class and began working on her case. Not wanting to misdiagnose the issue, I delved further into Elizabeth's case. I pulled her cumulative student file, a massive record, and began sifting through the data. She had failed most of her classes since first grade, earning Ds and Fs. Her teachers noted that she struggled in particular with reading and reading comprehension. She had been referred to the Department of Social Services in third grade, but the circumstances surrounding the case were confidential. Nonetheless, I discovered that the social worker still worked with the family so I spoke to her about my concerns. In collaborating with my administrator, he shared that he knew Elizabeth's father from patronizing the store where he worked. He offered to personally call him, asking him to come to the school to discuss Elizabeth at the end of the day.

When the father arrived, the administrator invited me into his office to take part in the conference. I shared the challenges Elizabeth was experiencing at school; the father began tearing up. He explained that he had recently been diagnosed with acute liver failure, making it impossible for him to report to work. They also had recently been evicted from their county apartment and were now living in a motel in the city—the only place he could afford. He was driving Elizabeth to school every day because the motel was out of zone and the school bus didn't come there. The fatigue and weakness from his illness made it difficult for him to move around, so Elizabeth was late to school because he was unable to get ready in time. Filled with prostitution and violent crimes, the area where they lived scared Elizabeth and she didn't sleep much. They were too afraid to go to the laundry across the street, a local gang hangout; and even if they could, he wouldn't be able to afford to wash their clothes there.

The administrator inquired about whether the father had short- and long-term plans to address his illness issues and financial concerns. He shared that his mother was coming to the area the next month and was allowing them to move into one of her homes. However, he didn't have enough money to pay for another week at the motel, and he wasn't sure what he was going to do. Knowing he was protected by the McKinney-Vento Homeless Education Assistance Improvements Act of 2001, a federal statue, the administrator and I went into immediate action, calling a motel the school had a partnership with. We made arrangements for them to stay within the county, which would allow Elizabeth to be bused to school. We also inquired about Elizabeth's meal plan, offering her free and reduced lunch. The father gratefully agreed.

Last, upon reviewing her student file, we expressed concern about her academic progress and wanted to have her assessed through the Student Support Team. Due to his relationship with the father, the administrator knew he couldn't read and had shared this with me prior to the meeting. Instead of giving him the consent form, telling him to read and sign it; I explained the Student Support Team process, read the consent form to him, explaining the verbose areas, and showed him where to sign if he was interested. This was all done in a respectful and nonjudgmental way, which gave the father room to ask questions and influence the decision-making process. He agreed and signed the form, allowing us to move forward. Before he left the school, I called a local church that we partnered with that manages a food bank in the basement of its building and receives clothing donations throughout the year. The church volunteered to have one of its members bring over a box of food that evening, agreeing to work with the family by supplying them with clothing and shoes. Last, I received the father's consent to touch base with the social worker who had handled their case through the Department of Social Services, allowing me to collaborate with her to provide support to Elizabeth throughout the school year in a seamless manner.

## Outcome

The next week, Elizabeth came to school extremely happy. She had moved to the new motel and was enjoying riding the bus again. Although not as trendy as she would have preferred, she donned weather-appropriate clothing, slightly used tennis shoes, and had a new book bag. Her grandmother arrived shortly after that, moving them into her house, and caring for Elizabeth's dad throughout his illness. The Student Support Team determined that Elizabeth was in great need of accommodations. She was formally assessed by the school psychologist,

diagnosed with attention-deficit/hyperactivity disorder—predominantly inattentive type, and assigned a 504 plan. She received one-on-one tutoring with her reading teacher twice a week, establishing a close relationship with her that blossomed into a mentorship. With accommodations and the collaboration of stakeholders, Elizabeth began to flourish, earning her way out of failure, and voted "most improved" by her teachers. In her eighth-grade career plan, Elizabeth shared that she aspired to becoming a teacher, helping students who struggled like her.

## Final Process Questions

Poverty can be a complex, emotionally taxing issue to deal with. It is not an issue that goes away with one intervention. As such, it's important to consistently monitor the student's well-being and check in with the student and family every so often.

- Do I have a strong network of school partnerships that I can call on when needed?

- Is my office knowledgeable about the culture of poverty and the barriers associated with it, so as to deal with it in a tactful and respectful manner?

Explore these issues; it will make a world of difference in how you serve your student population and the effectiveness of your interventions.

## Resources

There's a plethora of reading material regarding counseling disenfranchised youth in the school setting. The research in the multicultural and social justice fields is growing at such a rate that journal research is often the best way to keep one's finger on the pulse in this area. The American Counseling Association's *Journal of Counseling & Development* and the American School Counselor Association's *Professional School Counseling* journal are reliable resources.

Howard, K. A., & Solberg, V. S. (2006). School based social justice: The Achieving Success Pathways Program. *Professional School Counseling, 9,* 278–287.

U.S. Department of Education. (2006). *Report to the President and Congress on the implementation of the Education for Homeless Children and Youth Program under the McKinney-Vento Homeless Assistance Act.* Retrieved from http://www2.ed.gov/programs/homeless/rpt2006.doc

*Chapter 35*

# Working With Samantha, a Homeless Child

Elisabeth Bennett and Laurie Curran

## CASE BACKGROUND

Samantha ( "Sam" ) is a 9-year-old third-grade student in our Title I elementary school situated in the lowest socioeconomic section of our midsized city. For her young age, Sam has lived in at least 16 places, having spent the majority of her life in and out of homelessness. For Sam this has meant that her family has not had a permanent address of their own; rather, they have spent no more than seven consecutive nights sleeping in one of her mother's friend's or family's homes on the floor or a sofa before moving to the next person's home or the local shelter. Sam reports her shelter stays as the longest she recalls living in one place with consistent meals and her own bed, although her mother reports longer stays in the apartment of her mother's boyfriend on several occasions. Her mother has informed us that she is presently awaiting their own subsidized apartment and that she has recently found work that should keep them housed indefinitely.

When we discovered that Sam was homeless, she owned little clothing and one pair of shoes that did not fit. To date, Sam has all of her belongings in a backpack the school provided to her at the beginning of the year along with needed school supplies and added clothing. Sam keeps her backpack with her at all times and regularly checks its presence and contents throughout class time and at recess. She is sensitive to her living situation and tender to the thought that other students might know that her backpack is also her closet and dresser combined. As such, her pack is stuffed with her few clothes, a baby blanket she still uses to soothe herself, a broken-handled hairbrush, a book she won in second grade for making her reading goals, and her current library book and homework.

School records indicate that historically Sam has been well-liked by other students. Her teachers report her to be primarily attractive, kind, funny, and smart—traits that are more evident when her circumstances are most stable. Recently, though, Sam had been withdrawing from her friends following a comment from one of them regarding her repeated wearing of the same clothing over a few days. Sam's grades in school tend to be above average except during those periods when she reported she had "couch surfed" before staying in the shelter. Both Sam and her mother are conscientious about Sam's education. Her mother comments frequently that she wishes she could have attended college and that Sam *will go* to college, without question.

Despite Sam's mother's good intentions, it has been difficult for her to maintain stable housing primarily due to an on-again/off-again relationship with her boyfriend who struggles with substance abuse and alcohol-related domestic violence. Initially Sam's mother was worried about the school discovering that they were staying with friends and family outside the school's attendance area. She feared Sam would not be allowed to continue to attend her school, which would mean the loss of one of the most stable factors in Sam's life. It had become difficult for Sam's mother to transport Sam to school herself, which meant that many days Sam attended late or not at all. This warning sign alerted the school's secretary to their potential homelessness. Once the school informed Sam's mother of the McKinney-Vento Homeless Education Assistance Improvements Act (a conditional-funding federal act that requires districts to hire a liaison to assist in transportation, registration, and other benefits to students who are homeless to assure stability in their "home school"), she became open with school personnel. Sam's mother appreciated the connections with resources, supplies, and transportation support that the school provided to assist Sam in keeping up with her studies and staying put in the same supportive school despite her transience.

Sam's friendship group consists primarily of children in more stable living conditions; however, initially unbeknownst to Sam, at least two other children in that circle have experienced homelessness at least once in the last 3 years. Sam's interactions with her friends have been fairly typical of children Sam's age, though during the times that Sam's living situation has been more transient, Sam has been more withdrawn and appeared anxious and emotional. During these times, Sam has tended to be more isolated and has often not responded to the efforts of her classmates to be inclusive. Her mother sadly reports that Sam has missed a number of birthday parties. She had been invited, but Sam had elected not to show her mother the invitations, saying that she didn't really want to go. When pressed, Sam confessed that she did not want to bother her mother and did not believe they could afford a gift. She also reported being worried that they would not be in an apartment for her own birthday, which would mean she would not be able to invite anyone to a party of her own. Sam struggles with a sense of belonging in her friendship group and with low self-esteem related to her perceived differences from her classmates.

## INITIAL PROCESS QUESTIONS

- From a humanistic perspective, what core conditions are critical at the initial meeting and throughout all counseling situations with Sam and her mother?
- What challenges to the school counselor might exist in maintaining those core conditions for a homeless child such as Sam?
- What academic challenges might a counselor consider given Sam's disrupted living conditions throughout her early elementary school experience?
- How might those disruptions be related to Sam's inability to remain attentive, remain active in her friendship circles, be open and communicative with her teacher and counselor, and interact in a healthy manner with her peers, teachers, and other staff members?
- What issues are wise for the school counselor to address in a school setting that are most likely to assist Sam and her fellow students in maintaining a healthy learning environment? What issues are better addressed via a referral to services outside of the school setting?

- What kinds of techniques would be helpful for a school counselor to consider implementing with Sam to assist her in sharing her feelings and experiences and in helping to secure that her basic needs are met so as to ensure learning is optimal? What techniques might not be effective?
- Have all available resources been made available to this student and her parent? What other outside resources would be useful for referral?
- What ethical concerns must be considered in relation to Sam's situation?
- Why is it important to know the rights provided homeless students by the McKinney-Vento Homeless Education Assistance Improvements Act in Sam's case?
- How might a school counselor address other students both in assisting Sam's transition to yet another school and in preventative or secondary care to those who potentially are or could become homeless while a student in this school?

## ADDRESSING THE ISSUES

Sam's situation represents many of the common struggles for children without homes. Homelessness strikes students of every race and culture and all age levels. In our experience, many homeless families are headed by single-parent mothers who have a high rate of abuse in current and past relationships. Abuse is the most common reason reported to us by women leaving what living situations they have had with their children and opting for friends' homes, shelters, cars, or other living arrangements. For older children, housing becomes all the more difficult as older adolescents are often not allowed to reside in family shelters, but may not be safe staying alone in adult shelters. When the economy is unstable, the number of homeless children seems to rise. In addition to housing, four general issues for school counselors to consider when working with homeless children are (1) meeting of basic needs, (2) social difficulties, (3) emotional struggles, and (4) academic performance complications.

### Basic Needs

The very fact that a child is homeless makes clear the potential lack of meeting the child's basic needs. In Sam's case, unmet basic needs included security and shelter, and a sense of predictability of what might happen next. Homeless children often live without the regular meeting of other basic needs. Most can qualify for free breakfasts and lunches at school, but getting to school for many of these children can be difficult. Most parents are conscientious in maintaining resources to meet their children's basic needs; however, in homeless situations this is often very difficult and at times not possible. It is helpful for homeless children to have a place to go at school to secure breakfast, lunch, snacks, and a change of clothing (including a coat, gloves, and hat in the winter months). Some local and national businesses provide small grants for concrete services that allow schools to purchase clothing, school supplies, and other goods for homeless students. Once it was discovered that Sam was homeless, and in accordance with the McKinney-Vento Act, the school counselor was able to assure Sam and her mother that Sam could remain at that school despite her varied housing. The school district developed and supported a program to provide ongoing contact and assistance, which included a liaison between the school and agencies, organizations, and shelters. Sam was able to get consistent meals (breakfast and lunch on school days), two additional changes of clothing, and shoes that fit her. The school assisted her mother in securing transportation to school via district busing, and all of these efforts have promoted Sam's regular and punctual attendance. The shelter provides appropriate bedding, and Sam appears to be well-kept and prepared for school. School supplies and other necessary materials conducive to learning are also made available to Sam. The school remains connected with Sam and her mother as well as with the shelter and other services through the assigned shelter liaison.

A second issue related to basic needs was Sam's inability to seek help in having her needs met. She was ashamed and believed that she would likely only be ridiculed if others, including her teachers or school staff, knew she was homeless. Sam was provided information appropriate to her age regarding the laws and the school's intention to assist her to have a healthy learning environment. She was treated with respect and tenderness as well as confidentiality regarding her situation. Assertiveness training appropriate to her developmental level was provided so that she could comfortably state her needs to her teacher and counselor to secure food, warmth, school supplies, and other necessities essential for learning as well as her emotional well-being.

## Social Difficulties

Sam's social skills are generally developmentally appropriate, although many children who are homeless or have a history of extended periods of homelessness tend to lag behind their same-aged peers who are not homeless. Sam did experience decreased social support due to her limited opportunities to interact with others. Her withdrawal is typical of homeless children who tend to use withdrawal as a means of coping with the shame and uncertainty of their situation. Groups centered on friendship building and activities that connect children in social interaction are often helpful especially when the school counselor can provide modeling and instruction for healthy social behavior and support. The counselor must be sensitive to the ethical dilemmas of confidentiality while still recognizing the benefits that come from counseling groups of children who are homeless. Such connections can build a sense of universality and a venue for sharing thoughts and feelings related to homeless situations in a manner that relieves the children of their worries and fears. Related to social difficulties is the tendency of homeless children to identify themselves as "different." Such groups help to dissipate such negative identification.

## Emotional Struggles

Homeless children tend to have emotional struggles beyond feeling "different." Sam experienced worries and anxiety about a number of concerns such as the following: where she would sleep at night, if there would be food for dinner, if her mother would secure a job and apartment, if her friends would discover what she believed to be a shameful situation, and if she would be rejected by her peers should they discover her differences from them. She also worried about her clothes and the state of her appearance. Although Sam did not display evidence of depression, many homeless children do, along with a sense of hopelessness and pessimism. Because many homeless children have experienced domestic violence, there are often emotional difficulties such as excessive fears that would benefit from counseling and other interventions. Sam was invited to participate in a friendship group along with other children, two of whom were in her current friendship circle and who had recently experienced home-lessness. Shortly after these children shared their own homelessness situation with Sam, she became more interactive with her friends so much so that her teacher reported Sam's classroom and playground behaviors as engaged and typical of a happy child.

Given the population of a Title I school, it seemed prudent to provide some pre-ventative services. One of the first actions school counselors took was to educate their own faculty, administration, and staff regarding the signs of homelessness, the McKinney-Vento Act, and the district's program to address homelessness and individual student needs. This helped to ensure that all personnel were aware of the special needs of these children, the provisions of the law and district policy, and some of the resources available. It is important that when staff are dealing with serious issues such as home-lessness, that they model resilience and do not, themselves, lose hope.

Increased awareness and knowledge assisted teachers in more readily welcom-ing interventions in the classroom. Classroom guidance lessons can contribute to building an environment more conducive to acceptance of differences, including the students' home situations, and to friendly activity on the part of all students. Develop-mental guidance programs might include social skills building, communication skills, goal setting, and self-perception clarifications. It can be helpful to enlist students in roles that instill hope and develop leadership skills. Sam's class had the idea and pro-vided the leadership for involving the school in a coat drive for children to coincide with a local television station's coat drive. The students made posters, gathered and sorted coats, gave reports of their progress toward their goals, and even delivered the coats in person to the station. These activities further solidified Sam's self-perception as capable of taking at least some charge of her situation and her self-efficacy and worth as a leader in school. As a result, Sam's anxiety and related withdrawal sub-sided nearly completely, resulting in growth in social, personal, academic, and future life-planning arenas.

## Academic Performance Complications

Sam's grades and attention to and pride in her achievement were significantly lower than previous reports indicated. Academic struggles are common in children who are home-less. Consultation and assessment regarding the student's limits and strengths is typically warranted. The school counselor should be an active participant in team meetings, col-laboration, and subsequent plans to support student needs. Attending to the child's self-esteem and sense of personal adequacy, to the child's perceptions of the school climate, and to the relationships the child experiences with his teacher and classmates is important because each contributes to the learning environment for the identified student as well as the class as a whole. Consultation with the child's parents—particularly informing them of their rights under the McKinney-Vento Act—helps to create a sense of "team" in advo-cating for the child to ensure that wherever the child may be staying, the environment be as conducive as possible to the child's completion of her studies. In Sam's case, it had been clear by prior work and teacher reports that her struggles were not related to learn-ing disabilities or developmental delays. Emotional distress in the form of worry, with-drawal, and decreased self-esteem were more likely causes of her academic decline. Indeed, as her basic needs were met, and during times of greater living stability, Sam's academic issues subsided altogether.

The issues related to homeless children appear to be similar across various developmental levels. It is important to note, however, that the mid-teen years can be a time that homeless children are separated from their parents because many shelters do not allow older teens. This can create further issues for teens who are homeless and without family. Table 35-1 provides additional strategies and techniques for helping students who are homeless given five major paradigms across various academic levels.

**TABLE 35-1    Additional Strategies and Techniques for Helping Students Who Are Homeless**

| Paradigm | Elementary School | Middle School | High School |
|---|---|---|---|
| Psychodynamic | Analysis of ego development (fragile ego, under-/overdeveloped superego) and immature defense mechanisms (projection, regression, acting out); assisting in achieving initiative versus guilt and industry versus inferiority; analysis of cultural identity development; attachment assessment and introduction of stable adult figure | Analysis of ego development (fragile ego, under-/overdeveloped superego) and immature/neurotic defenses (projection, regression, acting out, splitting, devaluation); assisting in developing industry versus inferiority and identity versus role confusion; analysis of transference via free association | Ego development (fragile ego, under-/overdeveloped superego) and immature/neurotic defenses (projection, regression, acting out, splitting, devaluation, displacement, rationalization, intellectualization); assisting in achieving identity versus role confusion; process transference issues |
| Humanistic/Existential | Therapeutic conditions; role play; emotions identification and appropriate expression; examination of anxiety and behavioral issues and a sense of belonging to classmates, classroom, school, and community; counseling relationship; mentoring relationships | Therapeutic conditions; role play; "I" statements; examination of anxiety and behavioral issues related to safety, belonging, and personal and global responsibility and freedom; development of self as a contributing community member; counseling relationship; mentoring relationship | Therapeutic conditions; role play; "I" statements; examination of anxiety and behavioral issues related to safety, belonging, and personal and global responsibility and freedom as a contributing member of society; counseling relationship; mentoring relationship |
| Behavioral/CBT | Disputing irrational beliefs; self-talk; modeling; role playing; miracle question; flagging the minefield; psycho-education groups regarding friendship building, conflict resolution, and emotional regulation | Disputing irrational beliefs and self-talk related to one's role in class, school, and community; modeling; role playing; miracle question; flagging the minefield; psycho-education groups regarding friendship maintenance, conflict resolution, and emotional regulation | Disputing irrational beliefs and self-talk related to one's role as student, family member, employee, and community; modeling; role playing; miracle question; flagging the minefield; psycho-education regarding conflict resolution and emotional regulation; increasing awareness of how the world works |

(continued)

**TABLE 7-1** *(continued)*

| Paradigm | Elementary School | Middle School | High School |
|---|---|---|---|
| Family Systems | Caregiver training for identifying and assisting with behavioral, academic, and social issues typical for homeless children; building of patterns of communication conducive to emotional expression and meeting of needs; building appropriate working models | Caregiver training for identifying and assisting with behavioral, academic, and social issues typical for homeless adolescents; increasing communication conducive to emotional expression and meeting of needs; challenging unhealthy working models | Caregiver training for identifying and assisting with behavioral, academic, and social issues typical for homeless adolescents/adults; exploration of family patterns related to gaining/maintaining employment and shelter; challenging unhealthy working models |
| Emergent | Deconstruct/externalize problems; sparkling moments; gender role analysis; therapeutic alliance; role playing; mentoring | Deconstruct/externalize problems; sparkling moments; gender role analysis; therapeutic alliance; role playing; mentoring | Deconstruct/externalize problems; sparkling moments; gender role analysis; therapeutic alliance; role playing; mentoring |

## IN SESSION

The following is from a typical session with Sam. Her mother had let Sam know the night before that the subsidized housing was not going to be available on schedule. Sam had been more withdrawn in class than previously, and her teacher suggested she speak with the school counselor. The school counselor brought lunch for both of them into her office so that they could eat together and talk.

| | |
|---|---|
| COUNSELOR (C): | Mrs. Allen says you've been pretty quiet this morning. She sure does care about you and is worried you might be having a struggle today. |
| SAMANTHA (S): | I know. |
| C: | And I know that you are a very capable girl who usually does a really good job in class, but today you were having a hard time paying attention and getting your work done. You have told me that sometimes you are tired, hungry, or worried when you are having a hard time in class. |
| S: | Yeah. |
| C: | Tell me what's bothering you today, Sam. |
| S: | Well, we aren't getting the apartment yet, and they might make us leave the shelter, and I don't want to stay at Margo's house again, but we might have to go there or to my aunt's apartment before we can move to our apartment. |
| C: | No wonder you are distracted and worried. Tell me about having to wait for the apartment. |

S:  My mom picked me up last night, and she was crying and she said the apartment isn't ready yet. She said her job is hard, too. I know they said we could stay for 90 days at the shelter but that is up pretty soon I think. I don't think we can stay there long enough.

C:  No wonder you are worried. You are not sure how it will go for you and your mom. I am wondering if your mom has it figured out already. Sometimes when your mom is here, we are all happy to know she has already figured out lots of things we have been talking about.

S:  I didn't want to ask her about it because she was already crying.

C:  She was upset, and so you didn't want to worry her more than she already was.

S:  She doesn't cry very much, so I know she was upset.

C:  What if you and I think together and made a plan to find out what your mom has in mind and what you can do to be OK no matter what lies ahead for the two of you?

S:  OK.

C:  Thinking about what you've learned in our group, where do you think our plan should start?

S:  I know you are going to say that I am the kid, and I get to ask my mom about the things that make me worry.

C:  Very good, Sam! Yes! You don't have to be the grown-up and keep the worries inside. You get to be the child and ask your mom for the information you need. The first step of our plan is to ask. What is part two going to be?

S;  After I ask her about where we are going to live, you mean?

C:  Yes. What else do you need to do to make sure you are OK and ready to learn and to do your schoolwork super well as you usually do?

S:  I need to make sure I have other stuff I need that helps me learn and keeps me not worried.

C:  Yes. You got it. You need to get your worries out. Remember, too, that you can let me or let Mrs. Allen know if you need anything.

S:  I don't like to do that.

C:  Tell me more about not liking to ask for what you need.

S:  I just want to be like the other kids that don't have to ask for anything.

C:  You are worried that you are different, but you know what? Almost all kids need things just like you do, and they have to learn to ask for what they need, too.

> S:    I just want to be in our apartment so I can have my friends over.
>
> C:    Of course, you do. You want a home of your own where you can do all the things your classmates do. And your mom is working hard to make that happen. In the meantime, we need to make sure you are keeping up your studies in class and out. Tell me your plan again.
>
> S:    I'm going to tell my mom my worries about the apartment and ask if we can have friends over when we get moved. I will try to do my homework and not worry too much in class.
>
> C:    What good thinking and planning, Sam. I like the way you think ahead with hope for good things. Now, tomorrow I want to hear how the talk with your mom went. OK?

It is noteworthy that the school counselor has built a safe and strong relationship with Sam, allowing for fairly direct communication. It is helpful to note as well that Sam is able to problem solve with little prompting and is clearly aware of her own abilities to handle her situation. When working with any child, the counselor–student relationship is foundational to the outcomes of the work with the student. Relationship is even more important for homeless children who have experienced the world as unstable and unpredictable.

## Outcome

Samantha is presently an energetic, productive student just finishing third grade. She is active in her social group and developing a strong set of leadership skills. She and her mother are awaiting an imminent move to a subsidized apartment. Samantha has recovered academically and is presently near the top of her class academically. She is a strong reader and checks out a library book twice a week. She has a clear desire to go to college and expresses her hopeful intention of becoming a teacher and a mother. Her anxiety has presently subsided, and her ability to cope with worries and setbacks is evidenced by her resilience in the classroom and with her friends. She seeks assistance when needed from her teacher and counselor, and she reaches out to other children who have difficulties of any kind.

## Final Process Questions

- As the student's situation changes from homeless to housed or from housed to homeless, what issues might the child experience? What strategies and interventions might be appropriate to address those issues? What basic needs must be met as a foundation for a solid learning environment?
- What issues experienced by the child fall outside of the school counselor's expertise and should be referred to other experts/resources in the community?

- How might the school counselor partner with the community resources to best meet the student's needs? To support the parent(s)? How do the school district's policies and procedures reflect the district's responsibilities under the McKinney-Vento Act?
- What are gaps in knowledge or expertise regarding homelessness and its impact on students and student learning? How might the school counselor go about securing education, training, and/or supervision in order to assist the child and

create the best learning environment? How might the school counselor provide professional development for the school staff?
- Have all systems that interact with the student been brought to the table to collaborate and consult to promote the best interests of the student, family, school, and community?
- Specifically, what classroom guidance might intentionally be implemented to benefit an entire school population with a high prevalence of homelessness?

- What are ethical concerns (such as confidentiality) the counselor must be conscious of when working with this student, teachers, other staff, and community resources?
- What would be the elements of a good safety plan for students who are exposed to domestic violence? Are there any other safety concerns or needs that must be addressed?

## Resources

Educating Homeless Children, http://www.edc.org/newsroom/articles/educating_homeless_children

Educating Homeless Kids, http://www.npr.org/programs/morning/features/2002/apr/homeless

McKinney-Vento Act, http://portal.hud.gov/hudportal/HUD?src=/program_offices/comm_planning/homeless/lawsandregs/mckv

U.S. Department of Health & Human Services Grants, http://www.hhs.gov/homeless/grants/index.html

## Chapter 36

# Substance Use

KAMI WAGNER

## CASE BACKGROUND

I first met Samantha at the start of her 10th-grade year because of her low grades. As a school counselor, grades usually are the first pieces of data we have on a student that lead to offering some extra support. As Samantha and I began talking, it became clear that more was going on with her than just an unwillingness to work hard or an inability to grasp the concepts presented in class. I tried to ask probing questions without getting too personal during our first meeting. Questions such as, "What are you doing this weekend?" "Who lives with you at home?" and "What do you like to do with your friends after school?" tend to allow a student to know you are interested in her, but without digging too deep, too fast.

Samantha was a nice student and I quickly developed a positive relationship with her. I soon found out that she had an interest in becoming a substance abuse counselor as a career, and having a similar interest myself, our conversations became relaxed. She told me about her family's history of substance abuse and some instances of her current use. She revealed that a cousin she had been very close to died as the result of a drug overdose a few years earlier. That incident had a significant impact on Samantha's life for a variety of reasons, but most importantly, it began to drive her desire to help others in similar situations. Samantha's family pattern of substance abuse had also begun to shape Samantha's life, particularly her use of defense and coping mechanisms.

As we spent more time together over the last 2 years, Samantha's trust in me has grown. She respects me as a professional and as a consistent, stable adult in her life. I have seen her go through many ups and downs academically and personally. Although my primary focus continues to be on her academics, I am constantly aware that her personal struggles with her own and her family's substance use have a direct impact on her success in life.

## INITIAL PROCESS QUESTIONS

When working with students who struggle with substance abuse issues, the ethical and legal questions are varied and very significant. As a professional school counselor making decisions about students' treatment, my bottom line for every student is personal safety. In Maryland, children 14 years of age and older have the right to confidential treatment for substance use, unless they become a danger to themselves or others. As a practicing school counselor, I must be aware that sometimes that right is trumped by our duty to warn (which could vary by county and state). Substance use and abuse often pose a significant threat to a student's safety. Although this may seem obvious, the situation becomes much more complicated when one considers that the very people who are supposed to be keeping Samantha safe, her parents, are also abusing substances and refusing to take responsibility for their own or Samantha's problems.

Some of the questions to consider in a case such as Samantha's might be the following:

- Are Samantha's substance use behaviors putting her in danger?
- Would contacting Samantha's parents about her substance use break Samantha's trust in me?
- Are Samantha's parents aware of Samantha's substance use?
- Would Samantha's parents, who are struggling with their own abuse issues, make positive attempts to address Samantha's substance use behaviors?
- When I contact Samantha's parents, what are the critical points I must inform them of? What things, if shared, could threaten Samantha's relationship with and trust in me?
- Does the fact that Samantha's parents are users themselves make a difference in whether or when I contact them?
- Are there other people or resources in Samantha's life that could help provide more effective support than her immediate family?
- How might Samantha's family's culture or ethnic background affect how I interact with her and her family?
- What assumptions should I consider about her family if I decide to contact her parents?

Many of these questions do not have obvious answers, so it will be critical to consult with colleagues to inform the decisions and choices I make when working with this student.

## ADDRESSING THE ISSUES

Substance abuse issues are rare in elementary aged children, but common among middle and high school students. Additionally, identifying and treating substance abuse in schools is often complicated. Family issues, health concerns, and environmental factors are interrelated, so several theoretical counseling frameworks can and should be used (see Table 36-1).

If this topic were to come up in elementary school, it is likely that any use or abuse patterns would be in the early stages. Because elementary aged and most middle school aged children are minors, and therefore not afforded the same privilege as older students under minor consent laws, it would be imperative to contact the families immediately and refer the students and families to outside specialists for support services. It would be helpful to understand what the students know about this behavior, where the students learned this behavior, and to work to replace this behavior with more appropriate behaviors using resources the students can rely on as they grow up and experience increased life stressors.

| TABLE 36-1 | Additional Approaches to Addressing Substance Use Issues in Schools |
|---|---|
| **Paradigm** | **Approaches Applicable Across Elementary, Middle, and High School** |
| Psychodynamic | Analysis of transference and defense mechanisms; determination of events of childhood that may have an impact later in life; goal-driven behavior; determination of how the unconscious could play a role in recovery (Note: This paradigm is very difficult to use for short-term counseling in schools.) |
| Humanistic/ Existential | Therapeutic conditions; role play *and* "I" statements for social and behavioral issues; correcting misconceptions; focus on the present; redirecting energy or actions; helping students to trust themselves; reflection of feelings and how they contribute to negative behaviors; trying to understand factors underlying unhappiness |
| Behavioral/CBT | Positive reinforcement; token economy; Premack principle; behavior charts; behavior contracts; disputing irrational beliefs; cognitive restructuring; specifying automatic thoughts; self-talk; visual imagery; modeling; behavioral rehearsal; role playing; "picture in your mind"; exceptions; miracle question; overcorrection; response cost; flagging the minefield; conflicting feelings; misinformation; external stressors; examination of severe traumatic experiences; being sure to consider external factors |
| Family Systems | Parent behavior training for dealing with relevant behavioral, academic, and social issues, and family dynamics; analysis of communication within family; questions to encourage thinking about one's role in family |
| Emergent | Motivational interviewing; narrative therapy to deconstruct and externalize problems; examining personal constructs; improving personal support systems; miracle question; sparkling moments; empowerment; communication analysis; interpersonal incidents; role playing |

A concern that rises quickly among students struggling with substance abuse or whose families have a history of substance abuse is what degree family members treat this behavior as a secret. Most families that struggle with substance abuse are adept at keeping secrets as a mode of self-preservation. Frequently, students from families with substance addictions are very reserved, protective, and manipulative; or they are able to find different ways to cope than students who have not had to deal with parents in substance-altered states of mind.

Additionally, it is important as a school counselor to understand one's own perspective on substance abuse. Some believe these problems are solely the result of choices one makes, whereas others subscribe to the medical model belief that substance use is a disease. Still others' perspectives lie somewhere in between. One's personal beliefs about the causes and manifestations of substance abuse can heavily influence how one works with students. It is important to keep personal bias or opinion out of one's work and to focus primarily on how the student is being affected and how the school counselor can help to control the substance use and prevent further harm.

It is certainly possible to use elements of numerous theoretical frameworks when working with students struggling with substance abuse. For example, from a psychodynamic paradigm, substance abuse could be perceived as a defense mechanism to allow Samantha to deal with the complicated nature of her life without actually having to face the problems head-on. From the family systems paradigm, it is critical to understand the interrelationships within Samantha's family, and it would be important to work with the whole family to change some of the dynamics affecting use behaviors. As mentioned in Chapter 2, the emergent theory called motivational interviewing is a popular approach for treating chemical dependency. The theories I most subscribed to in working with Samantha were a combination of humanistic/existential and behavioral approaches, which are tightly aligned with motivational interviewing.

When beginning to work with a student struggling with substance abuse, it is critical to build a strong foundation of trust, maintain a nonjudgmental attitude, and encourage the student–counselor therapeutic alliance or relationship; these are the cornerstones of the humanistic/existential paradigm. Students usually understand the gravity of their decisions to use substances, especially because even legal substances such as alcohol and cigarettes are illegal for school-aged children. They have frequently seen their family members suffer legal consequences because of their decisions to abuse substances. Being nonjudgmental of the student's choices was critical in helping Samantha work toward positive solutions. Samantha's past had a significant influence on her choices, decision making, and ability to cope with stress. But in order for Samantha to move forward, the right versus wrong judgment must not be a focal point of the solution. Moralizing and continuing to talk about "the problem" would keep Samantha stuck in the past, rather than allowing her to focus on what is working and how to create a different path in moving forward (e.g., solution-focused approach).

The behavioral theories can also work effectively in certain situations depending on how serious the abuse of substances is. Often in middle or high school, students are just beginning to experiment with substances and are making choices about their frequency and patterns of use. For these students, the school counselor's trying the techniques of positive reinforcement, self-talk, modeling, and the miracle question can prove effective. Many of these students really need help restructuring thoughts and developing alternative coping mechanisms that may not have been previously learned or even considered. Teaching these students some alternative strategies could be very effective in helping them resist the behaviors they have seen modeled over the course of their lives.

## IN SESSION

Samantha and I continue our counseling sessions. As a school counselor, my primary focus of our discussions must remain on her academics. Yet I must continue to balance how much her home and outside life influence her ability to concentrate, do homework, follow through on projects, or stay after school for extra help. My goal is to continue to bring her focus back to the here and now, to how we can work together to improve her grades, time management, organization, study habits, and participation in class with the understanding that, from time to time, our discussion will stray from these topics and into the realm of substance use. At these times we center on how she is managing her own use of substances, coping with her parents' continuing pattern of abuse, and the family's unwillingness to address what has become a pervasive family problem. I've also helped her find organizations such as Alateen for opportunities to connect with other young people who struggle with similar family concerns. Support outside of the family is a critical part of successful treatment of students with these kinds of complicated family structures.

In our latest meeting, Samantha and I discussed a recent death in her family. This incident brought back many emotions related to her cousin's death a few years prior. Samantha made it clear to me that she needed to process this recent loss in relation to the previous loss of her cousin. Because this was Samantha's priority, we spent some time talking about how both losses have shaped her perspective on life and how previous events are affecting her current functioning (psychodynamic paradigm). She was so focused on her family and the emotions they were going through that she was having a really tough time managing everything else in her life, including school and grades.

In addition, Samantha really does have a story to tell (narrative theory). It is critical for Samantha to talk through her thoughts and emotions so she can create a more positive understanding of where she has been, identify her strengths and lessons learned, and determine where to go next. I tried to direct her to think about actions she could take to release stress in positive ways and even help her family members move through their pain. I asked her to try to experience the pain related to this situation without hiding or avoiding it. Historically, Samantha has learned from many of her family members (through modeling) that one of the ways to deal with stress is to use substances, so her willingness to try to feel those emotions without the cloud of alternative substances was a step in the right direction. Because she has to miss class time when she sees me and her issues are so complicated, she needs a counselor in an agency or private practice to provide continuing care. Samantha is ready to risk trusting an outside counselor, and we are planning for that referral and transition.

## Outcome

Samantha and I plan to work together until she graduates. Substance abuse is a complex issue that requires constant attention and can be difficult to resolve. Even if one has been clean for many years, the threat of relapse always lingers. My goal for Samantha is for her to learn as many effective coping strategies as possible so that when she begins college or a career, she will have alternatives and resources she can lean on when things get difficult and will know when to ask for help. It is also important for her to recognize the community resources that might be available to her and to teach her how to advocate for herself outside of school. I continue to communicate with Samantha's parents, especially when Samantha is having a particularly hard time with her own use or when I am concerned about her safety due to her elevated stress levels. In my experience, there does not seem to be a clear line for high school students when parent contact must be made. I usually rely on the American Counseling Association (2005) and American School Counselor Association (2010) codes of ethics, applicable state laws and regulations, and local school board policies to help me answer questions such as these: (1) "If this student goes home and does something related to what we were talking about today and her parents were not informed, could I be held accountable?" or (2) "If I were the parent, and was unaware of the information, how would I feel if something happened?"

For many, dealing with substance use is a lifelong struggle. Samantha and I continue to work hard together to make sure that struggle does not lead to foreclosure on her future career plans: helping others who struggle with substance abuse. Even though the future for Samantha and her relationships is still a challenge, I'm hopeful that our efforts in counseling, coupled with her maturity and openness to try new strategies, will pay off.

## Final Process Questions

Many of the same initial questions are ones that might also be asked at the end of a session or year with a student struggling with substance abuse. For example:

- Are Samantha's substance use behaviors putting her in dangerous situations?
- Did contacting Samantha's parents about her substance use result in some positive attempts to change her behavior?
- When I contact Samantha's parents, what are the critical points I should discuss? What issues, if discussed, might threaten Samantha's relationship with and trust in me?
- At what point do Samantha's behaviors become of such concern that I have no choice but to contact her parents?
- Are there other people or resources in Samantha's life who could help provide effective support?

- Has Samantha learned or used any coping mechanisms that are healthier than the use of substances?
- Might I have handled the situation differently if Samantha had a different cultural background?
- What additional resources might Samantha benefit from outside of school?

It is also important for professional school counselors to reflect on their work with students to help the counselors make better decisions when in similar situations in the future. It is critical not only to learn from each situation but also to understand that what works for one student may not be effective in a new situation. School counselors strive to help students struggling with substance abuse issues develop healthier and more appropriate tools to affect positive changes in behavior.

## Resources

Miller, G. (2010). *Learning the language of addiction counseling* (3rd ed.). Hoboken, NJ: Wiley.

Sheff, D. (2008). *Beautiful boy: A father's journey through his son's addiction.* New York, NY: Houghton Mifflin.

*Chapter 37*

# Adolescents, Sex, and STDs

SHANNON TRICE-BLACK AND MORGAN KIPER RIECHEL

## CASE BACKGROUND

Michaela, a 17-year-old Latina American high school senior, attends a large public high school in a suburban neighborhood in the southeastern United States. She lives with her mother, father, 24-year-old brother, and his 3-year-old daughter. Michaela's father was recently laid off from a manual labor position, and her mother was forced to quit her job as a store manager for medical reasons. In addition to other financial concerns, the family does not currently have health insurance coverage.

Michaela is a friendly, energetic student who interacts easily at school with both her peers and adults. She is involved in a number of extracurricular activities and is active in school leadership programs. Michaela has a part-time job after school to help pay for small expenses, and her family attends church regularly where Michaela participates in the bell choir.

Michaela requested to meet with me. During the initial counseling session, Michaela stated that she was seeking assistance with her dissatisfaction about some recent decisions she has made. Michaela discussed her concerns about an on-and-off sexual relationship with Daniel, a senior. Six months ago, during a yearly physical, Michaela's physician diagnosed her with chlamydia. She believed that Daniel was the source of the infection because she had not had any other sexual partners in the past 2 years. Michaela told her mother that she needed to fill a prescription from her doctor. When her mother asked her for more information, Michaela reluctantly told her that she had been diagnosed with chlamydia. Michaela stated that telling her mother was one of the most difficult things she had ever done in her life. Michaela's mother paid for the medication and told her that this would contribute to the financial difficulties facing their family. Michaela's parents did not discuss her diagnosis with her, but punished her by removing all privileges for a month. Michaela stated that her relationship with both parents has been strained since her original diagnosis. She discussed her feelings of isolation and shame.

Michaela said that she has been sexually active since the age of 14 years. She stated that she tries to practice "safe sex," but often does not use protection. Michaela said that she tried to break off the relationship with Daniel because he had been unfaithful to her in the past. She also said that she tried to tell Daniel about contracting chlamydia, but became too embarrassed to broach the subject. She stated that she still wanted to tell him and planned to do so.

The relationship with Daniel has continued, off and on, and at the time she first contacted me it was six months since her first diagnosis. Michaela was concerned that she might have been reinfected with chlamydia. She stated that she has not had sex with anyone recently due to the possibility of having this sexually transmitted disease. She reported that she asked her mother to take her to the doctor for a "simple follow-up" because she was afraid to tell her mother that she had possibly contracted chlamydia again. Her mother's response was that if Michaela had been practicing safe sex, she did not need to worry about seeing the doctor because it would be a waste of money, and the family could not afford it.

Michaela has multiple presenting issues. The main issue is her health and treatment for a potential sexually transmitted disease. Secondary issues include her decision-making skills regarding sexual relationships and a lack of effective communication within her family.

## INITIAL PROCESS QUESTIONS

- What would be your initial reaction to Michaela's situation? What might be your first response when she comes to you for help?
- Is it appropriate for professional school counselors to talk explicitly with students about their sexual experiences? Is it proper for school counselors to ask for information that the student has not offered regarding sexual practices?
- What concerns come to mind when talking to a student about sexually transmitted diseases or sex in general? What specific topics are difficult for you to talk about? How do you feel when discussing issues related to sexuality with students?
- How will you consider Michaela's culture and values in this situation?
- How does Michaela's family's socioeconomic status impact this situation?
- How can you help engage Michaela's parents in this situation? How will you determine what information to share with her parents?
- How might school, family, or community culture affect your interventions with Michaela? What are some ways you can help Michaela identify and use available resources in her family, school, and community?
- What ethical issues apply in this case?

## ADDRESSING THE ISSUES

I worked with Michaela using a solution-focused approach. After listening to Michaela recount her story and concerns, I instructed her to list her concerns in order of importance and stress level so she could focus on her goals (goal setting). In solution-focused counseling, it is recommended that clients identify their own goals because the goals must be personally important. As I suspected, she stated that the most important thing at that time was to visit a doctor to determine whether she had a sexually transmitted disease and, if so, how to get affordable medication. I asked Michaela whether she would mind if we brought the school nurse into our session. I explained that the school nurse was knowledgeable about sexually transmitted disease diagnosis, treatment options, and health care resources in the community. Michaela agreed, and together Michaela, the nurse, and I accessed information on the free health care clinic in the area. Michaela accessed this information online, where she learned how to make an appointment, and the location and hours of the clinic. We also discussed the importance of informing Daniel about the previous infection.

Michaela identified three main goals for herself: finding health care to address her medical needs, improving communication with her parents, and making better/healthier life decisions in sexual relationships (goal setting). Together, Michaela and I discussed the pros and cons of her potential options; explored her available, accessible resources; identified her personal strengths; and drew attention to previous experiences in which she achieved success in order to help generate solutions for her current situations. By identifying strengths and finding exceptions to previous difficulties, solution-focused counseling emphasizes possibilities and positive goals rather than problems and negative behaviors. This approach emphasizes what is currently working for the student and encourages the student who is often receiving multiple negative messages from others that, in fact, her behavior is not "all bad." Clients/students are placed in the role of expert in knowing what is best for them, which provides an element of control over their lives.

I encouraged Michaela to invite her parents to join us. Michaela said that she did not feel comfortable asking them herself, but said that I could contact them and invite them. When working with individual students on issues related to sex or sexuality, it is recommended that students involve their parents in the conversation (Stone, 2009). With Michaela's permission, I contacted her parents and invited them to attend our next meeting. Both parents were unavailable to meet with us, although a secondary benefit to making this call was that her parents became aware that I was working with Michaela and was available and willing to talk to them if they had any questions or concerns.

While working through some potential options for receiving heath care and medication, Michaela decided that she wanted and needed her parents' support (client is the expert; importance of defining goals for self). The medical community recommends routine health exams on a yearly basis, especially for sexually active students. Although the nurse and I were able to help her receive health care in this particular situation, she would need regular care beyond this one isolated case. Michaela discussed her own desire and personal goal for communication skills to talk with her parents in a "mature way" instead of yelling at each other, which is how they have communicated in the past. During our sessions, we focused on preparing Michaela for, and becoming more comfortable with, talking to her parents. Michaela practiced ways in which she could openly discuss her personal health care concerns and ways in which she could ask her parents for their support and assistance. Each week, I assigned Michaela homework, such as talking to her parents about a minor concern—for example, a test at school—or practicing good decision-making skills with friends. Homework is a core component of solution-focused counseling because it helps the client practice small steps toward goals. Because Michaela's family did not have health insurance, and because her mother was currently unemployed, it was important to connect Michaela's parents with health care providers in the community that could deliver services for a price the family could afford. Families such as Michaela's who have emigrated from another country may not be familiar with ways to access available resources. School counselors can act as advocates for families to receive needed health services.

A solution-focused brief counseling approach is appropriate for use with high school students dealing with issues related to sex and sexuality because it is student-centered and can be completed in a brief amount of time. This time factor is beneficial in the high school setting where students have little free time outside of their classes, and professional school counselors have many demands and often high caseloads of students. One of the most unique and applicable aspects of solution-focused counseling is its emphasis on the individual goals created by the student/client, which helps increase the student's personal investment in reaching goals she creates for herself. Table 37-1 provides additional strategies and techniques for working with students with sexuality-related issues.

**TABLE 37-1** Additional Approaches for Working With Students with Sexuality-Related Issues

| Paradigm | Elementary School | Middle School | High School |
|---|---|---|---|
| Psychodynamic | Object relations/ attachment theory; focus on development of "secure base" from which child can explore; establishing secure base to provide framework for healthy discussion of developmentally appropriate sexuality-related topics by modeling respectful handling of the subject, teaching anatomically correct terminology when referring to body parts, and encouraging appropriate modes to receive accurate information from parents and school personnel such as school nurse or counselor | Taking into consideration students experience enormous changes during middle school years: in their bodies, how they process information, and how they relate to others; creating trusting, "secure" relationship— how student relates to counselor is critical to meeting goals of counseling | Exploring past relationships, particularly how student relates to parents or closest caregiver, can impact current relationships, both sexual and platonic; depending on student ability and degree of insight, this approach can shed light on a student's current relationships and social functioning |
| Humanistic/ Existential | Providing support for school culture that embodies principles of genuineness, unconditional positive regard, and empathy, where students are valued and appreciated for their uniqueness; differences discussed and valued; teaching students to relate to others in positive and healthy manner; classroom guidance activities to reflect these values | Small group counseling sessions for practice of social and relational skills, and developing increased empathy; continuing to collaborate with other school personnel to create safe, inclusive environment; use of nonjudgmental stance due to this developmental group's sensitivity to cues expressing evaluation or judgment | Focus on present rather than past; increasing awareness of self, others, and world around them; continuing to collaborate with other school personnel, families, and communities to create safe, inclusive environment; use of nonjudgmental stance due to adolescents' sensitivity to cues expressing evaluation or judgment |

*(continued)*

**TABLE 37-1   (continued)**

| Paradigm | Elementary School | Middle School | High School |
|---|---|---|---|
| Behavioral/CBT | Emphasis on present rather than past; teaching skills to help child change personal thoughts and behaviors; modeling behaviors; role playing with students to act out new thoughts and behaviors; giving homework to help child practice new learned behaviors; classroom guidance lessons to teach and reinforce positive thoughts and behaviors | Emphasis on present rather than past; teaching skills to help adolescents change personal thoughts and behaviors; having students keep journals to record thoughts, feelings, and behaviors; assisting students in discovering thoughts and behaviors hindering success; helping them learn and practice new thoughts and behaviors | Emphasis on present rather than past; teaching skills to help adolescents change personal thoughts and behaviors; having students keep journals to record thoughts, feelings, and behaviors; assisting students in discovering thoughts and behaviors hindering success; helping them learn and practice new thoughts and behaviors |
| Family Systems | Teaching family members to accept differences in one another; emphasis on support for family members during changing family development; encouraging ability to adapt to changing needs of family as a whole | Addressing excessively diffuse or rigid boundaries within family system, which can lead to dysfunctional communication and unbalanced hierarchal system within family system; supporting and encouraging family members to adapt to changing needs of family as a whole | Addressing excessively diffuse or rigid boundaries within family system, which can lead to dysfunctional communication and unbalanced hierarchal system within family system; supporting and encouraging family members to adapt to changing needs of family as a whole |
| Emergent | Use of externalization to allow child to view the "problem as the problem," rather than child herself being the problem; especially important when child has little control over external circumstances that may influence her behavior | Preadolescents particularly sensitive to personal narratives ascribed by peers; giving student opportunity to re-author his or her life story to empower student looking for assurance that he or she holds intrinsic value as a person | Re-authoring personal narrative in later adolescence; students becoming more autonomous from parents and are tasked with creating a personal identity separate from their family of origin |

## IN SESSION (SESSION 2)

The following transcript was from session 2 with Michaela, and *italics* signify solution-focused techniques.

CounSELOR (C):   Hi, Michaela, what are you up to today?

MICHAELA (M):   I just have a lot on my mind right now. . . .

C:  Have a seat. What's going on?

[Michaela tells her story, with intermittent tears. She includes her goals in more concrete terms, which was her homework from the previous counseling session. As stated previously, she identified three main goals: finding health care to address her medical needs, improving communication with her parents, and making better/healthier life decisions in sexual relationships.]

C:  Thank you so much for sharing all of this, Michaela. It sounds like you have a lot on your plate right now. This has been enormously stressful for you. One amazing thing I'd like to point out is that you've already identified some goals for yourself. (*Compliment*) Let's talk about some potential solutions. What have you already considered?

M:  I don't know. I want my mom and dad to help me, but every time I talk to them about anything we end up screaming at each other. Sometimes I just want to move out.

C:  I see. So, home has turned into a pressure-cooker of sorts with all of the stressful things going on in your life right now and moving out seems like a good way to escape the pressure. It's pretty normal to feel like you want to get away when things are tough and you feel isolated. (*Normalizing*)

M:  I would be so much happier if I could just get away from my parents so we could stop arguing about everything.

C:  OK, so moving out could be one option. We can write that down. But it would not solve the problem of getting heath care for yourself, which you have identified as one of your main goals. What other solutions can you think of? Let's brainstorm all possible solutions, no matter how crazy they may sound initially.

M:  I don't know. I just feel like I can't do anything right these days. I feel like any decision I make is wrong. My parents certainly make that clear to me.

C:  OK, well, let's step back for a moment. You are concerned about your decision-making skills and that you believe you are unable to make good decisions. Can you tell me about a time recently that you did make a good decision, one that you were proud of? (*Exceptions*)

M:  Well . . . yesterday at lunch, I was with my friend Theresa and we wanted ice cream, so we went to the lunch line and picked up two, but when we went to pay, the lunch lady was in the back. Theresa said, "Let's go before she comes back so we don't have to pay." But I told her that she was stupid and that we needed to wait for the lunch lady to

|     |     |
| --- | --- |
|     | pay. Theresa was annoyed and said I was such a loser, but I still felt good about that decision. |
| C:  | Michaela, wow, it sounds like you made a great decision then. It would have been a lot easier to go along with your friend, but instead, you did what you felt to be the right decision, even though your friend teased you about it. (*Compliment*) |
| M:  | Yeah, I guess . . . |
| C:  | So, tell me what went through your mind at that time and how were you able to make that decision, even though it was difficult? |
| M:  | Well, I thought about how horrible I would feel if I stole that ice cream without paying, and how I would feel guilty every time I looked at the lunch lady for the rest of the year. Plus, I didn't want to get in trouble! |
| C:  | So, you have had success in the past making decisions that you are proud of and feel good about. That tells me that you have that ability to make good decisions, to problem solve, in other situations. Do you think you might be willing to try, even though this situation is much bigger, and more stressful? |
| M:  | I can try, but who knows. . . . |
| C:  | So, from what you've said, it sounds like what you want the most at this time is a way to talk to your parents and ask them for help with your health concerns in going to the doctor. |
| M:  | Yeah, that's definitely the most important right now. . . . I just don't know how to do it. |
| C:  | Let's just take it piece by piece, small steps. And you've already done some of those steps! (*Small, concrete steps of goals*) During our last meeting, we met with the nurse and found a free health clinic that you can tell your parents about. Can you think of some ways to begin this discussion with your parents? (*Clear, concrete goals*) |
| M:  | I don't know; they are always in such bad moods. The only time we are ever together and not arguing is on our way home from church on Sundays. And that usually doesn't last long. |
| C:  | Wow, that's great that you found a time when things are usually calm with your family. What do you think about talking to your parents on a Sunday afternoon? |
| M:  | We can talk about it. Can we practice in here? |
| C:  | Of course. Let's get started. |

## Outcome

Michaela and I had five consecutive sessions, once a week for 5 weeks, to define and clarify her goals, create solutions, and devise a plan. By our fourth session together, Michaela had successfully opened the conversation with her parents at home. After her parents' initial shock about Michaela contracting chlamydia for the second time, they were able to talk together without raising their voices, which pleased both Michaela and her parents. By the end of the fifth week, Michaela had successfully collaborated with the school nurse, her parents, and me, and made an appointment at the free health clinic. Her parents agreed to take her to the free health clinic after she made the appointment.

Michaela was diagnosed with chlamydia and was prescribed medication. Her parents required her to use her money from her part-time job to help pay for medication. By our fifth and final session together, Michaela and her parents had discussed the importance of practicing safe sex while discussing specific ways for Michaela to do so. It was interesting to note that Michaela had received safe sex information from multiple sources; however, prior to this counseling session, no one had helped her develop a specific plan for herself. Michaela's parents talked to her about their concerns for Michaela's health and explained that they wanted the best for her in life. They explained that they wanted her to be safe and happy.

Communication with Michaela's parents greatly improved in only 5 weeks, and Michaela and her parents were attempting to continue to repair the strained relationship. Michaela continued to "check in" with me periodically throughout her senior year. One of Michaela's goals was to make better, safer decisions regarding sexual relationships. Over time, Michaela applied the leadership and decision-making skills that she had learned in her after-school sports activities to sexual rela-

tionships outside of school. She became more confident in thinking about her decisions prior to acting on them and speaking up for what she felt the best decision to be. As part of her decision-making skills, Michaela informed Daniel about the two chlamydia infections. She also provided him with information about the free health clinic and urged him to make an appointment. She also determined that she would like to be in a relationship with more commitment than she had with Daniel and decided to end her relationship with Daniel. She also applied her skills in verbalizing and following through on her own personal decisions, including those regarding sexual activity and use of protection to help ensure safe sex practices.

Student issues regarding sex and sexually transmitted diseases are often difficult and ethically challenging. In Michaela's case, she was willing to talk to the nurse and to her parents about her diagnoses. American School Counselor Association's (2010) *Ethical Standards for School Counselors* state that professional school counselors should "consider the ethical responsibility to provide information to an identified third party, who by his/her relationship with the student, is at a high risk of contracting a disease that is commonly known to be communicable and fatal" (A.2.f). Chlamydia is a communicable, but not fatal disease. Nonetheless, it is a concern if a student is spreading the disease to sexual partners. In this case, Michaela informed Daniel of her diagnosis and gave him information on how to receive treatment. Stone (2009) recommends that, when working with students with problems related to sex, professional school counselors should seek consultation with other professionals. In this case scenario, the school counselor worked with the school nurse to help Michaela find treatment for chlamydia.

## Final Process Questions

- What are some prevention and intervention programs related to sexuality and risk-taking behavior that you can implement at each level (i.e., elementary, middle, and high school)?
- What resources are available in your community that you could partner with in delivering preventative education regarding sex and sexuality to both students and parents?

- How can you help students with poor decision-making skills and the impact on their self-esteem, as well as other negative consequences?
- What are some of the ethical issues that might influence your approach to this case?
- What are some of the ethical issues in this case that might be difficult for you?

## Resources

Bodenhorn, N. (2006). Exploratory study of common and challenging dilemmas experienced by professional school counselors. *Professional School Counseling, 10*, 195–202.

Lamb, S. (2006). *Sex, therapy, and kids.* New York, NY: Norton.

Lazovsky, R. (2008). Maintaining confidentiality with minors: Dilemmas of school counselors. *Professional School Counseling, 11*, 335–346.

*Chapter 38*

# Helping Students With Eating Disorders

NATALIE GRUBBS AND CATHERINE Y. CHANG

## CASE BACKGROUND

Haley, a 10-year-old White fifth-grade student from an upper middle-class family, attends a private elementary school. Her father is the sole financial provider. Haley's mother, a stay-at-home mother, is very involved in Haley's school, serving as "room mom" and "fifth grade coordinator." Haley's parents are separated and going through a hostile divorce. Haley has four siblings ranging in age from 9 to 20 years. Two of Haley's siblings are away in college. Haley lives primarily with her mother, her 9-year-old sister, and her 12-year-old brother.

Haley is a very bright student and consistently achieves honor roll status in school. She is very athletic and outgoing and has many friends both in school and in her neighborhood. I have known Haley since she was a first-grade student, and I have neither witnessed Haley struggle with her weight nor noticed any fluctuation in her weight. However, when we returned to school at the beginning of her fifth-grade year, I noticed that Haley had lost a great deal of weight and appeared to be well under a healthy weight for her age. After hearing a couple of parents at the school and a number of teachers comment on Haley's appearance, I consulted with the elementary school principal about these concerns regarding Haley's weight. The principal said that she, too, had noticed Haley's weight loss and planned to contact Haley's mother. Meanwhile, the principal and I decided to "keep an eye" on Haley. I also began to see Haley individually to discuss her parents' divorce and the family changes involved with the divorce (e.g., Dad moving out, going between Mom's and Dad's houses, etc.).

After my first few individual sessions with Haley, the principal informed me that she had met with Haley's mother and that Haley had been diagnosed by her pediatrician as having anorexia nervosa. Haley's mother and the principal requested that I increase my sessions with her to once every week. They also asked me *not* to bring up the anorexia because Haley was very embarrassed and upset about it. Haley's parents and the medical professionals acknowledged that the emergence of the eating disorder was likely related to Haley's parents' divorce. So instead of meeting with her about her eating disorder, they asked me to focus on the divorce.

## INITIAL PROCESS QUESTIONS

- What personal biases do you have about working with individuals who are diagnosed with eating disorders?
- What is your initial reaction to the diagnosis of anorexia?
- What are your thoughts on how to approach the issue of divorce in this case when another major issue (such as an eating disorder) is presented?
- How will you go about addressing Haley's experience of her parents' divorce while also addressing her eating disorder?
- What is your comfort level in working with individuals who are diagnosed with eating disorders, particularly in the case of an elementary school aged child?
- Who are the people you would consult with when preparing to respond to this child's issues?

## ADDRESSING THE ISSUES

School counselors can work with children experiencing eating disorders either individually or in small groups. Specific interventions used can be rooted in any of the five counseling paradigms summarized in Chapter 2. When working with children at various school levels (elementary, middle, and high school), age, maturity, and cultural background must be considered as school counselors seek out effective and culturally relevant interventions to implement with their student populations. In Haley's case, it was determined to undertake an interdisciplinary "wraparound" approach involving the school nurse, principal, teachers, medical professionals, Haley's mother, and me, the school counselor.

In general, my approach with Haley was based on the person-centered or child-centered theoretical approach to counseling with children. I wanted to respect Haley's mother's request for me not to bring up the eating disorder and to instead focus on the parental divorce. However, consistent with the child-centered theoretical approach, I allowed Haley to lead the conversation, being careful not to impose my own "agenda" in our session or allow my biases about divorce or eating disorders to affect our conversation. My goals for working with Haley included providing a safe, supportive environment, facilitating open dialogue, and establishing a relationship based on trust and genuineness. In allowing Haley to lead our sessions, she actually brought up her eating disorder during our third session. Although discussing the eating disorder was not necessarily a primary treatment goal, because I was able to create a safe, supportive environment, we spent most of our time together discussing her eating disorder. It became evident to me that the eating disorder was Haley's most pressing and confusing issue at this time in her life.

I focused our sessions on establishing our relationship by using effective communication skills. I was intentional about paraphrasing and reflecting feelings throughout our sessions. I also used interventions from a more emergent theoretical orientation, such as reading storybooks about divorce, viewing websites about eating disorders, drawing pictures, role playing, and providing information (i.e., psycho-education about eating disorders) when I felt the topic was relevant, when Haley was open to the information, or if she directly asked for some specific information.

Meanwhile, Haley had ongoing appointments and sessions with her pediatrician, a pediatric nutritionist, a psychiatrist, and a professional mental health counselor specializing in eating disorders. I secured Haley's parental permission to communicate with the mental health counselor in an effort to be a part of Haley's multidisciplinary support team. Haley's mental health counselor provided me with regular e-mail updates on Haley's overall progress and consulted with me on areas that I might emphasize during our counseling session and parent consultations, which would augment and reinforce their sessions. Many times I served as a liaison between Haley's medical team and the school, making sure the school was aware of and implementing any restrictions her medical team recommended (e.g., limited physical activity, sitting out of sports activities when necessary, monitoring Haley's adherence to her eating "rules" while at school).

In dealing with situations such as eating disorders, it is important for school counselors to be knowledgeable about ethical guidelines for dealing with what would be considered a serious medical condition. School counselors must also be aware that the scope of school counseling services is very limited in being able to address all of the concerns that are embedded in a condition such as an eating disorder. It is important to be mindful of the responsibility school counselors have to serve students and families facing an eating disorder within their level of competency, and to refer to or consult with medical and community professionals where appropriate.

The first thing I did was find out what medical attention Haley was getting and secure her family's permission for me to communicate with other professionals serving the family. Next, I found out what interventions Haley's medical team already had in place and what extensions of the interventions the school could implement while Haley is at school. Finally, I attempted to educate myself on helping young children with eating disorders by seeking information from reputable associations and organizations and by consulting with other school counselors.

While working with Haley, I maintained regular communication with Haley's mother and her mental health counselor, who sent me and the rest of Haley's medical team periodic updates and suggestions on how we all could work with Haley. In my mind, I took a "triage" approach, considering Haley's health to be our number-one concern to deal with before moving on to addressing Haley's parents' divorce, while also honoring her mother's request not to focus on her eating disorder. As previously stated, Haley was the first to talk about her eating disorder in counseling, and we were able to work from there. I was careful not to lead the sessions to focus on the eating disorder. In communicating with Haley's parents and teachers, my priority was to ensure that we all were doing all we could to support Haley's weight gain and road to health. In my sessions with Haley, although I allowed her to lead our conversations, we focused on her progress through the treatment of her eating disorder not only because of its priority position in her life but also because it was in the forefront of Haley's mind and often the first thing she spoke about in session once she learned that she had "a disease." As the school year progressed and Haley began to improve her eating and weight gain, she naturally began to talk less about her eating disorder and more about her parents' divorce, allowing us to move on to addressing her concerns about her changing family.

The information presented in Table 38-1 provides strategies and interventions school counselors can use when working with students with eating disorders. These interventions can be used in a group setting or in individual work with students.

| TABLE 38-1 | Strategies and Interventions for Working with Students with Eating Disorders | | |
| --- | --- | --- | --- |
| Paradigm | Elementary School | Middle School | High School |
| Psychodynamic | Play therapy; identifying and disclosing goal of behavior; parent consultations; encouraging | Exploring and processing attachment issues; identifying and disclosing goal of behavior; parent consultations; encouraging | Exploring and processing attachment issues; identifying and disclosing goal of behavior; parent consultations; encouraging |
| Humanistic/Existential | Play therapy; listening and reflecting feelings; encouraging; building relationship | Listening and reflecting feelings; encouraging; building relationship | Listening and reflecting feelings; encouraging; building relationship |
| Behavioral/CBT | Play therapy; parent or teacher consultation; role play; brainstorming; bibliotherapy/books on eating disorders and divorce; disputing irrational beliefs (e.g., "I am fat"); behavioral rehearsal | Role play; brainstorming; parent or teacher consultation; bibliotherapy/books on eating disorders and divorce; disputing irrational beliefs (e.g., "I am fat"); behavioral rehearsal | Role play; brainstorming; parent or teacher consultation; disputing irrational beliefs (e.g., "I am fat"); behavioral rehearsal |
| Systems | Play therapy; parent or teacher consultation; parent or teacher training on helping children with eating disorders | Parent or teacher consultation; parent or teacher training on helping children with eating disorders | Parent or teacher consultation; parent or teacher training on helping children with eating disorders |
| Emergent | Creating drawings about eating disorders; storytelling; providing student with age-appropriate information about various aspects of eating disorders; miracle question | Creating drawings about eating disorders; storytelling; providing student with age-appropriate information about various aspects of eating disorders; miracle question | Writing stories or narratives about eating disorders; storytelling; providing student with age-appropriate information about various aspects of eating disorders; miracle question |

## IN SESSION

Haley and I began to see each other one-on-one after she was referred to me for individual counseling. I met with her once or twice to discuss her family changes and allow her an opportunity to talk about her feelings about her parents' divorce. We did not discuss Haley's weight or nutrition plan during our first two sessions. The following is an excerpt from our third session.

| | |
| --- | --- |
| COUNSELOR (C): | Hi, Haley! How are you today? |
| HALEY (H): | OK, I guess. |

C:      How was your week since we saw each other last?

H:      Well, my mom said that I have a disease that makes me not very hungry. I have to try to eat more to gain weight.

C:      Really? When did your mom find out about the disease?

H:      I went in to the pediatrician's office and when they weighed me she was so worried about my weight that I had to go to the emergency room.

C:      That must have been very scary for you.

H:      Yeah, my mom was really scared. I have to go back to the pediatrician's office next week. I also have to see a nutritionist and a psychologist.

C:      That sounds like that could be overwhelming. How do you feel about all this?

H:      I hate it. Everyone is so mean and always telling me what I should be doing.

C:      It sounds like you have a lot of people who care about you and want to make sure that you are healthy. (*Pause . . . silence; Haley nods, acknowledging agreement with the statement*) What kinds of things do you have to do to gain more weight?

H:      I have to eat certain things for breakfast, and my teachers have to watch what I eat at lunch. My mom has to pick out what I'm going to eat for the week.

C:      How do you feel about all of that?

H:      I wish they would just let me eat what I want. I don't like for them to watch me all the time.

C:      I know that must be hard. But I think the good thing is that you are getting the food you need to be healthy. We really want to make sure you are at a healthy weight.

## Outcome

In the beginning, Haley was very uncooperative and hesitant with her medical team, sometimes even being dishonest about what she ate during lunch and "sneaking" into physical activities knowing she was to sit out instead. She would tell me that she "hated" going to all of her medical appointments and that she didn't like her counselor. She felt that everyone emphasized the negative and never said anything encouraging to her. She felt that even gaining a couple of ounces was making progress, but was frustrated that her doctors would express concern and dis-

appointment in her for not gaining as much as they wanted her to. However, as the school year went on and Haley began to make progress toward a healthy weight, she also began to display a more positive attitude about her plan. Haley told me that her mother began to allow her to make more decisions about what she ate and told me that she actually enjoyed some of the foods that her mother now prepared for her. Haley's mental health counselor also reported that Haley's attitude in session improved and that she seemed to be happier overall.

At the end of the school year, Haley had noticeably gained weight and was just under what would be considered a healthy weight. Her parents worked very closely together throughout all of Haley's medical treatments. They were spending less time fighting with each other and more time working cooperatively with Haley's doctors and counselors. Haley also received "rewards" for cooperating and following her health and nutrition plan. She was allowed to participate in a major field trip and physical activities. She also was allowed to go out of town with her classmates to Space Camp and to participate in an invitational track meet she had been eagerly anticipating.

An eating disorder is a very dangerous disorder, one of the deadliest mental illnesses. Haley's case is an example of the effectiveness of a wraparound approach, involving medical professionals, parents, and school faculty along with the school counselor. Haley's parents had the resources to access this approach to Haley's care. Many school counselors work in schools where parents may not necessarily have the resources to afford the level of medical and mental health care Haley received. School counselors must be aware of community-based and school-based resources available to assist families to appropriately address an eating disorder.

Haley's case is also an example of an instance where the eating disorder was fully disclosed. In many cases, eating disorders are hidden and not disclosed. It is imperative that school counselors learn to recognize warning signs of an eating disorder and have a procedure in place for notifying parents of concerns about a child's weight and/or eating habits. School counselors should also be prepared to educate the school community about the seriousness and warning signs of eating disorders and consult with parents and school staff on ways to best support a child with an eating disorder. One appropriate preventative approach school counselors could take would be to create a small group or guidance unit on healthy body image.

The National Eating Disorders Association (http://www.nationaleatingdisorders.org) offers many resources for parents and professionals, including ways to recognize eating disorders, advice for parents in supporting their children when an eating disorder is present, and advice on how to be supportive to a person with an eating disorder.

## Final Process Questions

- How can you continue to encourage the child as she works toward a healthy weight and healthy eating habits?
- How can you move from working with her on the stress caused by the eating disorder to working on the stress that may have caused the eating disorder in the first place?
- What interventions will help her process her emotions in a healthy way and learn healthy coping strategies?
- After reading this case scenario, what role do you think school counselors have in working with students who are experiencing an eating disorder? Has your response changed from the beginning of the case scenario?

## Resources

Boachie, A., & Jasper, K. (2011). *A parent's guide to defeating eating disorders: Spotting the stealth bomber and other symbolic approaches.* Philadelphia, PA: Jessica Kingsley.

Le Grange, D., & Lock, J. (2011). *Eating disorders in children and adolescents: A clinical handbook.* New York, NY: Guilford Press.

Lock, J., Le Grange, D., Agras, W., & Dare, C. (2001). *Treatment manual for anorexia nervosa: A family-based approach.* New York, NY: Guilford Press.

*Chapter 39*

# De-escalating Extreme Behaviors/Emotions

HELEN RUNYAN AND TIM GROTHAUS

## CASE BACKGROUND

Although his face was familiar, the first time I actually interacted with Aaron was in the aftermath of a confrontation between him and another student. I had come around the corner just in time to see several adults separating the two sixth graders who were shouting at each other and appeared ready to engage in a physical fight. While my colleague whisked one student away, I quickly stepped between Aaron and his adversary. Aaron was very agitated and tried to sidestep me in order to challenge the other student. I blocked his path and attempted to distract him by engaging him conversationally. As a fairly new counselor, this was my first encounter with a physical confrontation. Although Aaron was 12 years old, he likely weighed as much as I did. I guess it was serendipitous that it all happened so quickly—too fast for me to fear for my personal safety.

Shortly after the other student was out of our sight, I asked Aaron whether he wanted to take a walk and talk in order to cool down a bit. His only response was to glare down the hall toward his now absent co-combatant, spewing statements about people messing with him, and to pace back and forth. Because the hallways were cleared and he had a lot of energy to work off, I let him pace a bit before I resumed talking with him. I mentioned that people "messing with you" could be very aggravating and complimented his ability to calm himself down by "walking it off." As he continued to pace, he seemed to be listening and his fury appeared to be abating. Seeing his change in energy, I once again asked him about heading down to my office to talk it over. After a brief pause, he agreed and followed me.

After he told me about the incident and his frustration with some of his peers, I asked him what he wanted to do. He said he wanted "those people to leave him alone" and he wanted to get back to class. He appeared to have calmed down significantly and said he wasn't interested in further confrontation with his aforementioned adversary. He also agreed that I could talk to his team of teachers and our assistant principal to keep an eye out for peers who might hassle him. I told him that I would check in with him briefly after his class, and he said he was willing to meet the next day to strategize how to deal with "people who mess with him." We made a verbal contract that he would stay away from the other student, and then I walked with him back to class and had a brief conversation with his teacher.

## INITIAL PROCESS QUESTIONS

- Did my initial response to the situation pose an unnecessary risk to my physical safety?
- How else might I have tried to engage Aaron? Which alternative responses might have been worth trying?
- Did I get enough information to conclude that, in this case, Aaron was engaging in reactive (vs. proactive) aggression, or should I have used additional means of assessment and engaged in more precautionary measures (Bernes & Bardick, 2007; McAdams & Schmidt, 2007)?
- Was it safe to let Aaron go back to class?
- What are my ethical and legal duties to protect Aaron? To protect the other student?
- Which theoretical approach and techniques might be helpful in dealing with Aaron's concerns?
- How might I continue to develop a rapport with Aaron, especially considering the negative circumstances surrounding our first meeting?
- If I learn that Aaron has had issues with anger management previously, how might that change my approach in working with him?
- How might Aaron's various cultural identities and contextual/environmental issues affect how I proceed?

## ADDRESSING THE ISSUES

Unfortunately, extreme behaviors are commonplace in schools today. Accidentally "discovering" the panic button in my counseling office recently (a kind office worker from the main office responded and was understanding) led me to further reflect about the conditions that prompt the need for panic buttons, cameras, and security guards in our schools. It also made me ponder how school counselors might both respond and also work to prevent extreme behaviors.

In Aaron's case, my initial task was to find out more about him because he had been in our school for only a few weeks. I learned from his file that Aaron had already left the school grounds once when he was angry and that he had lost his lunch privileges to eat in the cafeteria for a week after a previous verbal altercation and outburst. A consultation with his elementary school counselor revealed that he had often reacted explosively to slights or frustrations he experienced and that school personnel had mostly been unsuccessful in their attempts to engage Aaron's parents. Talking with Aaron and his current teachers revealed that he appeared to be a target for teasing about his "shabby" clothes and his difficulties with reading.

A case such as Aaron's invites several possible responses. As part of the school's efforts to promote a positive, inclusive, safe, and accepting school climate, the administrators agreed to appoint a climate committee with culturally diverse representatives from the faculty, community, and several parents/guardians from the feeder neighborhoods. In addition, I met with the sixth-grade teachers to enlist their collaboration with the efforts to promote a more positive climate and scheduled classroom guidance sessions for the next few weeks starting with Aaron's sixth-grade "house." The topics on the agenda for these initial lessons were decision making, conflict resolution, appreciating differences, and harassment/bullying.

After several attempts, I was finally able to connect with Aaron's mother. I secured permission for Aaron to join a "friendship" group, and we agreed that I would enroll Aaron in the mentoring program. He would be assigned both a faculty member who would check in with him several times a week and also a trained and supervised "buddy" from the high school for the weekly after-school activities and homework sessions. In addition to working with Aaron's teachers to promote pro-social skills and decrease bullying, Aaron, his parents, his teachers, and I created a behavioral contract to assist Aaron in meeting the goals he named. The teachers agreed that they would call me should Aaron begin to get angry or frustrated during school and then send Aaron to my office if I was available. Also, I would meet with Aaron individually, using solution-focused and narrative theories as umbrella perspectives to guide our work on managing anger and building social skills. Incorporating "what works" (e.g., the behavior contract) is seen as congruent with solution-focused counseling. Table 39-1 delineates additional approaches for working with students exhibiting extreme behaviors.

## IN SESSION

As a counselor who favors the use of solution-focused (Murphy, 2008) and narrative counseling (Winslade & Monk, 2007) conceptualizations and interventions, I knew building rapport was essential to co-constructing an action plan with Aaron. I collaborated with Aaron by using his perspective/narrative of the various situations and employing his terms and goals. I suggested helpful solutions and invited his engagement in the

**TABLE 39-1  Additional Approaches for Working with Students Exhibiting Extreme Behaviors**

| Paradigm | Elementary School | Middle School | High School |
|---|---|---|---|
| Psychodynamic | Using play therapy as a tool to help self-acceptance; sand tray play and puppets; projection game such as "Parallels with Animals" in which counselor asks child what different animals look, act, and sound like when angry (Vernon, 2009a) | Verbal exploration of student's past and its effect on current behavior; use of various art mediums such as drawing or sculpture to allow students to explore and work through early childhood stressors | Verbal exploration of student's past and its effect on current behavior; "focus on the hurt, then address the anger" (Hanna, Hanna, & Keys, 1999, p. 398); recognition that many angry adolescents use anger to mask their hurt |
| Humanistic/ Existential | Avoidance of using desks in order to be more personal than authoritative; being genuine; respecting student regardless of acting-out behaviors (Hanna et al., 1999) | Avoidance of using desks in order to be more personal than authoritative; being genuine; using humor to lighten the mood; respecting student regardless of acting-out behaviors (Hanna et al., 1999) | Avoidance of using desks in order to be more personal than authoritative; being genuine; respecting student regardless of acting-out behaviors (Hanna et al., 1999) |

*(continued)*

**TABLE 39-1**   (*continued*)

| Paradigm | Elementary School | Middle School | High School |
|---|---|---|---|
| Behavioral/CBT | Assessing triggers through drawing, role play, puppets, etc.; having student fill out a behavior chart; assessing irrational/dysfunctional beliefs; postulating different points of view; practicing healthier self-talk | Assessing triggers through drawing, role play, puppets, sentence completion, etc.; having student fill out a behavior chart; assessing irrational/dysfunctional beliefs; helping students understand that people think (and therefore feel) differently; helping show how thoughts cause feelings; practicing overcoming negative thoughts through healthier self-talk | Assessing triggers through drawing, role play, puppets, sentence completion, etc.; having student fill out a behavior chart; assessing irrational/dysfunctional beliefs; helping students understand that people think (and therefore feel) differently; helping show how thoughts cause feelings; practicing overcoming negative thoughts through healthier self-talk |
| Family Systems | If family unavailable, asking students what they would be doing or saying if family were there; highlighting strengths (esp. those that oppose emotional outbursts) in existing system; if family present, assessing current ways of dealing with outbursts; using metaphors and/or narrative to indirectly guide students to healthier ways of behaving and coping | If family unavailable, asking students what they would be doing or saying if family were there; highlighting strengths (esp. those that oppose emotional outbursts) in existing system; if family present, assessing current ways of dealing with outbursts; using metaphors and/or narrative to indirectly guide students to healthier ways of behaving and coping | If family unavailable, asking students what they would be doing or saying if family were there; highlighting strengths (esp. those that oppose emotional outbursts) in existing system; if family present, assessing current ways of dealing with outbursts; using metaphors and/or narrative to indirectly guide students to healthier ways of behaving and coping |
| Emergent | Building rapport; listening to student's story without blame; exploring gender role (esp. in regard to "saving face"); posing miracle question; pointing out sparkling moments; empowering student in healthy ways to decrease feelings of helplessness; using content of current situations to process affect; role play of incidents surrounding outburst; identifying support system | Building rapport; listening to student's story without blame; exploring gender role (esp. in regard to "saving face"); posing miracle question; helping flesh out sparkling moments; helping identify healthy ways to obtain/retain power; using content of current situations to process affect; role play of incidents surrounding outburst; helping identify support system | Building rapport; listening to student's story without blame; exploring gender role (esp. in regard to "saving face"); posing miracle question; encouraging identification of sparkling moments; helping identify healthy ways to obtain/retain power; using content of current situations to process affect; role play of incidents surrounding outburst; encouraging identification and expansion of support system |

process to empower him to deal with his concerns. He externalized his undesirable reactions to frustration by naming them "Angry Man." Angry Man tried to get him to tell people off or fight them. Eventually, as his trust in me grew, he would seek me out when he felt angry. One segment of a session follows.

| | |
|---|---|
| COUNSELOR (C): | Can you tell me what's going on for you right now, Aaron? |
| AARON (A): | I'm mad because they keep messing with me when the teacher's not looking. Every time he turns his back, they take my books and pretend to be me. They act like they're stupid and can't understand what they're reading. Then, when I get mad, the teacher acts like I'm the one doing something wrong. |
| C: | It sounds like, even though you're mad, you're working really hard to not let Angry Man get control. What are some of the things that are helping you do that? |
| A: | You don't understand. I AM getting mad. |
| C: | Hmmm. I can hear the frustration in your voice and I can see that you are getting really mad. Still, you chose to come here to talk about it rather than fighting or yelling. I'm interested; how have you been able to keep Angry Man from "telling them off" today? |
| A: | So you're saying just because I'm mad doesn't mean Angry Man is in control? |
| C: | Is Angry Man in control right now? |
| A: | No. |
| C: | Are you mad right now? |
| A: | Yeah, but just because I'm mad, I don't have to be bad. |
| C: | Did you just make that up? |
| A: | (*Smiling and nodding*) |

## Outcome

An incident in a later class kept Aaron from realizing his behavior contract goals for that day but, overall, a measurable reduction in explosive behavior was evident for the remainder of the school year. Aaron proudly shared his tools and skills for dealing with Angry Man with his peers in the friendship group. He also volunteered to assist in creating the student-led production of an anti-bullying skit and message that aired during the school news in the spring.

As for the other interventions, his relationship with his faculty mentor was strained at times, but Aaron really enjoyed working with his high school buddy. He assured me that he would be a buddy for a sixth grader when he got to high school. The collaboration with Aaron's parents remained inconsistent but they did express pride in his improvement. The school and grade level efforts to improve the school climate yielded measurable positive results over the previous year. Aaron and his sixth-grade peers assisted by filling out surveys early and late in the school year, which documented the perceived improvement in school climate. We plan to meet with Aaron's seventh-grade team and school counselor early in the next school year to bring everyone on board to assist in consolidating his personal/social and academic gains as well as setting new goals.

## Final Process Questions

- How might I have helped Aaron develop and deploy his coping mechanisms more effectively in order to manage his frustration and anger?
- How might the interventions have looked using other theoretical approaches?
- Which collaborative efforts taken seemed most likely to be helpful? Whom might I enlist for additional efforts along these lines, and what might be done?

- Was the amount of time I invested in Aaron justifiable given a caseload of 450 students?
- What additional advocacy efforts might bear fruit for Aaron?
- What else might be done to address salient cultural issues?

## Resources

Beaty-O'Ferrall, M., Green, A., & Hanna, F. (2010). Classroom management strategies for difficult students: Promoting change through relationships. *Middle School Journal, 41*(4), 4–11.

Bernes, K. B., & Bardick, A. D. (2007). Conducting adolescent violence risk assessments: A framework for school counselors. *Professional School Counseling, 10,* 419–427.

Cochran, J. L., Cochran, N. H., Fuss, A., & Nordling, W. J. (2010). Outcomes and stages of child-centered play therapy for a child with highly disruptive behavior driven by self-concept issues. *Journal of Humanistic Counseling, Education, and Development, 49,* 231–246.

Fitzpatrick, M., & Knowlton, E. (2009). Bringing evidence-based self-directed intervention practices to the trenches for students with emotional and behavioral disorders. *Preventing School Failure, 53,* 253–266.

Hanna, F. J., Hanna, C. A., & Keys, S. G. (1999). Fifty strategies for counseling defiant, aggressive adolescents: Reaching, accepting, and relating. *Journal of Counseling & Development, 77,* 395–404.

McAdams, C., & Schmidt, C. D. (2007). How to help a bully: Recommendations for counseling the proactive aggressor. *Professional School Counseling, 11,* 120–128.

Murphy, J. J. (2008). *Solution-focused counseling in schools.* Retrieved from http://counselingoutfitters.com/vistas/vistas08/Murphy.htm

Vernon, A. (2009). *Counseling children & adolescents* (4th ed.). Denver, CO: Love.

Winslade, J. M., & Monk G. D. (2007). *Narrative counseling in schools: Powerful and brief* (2nd ed.). Thousand Oaks, CA: Corwin Press.

*Chapter 40*

# Gang Involvement

CHRISTINE WARD AND BIANCA BEKKER WILLMAN

## CASE BACKGROUND

My first encounter with Stefano outside of classroom guidance sessions occurred when he was escorted to my office by the principal for discussing gang-related behavior with other students and displaying gang-affiliated writing on his arm. Stefano greeted me with a defiant look and quickly told me in no uncertain terms, "I didn't do nothing!" I knew that Stefano struggled with sixth-grade academics and frequently presented a defensive attitude; in the past his teachers had told me that he was quick to anger and reacted aggressively when confronted by peers and authority figures.

The principal took me into the hallway and explained what had happened while Stefano sat in my office. It was my first year at this school, and the principal told me about some gang history in Stefano's family and how it had been affecting him lately. On this day, Stefano had been telling fellow students about a certain gang activity his older brother was involved in, and how he planned on joining his brother in participating in a "roll-in," which is when someone is beaten up by several gang members as an initiation into the gang. His teacher had overheard the conversation, seen Stefano's arm, which was covered in graffiti-type writing, and sent him to the office.

When I stepped back inside, Stefano looked me up and down, as if trying to figure out what I wanted from him. I was determined to build rapport with him so that he could see me as someone he could trust. I could tell Stefano was angry and embarrassed by the way he fidgeted in his chair, breathing rapidly and averting his eyes. I gave him a moment to relax and cool off. Because the school had a zero-tolerance policy on gang-related symbols and clothing, I asked Stefano whether he would like to take a few minutes to clean the writing off his arm and collect his thoughts before beginning our session. I escorted Stefano to the restroom in the main office and waited for him to return.

## INITIAL PROCESS QUESTIONS

- Is this student in danger or a danger to others?
- What are my legal obligations to the student, his parents, and other students?
- What is the school's policy on gang involvement?

- What are my boundaries in terms of confidentiality and privacy for the student?
- What is the best way to establish rapport and build a counseling relationship with this student?
- What is the extent of this student's gang involvement?
- To what degree are the student's parents aware of his involvement with gangs? Are they themselves involved?
- What is the nature of the student's relationship with his family, and particularly his older brother?
- What are my biases toward gangs and gang involvement, and how do I keep these biases in check when I work with this student?

## ADDRESSING THE ISSUES

I never enjoy beginning a counseling session with students when they are heated, upset, and have just been disciplined for some infraction. I find it can be difficult to establish a therapeutic relationship under these circumstances. However, as school counselors we are often called on to intervene in student disciplinary affairs. I choose to look at these situations as opportunities to understand and validate the student's feelings and help the student de-escalate and learn new coping skills. In Stefano's case, I allowed him time to de-escalate on his own prior to talking with me. My hope was that Stefano would see this gesture for what it was: an attempt to show him that I trusted him, saw him as capable and resourceful, and did not intend to punish him further for his actions.

While Stefano was scrubbing the marks from his arm, I reflected on my legal and ethical obligations with respect to this situation as well as my knowledge of gangs. When dealing with issues of gang involvement and, especially, gang-related violence, professional school counselors must first assess the situation and follow appropriate legal and ethical guidelines. As in any counseling situation, the counselor should inform the student of the limits to confidentiality. If the student is in danger or discloses an intention to harm someone or knows about a plan to harm someone else, school counselors should breach confidentiality and follow duty to warn and duty to protect protocol (if in a state that mandates these procedures). If the student or another member of the school or community is in imminent danger, the counselor should contact law enforcement immediately. The student's parent should be contacted and made aware of the student's gang involvement. In many schools, including mine, school policy also states that the school safety officer should be informed of any gang-related activity.

I also had time to reflect on my knowledge of gangs while Stefano took the time he needed to cool off and collect his thoughts. This was my first year in this suburban middle school and although gang activity was rare, I recognized that it was encroaching on the community. I also knew that although gang members are predominantly male (over 90%) and Black/African American and Hispanic/Latino (over 80%), gang activity is not limited to any specific demographic group (National Gang Center, n.d.). Of the approximately 250,000 gang members under the age of 18 years, the majority tends to be in high school, although middle and elementary school students are sometimes recruited to serve as "peewees" or "baby gangsters." The gang may use these students to act as lookouts or to hold drugs, money, or weapons. Furthermore, younger students (like Stefano) may have older siblings who are involved with gangs and therefore may feel an allegiance to their sibling's gang. I also learned from attending a recent gang awareness training sponsored by local law enforcement that the writing on Stefano's arm was not, in fact, "nothing." These symbols were tags for a local gang.

Student gang involvement is a delicate subject. Professional school counselors must validate a student's affiliation and allegiance to the gang while conveying to the student that gang activity, particularly violence, is dangerous and not acceptable in the schools. School counselors can establish this balance by integrating strategies and techniques from various paradigms. I intentionally pulled from humanistic/existential, family systems, psychodynamic, and behavioral paradigms in my work with Stefano. An explanation of these theories and their application for students of varying developmental levels follows.

As in any counseling relationship, school counselors working with gang-affiliated students must first build a foundation of trust with the student, regardless of the student's age or the nature of his or her gang involvement. Person-centered counseling (a humanistic/existential theory) is well-suited for establishing this foundation because of the importance it places on genuineness, unconditional positive regard, and empathy. When Stefano first entered my office I was frightened for him— he was only 11 years old and already displaying signs of delinquency. I was tempted to lecture him on the rights and wrongs of gang involvement; but I knew if I confronted Stefano in this way, he could potentially shut down and I would sabotage any chances I might have of establishing a therapeutic alliance with him. Furthermore, I was aware that many adolescents are drawn to gangs because of the sense of belonging, security, and loyalty that gangs offer their members—all of which imitate needs often provided by a biological family (Sharkey, Shekhtmeyster, Chavez-Lopez, Norris, & Sass, 2011). I knew it was not wise to infer that these things were inherently wrong. Thus, in my first session with Stefano, I avoided accusing him or his brother of gang involvement and instead expressed my genuine concern for his safety and validated the respect he felt for his brother and the gang. Novice school counselors may feel the need to "fix" problems like these, but would be well advised to first take the time to develop a relationship with students and avoid rushing to intervene. A student who believes that the school counselor is judging or trying to correct the student's behavior will not be a willing participant in counseling!

Following a humanistic/existential mind-set, the professional school counselor believes in the student's resourcefulness and abilities to recognize and solve his or her own problems. This assumption is critical when working with gang-affiliated populations. Students generally understand that gang involvement is dangerous, but may feel "stuck" in the gang and not see a way to escape. Existentialists recognize a student's resiliency in the face of adversity, and school counselors who embrace this paradigm will work with the student to identify the student's unique self and help the student make positive decisions about gang-related involvement now and in the future. The school counselor can also promote students' resiliency by understanding and fostering protective factors that serve to mitigate gang involvement and its dangerous consequences. These protective factors include extracurricular involvement, mentorship and support from a committed and caring adult role model, family involvement, supervision of activities, positive peer relationships, ability to communicate problems openly, and increased academic performance—all of which may increase self-esteem and foster a sense of belonging (Sharkey et al., 2011). Promoting these protective factors will often take the form of micro-level advocacy efforts and may be adapted for students at any developmental level.

Family systems theories are especially applicable for working with gang-affiliated students, as gang involvement often mirrors many aspects of families (Barrow, 2011; Sharkey et al., 2011). Furthermore, increased family involvement has been linked to decreased gang-related activities in children and adolescents (Li et al., 2002; Sharkey et al., 2011). School counselors should seek to understand and validate a student's and family's association with gangs and with one another, particularly for younger children and siblings, and to honor the love and respect the student feels for the gang-affiliated member. The school counselor can help the sibling of a gang member deconstruct the member's behaviors and the aspects of the sibling's character that the student identifies with or respects. At the same time, the school counselor can help Stefano differentiate as an individual separate from family (or gang) and, without denouncing the behaviors of his sibling, can encourage Stefano to identify ways to respect and interact with the sibling that do not involve gang activity.

Psychodynamic paradigms, particularly Adlerian counseling, can help a professional school counselor understand the rationale driving a student's involvement with a gang as well as help the counselor and student identify goals and subsequent techniques to use in counseling. Gangs may fulfill students' needs for belonging, identity, social support, security, protection, esteem, and respect (Sharkey et al., 2011). Conversely, students might engage in gang activity because they feel pressured, coerced, or threatened by peers or family. Once the relationship is established and the school counselor understands the forces driving a student's involvement in gangs, the school counselor may use behavioral techniques to help the student understand maladaptive beliefs about gang membership and establish constructive beliefs. As previously discussed, children and adolescents may seek gang membership because involvement in the gang fulfills a specific student need. Middle and high school counselors can help students identify these needs and seek socially appropriate alternatives that fulfill these needs.

Other specific techniques from across the various paradigms also can be used to help the student build protective factors. Identifying exceptions and the miracle question can help students recognize their own resourcefulness and abilities. Role play and role reversal can help students develop and practice pro-social skills. The use of "I" statements can help students communicate their feelings about gang involvement. Cognitive-behavioral techniques such as cognitive restructuring, thought stopping, modeling, and behavior rehearsal may increase student self-esteem. Assessment of family functioning (primarily intended for high school students) and parent/guardian education may help students connect with their families and may result in increased family involvement. Narrative approaches may help older and more advanced students externalize the problem (namely gang affiliation and its resulting consequences) and author a new direction for their lives. Additional approaches to addressing gang-related activity and violence in schools are outlined in Table 40-1.

## IN SESSION

When working with students who have committed disciplinary infractions—especially if the infraction involves potentially dangerous or criminal behavior—school counselors are charged with taking a more direct and investigatory role. School counselors who are involved in disciplinary situations like the one I was called upon to handle with Stefano can maintain their "counselor" hat by conveying empathy, genuineness, and

**TABLE 40-1  Additional Approaches to Addressing Gang-Related Activity and Violence in Schools**

| Paradigm | Elementary School | Middle School | High School |
|---|---|---|---|
| Psychodynamic | Analysis of defense mechanisms; understanding underlying forces driving behavior | Analysis of defense mechanisms; understanding underlying forces driving behavior | Analysis of defense mechanisms; understanding underlying forces driving behavior |
| Humanistic/ Existential | Therapeutic alliance/core conditions; role play and "I" statements to improve peer relationships | Therapeutic alliance/ core conditions; role play, role reversal, and "I" statements to improve peer relationships | Therapeutic alliance/core conditions; role play, role-reversal, and "I" statements to improve peer relationships |
| Behavioral/ CBT | Positive reinforcement; token economy; behavior charts and contracts; disputing irrational beliefs; cognitive restructuring and thought stopping; homework; self-talk; modeling; behavior rehearsal; role play; time-out; guided imagery/ relaxation; exceptions; miracle question | Positive reinforcement; token economy; response cost; behavior charts and contracts; disputing irrational beliefs; cognitive restructuring and thought stopping; homework; self-talk; modeling; behavior rehearsal; role play; time-out; guided imagery/ relaxation; exceptions; miracle question (Note: Exercise caution when challenging belief systems.) | Positive reinforcement; token economy; response cost; behavior charts and contracts; disputing irrational beliefs; cognitive restructuring and thought stopping; homework; self-talk; modeling; behavior rehearsal; role play; time-out; guided imagery/relaxation; exceptions; miracle question (Note: Exercise caution when challenging belief systems.) |
| Family Systems | Family as framework for understanding individual; parent skills training for promoting family connectedness and involvement | Family (and gang dynamics) as framework for understanding individual; "I" position; coaching; parent skills training for promoting family connectedness and involvement | Family (and gang dynamics) as framework for understanding individual; analysis of family dynamics and communication patterns; "I" position; coaching; parent skills training for promoting family connectedness and involvement |
| Emergent | Externalize problem; exceptions; miracle question; empowerment; role play; improving support systems | Deconstruct and externalize problem; exceptions; miracle question; empowerment; role play; improving support systems | Deconstruct and externalize problem; exceptions; miracle question; empowerment; role play; improving support systems |

unconditional positive regard for the student while simultaneously maintaining disciplinary policy. The primary objectives of my first session with Stefano were to ensure he was safe, to determine the extent of his involvement in gang-related activities, and to make certain he understood the gravity of his actions and the ensuing consequences. My secondary objective was to work individually with Stefano and collaborate with school and community stakeholders to promote Stefano's protective factors.

| | |
|---|---|
| COUNSELOR (C): | Hi, Stefano. The principal told me about what happened in class today. I can see that you are pretty angry right now. |
| STEFANO (S): | (*Silence*) |
| C: | Stefano, according to the school dress code, students are not allowed to have any kind of writing on their bodies. Would you like to take a few minutes to wash the writing off your arm and collect your thoughts? I will be right here when you get back. |
| | [While Stefano is in the restroom, I begin to document my interaction with him and organize my thoughts. When Stefano returns, I look up and smile at him but continue to do my work.] |
| C: | Let me know when you are ready to talk. |
| S: | (*After several minutes of silence*) I didn't do nothing. I was just talking to some kids. |
| C: | What were you talking about? |
| S: | My brother. |
| C: | I see. What is your brother's name? |
| S: | Jaime. |
| C: | So tell me about Jaime. |
| | [Stefano hesitates so I refocus the conversation, planning to return to Jaime later.] |
| C: | Can you tell me about the markings you had on your arm? |
| S: | It just means the area codes. It's nothing. |
| C: | I'm trying to understand why you had that writing on your arm. You say it's nothing, but I bet it must be something important to you if you would walk around with it written all over your arm. |
| S: | It's just stuff about my family. It don't mean nothing. |
| C: | It's about your family? About your brother Jaime? |
| S: | Yeah . . . (*Pauses and looks at the ground*) |
| C: | Seems like your brother is pretty important to you. |
| S: | Uh-huh. He takes care of me. Makes sure no one messes with me. |
| C: | (*Smiles*) He takes care of his baby brother, huh? |
| S: | Yeah. He don't let no one go dissin' on me or my mom or my sister and little brothers. They always try to mess with us cuz they know he's so important to the crew [another name for gang]. |
| C: | Stefano, is your brother a part of a gang? |
| C: | [When Stefano responded with silence, I pushed a bit further.] I understand you want to protect your brother like he |

|     | |
| --- | --- |
| | protects you. I think it's great that you care about him so much. But I also am worried about you. Your teacher says she heard you talking about participating in a roll-in with your brother. |
| C: | [When Stefano again responded with silence, I stated my interpretation of his silence.] It's hard to talk about this stuff. |
| S: | Yeah . . . I don't want him to get in trouble and I don't want him to get hurt. I was only gonna be a lookout, I swear! |
| C: | A lookout for the roll-in? |
| S: | Yeah. It's no big deal. |
| C: | Stefano, I think it's a big deal. Just like you don't want your brother to get in trouble or get hurt, I don't want *you* to get in trouble or get hurt. |
| S: | Why do you care so much? I told you it's nothing! |

At this point I could tell Stefano was becoming agitated and defensive, so I switched gears and explained to Stefano that I cared about him as a student, but didn't feel like I knew much about him. I asked Stefano to tell me more about his family and his interests. When I could see that Stefano's anger had subsided, I explained to him the code of conduct policy, and informed him that the principal would be calling his parent in for a conference to discuss the actions to be taken. I explained that I would be present at the meeting and reminded him of the limits of confidentiality. I asked Stefano whether he wanted to be a part of the meeting with his parent, and he replied that he did want to be there. I then walked him back to class and asked him whether it would be all right to check in on him when he returned from his suspension.

## Outcome

Stefano returned to class that day after speaking with me and was suspended the following day for his transgression. The day of the incident, per the school's code of conduct policy, the principal and I had a conference with his mother, who reported that she was unaware of the gang behavior her son had mentioned. With Stefano present in the room, we informed Stefano's mother of the limits of confidentiality. We told his mother about Stefano's intentions to engage in a roll-in, and she agreed to rigorously monitor Stefano's activities. I explained that I would be contacting the school resource officer to provide the resource officer with the information about the roll-in. I told her that the school resource officer was trained to handle situations such as these and would take precautions to protect Stefano's anonymity and safety. I also referred his mother to agencies in the community that offered family counseling. Because I knew that school success, relationships with caring adults, and involvement with structured activities (particularly after school hours when children and adolescents may be unsupervised and wander the streets) serve as protective factors against gang involvement, I continued to work behind the scenes and directly with Stefano and his mother to promote these protective factors. I followed up with his teachers about Stefano's behavior and made sure they knew that they could send Stefano to talk to me if they were having any issues with him in class. I also worked with his teachers to get Stefano involved with academic tutoring, set up a mentor to work with Stefano, included him in my social skills training group, introduced Stefano to the school's basketball coach, and encouraged him to attend basketball practice and try out for the team.

Throughout this time I never forced Stefano to come to my office to talk to me. However, from that day forward, every time I saw Stefano in the hallway or in the cafeteria, I made an effort to say hello and ask how he was doing and ask about his brother, his mentor, and basketball. He eventually began coming to my office on his own accord, to say hello and just vent. Over time, he shared more and more details about his family and his life with me, we discussed some of the dangers of gang life, and

I offered him specific coping strategies and ways to deal with pressure from family. Although he continued to get in trouble for minor things for the rest of the year, he never again came to school displaying gang writing on his person. However, although I felt that I had provided Stefano and his mother with resources and strategies to help boost his protective factors and mitigate against gang involvement, I knew that there was still a risk of Stefano's becoming involved in the gang, and so I pledged to continue monitoring Stefano and intervening when possible.

## Final Process Questions

- Is the student safe?
- Did I respect the student's right to confidentiality to the greatest extent possible?
- Did I follow appropriate legal and ethical guidelines and school policy?
- Did I follow up with the student after the incident?
- Did I respond to the behavior in an appropriate and professional manner?

- Did I establish a reasonable rapport with the student?
- Did I document the important aspects of the meeting and subsequent meetings and interactions with the student?
- Did I recognize the limits of my expertise and abilities, and seek external support when I reached these limits?

## Resources

American School Counselor Association. (2005). *Gang prevention for middle school students: A guidance unit for awareness and prevention*. Alexandria, VA: Author.

Arciaga, M., Sakamoto, W., & Jones, E. (2010, November). *Responding to gangs in the school setting.*

Retrieved from http://www.nationalgangcenter.gov/Content/Documents/Bulletin-5.pdf

Holmes, R. M., Tewksbury, R., & Higgins, G. (2012). *Introduction to gangs in America*. Boca Raton, FL: Taylor & Francis Group.

## Chapter 41

# Suicide Prevention

MEGAN KIDRON

## CASE BACKGROUND

I was sitting in my office, preparing for a group counseling session planned for later on in the day, when Rebecca, a high school student that I used to see quite regularly, knocked at my door. On this occasion she was concerned about a friend who had sent her a text message the night before saying she did not want to live anymore. Rebecca said she told her mom, and her mom called the sheriff. The sheriff was then supposed to contact Rebecca's friend's dad. I had Rebecca sit down and tell me who her friend was, what had happened, and what the text had said. My first thought was I had to see Rebecca's friend right away, and my second thought was there goes my schedule for the day.

I found the friend, named Sarah, in class, introduced myself, and we walked back to my office. I told her that a friend of hers had come to me worried about Sarah because of a text the friend had received from Sarah. I asked Sarah to tell me what was going on and how she was feeling.

## INITIAL PROCESS QUESTIONS

- Is this a new thought or behavior for the student?
- Do Sarah's parents know?
- Has there been previous suicide ideation or attempts?
- Which theoretical approach would work best when dealing with suicidal ideation?
- What are the ethical and legal aspects involved when working with suicidal students?
- How should I determine suicidal risk?
- What multicultural issues do I need to consider?
- What is the best way to establish a therapeutic relationship with this student?
- What techniques are best to get to the root of the problem?

## ADDRESSING THE ISSUES

When it comes to suicide, all precautions need to be taken. A lot of times in counseling there are gray areas about what a counselor should or should not do, but when it comes to suicide, certain very clear steps need to be taken. I had a good working knowledge of my school system's policies and procedures related to suicide intervention. I was also well aware of the ethical and legal implications related to suicide (Erford, Lee, Newsome & Rock, 2011; Linde, 2011; Stone, 2009), such as the 1991 *Eisel* case in Maryland that required parental contact in issues of potential self-harm. One thing I needed to learn right away was whether Sarah had in fact felt suicidal the night before and whether she was currently suicidal. In order to assess her potential for suicide, I asked her the following questions:

- Are you currently having any thoughts of suicide?
- Do you currently have the desire to kill yourself?
- Do you currently have a specific plan to kill yourself?

Suicide prevention is a crisis intervention/management strategy that interrupts a possible downward spiral as quickly as possible and is outside of any theoretical orientation. It basically consists of six components: immediacy, control, assessment, disposition, referral, and follow-up (Greenstone & Leviton, 2002). Based on my assessment and the answers to the aforementioned questions, I determined that suicide was not an imminent threat.

In order to help Sarah, I used an integrative theoretical approach. To establish a working relationship with her, I used some techniques and approaches from the humanistic/existential philosophy such as being nonjudgmental, having and showing empathy toward Sarah, being genuine and honest (Rogers, 1961), and being direct about why I had her come to my office.

Sarah and I talked about things that were happening in her life that were causing her to feel sad, what was currently going on that was upsetting her, and how she was feeling at the moment. She mentioned that a favorite uncle was sick, and she was having a hard time dealing with his illness. She also stated that she and her girlfriend had recently broken up, leaving her sad and emotionally drained.

During counseling I used the cognitive-behavioral approach by discussing with Sarah how she perceived her circumstances and how she wanted things to be. I used a reality therapy approach to discuss her wants and needs and whether she was moving in the right direction to meet them. Together we developed goals that Sarah wanted to accomplish and a plan to help her reach those goals. We talked about what in her life she could control and the steps she could take toward changing those things she was dissatisfied with (Corey, 2012; Kanel, 2011).

Sarah and I also developed a safety contract, or "no suicide contract," that she and I signed and that she took home to have her parents sign. This contract stated Sarah would not hurt herself in any way, and if she felt like hurting herself, she would let an adult know right away. We defined and discussed the different steps Sarah could take if she felt sad and started having thoughts of hurting herself (e.g., calling the suicide hotline, calling her best friend, talking to her grandmother). Sarah and I also left room in the contract so that we could add to it in the future, if necessary.

I had Sarah go next door to another counselor's room so that someone was watching her while I made two important telephone calls. First I called my supervisor to consult about the best possible steps to take next. I told my supervisor about the situation, what I had done already, and what steps I planned to take next. She agreed that the student was no longer an immediate danger to herself.

Next I called Sarah's father, who is a single parent, and told him about the text message Sarah sent to her friend saying goodbye, what Sarah said she was feeling last night, and that Sarah said she was not currently feeling like she wanted to end her life. I informed her dad that Sarah said she did not have a suicide plan, but that girls most often overdose on medication when attempting suicide so he could remove any medications that she had access to. I recommended taking Sarah to a doctor and telling the doctor that Sarah said she felt sad quite often. Sarah's father mentioned that his brother had bipolar disorder and asked whether Sarah could have that. I suggested that he discuss this possibility with the doctor, who would be more qualified to answer that question. I also advised Sarah's father to make arrangements for her to see an outside counselor on a regular basis. I said I would send home some information on suicide and ways that parents can talk to their children about suicide, as well as a list of outside counselors that Sarah's father could call to set up an appointment and check on what insurance they accepted.

I informed Sarah's father about the safety contract Sarah and I had created and that she would be bringing it home for him to read and sign, so he would know what we had agreed on. He was unable to get off of work to pick her up from school, so we agreed that Sarah would stay with me throughout the remainder of the day. After school, I would walk Sarah to the library where her grandmother worked, and Sarah would stay with her grandmother until her father got home. I suggested that it would be a good idea for someone to supervise Sarah whenever she was at home. I told her father that if he were ever concerned that Sarah was in immediate danger, he should call 911 or take her to the hospital to be evaluated. I also let Sarah's father know that Sarah was worried he would be mad at her. Sarah's father assured me that he was not and would convey that to Sarah. We talked about ways he could increase communication with Sarah.

Although this particular case involved a high school student, the steps when handling suicide ideations with middle and elementary school students are very similar. At any grade level the school counselor wants to ascertain the potential risk for suicide and follow the legal guidelines for handling suicidal thoughts when working with minors. Depending on the chronological age and developmental level of the student, the counselor would adjust his or her language to the student's level so the student can understand the questions and what the counselor is saying. Also, the younger the student, the more closely the school counselor will want to involve the parents or guardian of the child. As one gains experience in the counseling field, be prepared to deal with students with suicidal thoughts and/or behaviors at all grade levels. Table 41-1 provides additional approaches to working with students displaying suicidal ideation.

## IN SESSION

| | |
|---|---|
| COUNSELOR (C): | How were you feeling last night? |
| STUDENT (S): | Upset and sad, like I did not want to live anymore. |
| C: | Do you still feel that way today? |
| S: | I still feel sad, but I do not still feel like I want to kill myself. |
| C: | How often do you feel sad? |
| S: | A lot. |
| C: | How long have you felt that way and had thoughts of not wanting to live? |

| TABLE 41-1 | Additional Approaches to Working with Students with Suicide Ideation |
|---|---|
| **Paradigm** | **Interventions Appropriate Across All School Levels** |
| Psychodynamic | Exploring transference and countertransference issues, defense mechanisms, goals that drive behavior, and how the past influences student's current behavior |
| Humanistic/ Existential | Focus on the therapeutic relationship; role playing and "I" statements; focus on choice, taking responsibility for actions, and the present and future |
| Behavioral/CBT | Focus on behavior modification through positive reinforcement, token economy, behavior charts, and behavior contracts; developing coping strategies; disputing irrational beliefs; cognitive restructuring; exploring automatic thoughts; self-talk, visual imagery; modeling; behavioral rehearsal; role playing; exceptions; miracle question |
| Family Systems | Teaching parent(s) information and strategies for dealing with behavioral, academic, and social issues, and family dynamics; focus on interpersonal relationships |
| Emergent | Breaking problems down into pieces; miracle question; empowerment; focus on communication; interpersonal relationships; role playing |

| | |
|---|---|
| S: | I used to think about it before but have not thought about it before last night in a while. |
| C: | When you say before, how long ago do you mean? |
| S: | A couple of months ago. |
| C: | Have you ever attempted suicide before? |
| S: | No. |
| C: | When you were feeling upset last night and like you did not want to live, did you have a plan of how you would end your life? |
| S: | No. |
| C: | Was there something that happened to bring these thoughts up again? |
| S: | I broke up with my girlfriend a week ago, and I have just been feeling sad about things in general. |
| C: | You said that you were feeling better today. Did something happen to make you feel better? |
| S: | Last night when I was feeling upset, I talked to my grandma about how I was feeling and things that have been going on. |
| C: | Last night were you thinking and feeling like you wanted to kill yourself or were you thinking and feeling like you did not want to feel sad anymore? |
| S: | I just do not want to feel sad anymore. |

## Outcome

Sarah stayed with me for the rest of the school day. After school I walked her to the school library where her grandmother worked so she could stay with her until her dad got home. The next morning I met with her to see how she was feeling and how the discussion with her dad had gone. Sarah said she was having a good day so far, was feeling much better, and was relieved to have told her dad. We decided that we would meet once a week for the next couple of weeks just to check and see how things were going. For the rest of the school year, with her dad's per-

mission, we met occasionally to check in and talk about what was going on in Sarah's life, how she was feeling, and her progress toward her goals (Kanel, 2011).

It took a while for Sarah's family to make an appointment with an outside counselor, and once the family did, it was then canceled several times. However, as the school year came to a close, her family had an appointment set up for her to see a counselor by herself and an appointment for her and her family to go together.

## Final Process Questions

- Which aspects of the intervention need to be documented?
- Did I intervene within the limits of my training, background, and experience?
- How do I respect the client's rights to privacy and confidentiality as much as possible under the circumstances?
- Did my interventions account for multicultural considerations?
- How should follow-up with Sarah occur to ensure Sarah does not fall through the cracks?

## Resources

Jackson-Cherry, L., & Erford, B. T. (Eds.). (2011). *Crisis intervention and prevention*. Columbus, OH: Pearson Merrill.

Kanel, K. (2011). *A guide to crisis intervention* (4th ed.). New York, NY: Brooks/Cole.

Linde, L. (2011). Ethical, legal, and professional issues in school counseling. In B. T. Erford (Ed.), *Trans-forming the school counseling profession* (3rd ed., pp. 70–89). Columbus, OH: Pearson Merrill.

Stone, C. (2009). *School counseling principles: Ethics and law* (2nd ed.). Alexandria, VA: American School Counselor Association.

*Chapter 42*

# Helping Students Who Experience Disasters and Posttraumatic Stress

JEFFREY BROWN AND JILL M. THOMPSON

## CASE BACKGROUND

Courtney, a 10-year-old African American female, has attended my elementary school since prekindergarten. Her twin brother, Corey, also attends the school. Courtney consistently scores in the advanced range for both math and reading; however, when uninterested in a subject, she will disengage and perform poorly. Courtney and her brother alternate between living with their mother and their father in the midst of a contentious shared custody arrangement. The mother has another son who is almost 2 years old. The mother lives within walking distance of the school and the father lives in a nearby county. Both parents have been incarcerated at separate times. Each parent, separately, has alleged physical abuse of the children by the other parent. Both parents now have stable employment and are seeking full-time custody of both Courtney and Corey.

I have spent time talking with both parents about various behavioral issues. When summoned to the school, Courtney's mother responds as the primary caregiver. During October, Courtney refused to follow the direction of the adult supervising the recess break. Courtney left the school grounds and slowly walked away. I was alerted and found Courtney within a block of the school. Although Courtney was not considered a model student, this behavior was out of character for her. In the past, direct behavioral observations of Courtney within the school environment revealed disrespectful peer and teacher interactions. The most glaring behavioral observation was a disregard for authority when she felt she had been wronged; however, she usually can compose herself quickly.

Courtney joined me in my office after a brief conversation outside. I alerted her mother as well as the principal about the situation. Courtney divulged that a fire had occurred 2 weeks ago at her home and that she was afraid that harm would come to her family. She went on to state that the baby was in the basement where the fire started and, although everyone exited the house unharmed, Courtney remained afraid for her family's safety. Over the previous 2 weeks, school personnel had noted a spike in Courtney's negative behaviors including (1) walking out of class, (2) verbal assaults on both peers and adults, and (3) a decline in her academic performance. After an intake assessment, I discussed with her mother the possibility that Courtney might be suffering from the effects of the house fire and could benefit from speaking with someone outside of school who was trained in trauma counseling. Courtney's mother did not pursue this assistance.

## INITIAL PROCESS QUESTIONS

- What is the overarching responsibility of the school counselor when helping a student in crisis?
- What ethical guidelines must school counselors consider when working with students experiencing trauma?
- In what ways do cultural issues affect this case conceptualization process?
- To what extent should counselors address social issues in the practice of crisis intervention and school counseling?

## ADDRESSING THE ISSUES

Sudden natural disasters (e.g. floods, earthquakes, hurricanes) and human-caused traumas (e.g. fires, acts of violence, car accidents) can be particularly traumatic for children and adolescents. According to Gilliland and James (1997) and Green, Korol, Grace, and Vary (1991), a traumatic event affects youth both emotionally and physically. Trauma also transcends cultural differences. In addition to the destruction of property, loss of life, and disruption of daily activities, disasters result in various levels of trauma for those individuals affected by the event. The disastrous impact is heightened when the trauma directly affects the social support system of the family because a child's sense of security is decreased. In short, children's reactions often are influenced by the emotional reactions and coping skills of their caregivers (Green et al., 1991; Weems et al., 2010).

Most children are resilient when faced with disasters and trauma and as time passes can cope with the assistance of their caregivers and other adults. Some children, however, may be predisposed to severe reactions depending on extreme risk factors (Gard & Ruzek, 2006; La Greca, Silverman, Vernberg, & Roberts, 2002). These risk factors include (1) personal injury, (2) level of physical destruction, (3) level of caregiver support, (4) loss of immediate family members, and (5) relocation from home and community (Green et al., 1991; Jones, Fray, Cunningham, & Kaiser, 2001; Weems et al., 2010).

Common symptoms and reactions have been observed in children after a catastrophic event, and elementary school aged children exposed to disasters may be at increased risk for certain reactions. Developmentally, elementary aged students may be less able to process exposure to traumatic events and cope with the disruption. This often is true for older children and adults as well (Weems et al., 2010). As a result, elementary aged students can become fearful, insecure, and preoccupied with a need to talk repetitively about the experience. Elementary aged children also may become compulsive; have nightmares or sleep disturbance; become hostile; or display interpersonal problems, physical complaints, chronic sadness, or regression (Gilliland & James, 1997; Weems et al., 2010). Some common behaviors observed as a result of trauma include clinging to a primary caregiver, bedwetting, and thumb sucking (Erickson, 1998; Gilliland & James, 1997; Weems et al., 2010).

Middle school to high school aged adolescents usually display a more refined understanding of the disaster event, and adolescents' reactions frequently appear similar to adults' reactions to trauma. After a disaster, adolescents may view the world as dangerous and unsafe. To that end, they may experience personality changes, apathy, anxiety, physical complaints, conflicts, delinquent behaviors, acting-out behaviors, and change in attitudes about life (Erickson, 1998; Hale & Harris, 2006; Terr, 1995; Weems et al., 2010).

Some children and adolescents who experience a catastrophic event may develop ongoing difficulties known as posttraumatic stress disorder (PTSD; Erickson, 1998;

Gilliland & James, 1997; Lonigan, Shannon, Taylor, & Salee, 1994). According to the fifth edition of the *Diagnostic and Statistical Manual of Mental Disorders* (*DSM-5*; American Psychiatric Association [APA], 2013), symptoms of PTSD can include those behaviors and attitudes listed previously, exhibited over an extended period of time. Other symptoms of PTSD may include reexperiencing the disaster or traumatic event during play and/or dreams or anticipating or feeling that the disaster is happening again. Hyperarousal and intrusive symptoms eventually may become so distressing that the individual strives to avoid contact with everything and everyone. Avoidance may be applied even to one's own thoughts, which can arouse memories of the trauma and thus cause the intrusive and hyperarousal states to persist. Students with PTSD may isolate or become detached from their feelings, displaying a restricted range of emotional response and experiencing emotional detachment ("aloofness"). When experiencing serious mental health problems such as PTSD or depression, some adolescents may be at risk for suicide (Gilliland & James, 1997; Hale & Harris, 2006; Weems et al., 2010). Students who exhibit these symptoms should be referred for appropriate mental health evaluation and intervention.

School counselors need to encourage and provide opportunities for students to talk about their thoughts, feelings, and behaviors in a safe and accepting environment. In addition, counselors must allow students to express concerns and ask questions, while promoting the use of effective coping and problem-solving skills. The client-centered theoretical frame of reference seems most appropriate for use with a student after a disaster event because the student is stabilized and has returned to an approximate state of process equilibrium. In Courtney's case, the session began with questions to conceptualize the behavioral, cognitive, and affective symptoms related to the trauma. Specifically, the counselor asked questions to determine the presence of any (1) behavioral avoidance patterns or immobility, (2) cognitive transgression, threats, or denial, and (3) affective function of anger, hostility, fear, or sadness. Table 42-1 provides additional approaches and strategies for helping students experiencing disasters, trauma, or PTSD.

## IN SESSION

A humanistic/existential approach is demonstrated in the following discussion by establishing a climate of trust, unconditional respect, and genuine acceptance. This approach allows Courtney to talk freely about the disaster event and any anxieties related to the event (Corey, 2012). The scope of the event was defined through the use of opened-ended questions. The focus of the session was on the "now" and "how."

| | |
|---|---|
| COUNSELOR (C): | I want you to tell me about the day of the fire and how you felt. |
| STUDENT (S): | We were sitting on my mama's bed, so my mama left the baby there because my cousin didn't work. So I went off upstairs and ask her do you want me to bring the baby, and she said no he is asleep. So me and Duke went downstairs for a few minutes and we sat on the bed. We said what is that smell? I went back to the washing machine and on top of it the stuff and the pillow was on fire. I told my cousin and she had to put it out. |
| C: | The fire started when a pillow at or near the washing machine was ignited by sparks or flames from the fireplace. |
| S: | No, the fire started down by the thing, I don't know what it's called. |

**TABLE 42-1    Additional Approaches and Strategies for Helping Students Experiencing Disasters, Trauma, or PTSD**

| Paradigm | Elementary School | Middle School | High School |
|---|---|---|---|
| Psychodynamic | Transference issues; goals that drive faulty behavior; how current behaviors are connected to past experiences | Transference issues; defense mechanisms; goals that drive faulty behavior; how current behaviors are connected to past experiences | Transference issues; defense mechanisms; goals that drive faulty behavior; how current behaviors are connected to past experiences |
| Humanistic/ Existential | Establishing an accepting, authentic therapeutic relationship; "I" statements; focus on choice and taking responsibility | Establishing an accepting, authentic therapeutic relationship; "I" statements; focus on choice and taking responsibility | Establishing an accepting, authentic therapeutic relationship; role playing; "I" statements; focus on choice and taking responsibility |
| Behavioral/CBT | Assisting with elimination of anxiety, fears, irrational or illogical thoughts; modifying maladaptive behaviors; behavior contracts; teaching coping skills; bibliotherapy; cognitive restructuring; play therapy | Assisting with elimination of anxiety, fears, irrational or illogical thoughts; modifying maladaptive behaviors; behavior contracts; teaching coping skills; cognitive restructuring | Assisting with elimination of anxiety, fears, irrational or illogical thoughts; modifying maladaptive behaviors; behavior contracts; teaching coping skills; positive imagery; cognitive restructuring |
| Family Systems | Focus on interpersonal relationships by facilitating primary caregivers' ability to foster positive parent–child relationships; teaching coping strategies and strategies to deal with regressive behaviors that affect academic and social development | Focus on interpersonal relationships by facilitating primary caregivers' ability to foster positive parent–child relationships; teaching coping strategies and strategies to deal with regressive behaviors that affect academic and social development | Focus on interpersonal relationships by facilitating primary caregivers' ability to foster positive parent–child relationships; teaching coping strategies and strategies to deal with regressive behaviors that affect academic and social development |
| Emergent | Breaking problems down into pieces; miracle question; empowerment; focus on communication | Breaking problems down into pieces; miracle question; empowerment; focus on communication; interpersonal relationships | Breaking problems down into pieces; miracle question; empowerment, focus on communication; interpersonal relationships; role playing |

| | |
|---|---|
| C: | Downstairs where you do the laundry. |
| S: | Yes. |
| C: | Did everyone get out safe? |
| S: | Yes, I told my cousin and I took the baby [Terrell] outside with me. |
| C: | Tell me what you felt. How did you feel when you smelled the smoke and saw the fire? |

| S: | I was scared because it was my first time, because I never saw nothing like that. |
|---|---|
| C: | You were brave to tell the adults and take the baby with you. How are you sleeping? |
| S: | OK. |
| C: | How did you feel about coming to school after the fire? |
| S: | I wanted to come to school. I ask my mama could I bring Terrell to school. |
| C: | Why did you want to bring him to school? |
| S: | I just wanted to keep him safe. |
| C: | You did something that not everyone would have done. You care a lot about Terrell. . . . |

## Outcome

Immediately after our first meeting following the fire, Courtney and I met at school twice weekly for 3 consecutive weeks to fulfill three primary goals.

1. To assess how she was feeling following the fire. Every morning as the students assembled, I spoke with Courtney to gain a visual assessment of how she transitioned from school to home. This was particularly important as she split time between parents and did not handle that transition well. During the sessions with Courtney, the focus would be on the residual effects from the fire (i.e., fear of going to the basement, nightmares, clinging onto or fear of not being near her younger brother).
2. To assess Courtney's ability to focus on her class work, ability to stay on task, concentrate, and not have thoughts of the fire inhabiting her educational experience.
3. To assess her perception of how her family was coping with the fire. We formulated an action plan in the event there were lingering effects from the fire and provided Courtney with the tools to move forward confident that she was equipped with the ability to transition into middle school absent any residual effects from the fire.

Courtney appears to have returned to a safe place in her understanding about fires, but continues to feel anxious about leaving her baby brother in the house while she attends school. I told her that we would continue to meet for the next 4 weeks to develop effective ways to cope with leaving her brother in the house while she attends school. She smiled and we walked back to her classroom.

## Final Process Questions

- How was the student's level of development considered in the counseling relationship?
- How would you proceed in a counseling relationship with Courtney?
- Would you encourage the mother to seek outside counseling for Courtney? Be sure to consider issues of culture.

## Resources

James, R. K., & Gilliland, B. E. (2012). *Crisis intervention strategies* (7th ed.). Belmont, CA: Brooks/Cole.

Kanel, K. (2011). *A guide to crisis intervention* (4th ed.). Belmont, CA: Brooks/Cole.

Kerr, M. M. (2008). *School crisis prevention and intervention.* Upper Saddle River, NJ: Prentice Hall.

*Chapter 43*

# Responsible Use of Technology (Social Networking)

Stefanie Johnson and Jeffrey M. Warren

## CASE BACKGROUND

My first experience with Amanda, a 15-year-old European American female 10th grader, was through a referral from the school administrator. As she sat in my office, tears poured down her face as she told the story of her broken heart. Her girlfriend had recently broken up with her. She presented as confused and upset by the loss of this relationship. This breakup appeared to be affecting Amanda academically and was causing her to have conflict with teachers and peers. Although Amanda was in the top 3% of her class academically, and classroom discipline had never been a concern, she often struggled with peer interactions. She frequently became irritated when her expectations of others were not met, made poor decisions, and failed to take into account the consequences of her actions.

Over the months since then, Amanda and I have developed and maintained a rapport that would set the stage for intimate conversations about school and life in general. Amanda and I frequently met in my office during her lunch break to talk about her day and any developments in her life in regard to relationships, school issues, grades, college, and work. Our sessions weaved their way through Amanda's struggles with identity, high expectations, low self-esteem, poor decision making, and self-injurious behaviors. The relationship we built across these sessions provided Amanda with safety and reassurance that I was going to listen to her and accept her no matter what.

One day during a session, Amanda, now 16 years old, told me she had met a "great guy" named Jake. I began to inquire about this new relationship and how they became acquainted. Amanda was very open and forthcoming about meeting Jake, a 23-year-old Marine, on a dating website. I was aware of Amanda's use of social networking sites, such as Facebook and MySpace, as a means of communication, maintaining friendships, and entertainment. However, it was not until this session that I became aware of her exploration with online dating.

## INITIAL PROCESS QUESTIONS

The questions listed here appear to be most pertinent to addressing issues related to the use of social networking sites. Although the focus of this chapter is on social networking, I realize this case scenario may also engender concerns or questions related to other issues, and these will be mentioned later.

- What immediate danger might Amanda be experiencing?
- What do Amanda's parents know about her online dating?
- In what ways is Amanda's behavior developmentally appropriate or the result of low self-esteem and poor decision making?
- What, if any, multicultural issues should be considered when working with Amanda? What theoretical approaches and strategies would be most effective in addressing this situation?

## ADDRESSING THE ISSUES

The use of social networking sites is more prevalent than ever among teenagers. A recent report suggested that during a typical school day, approximately one out of every 10 teenagers spends 3 hours or more on social networking sites (Johnson, 2011). Teenagers use these sites to enhance social relations, manage their identity, and promote their lifestyle (Livingstone, 2008). However, these "hyper-networkers" are more likely to engage in risky behavior such as having sex with multiple partners. Furthermore, hyper-networkers were also found to be at high risk for mental health issues including stress, depression, and suicide. In general, there appears to be a negative correlation between teenagers' increased use of social networking sites and their mental and behavioral health.

Research also indicated that teenage users interact with social networking sites based on their personality traits (e.g., individuals reporting high levels of shyness also reported stronger associations between social networking usage and friendship quality when compared to less shy individuals; Baker & Oswald, 2010; Buffardi & Campbell, 2008). These networking sites appear simply to be social microcosms of the students' lives. School counselors must remain informed of research on and advancements in social networking communities in order to effectively meet the needs of their students. The ability to address social networking issues with students within the context of counseling paradigms is exceedingly valuable and necessary.

In this case scenario, Amanda responded to my use of a trans-theoretical approach spanning several paradigms across the counseling relationship. Theoretical concepts and strategies within the humanistic/existential, behavioral/cognitive-behavioral, and family systems paradigms were integrated during many of the counseling sessions. When addressing the issues presented during this particular session, I used person-centered counseling with complementary strategies from rational emotive behavior therapy (REBT) and family systems theory.

I used person-centered concepts to focus on the counselor–student relationship. I met Amanda where she was by listening with empathy throughout the session. Genuineness was clearly demonstrated when I emphasized concern for Amanda's safety and happiness. I also displayed unconditional positive regard for Amanda and was accepting of her, without being judgmental. Many basic helping skills (counseling micro skills), such as open-ended questions, simple and minimal verbalizations, reflection of feeling, and summarizing, were used throughout the session. The implementation of these skills allowed me as the counselor to explore Amanda's mental health status and determine the most appropriate course of action for addressing this situation. Amanda responded positively to the person-centered approach: She was very forthcoming with her thoughts and feelings, while providing detailed information about the events that transpired as a result of social networking.

Strategies embedded within an REBT framework were instinctively used during this session as well. I employed humor and confrontation while working with Amanda. Ellis and MacLaren (2005) suggested that humor can be very effective when counseling clients. When incorporating humor in a counseling relationship or session, it is important not to "joke" about the person, but to direct the humor at the situation or specific thoughts about the situation. Furthermore, humor should be used with caution, and only once rapport has been established between the counselor and the client.

Amanda and I had clearly established a strong counseling alliance by the time of this session. Earlier in the counseling relationship, we created a joke related to self-acceptance. Amanda began this session by referencing that joke. My acceptance of Amanda's joke provided her the space to elaborate. The joke was again referenced at the end of the session.

REBT is an active approach to counseling that directs the client to the root of the problem (Dryden, 2009a). REBT encourages counselors to be confrontational in therapeutic ways. However, Dryden (2009b) cautioned that the premature use of confrontation is often detrimental to the counseling process. Once rapport has been established, then counselors may become confrontational in an attempt to assist the client in rethinking thoughts inconsistent with reality. For example, a counselor may say, "I'm confused! You say one thing but do the complete opposite, despite the consequences." This statement may lead the client toward increased self-awareness or ultimate change.

The strong therapeutic relationship that Amanda and I had established led me to comfortably employ confrontation during our sessions. During this particular session, Amanda indicated that she "magically" knew she would be fine at Jake's house. I actively confronted Amanda by posing the question, "What if he wasn't a great guy?" This confrontation was intended to help Amanda realize that she could have easily met danger at Jake's house. I continued the confrontation by suggesting Jake could have lied about his age, just as Amanda had. Together, these confrontations were aimed at bringing about awareness and behavioral change.

The ability to understand a child within the context of his or her family is of great benefit to a counselor (Vernon, 2009b). As described in Chapter 2, a family systems approach is useful in addressing communication issues between students and families. During this session, I utilized the "I" position to help Amanda become aware of how her mother might perceive her behavior. By using this strategy, I quickly determined that Amanda's relationship with her mom was currently unstable. From a family systems perspective, the apparent discord between Amanda and her mom was a great concern, one I knew would need to be addressed.

Although I used a trans-theoretical approach when working with Amanda, there are many other techniques or strategies, derived from other paradigms, useful in addressing issues related to social networking. Often an integrative approach is most effective in working with students, as suggested in Chapter 2. It is important for the school counselor to have general knowledge of each paradigm and a clear rationale for using a specific strategy. Table 43-1 provides additional strategies for addressing issues related to social networking.

## IN SESSION

Amanda appeared to experience difficulty in many areas of her life. From a developmental perspective, it was first important to acknowledge what issues were common among adolescents. Some issues are a healthy part of the process of maturing, whereas

| TABLE 43-1 | Recommended Strategies for Addressing Issues Related to Social Networking | | |
|---|---|---|---|
| Paradigm | Elementary School | Middle School | High School |
| Psychodynamic | Interpreting the reason for behavior based on dialogue, drawings, or dreams; exploring relationships between current behavior and past or current life events | Exploring relationships between current behavior and past experiences related to relationships; addressing issues related to transference | Exploring relationships between current behavior and past experiences related to relationships; addressing issues related to transference |
| Humanistic/ Existential | Demonstrating acceptance, unconditional positive regard, and a genuine interest in student's well-being and safety; role playing potential scenarios relevant to responsible and irresponsible social networking | Demonstrating acceptance, unconditional positive regard, and a genuine interest in student's well-being and safety; using role play and reverse role play to assist student in finding meaning of current behavior while encouraging responsibility | Demonstrating acceptance, unconditional positive regard, and a genuine interest in student's well-being and safety; providing decision-making models for present and future use; exploring scenarios using empty chair |
| Behavioral/CBT | Exploring thoughts and feelings related to the pattern of social networking; creating a behavior contract focused on healthy social networking; instructing parents to assist in helping student change behavior | Exploring thoughts and feelings related to the pattern of social networking; assisting client in challenging irrational beliefs; encouraging positive self-talk related to social networking | Exploring thoughts and feelings related to the pattern of social networking; presenting ABCDE model to student; encouraging student to use this framework to develop healthy thoughts related to social networking |
| Family Systems | Exploring family dynamics with a genogram; encouraging parental involvement and support; educating parents on ways they may contribute to child's behavior and exploring alternative solutions | Exploring family dynamics with a genogram; encouraging parental involvement; educating family members on ways they may contribute to child's behavior | Use "I" positions and relationship experiments to foster familial growth; encouraging parental involvement and support; educating family members on ways they may contribute to child's behavior |
| Emergent | Assisting student in developing positive social networks; assisting student in creating a story about the situation and identifying a more favorable outcome | Encouraging healthy relationships based on equal distribution of power; assisting student in developing positive social networks; organizing beliefs of self with card sort | Encouraging healthy relationships based on equal distribution of power; assisting student in developing positive social networks; using card sort to organize beliefs of self |

others may be unhealthy and in need of intervention. During mid-adolescence, it is plausible for a child Amanda's age to experience identity issues, as suggested by Erikson's model of social-emotional development (Crain, 2010). During the stage of identity versus confusion, mid-adolescents often experience opportunity and challenges, frequently leading to anxiety (Vernon, 2009b). Rebellion, delinquency, and self-doubt are not uncommon among minors.

As I was aware that Amanda struggled with significant mental health issues related to a diagnosis of a mood disorder, I also took note of her affect in this particular session. From a diagnostic perspective, during the session she appeared to exhibit several symptoms of a manic episode; however, it was unclear whether this might just be normal teenage excitement. I witnessed Amanda with what seemed like an inflated self-esteem. She appeared to be more talkative than usual and pressured to keep talking. She also was very distracted and excitable. These symptoms appeared to extend beyond what is typical of mid-adolescent behavior. I was unsure whether Amanda met the other criteria of mood disorder at this time, but remained aware of the potential due to my knowledge of her background and the relationship we had formed.

| | |
|---|---|
| Counselor (C): | That's a big smile you have on your face. |
| Student (S): | I know. I can't help it. I met someone. He is great. I am excited. . . . |
| C: | Tell me more about your excitement. |
| S: | Well, Ms. Johnson, it doesn't fit into your box. |
| | [This was an ongoing joke Amanda and I had created to emphasize the importance of self-acceptance versus peer acceptance.] |
| C: | (*Laughter*) It's OK. I think I can handle it, whatever it is. |
| S: | I met a great guy this weekend. |
| C: | Really? |
| S: | Yeah, I met him online and was talking to him. I gave him my phone number and we started texting. He is in the military and was on base; we were chatting and then he said he couldn't come this way but I could come that way and I did. I drove up there after school and met him at his place. |
| C: | So you met him on Facebook? |
| S: | No, Ms. Johnson. I told you this doesn't fit into your box. (*Laughter*) I met him on a dating website. I set up a profile and he started talking to me on there and then last night was just great. |
| C: | You met him on a dating website. . . . Can you do that at your age? |
| | [Using basic helping skills, I attempted to gather more information about Amanda's use of social networking sites.] |
| S: | Well, my profile says I am 18, not 16. |
| C: | So this guy thinks your 18? |

S: Yeah, I look older than 16 anyway. He thinks I am a senior in high school and he seemed to be OK with that. So, I went there and I met up with him. His roommate was there so it wasn't like I was all alone with him.

[During the next several exchanges, I helped Amanda process the decision she made to visit Jake without telling anyone.]

C: Well, I'm glad that someone else was there, but you didn't know either one of them. Did someone know where you were?

S: Not really. Jenna kind of knew but she didn't really know where I was going.

C: It sounds like Jenna couldn't have found you if she needed to.

S: She could have called me or texted me.

C: I'm wondering if there was the possibility for you not to have access to your phone.

S: True, it was OK though. . . . Ms. Johnson, I am here and he is great and we're still texting. He has texted me already today.

C: Did your mom or dad know where you were?

S: Definitely, not. My mom thought I was with Jenna at the mall.

C: I wonder what she would have said if you had asked her if you could go meet him.

S: She would make me delete my page! That's for sure . . . and she probably wouldn't have let me go to his place! Actually, she definitely wouldn't have let me go by myself!

[I changed the direction of the session at this point to assess what happened while Amanda was at Jake's house.]

C: Maybe we can talk more about your decision to visit with him in a bit. . . . I'd like to hear more about what happened while you were there. What did you do when you got there?

S: I didn't sleep with him, Ms. Johnson; we just made out. He likes me and I like him. He is older and he thinks I am too . . . and, I mean, I am mature for my age.

C: He is older and thinks you are too.

S: Yeah, he is 23. I think he is closer to your age than mine. (*Laughter*)

C: Was he who you thought he would be?

[I returned to Amanda's thoughts related to meeting Jake.]

S: Yeah, he's older, mature, has goals, a job, and knows how to use a gun. (*Laughter*)

C: Some of those are good things if you're at that place in your life; do you think you are really looking for someone who has settled down?

S: Yeah, I mean I am that kind of person anyway, and I am tired of all this high school stuff.

C:  So, what were you thinking on the way up there?

S:  I was just excited. I mean he must have thought I was cute if he started talking to me on the website.

C:  Did you ever question whether it was safe or not?

S:  Not really. I knew I would be fine. He is in the military; he wouldn't take advantage of me . . . he would get in trouble!

[I used confrontation in the next exchanges to challenge Amanda's thought that meeting Jake "would be fine."]

C:  What if he wasn't a "great guy"? You had lied about your age; do you think it's possible that he could have lied about his age, his profession, or his character?

S:  I would have left or called Jenna. But he didn't lie! He really is a great guy and, I mean, he is obviously in the military and they have to have some kind of character.

C:  That easy?

S:  I think so, Ms. Johnson! Aren't you excited for me . . . this means I'm over Kendra. This is good. I finally am moving on to something different and dating a guy . . . a good guy!

C:  I am glad to see you moving on. I just want to make sure you are making safe decisions and are happy with the choices you are making, whether it fits in my box or not.

[I conclude the session by supporting Amanda in her efforts to move on from a past relationship, while encouraging decisions that lead to safety and happiness.]

S:  Thanks, Ms. Johnson. I know!

## Outcome

School counselors are often faced with complex and multidimensional situations, and this case scenario of Amanda's use of social networking sites is no exception. Although Amanda's experiences related to social networking are at the forefront of this counseling session, there are clearly other precipitating issues that are of concern. Amanda's struggles with a mood disorder, a recent breakup, identity issues, and common developmental issues may influence her social networking decisions. To best understand and help students, school counselors must take into account the whole student and not simply isolated incidents. In this case scenario, I was aware of Amanda's social-emotional history as a result of our preestablished counseling relationship.

As I considered all aspects of Amanda's life, multiple outcomes emerged from this session.

In a follow-up session, Amanda and I explored the nature of social networking. I informed Amanda about healthy and unhealthy social networking practices. Amanda learned strategies for safe use of the Internet and the dangers of releasing personal information online. We also completed several activities exploring the misconceptions and vulnerabilities of social networking.

Due to the potential for Amanda to perhaps be experiencing symptoms related to a manic episode, I encouraged her and her mother to schedule an appointment with the therapist at a nearby practice. With her mom's permission, I also consulted with the therapist on several occasions, addressing concerns related to Amanda's mental health. The therapist and I collaborated on Amanda's treatment and explored avenues for positive parental, social, and school involvement.

I did have legal and ethical concerns related to the intimate nature of Amanda's encounter with Jake. Because Amanda was only 16 and Jake was 23, I questioned what legal action, if any, should be taken. I was also unsure of my ethical obligations in this matter. As a result, I consulted with several other professionals to determine what I should do. The resource officer assigned to the school, the school's lead counselor, and the Director of Student Services provided valuable insight. As a team, we were able to navigate the laws in my state as well as the *Ethical Standards for School Counselors* (American School Counselor Association [ASCA], 2010). The resource officer advised the team that legal recourse did not appear to be an option. Several factors, including Amanda's age and the nature of the interaction (consensual and nonsexual), ultimately led the team members to agree with the resource officer's judgment.

As a school counselor, I considered my ethical obligation to Amanda. Out of my concern for Amanda's well-being, I wanted to ensure that her social-emotional needs were met and that she had a support network in place. I expressed these concerns to Amanda's mother and the therapist, and both indicated they would address the risky behavior and monitor Amanda's mental health. After reviewing the decision-making model, Solutions to Ethical Problems in Schools (STEPS; Stone, 2009), recommended by ASCA (2010), the lead school counselor and I were confident the team had taken the appropriate course of action.

Amanda and I continued our counseling relationship until her graduation. I would often "check in" with Amanda to monitor her overall well-being and get updates on recent events in her life. Several other issues arose during that time; however, Amanda was able to work through each of them with the support of her therapist, her mother, and me. I also maintained communication and encouraged collaboration with Amanda's mother and the therapist. Providing Amanda with appropriate supports appeared vital to her success and well-being. As the school counselor, I provided Amanda with a safe environment to vent her frustrations, problem solve, and grow. Amanda knew that she could count on me to be there for her unconditionally, "whether she fit into my box or not!"

## Final Process Questions

- Did I respond appropriately to Amanda's needs? Would you have responded differently?
- Were the legal and ethical concerns adequately addressed in this case scenario?
- Were there multicultural issues impacting this case scenario that I should have explored?

- In what ways can school counselors promote the responsible use of technology among K through 12 students?
- What counseling strategies or techniques might have been useful when working with Amanda?

## Resources

Bauman, S., & Tatum, T. (2009). Websites for young children: Gateway to online social networking? *Professional School Counseling, 13*, 1–7.

Burrow-Sanchez, J., Call, M., Zheng, R., & Dew, C. (2011). How school counselors can help prevent online victimization. *Journal of Counseling & Development, 89*, 3–10.

Ybarra, M. L., & Mitchell, K. J. (2008). How risky are social networking sites: A comparison of places online where youth sexual solicitation and harassment occurs. *Pediatrics, 121*, e350–e357. doi:10.1542/peds.2007-0693

*Chapter 44*

# FERPA Issues in School Counseling

Charlotte Daughhetee and James Jackson

## CASE BACKGROUND

Tim was a fifth-grade student at a small rural elementary school. The local community was very involved in the school and, like most small towns, everyone knew everyone else's business. Tim's parents, Jack and Sue, divorced when Tim was 3 years old. Jack and Sue were awarded joint custody, and Tim saw his father every other weekend until he was 4 years old. Just after Tim's fourth birthday, Jack was sentenced to 20 years in prison for drug trafficking. After Jack was imprisoned, his contact with Tim was limited to sending the occasional card or letter. However, Tim did continue to visit with his paternal grandparents, who kept Jack abreast of how Tim was doing.

When Tim was enrolled in kindergarten, the school did not ask for a copy of the custody agreement because everyone knew his father, Jack, was in jail and assumed he was out of the picture. During Tim's kindergarten year, Sue, Tim's mother, remarried. It was generally understood that the community was very happy that Tim now had a father figure, Ben, in his life.

Ben was a very involved stepfather and a positive influence in Tim's life. Ben was one of the coaches of Tim's little league basketball team and was always present at Tim's school events. Ben and Sue had a child together, and Ben continued to treat Tim as his own son. Although Ben wanted to adopt Tim, no action was taken due to concerns about Jack's likely unwillingness to relinquish his parental rights. Even though Ben hadn't officially adopted Tim, they both felt as though they were truly father and son, and by second grade, Tim began signing his school papers with Ben's last name. Although Tim's surname was still legally the same as Jack's, teachers overlooked the matter because everyone thought of Ben as Tim's "real" dad.

When Tim was in fifth grade, Jack entered the school's main office on a teacher workday when no children were present and identified himself as Tim's biological father. A combination of prison overcrowding and good behavior on Jack's part had led to his early release from prison. Jack wanted to meet with Tim's teacher and review Tim's school records. The principal called the school counselor and laid out the situation: "What do we do? Tim's mother won't want him to see Tim's information. Jack is an ex-con—does he even have a right to view Tim's school records?" Having no documentation regarding the custody agreement, the school had no reason to believe that Jack's rights as Tim's biological father had been terminated.

## INITIAL PROCESS QUESTIONS

- Does Jack have a right to view his son's educational records?
- Because it is recommended that schools obtain a copy of custody agreements, why do you think Tim's school failed to ask for copies of these documents?
- What might be the fallout if the school refuses to show Jack his son's records?
- What might be the fallout if the school does show Jack the records?
- Does Ben have a right to view Tim's educational records?
- What effect might Jack's return have on Tim?

## ADDRESSING THE LEGAL ISSUES

A common concern among school counselors is how to address situations in which noncustodial parents request access to a student's educational records (Bodenhorn, 2006). The federal legislation that addresses the disclosure and accessibility of student educational records is the Family Educational Rights and Privacy Act of 1974 (FERPA, 1974), also known as the Buckley Amendment. The American School Counselor Association's *Ethical Standards for School Counselors* (2010) reference FERPA in section A.8.e dealing with counselors' responsibilities in regard to student records. ASCA standards state that counselors must "understand and abide by the Family Educational Rights and Privacy Act (FERPA, 1974), which safeguards student's records and allows parents to have a voice in what and how information is shared with others regarding their child's educational records" (ASCA, 2010).

FERPA provides rights equally to custodial and noncustodial parents concerning the educational records of their children, unless evidence of a state law or court order specifically revoking these rights is provided to the school. In the absence of such a legal document, both custodial and noncustodial parents must be permitted access to their children's educational records. It should be noted that although parents can grant authorization for others to view their child's educational records by simply providing a letter to this effect to the school, parents cannot rescind the rights of others through the same means. For example, the custodial parent cannot legally control the rights of the noncustodial parent to view his or her child's educational records (*Page v. Rotterdam-Mohonasen Central School District*, 1981). If a legal decree is issued (e.g., a legally binding document such as a court order or state statute) that specifically revokes a person's reviewing rights of student records, parents are responsible for providing the school with that documentation in order for those rights to be revoked.

An important point regarding the FERPA legislation is the criteria by which a person may be considered as serving in the capacity of a parent. Under FERPA, a parent includes a biological parent, a legal guardian, and "an individual acting as a parent in the absence of a parent or a guardian." According to 34 CFR § 99.3, "Parent" means a parent of a student and includes a natural parent, a guardian, or an individual acting as a parent in the absence of a parent or a guardian (Authority: 20 U.S.C. 1232g). The Department of Education considers a person who is the age of majority and is providing care and supervision of the child on a day-to-day basis to be "acting as a parent." Once a parent has requested to review his or her child's educational record, FERPA mandates that the school must comply with the request within 45 days (20 U.S.C. §1232g(a)(1)(A)). Remley and Huey (2002) recommended that, when dealing with legal issues with parents or guardians, school counselors should either refer the parent or legal guardian to the school principal or consult with the principal on how to resolve the concern.

## IN SESSION

After a quick consultation between the school counselor and the principal, it was agreed that Jack had the right to view Tim's records. The teacher was nervous about meeting with Jack and asked whether the school counselor could be present; the counselor agreed and the three met to review Tim's school records and current grades. Jack exhibited a great deal of pride at his son's honor roll awards and was interested in hearing about whether or not his son had friends and how his son was doing in basketball. The teacher began to relax. After all, this was just another interested parent wanting to hear about school progress, and because Tim was a good student, well liked and was not a discipline problem, there was plenty of good news to share.

Only one glitch occurred. When showing Jack the current folder of Tim's most recent work, the father bristled at the fact that Tim was signing Ben's last name.

| | |
|---|---|
| COUNSELOR (C): | It's difficult for you to find out that Tim is not signing your name. |
| JACK (J): | Yes, I love the little guy and he was what kept me going all these years in prison. I know I haven't been there for him, but he was there for me every day in my thoughts. I lived to get letters from my mom about what he was doing. (*Jack begins to cry*) |
| | [After a few minutes of silence . . .] |
| C: | It hurts that you haven't been able to have Tim in your life for the past 6 years, but you've had him in your thoughts and wanted so many good things for him. He's doing really well. You can be very proud of him. |
| J: | I know I should be happy that he's had someone there for him, and maybe I'll be able to be happy about that someday. But for now it hurts to see Ben's name and not mine on those papers. Do you think Sue will let me see Tim? |
| C: | That is something you and your ex-wife will have to work out, but it seems that seeing how he's doing was very meaningful for you today. |

## Outcome

Sue was not happy that her ex-husband had come to the school, but after checking with her lawyer, she admitted that there was nothing legally that could prevent him from having a parent–teacher conference. This case scenario points out two major issues. First, noncustodial parents have a right to view the educational records of their children, and unless there is some type of court documentation forbidding it, the noncustodial parent must be accommodated. Second, the school was remiss in not requesting copies of the custodial agreement. It was a small town and everyone "knew everyone else's business" so they didn't ask for documentation. Everyone at the school assumed that Tim's father would be out of the picture for another 14 years; therefore, no one considered the documentation necessary. Remember, *never* make assumptions and *always* get the necessary documentation.

## Final Process Questions

- What concerns on the part of the teacher might have motivated the request for the school counselor to participate in the meeting?
- What do you think of how the counselor addressed Jack's reaction to seeing his son signing the stepfather's last name? Would you have done anything differently?
- Would it be appropriate for the school to keep Jack informed of and involved with Tim's educa-

tional activities in the future? If so, what steps would be appropriate for the school to take to encourage Jack's ongoing participation?
- Assuming Jack continues to be involved in Tim's education, what situations might require special planning to minimize the potential for conflict among the parents and/or school?

## Resources

American School Counselor Association. (ASCA). (2010). *Ethical standards for school counselors.* Retrieved from http://www.schoolcounselor.org/files/EthicalStandards2010.pdf

Murphy, D., & Dishman, M. (2010). *Educational records: A practical guide for legal compliance.* Lanham, MD: Rowland & Littlefield.

U.S. Department of Education, *Family Educational Rights and Privacy Act (FERPA)*, http://www2.ed.gov/policy/gen/guid/fpco/ferpa/index.html

Williams, R. (2010). *HIPPAA or FERPA or not?* Retrieved from http://www.ascaschoolcounselor.org/article_content.asp?edition=91&section=140&article=1159

## Chapter 45

# Confidentiality With Minors

KATIE LIEBERS

## CASE BACKGROUND

I had just begun my first school counseling job in a middle school when I started meeting with Hannah. Hannah would frequently come to my office to talk about frustrations she was experiencing at home, where she lived with her father and stepmother. Hannah's biological mother had left a year earlier and moved 12 hours away to another state with Hannah's older sister, Mary. Not only did Hannah's mother leave her behind when she moved, but she did not even tell Hannah she was moving, nor did she say good-bye. Hannah often spoke to me about her conflicting emotions regarding her mother; one part of Hannah was very angry at her mother for abandoning her, but the other part missed her mother and sister terribly. Hannah desperately wanted to talk to her mother; there were several questions she needed answered in order to resolve the emotional conflict she was experiencing. For instance, Hannah stated that she wanted to ask her mother, "Why did you leave me behind? Why did you take Mary with you and not me? Are you coming back? Will I get to see you again? Did I do something wrong?" What was most frustrating to Hannah was that she knew her mother had frequently tried to contact her, but her father, trying to protect Hannah from getting hurt again, refused to let them talk.

Most of my sessions with Hannah revolved around her frustrations with her father's forbidding her to talk to her mother or sister. One afternoon, Hannah came down to my office clearly upset and agitated. When I vocalized this observation, Hannah's eyes filled with tears and she said, "Yeah, I've had a terrible week. My dad said he is going to call you and see what I have been saying to you. He said you have to tell him everything, and I really don't want him to know that I miss my mom. He already grounded me because my mom messaged me on Facebook, and I wrote her back and told her that I missed her and wanted her to come back. If you tell my dad that I talk to you about my mom and Mary, he will be so mad at me." I asked Hannah whether she remembered our discussion about confidentiality from our very first session. She shrugged her shoulders and said, "I remember talking about that, but I don't really remember exactly what you said." I reminded Hannah that part of my job is to help parents understand the importance of honoring students' confidentiality. I further explained that I am required to break confidentiality only in instances of child abuse, or if she was at risk for harming herself or others. Hannah was immediately relieved that none of the things she has told me fell into these categories. After this interaction, I realized that Hannah's not being able to recall information related to confidentiality, demonstrates the importance of reminding clients of the exceptions to confidentiality throughout counseling. As counselors, we should not tell students these exceptions only at the beginning of the relationship and expect them to remember this important information. We must remind students, especially when we feel they might be about to reveal something that would require a break in confidentiality.

## INITIAL PROCESS QUESTIONS

As school counselors, we are frequently confronted by other people that want to know what a student discusses during counseling. School counselors should be prepared to appropriately respond to these requests from not only parents but also teachers, administrators, and outside counseling agencies. In these situations, here are some questions to consider:

- What do the ethical codes say about confidentiality and minor clients?
- What is my legal responsibility in regard to protecting the confidentiality of minor clients?
- What are the ethical responsibilities to my client?
- What are my legal responsibilities to parents or guardians?
- If subpoenaed to court, what are the laws in my state about privileged communication for school counselors?
- How can I validate the concerns of the parent, while also advocating for the rights of the student?

## ADDRESSING THE ISSUES

For school counselors, navigating between students' rights to confidentiality and the legal rights of parents can be confusing and frustrating. School counselors are ethically obligated to maintain minor clients' confidentiality. Yet this obligation often conflicts with laws that state parents have the right to information regarding treatment for their children (Glosoff & Pate, 2002). Though the ethical codes and the law are in agreement that confidentiality must be broken in cases of child abuse or when harm to self or others is suspected, there is much ambiguity as to what school counselors should do when parents demand to know what their child has said in counseling (Mitchell, Disque, & Robertson, 2002). Even the *Ethical Standards for School Counselors* of the American School Counselor Association (ASCA; 2010) can cause confusion regarding confidentiality for minors. For instance, code A.2.d. states:

> Professional school counselors: . . . Recognize their primary obligation for confidentiality is to the students but balance that obligation with an understanding of parents'/guardians' legal and inherent rights to be the guiding voice in their children's lives, especially in value-laden issues. Understand the need to balance students' ethical rights to make choices, their capacity to give consent or assent and parental or familial legal rights and responsibilities to protect these students and make decisions on their behalf. (p. 2)

Thus, school counselors face the difficult task of protecting the confidentiality of students while also making reasonable efforts to honor the legal requirements to, and wishes of, parents. Courts continue to assert parents' legal ability to make decisions governing their children. If parents request disclosure of information their child reveals in counseling, they likely have the legal right to this information (Huey & Remley, 1988). Fortunately, there are several things school counselors can do to fulfill parents' wishes without breaking confidentiality and losing the trust of the student.

First, parents/guardians need to have their feelings validated. When school counselors are approached by concerned parents, they should begin by building rapport and using empathic listening skills (Mitchell et al., 2002). Often, when parents feel validated, the problem will diffuse and the counselor will no longer be faced with a dilemma.

Another option for school counselors when faced with demanding parents is to help the parents see the positives of the situation instead of the negatives. For instance, school counselors should help parents recognize that their child is demonstrating great autonomy, maturity, and independence by seeking adult help when faced with a problem. Communicate to parents that they have clearly done a great job at instilling these values in their child. Sometimes parents need to be reminded that counseling services are designed to help and support their child, not to keep secrets from the parents.

Last, some parents do not understand how counseling works and simply need to be educated about the role confidentiality plays in counseling. For instance, the school counselor should explain the importance of providing a safe, trusting environment for students. If students do not believe that they can trust the counselor, they will likely choose not to share or even use counseling services at all. Additionally, school counselors should explain what the laws and ethical codes state about when confidentiality must be broken (Mitchell at al., 2002). Some parents are relieved to know that they will be notified if their child is in danger, which helps them feel more comfortable with the counseling process.

Through my work with Hannah, I integrated strategies from the humanistic/existential and family systems paradigms. Person-centered strategies were essential in developing trust in the counseling relationship. Hannah rarely had her feelings validated by an adult; my demonstration of empathy, genuineness, and unconditional positive regard allowed her to openly express her feelings and concerns.

The next step I took with Hannah was further exploring her family dynamics to help both of us gain a greater understanding of the presenting issues. Through this exploration, Hannah reported that though she misses her mother terribly, she prefers living with her father because he provides a loving, stable home that her mother could not offer. I believed it would greatly benefit both Hannah and her father if she would share this realization with him. My conversation with Mr. Johnson showed me that he was likely unaware of Hannah's love and appreciation for him, as he seemed overwhelmingly concerned with her missing her mother. Through role play activities, I helped Hannah prepare for discussing her feelings with her father. Role playing not only helped Hannah explore and verbalize her feelings, but she also reported feeling less anxious about talking to her father face-to-face. Encouraging Hannah to discuss her feelings with her father was not only therapeutic for her, but it also allowed me to maintain Hannah's confidentiality, therefore preserving trust within the counseling relationship.

School counselors may not only refer to theories and techniques through work with students but may demonstrate them with parents as well. During my initial telephone conversation with Mr. Johnson, I referred to the basic principles of the person-centered approach. By demonstrating active listening, empathy, and unconditional positive regard, my goal was to show Mr. Johnson that I understood his frustrations and concerns. Additionally, I used a technique from the family systems paradigm when I tried to help Mr. Johnson understand that Hannah's seeking support outside of the family suggests great independence and maturity that is appropriate for adolescents. There are several other techniques from each of the paradigms that could be used to address issues related to confidentiality. Table 45-1 outlines additional strategies for working with issues of privacy and confidentiality across all school levels.

**TABLE 45-1   Recommended Strategies for Addressing Issues Related to Privacy and Confidentiality for Minor Students**

| Paradigm | Elementary School | Middle School | High School |
|---|---|---|---|
| Psychodynamic | Adlerian play therapy to discover and assess child's logic and lifestyle; exploring how student's past experiences affect current behavior; exploring behaviors through drawings or dream analysis; teaching parents techniques for encouraging child/adolescent; implementing Adlerian family counseling to assist family in operating cooperatively; exploring family constellation and atmosphere | Exploring how student's past experiences affect current behavior; analyzing student's familial relationships throughout childhood; exploring student's perception of the ideal situation by acting "as if"; teaching parents techniques for encouraging child/adolescent; implementing Adlerian family counseling to assist family in operating cooperatively; exploring family constellation and atmosphere | Exploring how student's past experiences affect current behavior; analyzing student's familial relationships throughout childhood; exploring student's perception of the ideal situation by acting "as if"; helping student accept and demonstrate responsibility for life choices; teaching parents techniques for encouraging child/adolescent; implementing Adlerian family counseling to assist family in operating cooperatively; exploring family constellation and atmosphere |
| Humanistic/ Existential | Validating student's concerns through empathy, active listening, and unconditional positive regard; through play therapy, having student play out feelings relating to confidentiality/privacy, instead of talking about them; using puppets to act out and express any familial issues; teaching parents to use esteem-building activities with child/adolescent; working directly with parents to explore and validate feelings/thoughts | Validating student's concerns through empathy, active listening, and unconditional positive regard; using role-play scenarios to allow student to practice sharing problems or concerns with parents; providing opportunities for safe exploration of feelings and thoughts surrounding privacy and confidentiality; teaching parents to use esteem-building activities with child/adolescent; working directly with parents to explore and validate feelings/thoughts | Validating student's concerns through empathy, active listening, and unconditional positive regard; providing opportunities for safe exploration of feelings and thoughts surrounding privacy and confidentiality; exploring feelings and practicing appropriate communication through empty chair technique; teaching parents to use esteem-building activities with child/adolescent; working directly with parents to explore and validate feelings/thoughts |

| Paradigm | Elementary School | Middle School | High School |
|---|---|---|---|
| Behavioral/CBT | Exploring and analyzing student's shoulds, oughts, musts, catastrophizing, and awfulizing relevant to privacy and confidentiality; assessing irrational beliefs through drawing, role playing, puppets, or sentence completion; teaching parents about common irrational beliefs of children and parents surrounding familial communication and privacy | Exploring and analyzing student's shoulds, oughts, musts, catastrophizing, and awfulizing relevant to privacy and confidentiality; encouraging journaling about feelings or thoughts; teaching parents about common irrational beliefs of children and parents surrounding familial communication and privacy | Exploring and analyzing student's shoulds, oughts, musts, catastrophizing, and awfulizing relevant to privacy and confidentiality; teaching about choice theory and helping student make list of choices made that have contributed to current situation or beliefs about situation; teaching parents about common irrational beliefs of children and parents surrounding familial communication and privacy |
| Family Systems | Assisting student in discussing feelings with parents; trying to learn what values are important to student's family; developing a genogram to further explore family dynamics; helping parents recognize and avoid harmful communication patterns; emphasizing family and individual family member strengths | Assisting student in discussing feelings with parents; trying to learn what values are important to student's family; developing a genogram to further explore family dynamics; helping parents understand changing parent–child relationships and need for independence that comes with adolescence; helping parents recognize and avoid harmful communication patterns; emphasizing family and individual family member strengths | Assisting student in discussing feelings with parents; trying to learn what values are important to student's family; developing a genogram to further explore family dynamics; helping parents understand changing parent–child relationships and need for independence that comes with adolescence; helping parents recognize and avoid harmful communication patterns; emphasizing family and individual family member strengths |
| Emergent | Helping student deconstruct current problem-focused story and encouraging her to rewrite a new story that is strength based; using empowerment to help decrease student's feelings of helplessness; working on appropriate communication skills; empowering parents to re-author a more successful story surrounding relationship with child/adolescent | Helping student deconstruct current problem-focused story and encouraging her to rewrite a new story that is strength based; using empowerment to help decrease student's feelings of helplessness; working on appropriate communication skills; empowering parents to re-author a more successful story surrounding relationship with child/adolescent | Helping student deconstruct current problem-focused story and encouraging her to rewrite a new story that is strength based; using empowerment to help decrease student's feelings of helplessness; working on appropriate communication skills; empowering parents to re-author a more successful story surrounding relationship with child/adolescent |

## IN SESSION

As mentioned, and as Hannah promised, her father called me later that day. What follows is a conversation with Mr. Johnson, Hannah's father:

| | |
|---|---|
| Mr. Johnson (J): | Hello. This is Hannah Johnson's father. Hannah told me that she has been coming to talk to you. I need you to tell me everything she has said to you. |
| Counselor (C): | Mr. Johnson, confidentiality is very important in counseling. It ensures that our students feel they have a safe place to turn when they have a problem. However, there are exceptions to confidentiality that I would like to bring to your attention. Legally, I am required to break confidentiality in cases of child abuse. Or if I believe Hannah is a threat to herself or someone else, I would notify you immediately. I want to assure you that Hannah has never expressed anything of concern; if this were to ever change, I would absolutely contact you. |
| J: | Well, I *am* concerned! I have a lawyer and I know my rights. I know that you have to tell me everything she says because I never gave you permission to talk to my daughter in the first place! Why have you been talking to my daughter without my permission? |
| C: | I understand your frustration, Mr. Johnson. Counseling is a regular educational service provided by the school, available for all students. However, you do have the option to request that Hannah not receive counseling services. |
| J: | If you aren't going to tell me what she says, then I don't want you talking to my daughter! |
| C: | Mr. Johnson, I understand that it must be frustrating that Hannah is talking to someone else when you clearly care very much about her. However, this really shows that you have instilled in Hannah the importance of seeking help from an adult when she is in need of support and/or assistance. The fact that Hannah sought counseling services on her own demonstrates great maturity and independence. |
| J: | That may be so, but I don't want her talking to you or any of the counselors there until I talk to my lawyer! |

## Outcome

Hannah's father was very angry at first when I did not reveal what Hannah had discussed with me. After our conversation, he immediately contacted the school principal and the director of schools. Though Mr. Johnson threatened a lawsuit, both the principal and the director reiterated what I had told Mr. Johnson and emphasized the importance of confidentiality in maintaining trust in the counseling relationship. Later that week, a representative from the school system's central office came to speak with me about the incident with Mr. Johnson. She wanted to confirm that Hannah had not told me anything indicating harm to self or others that would need to be relayed to Mr. Johnson, and I assured her that Hannah hadn't. During our conversation, I explained the importance of protecting students' confidentiality in developing and maintaining a trusting relationship. If students do not feel they are in a safe, trusting relationship, they will not be likely to seek support through counseling services. The representative from central office was extremely understand-

ing and validated that we acted in the best interest of the student. As school counselors, it is important to educate not only parents about the importance of confidentiality but also teachers, administrators, and other stakeholders.

A week after our first telephone conversation, Mr. Johnson came to the school to apologize to the principal and me. He also requested that Hannah continue to meet with me because he wanted for her to have a safe place to go when she was feeling upset. Mr. Johnson said he realized that Hannah feels very comfortable talking to me about her problems, and he wanted her to have another adult in her life that she trusted.

## Final Process Questions

- How can I make parents aware of the importance of confidentiality in counseling before a situation like this happens?
- As a school counselor, how could I have facilitated better communication between Hannah and her father?

- How could I have encouraged Hannah to talk to her father about her feelings regarding missing her mom?
- Are there differences in how school counselors should define "harm to self" based on the age of the student?

## Resources

American School Counselor Association. (ASCA). (2010). *Ethical standards for school counselors.* Retrieved from http://www.schoolcounselor.org/files/EthicalStandards2010.pdf

Glosoff, H. L., & Pate, R. H. (2002). Privacy and confidentiality in school counseling. *Professional School Counseling, 6,* 20–27.

Huey, W. C., & Remley, T. P., Jr. (1988). *Ethical and legal issues in school counseling.* Alexandria, VA: American School Counselor Association.

Isaacs, M. L., & Stone, C. (1999). School counselors and confidentiality: Factors affecting professional choices. *Professional School Counseling, 2,* 258–266.

Melton, B. (2008). *What parents need to know about confidentiality.* Alexandria, VA: American School Counselor Association.

Mitchell, C. W., Disque, J. G., & Robertson, P. (2002). When parents want to know: Responding to parental demands for confidential information. *Professional School Counseling, 6,* 156–161.

Remley, T. P., Jr., & Huey, W. C. (2002). An ethics quiz for school counselors. *Professional School Counseling, 6,* 3–11.

Stone, C. (2009). *School counseling principles: Ethics and law* (2nd ed.). Alexandria, VA: American School Counselor Association.

# REFERENCES

Abrams, K., Theberge, S. K., & Karan, O. C. (2005). Children and adolescents who are depressed: An ecological approach. *Professional School Counseling, 8*, 284–292.

American Counseling Association (2005). *ACA code of ethics*. Retrieved from http://www.counseling.org/resources/codeofethics/TP/home/ct2.aspx

American Psychiatric Association (APA). (2013). *Diagnostic and statistical manual of mental disorders* (5th ed.). Washington, DC: Author.

American School Counselor Association (ASCA). (2007). *The professional school counselor and LGBTQ youth*. Retrieved from http://asca2.timberlakepublishing.com/files/ PS_LGBTQ.pdf

American School Counselor Association (ASCA). (2010). *Ethical standards for school counselors*. Retrieved from http://www.schoolcounselor.org/files/EthicalStandards2010.pdf

American School Counselor Association (ASCA). (2012). *The ASCA national model: A framework for school counseling programs* (3rd ed.). Alexandria, VA: Author.

Anderson, H. (1993). On a roller coaster: A collaborative language systems approach to therapy. In S. Friedman (Ed.), *The new language of change: Constructive collaboration in psychotherapy* (pp. 323–344). New York, NY: Guilford.

Arredondo, P., Toporek, M. S., Brown, S., Jones, S., Locke, D. C., Sanchez, J., & Stadler, H. (1996). *AMCD multicultural competencies*. Retrieved from http://www.counseling.org/resources/competencies/multcultural_competencies. pdf

Baker, L. R., & Oswald, D. L. (2010). Shyness and online social networking services. *Journal of Social and Personal Relationships, 27*, 873–889. doi: 10.1177/0265407510375261

Banning, J. H. (1989). *Ecotherapy: A life space application of the ecological perspective*. Retrieved from http://www.campusecologist.com/1989/01/05/volume-7-number- 3-1989/

Barrow, E. C. (2011). *The role of professional school counselors in working with students in gangs: A grounded theory study* (Doctoral dissertation). Available from ProQuest Dissertations and Theses database. (UMI No. 3497190)

Bartholomew, C. (2003). *Gender-sensitive therapy: Principles and practices*. Prospect Heights, IL: Waveland Press.

Bem, S. L. (1981). *Bem Sex-Role Inventory: Professional manual*. Palo Alto, CA: Consulting Psychologists Press.

Berg, I. K., & Miller, S. (1992). *Working with the problem drinker*. New York, NY: Norton.

Berk, L. E. (Ed.). (2007). *Development through the lifespan* (4th ed.). New York, NY: Pearson.

Bernes, K. B., & Bardick, A. D. (2007). Conducting adolescent violence risk assessments: A framework for school counselors. *Professional School Counseling, 10*, 419–427.

Black, J., & Underwood, J. (1998). Young, female, and gay: Lesbian students and the school environment. *Professional School Counseling, 1*, 15–21.

Blanco, J. (2010). *Please stop laughing at me*. Avon, MA: Adams Media.

Blanco, J. (2012). *It's NOT just joking around™ seminar*. Retrieved from http://www.jodeeblanco.com/seminars.htm

Bodenhom, N. (2006). Exploratory study of common and challenging ethical dilemmas experienced by professional school counselors. *Professional School Counseling, 10*, 195–202.

Bowen, M. (1966). The use of family theory in clinical practice. *Comprehensive Psychiatry, 7*, 345–374.

Bowen, M. (1976). Theory in the practice of psychotherapy. In P. J. Guerin (Ed.), *Family therapy: Theory and practice* (pp. 42–90). New York, NY: Gardner Press.

Bradley, L. J., Parr, G., & Gould, L. J. (1999). Counseling and psychotherapy: An integrative perspective. In D. Capuzzi & D. R. Gross (Eds.), *Counseling and psychotherapy: Theories and interventions* (pp. 345–379). Upper Saddle River, NJ: Prentice Hall.

Broderick, P. C., & Blewitt, P. (2010). *The life span: Human development for helping professionals* (3rd ed.). Upper Saddle River, NJ: Pearson Merrill/Prentice Hall.

Bronfenbrenner, U. (1979). *The ecology of human development*. Cambridge, MA: Harvard University Press.

Buffardi, L. E., & Campbell, W. E. (2008). Narcissism and social networking web sites. *Personality and Social Psychology Bulletin, 34*, 1303–1314. doi: 10.1177/0146167208320061

Byrd, R., & Hays, D. (2012). School counselor competency and lesbian, gay, bisexual, transgender, and questioning (LGBTQ) youth. *Journal of School Counseling, 10*(3). Retrieved from http://jsc.montana.edu/articles/v10n3.pdf

Callahan, C. J. (2001). Protecting and counseling gay and lesbian students. *Journal of Humanistic Counseling, Education and Development, 40*(1), 5–11.

Callahan, R. M. (2005). Tracking and high school English learners: Limiting opportunity to learn. *American Educational Research Journal, 42*, 305–328.

Cass, V. C. (1979). Homosexual identity formation: A theoretical model. *Journal of Homosexuality, 4*, 219–235.

Centers for Disease Control and Prevention. (2010, June 4). Youth risk behavior surveillance—United States 2009. CDC Surveillance Summaries. *Morbidity and Mortality Weekly Report, 59*(SS-5), 1–148.

Chang, C. Y., & Gnilka, P. (2014). Social advocacy: The fifth force in counseling. In D. G. Hays & B. T. Erford (Eds.), *Developing multicultural counseling competency: A systems approach* (2nd ed., pp. 53–71). Columbus, OH: Pearson Merrill.

Chang, V. N., Scott, S. T., & Decker, C. L. (2009). *Developing helping skills: A step-by-step approach*. Belmont, CA: Brooks/Cole.

Chester, A., & Bretherton, D. (2001). What makes feminist counseling feminist? *Feminism & Psychology, 11*, 527–545.

Chodron, T. (1990). *Open heart, clear mind*. Ithaca, NY: Snow Lion.

Conners, C. K. (2008). *Manual for the Conners 3*. North Tonawanda, NY: Multi-Health Systems.

Corey, G. (2012). *Theory and practice of counseling and psychotherapy* (9th ed.). Belmont, CA: Brooks/Cole Cengage.

Cottone, R. R. (1992). *Theories and paradigms of counseling and psychotherapy*. Boston, MA: Allyn & Bacon.

Counselors for Social Justice. (2011). *What is social justice in counseling?* Retrieved from http://counselorsforsocial justice.com/

Covey, S. (1998). *The seven habits of highly effective teens*. New York, NY: Fireside.

Crain, W. (2010). *Theories of development: Concepts and applications* (6th ed.). Upper Saddle River, NJ: Prentice Hall.

D'Augelli, A. R., Grossman, A. H., & Starks, M. T. (2006). Childhood gender atypicality, victimization, and PTSD among lesbian, gay, and bisexual youth. *Journal of Interpersonal Violence, 21*, 1462–1482. doi: 10.1177/0886260506293482

Davis, K. (2011). Students with severe acting out behavior: A family intervention approach. In C. A. Sink (Ed.), *Mental health issues for school counselors* (pp. 123–134). Florence, KY: Brooks/Cole Cengage.

de Shazer, S. (1988). *Clues: Investigating solutions in brief therapy*. New York, NY: Norton.

de Shazer, S. (1991). *Putting difference to work*. New York, NY: Norton.

DeVoss, J. A., & Andrews, M. F. (2006). *School counselors as educational leaders*. Boston, MA: Houghton Mifflin.

Dougherty, A. M. (2009). *Psychological consultation and collaboration in school and community settings* (5th ed.). Belmont, CA: Brooks/Cole.

Dowling, E. (2008). *English language learners and special education issues*. Retrieved from http://www.planesllessons.com/2008/12/english-language-learners-and-special-education-issues/

Dryden, W. (2009a). *Rational emotive behavior therapy: Distinctive features*. New York, NY: Routledge.

Dryden, W. (2009b). *How to think and intervene like an REBT therapist*. New York, NY: Routledge.

Dryden, W., & Neenan, M. (2006). *Rational emotive behaviour therapy: 100 key points and techniques*. New York, NY: Routledge.

Duany, J. A. (2001). *Believers together with glad and sincere hearts: Special needs of Sudanese girls*. Retrieved from http://southsudanfriends.org/specialneeds.html

Dutton, D. G., & Starzomski, A. J. (1997). Personality predictors of the Minnesota Power and Control Wheel. *Journal of Interpersonal Violence, 12*, 70–82.

Ellis, A. (1996). *Better, deeper, and more enduring brief therapy: The rational emotive behavior therapy approach*. New York, NY: Brunner/Mazel.

Ellis, A. (2005). *The myth of self-esteem: How rational emotive behavior therapy can change your life forever*. Amherst, NY: Prometheus Books.

Ellis, A. (2007). *Overcoming resistance: A rational emotive behavior therapy integrated approach* (2nd ed.). New York, NY: Springer.

Ellis, A. (n.d.). *Emotional disturbance and its treatment in a nutshell*. New York, NY: Albert Ellis Institute.

Ellis, A., & MacLaren, C. (2005). *Rational emotive behavior therapy: A therapist's guide* (2nd ed.). Atascadero, CA: Impact.

Ellis, B., MacDonald, H. Z., Lincoln, A. K., & Cabral, H. J. (2008). Mental health of Somali adolescent refugees: The role of trauma, stress, and perceived discrimination. *Journal of Consulting and Clinical Psychology, 76*, 184–193.

Engberg, M. E., & Wolniak, G. C. (2010). Examining the effects of high school contexts on postsecondary enrollment. *Research in Higher Education, 51*, 132–153. doi: 10.1007/s11162-009-9150-y

Erford, B. T., Eaves, S., Bryant, E., & Young, K. (2010). *35 techniques every counselor should know*. Columbus, OH: Pearson Merrill.

Erford, B. T., Lee, V., Newsome, D., & Rock, E. (2011). Systemic approaches to counseling students experiencing complex and specialized problems. In B. T. Erford (Ed.), *Transforming the school counseling profession* (3rd ed., pp. 288–313). Columbus, OH: Pearson Merrill.

Erickson, M. T. (1998). *Behavior disorders of children and adolescents: Assessment, etiology, and intervention* (3rd ed.). Upper Saddle River, NJ: Prentice Hall.

Espelage, D., & Swearer, S. (2008). Addressing research gaps in the intersection between homophobia and bullying. *School Psychology Review, 37*, 155–159.

*Family Educational Rights and Privacy Act* of 1974 (FERPA). (1974). 20 USC § 1232g; 34 CFR.

Farmer, T. W., Hall, C. M, Estell, D. B., Leung, M., & Brooks, D. (2011). Social prominence and the heterogeneity or rejected status in late elementary school. *School Psychology Quarterly, 26*, 260–274.

Fineran, S. (2001). Sexual minority students and peer sexual harassment in high school. *Journal of School Social Work, 11*, 50–59.

Foley, R. M., & Lan-Szo, P. (2006). Alternative education programs: Program and student characteristics. *High School Journal, 89*(3), 10–21.

Frank, D. A., II, & Cannon, E. P. (2009). Creative approaches to serving LGBTQ youth in schools. *Journal of School Counseling, 7*(35), 1–25.

Frankl, V. (1963). *Man's search for meaning*. Boston, MA: Beacon.

Gagne, P., Tewksbury, R., & McGaughey, D. (1997). Coming out and crossing over: Identity formation and proclamation in a transgender community. *Gender & Society, 11*, 478–508.

Gard, B. A., & Ruzek, J. I. (2006). Community mental health response to crisis. *Journal of Clinical Psychology, 62*, 1029–1041.

Garner, N. E., & Valle, J. P. (2008). Solution-focused theory applied to career counseling. In G. Eliason & J. Patrick (Eds.), *Career development in the schools* (pp. 155–183). Greenwich CT: Information Age.

Gay, Lesbian, and Straight Education Network (GLSEN). (2007). *Gay-straight alliances: Creating safer schools for LGBT students and their allies*. (GLSEN Research Brief). New York, NY: Author.

Gay, Lesbian, and Straight Education Network (GLSEN). (2008). *ThinkB4YouSpeak: Educator's Guide*. New York, NY: Author.

Gelhaar, T., Seiffge-Krenke, I., Borge, A., Cicognani, E., Cunha, M., Loncaric, D., . . . Metzke, C. (2007). Adolescent coping with everyday stressors: A seven-nation study of youth from central, eastern, southern, and northern Europe. *European Journal of Developmental Psychology, 4*, 129–156. doi: 10.1080/17405620600831564

Gilbert, L. A., & Scher, M. (1999). *Gender and sex in counseling and psychotherapy*. Boston, MA: Allyn & Bacon.

Gilliland, B. E., & James, R. K. (1997). *Crisis intervention strategies* (3rd ed.). Pacific Grove, CA: Brooks/Cole.

Gladding, S. T. (2012). *Counseling: A comprehensive profession* (6th ed.). Upper Saddle River, NJ: Prentice Hall.

Glasser, W. (1999). *Counseling with choice theory*. New York, NY: HarperCollins.

Glosoff, H. L., & Pate, R. H. (2002). Privacy and confidentiality in school counseling. *Professional School Counseling, 6*, 20–27.

Gollnick, D. M., & Chinn, P. C. (2009). Language. In D. M. Gollnick & P. C. Chinn (Eds.), *Multicultural education in a pluralistic society* (8th ed., pp. 199–233). Upper Saddle River, NJ: Pearson Merrill.

Gonsiorek, J. (1988). Mental health issues of gay and lesbian adolescents. *Journal of Adolescent Health Care, 9*, 114–122. doi:10.1016/0197-0070(88)90057-5

Goodrich, K. M., & Luke, M. (2009). LGBTQ responsive school counseling. *Journal of LGBT Issues in Counseling, 3*(2), 113–127. doi: 10.1080/15538600903005284

Goodrich, K. M., & Luke, M. (2010). The experiences of school counselors-in-training in group work with LGBTQ adolescences. *The Journal for Specialists in Group Work, 35*, 143–159. doi: 10.1080/01933921003705966

Graham-Kevan, N., & Archer, J. (2008). Does controlling behavior predict physical aggression and violence to partners? *Journal of Family Violence, 23,* 539–548.

Green, B. L., Korol, M., Grace, M. C., & Vary, M. G. (1991). Children and disaster: Age, gender, and parental effects on PTSD symptoms. *Journal of the American Academy of Child & Adolescent Psychiatry, 30,* 6.

Greenstone, J. L., & Leviton, S. C. (2002). *Elements of crisis intervention: Crises and how to respond to them* (2nd ed.). Belmont, CA: Brooks/Cole.

Grodsky, E., & Riegle-Crumb, C. (2010). Those who choose and those who don't: Social background and college orientation. *The ANNALS of the American Academy of Political and Social Science, 627,* 14–25.

Halbur, D. A., & Halbur, K. V. (2006). *Developing your theoretical orientation in counseling and psychotherapy.* Boston, MA: Pearson/Allyn & Bacon.

Hale, R. P., & Harris, C. M. (2006). *Pedagogy of indignation: Race, class and Hurricane Katrina.* Santa Barbara, CA: Women Educators.

Hanna, F. J., Hanna, C. A., & Keys, S. G. (1999). Fifty strategies for counseling defiant, aggressive adolescents: Reaching, accepting, and relating. *Journal of Counseling & Development, 77,* 395–404.

Hansen, J. T. (2006a). Counseling theories within a postmodern epistemology: New roles for theories in counseling practice. *Journal of Counseling & Development, 84,* 291–297.

Hansen, J. T. (2006b). Humanism as moral imperative: Comments on the role of knowing in the helping encounter. *Journal of Humanistic Counseling, Education, and Development, 45,* 115–125.

Harrison, T. (2003). Adolescent homosexuality and concerns regarding disclosure. *Journal of School Health, 73,* 107–112.

Head, C. J. (2010). Partnerships and addressing tough issues in promoting health among GLBTQ youth: An interview with Jesus Ramirez-Valles. *Health Promotion Practice, 11,* 15S–18S.

Heegaard, M. E. (1996). *When someone very special dies.* Chapmanville, WV: Woodland Press.

Henderson, D. A., & Thompson, C. L. (2011). *Counseling children* (8th ed.). Belmont, CA: Brooks/Cole.

Hickman, L. J., Jaycox, L. H., & Aronoff, J. (2004). Dating violence among adolescents: Prevalence, gender distribution and prevention program effectiveness. *Trauma, Violence & Abuse, 5,* 123–142.

Hoffman, R. M. (2001). The measurement of masculinity and femininity: Historical perspectives and implications for counseling. *Journal of Counseling & Development, 79,* 472–485.

Holcomb-McCoy, C., & Chen-Hayes, S. F. (2011). Culturally competent school counselors: Affirming diversity by challenging oppression. In B. T. Erford (Ed.), *Transforming the school counseling profession* (3rd ed., pp. 90–109). Upper Saddle River, NJ: Pearson Education.

Horn, S. S., Kosciw, J. G., & Russell, S. T. (2009). Special issues introduction: New research on lesbian, gay, bisexual, and transgender youth: Studying lives in context. *Journal of Youth and Adolescence, 38,* 863–866.

Howard, K. A. S., & Solberg, S. H. (2006). School-based social justice: The Achieving Success Identity Pathways Program. *Professional School Counseling, 9,* 278–287.

Hoyle, J. R., & Kutka, T. M. (2008). Maintaining America's egalitarian edge in the 21st century: Unifying K–12 and postsecondary education for the success of all students. *Theory into Practice, 47,* 353–362.

Huegel, K. (1998). *Young people and their chronic illness.* Minneapolis, MN: Free Spirit.

Huey, W. C., & Remley, T. P., Jr. (1988). *Ethical and legal issues in school counseling.* Alexandria, VA: American School Counselor Association.

Human eSources. (2011). *Learning style inventory.* Retrieved from http://www.connection.naviance.com/cshs

Ivey, A. E., & Ivey, M. B. (2007). *Intentional interviewing and counseling: Facilitating client development in a multicultural society* (6th ed.). Belmont, CA: Thomson Brooks/Cole.

Jay, M. (2009). Race-ing through the school day: African American educators' experiences with race and racism in schools. *International Journal of Qualitative Studies in Education, 22,* 671–685. doi: 10.1080/09518390903333855

Johnson, P. (2002). Predictors of family functioning within alcoholic families. *Contemporary Family Therapy, 24,* 371–384.

Johnson, T. D. (2011). Excessive texting, social networking linked to health risks for teenagers. *The Nation's Health, 40*(10), 11.

Jones, K. D., & Nugent, F. A. (2008). *Introduction to the profession of counseling* (5th ed.). Upper Saddle River, NJ: Pearson Merrill.

Jones, R. T., Fray, R., Cunningham, J. D., & Kaiser, L. (2001). The psychological effects of Hurricane Andrew on ethnic minority and Caucasian children and adolescents: A case study. *Cultural Diversity and Ethic Minority Psychology, 7,* 103–108.

Jones-Smith, E. (2012). *Theories of counseling and psychotherapy: An integrative approach.* Thousand Oaks, CA: Sage.

Kaffenberger, C. J. (2010). *Handbook for school support teams* (4th ed.). McLean, VA: Author. Retrieved from http://www.fcps.edu/cco/prc/resources/events/docs/workshops_2010-11/Handbook_Manual_revised_2010.pdf

Kanel, K. (2011). *A guide to crisis intervention* (4th ed.). New York, NY: Brooks/Cole.

Kelleher, C. (2009). Minority stress and health: Implications for lesbian, gay, bisexual, transgender, and questioning (LGBTQ) young people. *Counselling Psychology Quarterly, 22,* 373–379.

Kelly, G. A. (1963). *A theory of personality.* New York, NY: Norton.

Kelly, J. B., & Lamb, M. E. (2003). Developmental issues in relocation cases involving young children: When, whether, and how? *Journal of Family Psychology, 17,* 193–205.

Kerr, M., & Bowen, M. (1988). *Family evaluation.* New York, NY: Norton.

Kingery, J. N., Erdley, C. A., & Marshall, K. C. (2011). Peer acceptance and friendship as predictors of early adolescent adjustment across middle school transition. *Marshall-Palmer Quarterly, 57,* 215–243.

Klungman, J. R., & Butler, D. (2008). *Opening doors and paving the way: Increasing college access and success for talented low-income students.* Retrieved from http://www.princeton.edu/~tprep/pupp/forum/publications.htm

Kosciw, J. G., Diaz, E. M., & Greytak, E. A. (2008). *2007 National School Climate Survey: The experiences of lesbian, gay, bisexual and transgender youth in our nation's schools.* New York, NY: GLSEN.

Kosciw, J. G., Greytak, E. A., Diaz, E. M., & Bartkiewicz, M. J. (2010). *The 2009 National School Climate Survey: The experiences of lesbian, gay, bisexual and transgender youth in our nation's schools.* New York, NY: GLSEN.

Kübler-Ross, E. (1969). *On death and dying.* New York, NY: Simon & Schuster.

LaFountain, R. M., & Garner, N. E. (1998). *A school with solutions: Implementing a solution-focused/Adlerian based comprehensive school counseling program.* Alexandria, VA: American School Counselor Association.

La Greca, A. M., Silverman, W. K., Vernberg, E. M., & Roberts, M. C. (Eds.). (2002). *Helping children cope with disasters and terrorism.* Washington, DC: American Psychological Association.

Landreth, G. (2002). *Play therapy: The art of the relationship* (2nd ed.). New York, NY: Brunner-Routledge.

Landreth, G., Baggerly, J., & Tyndall-Lind, A. (1999). Beyond adapting adult counseling skills for use with children: The paradigm shift to child-centered play therapy. *Journal of Individual Psychology, 55,* 272–287.

Lee, W. M. L., Blando, J. A., Mizelle, N. D., & Orozco, G. L. (2007). *Introduction to multicultural counseling for helping professionals* (2nd ed.). New York, NY: Routledge.

Lehr, C. A., & Lange, C. M. (2003). Alternative schools serving students with and without disabilities: What are the current issues and challenges? *Preventing School Failure, 47*(2), 59.

Lemoire, S. J., & Chen, C. (2005). Applying person-centered counseling to sexual minority adolescents. *Journal of Counseling & Development, 83,* 146–160.

Lewis, J., Arnold, M., House, R., & Toporek, M. S. (2003). *Advocacy competencies.* Retrieved from http://www.counseling.org/resources/competencies/advocacy_competencies.pdf

Li, X., Stanton, B., Pack, R., Harris, C., Cottrell, L., & Burns, J. (2002). Risk and protective factors associated with gang involvement among urban African American adolescents. *Youth and Society, 34*(2), 172–194. doi: 10.1177/004411802237862

Linde, L. (2011). Ethical, legal, and professional issues in school counseling. In B. T. Erford (Ed.), *Transforming the school counseling profession* (3rd ed., pp. 70–89). Columbus, OH: Pearson Merrill.

Livingstone, S. (2008). Taking risky opportunities in youthful content creation: Teenagers' use of social networking sites for intimacy, privacy and self-expression. *New Media Society, 10,* 393–411. doi: 10.1177/1461444808089415

Lonigan, C. J., Shannon, M. O., Taylor, C. M., & Salee, F. R. (1994). Children exposed to disaster: II Risk factors for the development of post traumatic symptomatology. *Journal of the American Academy of Child and Adolescent Psychiatry, 33,* 94–105.

Matthews, C. R., & Bieschke, K. J. (2001). Adapting the ethnocultural assessment to gay and lesbian clients: The sexual orientation enculturation assessment. *Journal of Humanistic Counseling, Education, and Development, 40,* 58–73.

May, R. (1977). *The meaning of anxiety* (Rev. ed.). New York, NY: Norton.

McAdams, C. R., & Schmidt, C. D. (2007). How to help a bully: Recommendations for counseling the proactive aggressor. *Professional School Counseling, 11,* 120–128.

McCabe, P. C., & Rubinson, F. (2008). Committing to social justice: The behavioral intention of school psychology and education trainees to advocate for lesbian, gay, bisexual and transgendered youth. *School Psychology Review, 37,* 469–486.

McWhirter, B. T., & Ishikawa, M. I. (2005). Individual counseling: Traditional approaches. In D. Capuzzi & D. R. Gross (Eds.), *Introduction to the counseling profession* (4th ed., pp. 155–172). Upper Saddle River, NJ: Prentice Hall.

Meichenbaum, D. (1995). Cognitive-behavioral therapy in historical perspective. In B. M. Bongar & L. E. Beutler (Eds.), *Comprehensive textbook of psychotherapy: Theory and practice* (pp. 140–158). London, UK: Oxford University Press.

Mitchell, C. W., Disque, J. G., & Robertson, P. (2002). When parents want to know: Responding to parental demands for confidential information. *Professional School Counseling, 6,* 156–161.

Monk, G., Winslade, J., Crocket, K., & Epston, D. (1997). *Narrative therapy in practice.* San Francisco, CA: Jossey-Bass.

Murphy, J. J. (2008). *Solution-focused counseling in schools* (2nd ed.). Alexandria, VA: American Counseling Association. Retrieved from http://counselingoutfitters.com/vistas/vistas08/Murphy.htm

Myers, E. (2006). *Teens, loss, and grief.* Lanham, MD: Rowland & Littlefield.

National Association for Children of Alcoholics (NACoA). (1995). *Alcoholism affects the entire family.* Retrieved from http://www.nacoa.net/coa3.htm

National Association for Children of Alcoholics (NACoA). (2001). *A kit for educators* (4th ed.). Rockville, MD: Author. Retrieved from http://www.nacoa.org/pdfs/EDkit_web_06.pdf

National Cancer Institute. (NCI). (2011). *Grief, bereavement, and coping with loss (PDQ®).* Retrieved from http://www.cancer.gov/cancertopics/pdq/supportivecare/bereavement/Patient

National Gang Center. (n.d.). *National Youth Gang Survey analysis.* Retrieved from http://www.nationalgangcenter.gov/Survey-Analysis

Nichols, M. P., & Schwartz, R. C. (2005). *The essentials of family therapy.* Boston, MA: Allyn & Bacon.

Niles, S. G., & Harris-Bowlsbey, J. (2009). *Career development interventions in the 21st century* (3rd ed.). Upper Saddle River, NJ: Pearson.

No Child Left Behind Act of 2001. (NCLB). Public Law 107-110, 107th Congress, 1st Session (2002). Retrieved from http://www.ed.gov/policy/elsec/leg/esea02/107-110.pdf

O'Connell, B. (2005). *Solution-focused therapy* (2nd ed.). London, UK: Sage.

O'Hanlon, W. H., & Weiner-Davis, M. (1989). *In search of solutions: A new direction in psychotherapy.* New York, NY: Norton.

Olweus, D. (1993). *Bullying at school: What we know and what we can do.* Oxford, UK: Blackwell Publishers.

Pachter, L. M., Bernstein, B. A., Szalacha, L. A., & Coll, C. G. (2010). Perceived racism and discrimination in children and youths: An exploratory study. *Health & Social Work, 35*(1), 61–69.

*Page v. Rotterdam-Mohonasen Central School District,* 441 N.Y.S. 2d 323, 109 Misc. 2d 1049 (N.Y. 1981).

Palahnuik, C. (1999). *Invisible monsters.* New York, NY: Norton.

Palpant, R. G., Steimnitz, R., Bornemann T. H., & Hawkins, K. (2006). The Carter Center mental health program: Addressing the public health crisis in the field of mental health through policy change and stigma reduction. *Preventing Chronic Disease, 3*(2), A62.

Perls, L. (1970). One Gestalt therapist's approach. In J. Fagan & I. Shepherd (Eds.), *Gestalt therapy now* (pp. 125–129). New York, NY: Harper & Row (Colophon).

Policies & Laws. (2012). *State anti-bullying laws & policies.* Retrieved from http://www.stopbullying.gov/laws/index.html

Prochaska, J. O., & DiClemente, C. C. (1982). Transtheoretical therapy: Toward a more integrative model of change. *Psychotherapy: Theory, Research and Practice, 20,* 161–173.

Ratts, M. (2009). Social justice counseling: Toward the development of a fifth force among counseling paradigms. *Journal of Humanistic Counseling, Education, and Development, 48,* 160–172.

Ratts, M. J., DeKruyf, L., & Chen-Hayes, S. F. (2007). The ACA advocacy competencies: A social justice advocacy framework for professional school counselors. *Professional School Counseling, 11,* 90–97.

Raywid, M. (1994). Alternative schools: The state of the art. *Educational Leadership, 52*(1), 26.

Remley, T. P., & Herlihy, B. (2010). *Ethical, legal, and professional issues in counseling* (3rd ed.). Upper Saddle River, NJ: Pearson.

Remley, T. P., Jr., & Huey, W. C. (2002). An ethics quiz for school counselors. *Professional School Counseling, 6*, 3–11.

Ringel, J. S., & Sturm, R. (2001). National estimates of mental health utilization and expenditures for children in 1998. *Journal of Behavioral Health Services and Research, 28*, 319–333.

Rogers, C. (1951). *Client-centered therapy*. Boston, MA: Houghton Mifflin.

Rogers, C. (1957). The necessary and sufficient conditions of therapeutic personality change. *Journal of Consulting Psychology, 21*, 95–103.

Rogers, C. R. (1961). *On becoming a person*. Boston, MA: Houghton Mifflin.

Rogers, C. R. (1980). *A way of being*. Boston, MA: Houghton Mifflin.

Satcher, J., & Leggett, M. (2007). Homonegativity among professional school counselors: An exploratory study. *Professional School Counseling, 11*(1), 10–16.

Savage, T., & Harley, D. (2009). A place at the blackboard: LGB-TIQ. *Multicultural Education, 16*, 2–9.

Sharkey, J. D., Shekhtmeyster, Z., Chavez-Lopez, L., Norris, E., & Sass, L. (2011). The protective influence of gangs: Can schools compensate? *Aggression and Violent Behavior, 16*, 45–54. doi: 10.1016/j.avb.2010.11.001

Shostrom, E. (Producer). (1965). *Three approaches to psychotherapy* [Film]. Orange, CA: Psychological Films.

Sklare, G. B. (2005). *Brief counseling that works: A solution-focused approach for school counselors and administrators* (2nd ed.). Thousand Oaks, CA: Corwin Press.

Smead, R. (1994). *Skills for living: Group activities for elementary students*. Champaign, IL: Research Press.

Smead, V. (1982). "I am hurt, but I am not sick": Individual psychotherapy provided within an ecological/environmental framework. *Psychotherapy: Theory, Research, and Practice, 19*, 307–316.

Sobhy, M., & Cavallaro, M. (2010). Solution-focused brief counseling in schools: Theoretical perspectives and case application to an elementary school student. *VISTAS, 1*–12. Retrieved from http://counselingoutfitters.com/vistas/vistas10/Article_81.pdf

Stone, C. (2003). Counselors as advocates for gay, lesbian, and bisexual youth: A call for equity and action. *Journal of Multicultural Counseling and Development, 31*, 143–152.

Stone, C. (2009). *School counseling principles: Ethics and law* (2nd ed.). Alexandria, VA: American School Counselor Association.

Stuart, S., & Robertson, M. (2003). *Interpersonal psychotherapy: A clinician's guide*. London, UK: Edward Arnold.

Sue, D., Arredondo, P., & McDavis, R. J. (1992). Multicultural counseling competencies and standards: A call to the profession. *Journal of Counseling & Development, 70*, 477–486.

Swearer, S. M., Turner, R. K., Givens, J. E., & Pollack, W. S. (2008). "You're so gay!": Do different forms of bullying matter for adolescent males? *School Psychology Review, 37*, 160–173.

Sweeney, T. J. (1998). *Adlerian counseling: A practitioner's approach* (4th ed.). Philadelphia, PA: Accelerated Development.

Terr, L. C. (1995). Children traumas: An outline and overview. In G. S. Everly Jr. & J. M. Lating (Eds.), *Psychotraumatology* (pp. 301–320). New York, NY: Plenum.

Thompson, R. A. (2012). *Professional school counseling: Best practices for working in schools* (3rd ed.). New York, NY: Routledge.

U.S. Department of Education. (2006). *Report to the President and Congress on the implementation of the Education for Homeless Children and Youth Program under the McKinney-Vento Homeless Assistance Act*. Retrieved from http://www2.ed.gov/programs/homeless/rpt2006.doc

U.S. Department of Health and Human Services, Substance Abuse and Mental Health Services Administration. (SAMHSA). (2001). *Mental health: Culture, race, and ethnicity—A supplement to mental health: A report of the Surgeon General*. Retrieved from http://www.ncbi.nlm.nih.gov/books/NBK44243/

Vare, J., & Norton, T. (1998). Understanding gay and lesbian youth: Sticks, stones and silence. *The Clearing House, 71*, 327–331. doi:10.1080/00098659809599584

Verdugo, R. R., & Glenn, B. C. (2006). *Race and alternative schools* (NCJ No. 226234). Retrieved from https://www.ncjrs.gov/pdffiles1/ojjdp/grants/226234.pdf

Vernberg, E. M., Greenhoot, A. F., & Biggs, B. K. (2006). Intercommunity relocation and adolescent friendships: Who struggles and why? *Journal of Consulting and Clinical Psychology, 74*, 511–523.

Vernon, A. (2009a). *Counseling children & adolescents* (4th ed.). Denver, CO: Love.

Vernon, A. (2009b). Working with children, adolescents, and their parents: Practical application of developmental theory. In A. Vernon (Ed.), *Counseling children & adolescents* (4th ed., pp. 1–34). Denver, CO: Love.

Walker, L. E. A. (1979). *The battered woman*. New York, NY: Harper & Row.

Walter, J. L., & Peller, J. E. (1992). *Becoming solution-focused in brief therapy*. New York, NY: Brunner/Mazel.

Weems, C. F., Taylor, L. K., Cannon, M. F., Marino, R. C., Romano, D. M., Scott, B. G., Perry, A. M., & Triplett, V. (2010). Post traumatic stress context, and the lingering effects of the Hurricane Katrina disaster among ethnic minority youth. *Journal of Abnormal Child Psychology, 38*, 49–56.

Weiler, E. (2004). Legally and morally, what our gay students must be given. *Education Digest: Essential Readings Condensed for Quick Review, 69*, 38–43.

White, M., & Epston, D. (1990). *Narrative means to therapeutic ends*. New York, NY: Norton.

Wilson, F. R. (2003). *What is ecological psychology?* Retrieved from http://www.cech.uc.edu/ecological_counseling/ecological_psychotherapy/

Winslade, J. M., & Monk, G. D. (2007). *Narrative counseling in schools: Brief and powerful* (2nd ed.). Thousand Oaks, CA: Corwin Press.

Wood, J. T. (2005). *Gendered lives: Communication, gender, and culture* (6th ed.). Belmont, CA: Wadsworth/Thomson Learning.

Wubbolding, R. E. (1991). *Understanding reality therapy*. New York, NY: HarperCollins.

Wyner, J. S., Bridgeland, J. M., & Diiulio, J. J. (2007). *Achievement trap: How America is failing millions of high-achieving students from lower-income families*. Retrieved from http://www.promoteprevent.org/resources/achievement-trap-how-america-failing-millions-high-achieving-students-lower-income-familie

Yalom, I. D. (2002). *The gift of therapy: An open letter to a new generation of therapists and their patients*. New York, NY: HarperCollins.

# INDEX